# ADVERSARIAL ROBUSTNESS FOR MACHINE LEARNING

# ADVERSARIAL ROBUSTNESS FOR MACHINE LEARNING

**PIN-YU CHEN**
IBM Research
Yorktown Heights, NY, United States

**CHO-JUI HSIEH**
University of California, Los Angeles
Los Angeles, CA, United States

ACADEMIC PRESS
An imprint of Elsevier

Academic Press is an imprint of Elsevier
125 London Wall, London EC2Y 5AS, United Kingdom
525 B Street, Suite 1650, San Diego, CA 92101, United States
50 Hampshire Street, 5th Floor, Cambridge, MA 02139, United States
The Boulevard, Langford Lane, Kidlington, Oxford OX5 1GB, United Kingdom

**Notices**

Knowledge and best practice in this field are constantly changing. As new research and experience
broaden our understanding, changes in research methods, professional practices, or medical
treatment may become necessary.

Practitioners and researchers must always rely on their own experience and knowledge in
evaluating and using any information, methods, compounds, or experiments described herein. In
using such information or methods they should be mindful of their own safety and the safety of
others, including parties for whom they have a professional responsibility.

To the fullest extent of the law, neither the Publisher nor the authors, contributors, or editors,
assume any liability for any injury and/or damage to persons or property as a matter of products
liability, negligence or otherwise, or from any use or operation of any methods, products,
instructions, or ideas contained in the material herein.

ISBN: 978-0-12-824020-5

For information on all Academic Press publications
visit our website at https://www.elsevier.com/books-and-journals

*Publisher:* Mara E. Conner
*Acquisitions Editor:* Tim Pitts
*Editorial Project Manager:* Sara Greco
*Production Project Manager:* Nirmala Arumugam
*Cover Designer:* Christian J. Bilbow

Typeset by VTeX

Working together
to grow libraries in
developing countries

www.elsevier.com • www.bookaid.org

*We would like to give our sincerest gratitude to our colleagues, collaborators, the research community, and our beloved family members and friends for their continuous support and contributions.*

*The first version of this book was prepared and written during the COVID-19 pandemic period (2020–2022).*

*May the adversarial be abated, and the good be elevated.*

# Contents

# PART 5   Applications beyond attack and defense

# Biography

## Dr. Pin-Yu Chen (1986–present)

Dr. Pin-Yu Chen is currently a principal research staff member at IBM Thomas J. Watson Research Center, Yorktown Heights, NY, USA. He is also the chief scientist of RPI-IBM AI Research Collaboration and PI of ongoing MIT-IBM Watson AI Lab projects. Dr. Chen received his Ph.D. degree in electrical engineering and computer science and M.A. degree in Statistics from the University of Michigan, Ann Arbor, USA, in 2016. He received his M.S. degree in communication engineering from National Taiwan University, Taiwan, in 2011 and B.S. degree in electrical engineering and computer science (undergraduate honors program) from National Chiao Tung University, Taiwan, in 2009. Dr. Chen's recent research focuses on adversarial machine learning and robustness of neural networks. His long-term research vision is building trustworthy machine learning systems. He has published more than 40 papers related to trustworthy machine learning at major AI and machine learning conferences, given tutorials at AAAI'22, IJCAI'21, CVPR('20,'21), ECCV'20, ICASSP'20, KDD'19, and Big Data'18, and organized several workshops for adversarial machine learning. His research interest also includes graph and network data analytics and their applications to data mining, machine learning, signal processing, and cybersecurity. He was the recipient of the Chia-Lun Lo Fellowship from the University of Michigan Ann Arbor. He was also the recipient of the IEEE GLOBECOM 2010 GOLD Best Paper Award. At IBM Research, Dr. Chen has coinvented more than 30 U.S. patents and received the honor of IBM Master Inventor. In 2021, he received an IBM Corporate Technical Award for his contributions to trustworthy machine learning. More details about him can be found at www.pinyuchen.com.

## Dr. Cho-Jui Hsieh (1985–present)

Dr. Cho-Jui Hsieh is currently an assistant professor of Computer Science at University of California, Los Angeles. He received his Ph.D. degree in computer science from the University of Texas at Austin in 2015. He received his M.S. and B.S. degrees in computer science and information engineering from National Taiwan University in 2009 and 2007, respectively. His main research focuses on developing efficient, reliable and automatic machine learning algorithms. His work has received best/outstanding paper awards at KDD'10, ICDM'12, ICPP'18, ICLR'21 as well as three other paper award finalists. He was the recipient of NSF Career Award, Samsung AI Researcher of the Year, and several other research awards from Google, Intel, and Facebook. Further, his algorithms have been implemented in widely used machine learning libraries such as LIBLINEAR, scikit-learn, Pytorch, Tensorflow, DGL. The verification toolbox developed by his team won the 2021 VNN-Comp (International Verification of Neural Network Competition). His optimization algorithms have been chosen by the MLPerf as default solver for large-batch training tasks (e.g., BERT) and have been widely used in industry.

# Preface

With the recent advances in machine learning theory and algorithms, the design of high-capacity and scalable models such as neural networks, abundant datasets, and sufficient computing resources, machine learning (ML), or more broadly, artificial intelligence (AI), has been transforming our industry and society at an unprecedented speed.

While we are anticipating positive impacts enabled by machine learning technology, we may often overlook potential negative effects, which may bring considerable ethical concerns and even setbacks due to law regulations and catastrophic failures, especially for mission-critical and high-stakes decision making tasks. Therefore, beyond accuracy, trustworthy machine learning is the last milestone for ML-based technology to achieve and thrive. Trustworthy machine learning encompasses a broad set of essential topics such as adversarial robustness, fairness, explainability, accountability, and ethics.

This book focuses on fulfilling the endeavor of evaluating, improving, and leveraging adversarial robustness of machine learning algorithms, models, and systems toward better and more trustworthy versions. Exploiting untrusted machine learning as vulnerabilities create unattended gateways for intended parties to manipulate machine predictions while evading human's attention to gain their own benefits. No matter what one's role is in ML, as a model developer, a stakeholder, or a user, we believe it is essential for everyone to understand adversarial robustness for machine learning, just like knowing the capabilities and limitations of your own vehicle before driving. For model developers, we advocate proactive in-house robustness testing of your own models and systems for error inspection and risk mitigation. For stakeholders, we advocate acknowledgment of possible weaknesses in products and services, as well as honest and thorough risk and threat assessment in a forward-thinking manner to prevent revenue/reputation loss and catastrophic damage to the society and environment. For users using machine learning byproducts, we advocate active understanding of their limitations for safe use and gaining awareness about possible misuses. These aspects related to adversarial robustness, along with the available techniques and tools, are elucidated in this book.

Generally speaking, adversarial robustness centers on the study of the *worst-case* performance in machine learning, in contrast to the standard machine learning practice, which focuses on the *average* performance, e.g., prediction accuracy on a test dataset. The notion of worst-case analysis is motivated by the necessity of ensuring robust and accurate predictions for machine learning against changes in the training environments and deployed scenarios. Specifically, such changes can be caused by natural occurrences (e.g., data drifts due to varying lighting conditions) or by malicious attempts (e.g., hackers aiming to compromise and gain control over the system/service based on machine learning). Consequently, instead of asking "How well can machine learning perform on this given dataset/task?", in adversarial robustness, we ask "How robust and accurate can machine learning be if the dataset or the model can undergo different quantifiable levels of changes?" This interventional process often involves introducing a virtual adversary in machine learning for robustness assessment and improvement, which is a key ingredient in adversarial machine learning.

This book aims to offer a holistic overview of adversarial robustness spanning the lifecycle of machine learning, ranging from data collection, model development, to system integration and deployment. The contents provide a comprehensive set of research techniques and practical tools for studying adversarial robustness for machine learning. This book covers the following four research thrusts in adversarial robustness: (i) *Attack* – Finding failure modes for machine learning; (ii) *Defense* – Strengthening and safeguarding machine learning; (iii) *Certification* – Developing provable robustness performance guarantees; and (iv) *Applications* – Inventing novel use cases based on the study of adversarial robustness.

We summarize the contents of each part in this book as follows. In Part 1, we introduce preliminaries for this book, connect adversarial robustness to adversarial machine learning, and provide intriguing findings to motivate adversarial robustness. In Part 2, we introduce different types of adversarial attacks with varying assumptions in attackers' capabilities in the lifecycle of machine learning, knowledge of the target machine learning system, realizations in digital and physical spaces, and data modalities. In Part 3, we introduce certification techniques for quantifying the level of provable robustness for neural networks. In Part 4, we introduce defenses for improving the robustness of machine learning against adversarial attacks. Finally, in Part 5, we present several novel applications inspired from the study of adversarial robustness for machine learning.

Pin-Yu Chen and Cho-Jui Hsieh

PART 1

# Preliminaries

# CHAPTER 1

# Background and motivation

## 1.1 What is adversarial machine learning?

Adversarial machine learning (AdvML) refers to the methodology of introducing a virtual adversary for evaluating and improving the performance of a machine learning (ML) system throughout its lifecycle of development and deployment, ranging from training (e.g., data collection, model selection and tuning, etc), model testing (e.g., vulnerability assessment, performance benchmarking, etc), hardware implementation, and system integration to continuous system status monitoring and updates.

We list two primary scientific and engineering goals considered in AdvML:

1. The practice of virtual adversary for proactive risk evaluation to prevent or mitigate different kinds of failure modes of machine learning systems when deployed in the real world. The failure modes include natural changes such as domain shifts in data inputs and lacking generalization to unseen or out-of-domain data, as well as potential adversarial threats (from real adversary) such as training-phase and deployment-phase attacks aiming to compromising machine learning algorithms and systems.

2. The use of virtual adversary to deliver new machine learning algorithms for performance improvement. Comparing to standard ML without the notion of adversary, the interplay between the model of interest and virtual adversary, either in cooperative or competitive manner, can help developing more effective and robust machine learning models and algorithms. One well-known example is the training of generative adversarial network (GAN) (Goodfellow et al., 2014), which attains a high-quality generator via introducing a discriminator.

Despite the fact that the second goal touches upon many related research topics associated with AdvML, such as GANs, multiagent systems, and game-oriented learning, this book focuses on the topics underlying adversarial robustness in machine learning algorithms and systems. These topics cover both aforementioned goals and deliver important insights to ML applications concerning safety, security, and reliability.

*Adversarial Robustness for Machine Learning*
https://doi.org/10.1016/B978-0-12-824020-5.00009-0
3

**Table 1.1** Commonly used mathematical symbols and their meanings.

| Symbol | Meaning |
| --- | --- |
| $(x, y) \sim \mathcal{D}$ | data sample $x$ and one-hot coded label $y$ drawn from the data distribution $\mathcal{D}$ |
| $K$ | number of classes in a classification task |
| $\theta$ | parameters of a machine learning model |
| $f_\theta : \mathbb{R}^d \mapsto [0, 1]^K$ (or $F_\theta$) | $K$-way classifier (e.g., a neural network parameterized by $\theta$) |
| $\delta$ (or $\Delta$) | input perturbation |
| $\epsilon$ | perturbation budget |
| $\nabla_z J(\cdot)$ | gradient of a scalar function $J$ with respect to $z$ |
| $\mathcal{L}$ (or loss, $J$) | loss function |
| $[K]$ | integer set $\{1, 2, \ldots, K\}$, where $K \geq 1$. |
| $\|x\|_p$ $(p \geq 1)$ | vector $p$-norm of $x = [x_1, \ldots, x_d]$, defined as $\|x\|_p = \left(\sum_{i=1}^d \|x_i\|^p\right)^{1/p}$ |
| $\|x\|_\infty$ | infinity norm of $x = [x_1, \ldots, x_d]$, defined as $\|x\|_\infty = \max_{i \in [d]} \|x_i\|$ |
| $\text{sign}(\cdot)$ | elementwise sign operation; $\text{sign}(z) = 1$ if $z \geq 0$ and $\text{sign}(z) = -1$ otherwise. |

## 1.2 Mathematical notations

Throughout this book, unless specified otherwise, we will use the following convention for mathematical notations. Regular letters (e.g., $x$ or $X$) are used to denote scalars, index, or an element in a set. Bold-faced lowercase letters (e.g., $x$) are used to denote column vectors. Bold-faced uppercase letters (e.g., $X$) are used to denote matrices. Uppercase letters in calligraphic fonts (e.g., $\mathcal{X}$) are used to denote sets or probability distributions. All vectors and matrices are assumed to be real-valued. The subscript $x_i$ ($X_{ij}$) denotes the $i$th element (the element at the $i$th row and the $j$th column) of a vector $x$ (a matrix $X$). $[x]_j$ (or $x_j$) means the $j$th element of the vector $x$. The notation $\mathbb{R}^d$ denotes the space of $d$-dimensional real-valued vectors. The notation $\cdot^T$ denotes the transpose of a vector or a matrix.

Table 1.1 summarizes commonly used mathematical symbols and their meanings in this book. In each chapter the associated mathematical notations and their meanings will be formally defined. Depending on the context, the notation $f_\theta(\cdot)$ (or $F_\theta(\cdot)$) for model output may refer to the top-1 (mostly likely) class based on the model prediction. Similarly, the notation $y$ may be used to denote the groundtruth class label of a data sample $x$.

## 1.3 Machine learning basics

Machine learning is the methodology of teaching machines for problem/task solving based on the observable data (or the interaction with training environments) and the underlying computational/statistical learning mechanism. The learning component, also known as model training, involves a parameterized model whose parameters (or model weights) are updated by a designated loss function, measured by the available data or rewards from the training environment. The updates of the model parameters are often accomplished by gradient-based optimization algorithms such as stochastic gradient descent. Here "stochastic" means that in each iteration of the optimization process, a subset of data samples are sampled from the whole training dataset (i.e., a minibatch) for evaluating the loss and calculating the gradient with respect to the model parameters for updates. The science and engineering of machine learning have been a mainstream research field and dominant technology in artificial intelligence and computer science, with far-reaching applications to specific domains such as computer vision, natural language processing, policy learning, robot planning, speech processing, healthcare, data science, to name a few.

Supervised machine learning is a major branch of machine learning, which uses a set of labeled training data samples $\{x_i, y_i\}_{i=1}^{n}$ and a designated loss function $\mathcal{L}$ for training the parameters $\theta$ associated with a machine learning model $f_\theta$. Most of the supervised learning methods follow the Empirical Risk Minimization (ERM) framework, where the model parameters $\theta$ is obtained by solving the following optimization problem:

$$\min_\theta \frac{1}{n} \sum_{i=1}^{n} \mathcal{L}(f_\theta(x_i), y_i),$$

where the loss function $\mathcal{L}(\cdot, \cdot)$ measures how the model's prediction fits the label. This optimization problem can be typically solved by Stochastic Gradient Descent (SGD) or other gradient-based optimizers such as Adagrad (Duchi et al., 2011) and Adam (Kingma and Ba, 2015). The loss function can be designed according to the application. Popular loss functions include the mean squared error (MSE) loss defined as $\mathcal{L}_{\mathrm{MSE}}(f_\theta(x), y) = \|f_\theta(x) - y\|_2^2$, and the cross entropy (CE) loss defined as $\mathcal{L}_{\mathrm{CE}}(f_\theta(x), y) = -\sum_{k=1}^{K} [y]_k \log[f_\theta(x)]_k$, where in the CE loss $f_\theta$ outputs a vector on the $K$-dimensional probability simplex such that $f_\theta(\cdot) \in [0, 1]^K$ and $\sum_{k=1}^{K} [f_\theta(\cdot)]_k = 1$.

Semisupervised machine learning refers to the problem setting of leveraging a labeled dataset (usually limited) and an unlabeled dataset (usually abundant) for machine learning. Unsupervised machine learning means learning representations of the data inputs without using any data labels. In particular, self-supervised machine learning uses self-generated pseudo-labels or tasks for learning good representations. For unsupervised or self-supervised machine learning schemes, the practice is to follow the strategy of pretraining (on a large unlabeled dataset) and fine-tuning (on a task-specific labeled dataset). Transfer learning refers to fine-tuning a task-specific model trained in a source domain to solve a related task in a target domain using the labeled target-domain data.

*Scope of this book.* Most of the considered machine learning tasks and models in this book are within the scope of supervised machine learning, such that the goal of the adversary can be defined in a straightforward manner. Nonetheless, the methodology can be extended to unsupervised or self-supervised machine learning settings, as discussed in Chapter 21. In this book, the studied machine learning model, task, and loss function will be introduced and clearly defined in each chapter; we defer the readers interested in the in-depth background of machine learning to seminal books such as (Bishop, 2006).

*Neural networks.* A neural network is the default machine learning model in deep learning (LeCun et al., 2015), a powerful and high-capacity tool for representation learning. Deep neural networks (DNNs) have achieved state-of-the-art performance in many machine learning tasks. In general, neural networks perform a set of layered operations on data inputs, in either sequential or recurrent manner, with layers of trainable parameters (mostly linear or convolutional transformations), nonlinear activation functions, or dimension reduction through max/average pooling. The fact that neural networks can be "deep" means that a large number of such layers can constitute a high-capacity machine learning model with a strong expressive power of data representations and function approximations. With sufficient training data and compute power, neural networks are capable of capturing the complex relationship between data samples and associated labels, as well as learning generalizable representations for different data modalities. In this book, we will primary focus on the adversarial robustness of neural networks because they are state-of-the-art machine learning models. Nonetheless, the methodology naturally applies to other machine learning models such as support vector machines, random forests, gradient-boosted trees, etc. In fact, the black-box adversarial attacks introduced in Chapter 3 are agnostic to the underlying machine learning model used for classification. The necessary details of the studied neural networks will be given in the corresponding chapters.

*Commonly used datasets.* Below we summarize some commonly used datasets for image classification.

- MNIST (LeCun et al., 1998): The MNIST database (Modified National Institute of Standards and Technology database) is a large database of handwritten digits (0 to 9). It has a training set of 60,000 examples and a test set of 10,000 examples.

- CIFAR-10 (Krizhevsky et al., 2009): CIFAR-10 data samples are labeled subsets of the 80 million tiny images dataset. The dataset consists of 60,000 $32 \times 32$ color images in 10 classes, with 6,000 images per class. There are 50,000 training images and 10,000 test images.

- ImageNet (1K) (Deng et al., 2009): ImageNet is an image database organized according to the WordNet hierarchy (currently only the nouns), in which each node of the hierarchy is depicted by hundreds and thousands of image. We refer the ImageNet dataset to the Large Scale Visual Recognition Challenge 2012 (ILSVRC2012), which is a subset of the large hand-labeled ImageNet dataset (10,000,000 labeled images depicting 10,000+ object categories). The training data is a subset of ImageNet containing the 1,000 categories and about 1.2 million images. The test data has 50,000 images.

## 1.4  Motivating examples

This section provides two motivating examples to highlight the importance of studying adversarial robustness for machine learning.

### Adversarial robustness $\neq$ accuracy – what standard accuracy fails to tell

The prediction accuracy has been the long-lasting and sole standard for comparing the performance of different image classification models, including the yearly ImageNet competition (Russakovsky et al., 2015) held from 2010 to 2017. Many significant advances in the architecture design and training of neural networks can be attributed to this task. In the competition a model with a higher standard accuracy (e.g., top-1 or top-5 prediction accuracy on the test dataset) implies that a model is "better". However, surprisingly, (Su et al., 2018) performed a large-scale adversarial robustness study on 18 different publicly available ImageNet models and discovered that the empirical $\ell_2$ and $\ell_\infty$ distortion metrics scale linearly with the logarithm of classification error. Their results suggest that when using the standard accuracy as the sole metric to benchmark, the model performance may give a false sense of progress in machine learning, because the models having higher standard accuracy (lower classification error) are also shown to be more sensitive to input perturbation leading to prediction changes.

For each of the 18 models, Su et al. (2018) apply different attacks to generate adversarial examples for a common set of originally correctly classified data samples to find out the smallest additive distortions (measured by $\ell_p$ norms) required to flip the model prediction. They study the empirical relation between adversarial robustness and (standard) accuracy of different ImageNet models, where the robustness is evaluated in terms of the minimum $\ell_\infty$ and $\ell_2$ distortion metrics from successful I-FGSM (Kurakin et al., 2016) and C&W (Carlini and Wagner, 2017b) attacks, respectively.

The scatter plots of distortions v.s. top-1 prediction accuracy are displayed in Fig. 1.1. We define the classification error as 1 minus top-1 accuracy (denoted as 1-acc). By regressing the distortion metric with respect to the classification error of networks on the Pareto frontier of robustness-accuracy distribution (i.e., AlexNet, VGG 16, VGG 19, ResNet_v2_152, Inception_ResNet_v2, and NASNet), they find that the distortion scales linearly with the logarithm of classification error. That is, the distortion and classification error has the following relation: distortion $= a + b \cdot$ log (classification-error). The fitted parameters of $a$ and $b$ are given in the captions of Fig. 1.1. Taking I-FGSM attack (Kurakin et al., 2016) as an example, the linear scaling law suggests that to reduce the classification error by a half, the $\ell_\infty$ distortion of the resulting network will be expected to reduce by approximately 0.02, which is roughly 60% of the AlexNet distortion. Following this trend, if we naively pursue a model with low test error, then the model's adversarial robustness may suffer. Consequently, when designing new networks for ImageNet, standard accuracy is not sufficient to characterize the model performance against adversarial attacks. Similar trend is observed by Su et al. (2018) when using an attack-agnostic adversarial robustness metric (the CLEVER score (Weng et al., 2018b)) as the $y$-axis.

This undesirable trade-off between standard accuracy and adversarial robustness suggests that one should employ the techniques discussed in this book to evaluate and improve adversarial robustness for machine learning.

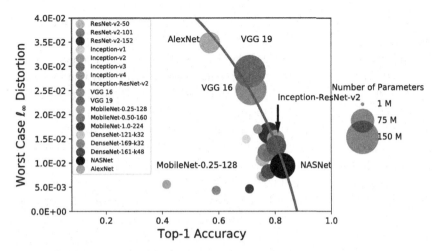

(a) Fitted Pareto frontier of $\ell_\infty$ distortion (I-FGSM attack) vs. top-1 accuracy:
$$\ell_\infty \text{ dist} = [2.9 \cdot \ln(1\text{-acc}) + 6.2] \times 10^{-2}$$

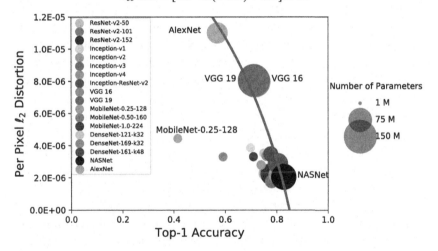

(b) Fitted Pareto frontier of $\ell_2$ distortion (C&W attack) vs. top-1 accuracy:
$$\ell_2 \text{ dist} = [1.1 \cdot \ln(1\text{-acc}) + 2.1] \times 10^{-5}$$

**Figure 1.1** Robustness vs. classification accuracy plots of I-FGSM attack (Kurakin et al., 2016), C&W attack (Carlini and Wagner, 2017b), and on random targets over 18 ImageNet models (Su et al., 2018).

## Fast adaptation of adversarial robustness evaluation assets for emerging machine learning models

As another motivating example, once we have sufficient practice in studying adversarial robustness, when new machine learning models emerge, we can quickly adapt the existing adversarial robustness tools for evaluation and profiling.

For instance, transformers are originally applied in natural language processing (NLP) tasks as a type of deep neural network (DNN) mainly based on the self-attention mechanism (Vaswani et al., 2017; Devlin et al., 2018; Brown et al., 2020b), and transformers with large-scale pretraining have achieved state-of-the-art results on many NLP tasks (Devlin et al., 2018; Liu et al., 2019e; Yang et al., 2019b; Sun et al., 2019b). Recently, Dosovitskiy et al. (2020) applied a pure transformer directly to sequences of image patches (i.e., a vision transformer, ViT) and showed that the Transformer itself can be competitive with convolutional neural networks (CNNs) on image classification tasks. Since then, transformers have been extended to various vision tasks and show competitive or even better performance compared to CNNs and recurrent neural networks (RNNs) (Carion et al., 2020; Chen et al., 2020b; Zhu et al., 2020b).

Using existing tools for adversarial robustness evaluation, Shao et al. (2021a) examine the adversarial robustness of ViTs on image classification tasks and make comparisons with CNN baselines. As highlighted in Fig. 1.2, their experimental results illustrate the superior robustness of ViTs than CNNs in both white-box and black-box attack settings, based on which they make the following important findings:

- Features learned by ViTs contain less low-level information and benefit adversarial robustness. ViTs achieve a lower attack success rate (ASR) of 51.9% compared with a minimum of 83.3% by CNNs in Fig. 1.2. They are also less sensitive to high-frequency adversarial perturbations.
- Using denoised randomized smoothing (Salman et al., 2020b), ViTs attain significantly better certified robustness than CNNs.
- It takes the cost of adversarial robustness to improve the classification accuracy of ViTs by introducing blocks to help learn low-level features as shown in Fig. 1.2.
- Increasing the proportion of transformer blocks in the model leads to better robustness when the model consists of both transformer and CNN blocks. For example, the attack success rate (ASR) decreases from 87.1% to 79.2% when 10 additional transformer blocks are added to T2T-ViT-14. However, increasing the size of a pure transformer model cannot guarantee a similar effect, e.g., the robustness of ViT-S/16 is better than that of ViT-B/16 in Fig. 1.2.
- Pretraining without adversarial training on larger datasets does not improve adversarial robustness though it is critical for training ViT.

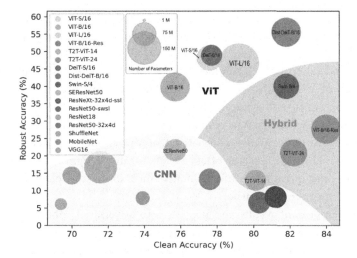

(a) Robust Accuracy v.s. Clean Accuracy

(b) Model Architecture

**Figure 1.2** (a) Robust accuracy v.s. clean accuracy. The robust accuracy is evaluated by AutoAttack (Croce and Hein, 2020). The "Hybrid" class includes CNN-ViT, T2T-ViT and Swin-T as introduced by Shao et al. (2021a). Models with attention mechanisms have their names printed at the center of the circles. ViTs have the best robustness against adversarial perturbations. Introducing other modules to ViT can improve clean accuracy but hurt adversarial robustness. CNNs are more vulnerable to adversarial attacks. (b) Illustration of considered vision transformers and CNNs in Shao et al. (2021a).

- The principle of adversarial training through min-max optimization (Madry et al., 2017; Zhang et al., 2019b) can be applied to train robust ViTs.

Paul and Chen (2022) conduct a comprehensive study on the general robustness of ViT against common corruptions, adversarial perturbations, distribution shifts, and natural adversarial examples. They use six different diverse ImageNet datasets concerning robust classification to conduct a comprehensive performance comparison of ViT models and state-of-the-art CNNs. Through a series of six systematically designed experiments, they show both quantitative and qualitative indications to explain why ViTs are indeed more robust learners.

These important results and insights into adversarial robustness could not be obtained shortly after the emergence of new machine learning models such as ViTs without reusing the available assets and tools in studying existing machine learning models. More importantly, as long as we acknowledge that ensuring adversarial robustness is a necessary step for making realistic and sustainable improvement in machine learning, stronger momentum will be generated to accelerate the progress in developing advanced machine learning.

## 1.5  Practical examples of AI vulnerabilities

Here are some public resources summarizing real-world incidences and vulnerabilities in an ML-based system.
- Adversarial ML Threat Matrix:
  https://github.com/mitre/advmlthreatmatrix.
- AI Incidence Database: https://incidentdatabase.ai/.

## 1.6  Open-source Python libraries for adversarial robustness

Here are some resources of open-source Python-based libraries for studying adversarial robustness:
- IBM adversarial robustness toolbox: https://github.com/Trusted-AI/adversarial-robustness-toolbox.
- CleverHans: https://github.com/cleverhans-lab/cleverhans.
- Foolbox: https://github.com/bethgelab/foolbox.
- RobustBench: https://robustbench.github.io/.
- TextAttack: https://github.com/QData/TextAttack.

# PART 2

# Adversarial attack

# CHAPTER 2

# White-box adversarial attacks

Prediction-evasive adversarial attacks are procedures to generate adversarial examples on a given machine learning model. For a target model $F_\theta$ (also called the victim model from the security point of view), the most general definition of adversarial example is an input $x$ such that the model prediction $F_\theta(x)$ is clearly inconsistent with human perception, where $\theta$ is the set of model parameters. For brevity, we will use $F$ to denote the target model in the remaining chapter. To construct an adversarial example, a typical procedure is to start with a natural data input (e.g., an image) that is correctly classified by the machine learning model and then add a human imperceptible perturbation to change the predicted label. This is also called evasion attack or test-time attack, since the attacker is trying to add a small perturbation in the test time to make the machine learning model misclassify without interfering the training procedure. Fig. 2.1 gives an example of an adversarial attack, where the original bagel image is correctly classified as a *bagel*, but the perturbed example, after adding a human imperceptible noise, will be classified as a *piano*. In practice, an adversarial perturbation could lead to catastrophic damage to a real-time system. For instance, researchers have demonstrated that it is possible to slightly perturb a stop sign to make it being recognized as a speed limit sign by a machine learning-based image recognition system (Eykholt et al., 2018).

In this chapter, we discuss how to conduct adversarial attacks in the *white-box setting*. In this setting the attacker is assumed to have full knowledge of the victim machine learning model. For instance, if the victim

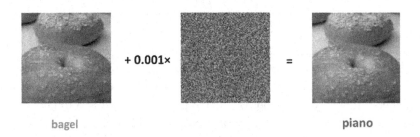

**Figure 2.1** An illustration of adversarial example from (Chen et al., 2017a).

*Adversarial Robustness for Machine Learning*
https://doi.org/10.1016/B978-0-12-824020-5.00011-9

model $F$ is a neural network, we will assume that the attacker knows both the architecture and weights of this network in the white-box setting. Since the attacker can leverage full knowledge to attack the victim model, white-box attacks are the easiest way to construct adversarial examples and also lead to the highest successful rate and smallest perturbations. In practice, the white-box assumption is often too strong since the underlying model used in production is usually hidden to the attacker, and we will discuss how to conduct the attacks under those more realistic settings in the next chapter. Despite being unrealistic, white-box attacks are more reliable ways to evaluate the robustness of a model, since they usually lead to strongest attacks that can be used to evaluate the worst-case performance of a system. Therefore white-box attacks can be used by model developers to provide in-house performance evaluation.

## 2.1 Attack procedure and notations

Now we formally define the procedure of an adversarial attack. For simplicity, we will mainly focus on the multiclass classification problem in this chapter. For a $K$-way multiclass classification problem, we define the model as $F : \mathbb{R}^d \rightarrow \{1, \ldots, K\}$ that maps an input $x$ to a predicted class label. We assume that the model makes the final decision by first computing a score for each class and then choosing the class with the maximum score. Mathematically, we use $f_j(x)$ to denote the predicted score for the $j$th class, and the label with highest score will be the final decision of the model: $F(x) = \text{argmax}_{j \in \{1,\ldots,K\}} f_j(x)$.

Assuming that $x_0 \in \mathbb{R}^d$ is a natural example with the ground truth label $y_0 \in \{1, \ldots, K\}$, a prediction-evasion attack will try to find a small perturbation $\Delta$ such that $F(x_0 + \Delta) \neq y_0$. The perturbed example $x^* = x_0 + \Delta$ is known as an *adversarial example*; this perturbed example is supposed to belong to class $y_0$ since $x^*$ is only slightly perturbed from the original example $x_0$, but the model will misclassify $x^*$ as another label. The overall procedure is illustrated in Fig. 2.2. The notion of "perturbation" can be generalized to other meaningful data manipulations beyond additive noises.

*Untargeted v.s. targeted attack.* Multiple attack methods have been introduced for crafting adversarial examples to attack a machine learning model. In general, there are two kinds of "attack goals", targeted and untargeted. For untargeted attack, the attack is successful if the input image is predicted with the wrong label. Take Fig. 2.2 as an example: as long as the bagel image is not classified as a bagel, the attack is considered successful. For

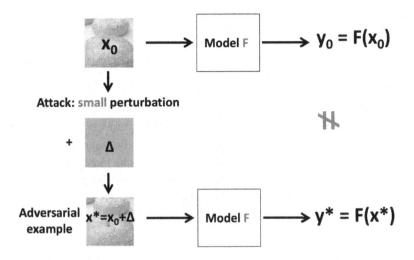

**Figure 2.2** The procedure of adversarial attacks.

targeted attack, the attack is successful only when the adversarial example is classified as the target class. In this example, if the target class is piano, then the attack is considered successful only when the perturbed image on the right-hand side is labeled as piano by the victim classifier.

## 2.2 Formulating attack as constrained optimization

Given the original example $x_0$, an adversarial attack aims to find an adversarial example $x^* = x_0 + \Delta$ that can successfully achieve the attack goal (either targeted or untargeted attack) under the constraint that $\Delta$ should be small. This can be formulated as a constrained optimization problem: we aim to find an adversarial example $x$ that maximizes the "attack successfulness" (or minimizes the attacker's loss function), whereas $x$ is constrained to be close to the original example $x_0$. This can be mathematically written as the following problem:

$$\operatorname*{argmax}_{x} g(x) \text{ s.t. } x \in B(x_0), \tag{2.1}$$

where $g(x)$ measures the successfulness of the attack, and $B(x_0)$ is a small region around $x_0$ indicating the feasible perturbation range.

The definition of $g(x)$ can be defined differently for different attacks. As described in Chapter 1, neural network training usually involves minimizing the cross-entropy (CE) loss, defined as the negative log-likelihood of predicting label $y_0$:

$$\ell_{\text{CE}}(f(\boldsymbol{x}_0), y_0) := -\log P(y_0 \mid \boldsymbol{x}_0), \quad \text{where } P(y_0 \mid \boldsymbol{x}_0) := \frac{e^{f_{y_0}(\boldsymbol{x}_0)}}{\sum_{j=1}^{K} e^{f_j(\boldsymbol{x}_0)}}. \quad (2.2)$$

Here $f_j(\boldsymbol{x}_0)$ is the class prediction score of class $j$, and the prediction probability of class $j$ is computed using a softmax operation for normalization. We can define the $g(\boldsymbol{x})$ for adversarial attacks by slightly changing this loss function. For untargeted attack, the goal of "making model predicts another label" can be formulated as "minimizing the probability of predicting class $y_0$". This can be naturally achieved by setting

$$\text{Untargeted CE loss: } g(\boldsymbol{x}) := \ell_{\text{CE}}(f(\boldsymbol{x}), y_0). \quad (2.3)$$

Since here we want to maximize $g(\boldsymbol{x})$ instead of minimizing it, the perturbation will try to maximally increase the cross-entropy loss to achieve the worst prediction.

For targeted attack, we aim to maximize the predicted probability of the target class $t$. The attack successfulness can thus be defined as

$$\text{Targeted CE loss: } g(\boldsymbol{x}) := -\ell_{\text{CE}}(f(\boldsymbol{x}), t), \quad (2.4)$$

which is the log-likelihood of the target class probability.

The constraint set $B(\boldsymbol{x}_0)$ is usually defined as a small region around $\boldsymbol{x}_0$. If the $\ell_p$ norm is used for measuring distance, then we can define

$$B(\boldsymbol{x}_0) = \{\boldsymbol{x} : \|\boldsymbol{x} - \boldsymbol{x}_0\|_p \leq \epsilon\},$$

where $\epsilon$ is a predefined small constant, known as the perturbation threshold or budget. For example, on the CIFAR-10 image classification dataset (which is a standard benchmarking dataset for evaluating adversarial attacks), the $\epsilon$ is often set as $8/255$ (for $\ell_{\infty}$ norm) when each pixel is in the range of $[0, 255]$. Note that for computer vision applications, we usually need to enforce an additional elementwise lower and upper bounds to ensure that the adversarial example $\boldsymbol{x}$ is still a valid image, so the constraint set will become the intersection of $\ell_p$ ball and $\boldsymbol{x} \in [0, 255]^d$. For simplicity, we will omit this constraint in our derivations since they can often easily done by a simple elementwise projection to the feasible data space.

Once we formulate an adversarial attack as a constraint optimization problem, any existing optimization algorithm can be used for solving this problem to generate an adversarial example. For example, a projected gradient descent method can be applied: at each iteration, we update the current solution $x_t$ by

$$x_{t+1} \leftarrow \Pi(x_t + \alpha \nabla g(x)), \tag{2.5}$$

where $\alpha$ is the learning rate of gradient descent, and $\Pi(\cdot)$ projects the vector to $B(x_0)$. However, in practice, we may find that this plain projected gradient descent update is not very effective in solving the attack problem, especially when we use $\ell_\infty$ norm constraint, which is the most common choice in the computer vision community. In the $\ell_\infty$ norm case the constraint set $B(x)$ is a hyperrectangle (high-dimensional rectangle), and the successful attacks are often (but not always) lying on the corner of this rectangle, i.e., most of the elements of a successful adversarial example $x_i^*$ should be close to $(x_0)_i \pm \epsilon$. If the plain projected gradient descent update (2.5) is used, then some coordinates will require many iterations to reach $\pm \epsilon$, leading to slow convergence. Therefore it is a common practice to use the *steepest descent algorithm* for conducting an attack, as detailed below.

## 2.3 Steepest descent, FGSM and PGD attack

In this section, we will first consider the $\ell_\infty$ norm attack (i.e., $B(x) = \{x : \|x - x_0\|_\infty \le \epsilon\}$). Let us consider the problem of conducting only *one update* to approximately solve (2.1). The idea of steepest descent update is forming a linear approximation of the objective function and finding the best update to maximize this linear approximation. Concretely, we can conduct the first-order Taylor expansion of $g(x)$ on the initial solution $x_0$ (assuming that we start from the original natural example):

$$g(x) \approx g(x_0) + \nabla g(x_0)^T (x - x_0).$$

We can then solve the following constraint optimization problem, which is an approximation of (2.1):

$$\underset{x}{\mathrm{argmax}}\, \nabla g(x_0)^T (x - x_0) \quad \text{s.t.} \quad x \in \|x - x_0\|_\infty \le \epsilon. \tag{2.6}$$

Note that we drop the $g(x_0)$ term in the Taylor expansion since it is a constant irrelevant to $x$. Now we can easily see that (2.6) has a closed-form solution

$$x_1 = x_0 + \epsilon \mathrm{sign}(\nabla g(x_0)). \tag{2.7}$$

Here sign($\cdot$) $\in \{+1, -1\}$ denotes elementwise sign values. This is the one-step steepest descent update, and surprisingly, it has been found that even this simple step is very effective for constructing adversarial examples. This rule in (2.7) is known as the fast gradient sign method (FGSM), first proposed by Goodfellow et al. (2015).

A straightforward extension of FGSM is to run steepest descent for multiple iterations. In this case, we need to choose a step size $\alpha$ for each iteration, that is, from the current iteration $x_t$ we allow the update in $\{x_{t+1} : \|x_{t+1} - x_t\|_\infty \leq \alpha\}$ and minimize the linear approximation within this region. This will lead to the same subproblem with (2.6) with $\epsilon$ being replaced by $\alpha$, so the optimal update is $x_t + \alpha \text{sign}(\nabla g(x_t))$. Another issue when running multiple iterations is that the variables may go outside the constraint set $B(x_0)$ after few iterations. Therefore we have to further project the update back to the constraint set, leading to the following iterative steepest descent update:

$$x_{t+1} = \Pi(x_t + \alpha \text{sign}(\nabla g(x_t))) \quad \forall t = 0, \ldots, T-1. \qquad (2.8)$$

If we run this update for $T$ iterations, then the final solution $x_T$ is supposed to be better than FGSM. This is called the iterative FGSM (I-FGSM) attack by Kurakin et al. (2016), also called the (basic) PGD attack by Madry et al. (2018). This PGD attack is one of the most effective first-order (gradient-based) algorithms for constructing adversarial examples. Furthermore, it is very easy to incorporate in the adversarial training algorithm to train a robust model, which will be discussed in Chapter 11.

One issue for running PGD attack is to choose a suitable step size $\alpha$. If $\alpha < \frac{\epsilon}{T}$, then the solution $x_T$ will not reach the boundary of $B(x_0)$, and so the attack will not be very effective. In practice, $\alpha$ is usually set as a number slightly larger than $\frac{\epsilon}{T}$. Its value can also vary per attack iteration. Also, one can randomly initialize $x_0$ inside $B(x_0)$ and possibly repeat this process multiple times for finding adversarial examples.

## 2.4 Transforming to an unconstrained optimization problem

Instead of solving the constrained optimization problem in (2.1), we can actually transform it into an unconstrained optimization problem and apply standard gradient descent or other first-order methods (without projection) to solve the problem. This is done by solving the following "soft-constrained" form, where we remove the constraint and add a penalty in the objective function to enforce small perturbation:

$$\operatorname*{argmin}_{x} -g(x) + \lambda \cdot \|x - x_0\|_p, \tag{2.9}$$

where $\lambda > 0$ is a constant to control the balance between the two terms. A larger $\lambda$ will lead to a smaller perturbation in $\ell_p$ norm but lower attack successfulness, whereas a smaller $\lambda$ will find larger perturbations with higher attack success rate.

Note that we can find adversarial examples within a certain $\epsilon$ perturbation constraint by solving a series of unconstrained problems (2.9). Let $x^*(\lambda)$ be the solution of (2.9) with a constant $\lambda$; then the perturbation $\|x^*(\lambda) - x_0\|_p$ will be a decreasing function of $\lambda$. Therefore we can find the ideal $\lambda$ that produces $\|x^*(\lambda) - x_0\|_p = \epsilon$ by binary search. This approach has been used in the Carlini and Wagner (C&W) attack (Carlini and Wagner, 2017b), which solves the unconstrained form with a different loss function defined below.

## 2.5 Another way to define attack objective

Defining the attack successfulness $g(x)$ by cross-entropy loss is intuitive, but it has been found that sometimes the nonconvexity introduced by cross-entropy loss makes PGD attack converge slowly and sometimes result in a bad local minimum. Therefore several alternative definitions of $g(x)$ have been studied in the literature. Among them, Carlini and Wagner (2017b) showed that defining $g(x)$ with a so-called "hinge loss" is most effective. Attacks using this approach are called C&W attack. For untargeted attack, the C&W loss can be written as

$$\text{Untargeted C\&W loss: } g(x) = -\max\{f_{y_0}(x) - \max_{j \neq y_0} f_j(x), -\kappa\}, \tag{2.10}$$

where $y_0$ is the ground truth class, and $\kappa \geq 0$ is a constant. For $\kappa = 0$, this function will be negative if the model predicts the original class ($f_{y_0}(x) \geq \max_{j \neq y_0} f_j(x)$) and zero when the model gives any top-1 prediction other than $y_0$ (i.e., the "wrong" prediction). Therefore maximizing this function will obtain a successful attack. Setting $\kappa$ to be some positive value can enforce a margin between $f_{y_0}(x)$ and $\max_{j \neq y_0} f_j(x)$, but this is usually only used in special circumstances when we want to have stronger adversarial examples that are further away from the decision boundary. With a similar intuition, the loss for C&W targeted attack can be written as

$$\text{Targeted C\&W loss: } g(\boldsymbol{x}) = -\max\{\max_{j \neq t} f_j(\boldsymbol{x}) - f_t(\boldsymbol{x}), -\kappa\}, \qquad (2.11)$$

where $t$ is the target class. It has been observed that this loss function leads to better attack, especially for the $\ell_2$ perturbation case.

## 2.6 Attacks with different $\ell_p$ norms

For computer vision, the commonly used $\ell_p$ norms for adversarial perturbations include $\ell_\infty$, $\ell_2$, $\ell_1$, and $\ell_0$ norms.[1] The family of $\ell_p$ norms carry physical meanings when crafting adversarial examples. The $\ell_\infty$ norm confines the maximal change in all dimensions, the $\ell_2$ norm measures the Euclidean distance between $\boldsymbol{x}$ and $\boldsymbol{x}_0$, the $\ell_1$ norm measures the sum of total changes (in absolute value) between $\boldsymbol{x}$ and $\boldsymbol{x}_0$, and the $\ell_0$ norm measures the number of modified elements (e.g., modified pixels for images). Depending on the context, we can use mixed norms for adversarial attacks, either in the form of constraints or penalty functions in the optimization formulation. For instance, Chen et al. (2018b) proposed the elastic–net attack to deep neural networks (EAD attack), which uses a mixture of $\ell_1$ and $\ell_2$ norms to find sparse adversarial examples and is shown to improve the attack performance of C&W attack. Su et al. (2019) proposed an $\ell_0$-norm based attack that only modifies few pixels to cause prediction changes. We can also leverage the convolution filters and use group norms to design structured adversarial attacks as proposed by Xu et al. (2019b).

## 2.7 Universal attack

Up to now, all the attacks we introduced are generating a perturbation $\boldsymbol{\Delta}$ for each image, and the perturbations for each image are different. An interesting question studied in the literature is "Can we use the same adversarial perturbation on all the images to fool the victim model?" Moosavi-Dezfooli et al. (2017) first introduced this concept and call it *universal adversarial perturbation*. Note that the perturbation, although universal to all the images, is designed for each particular machine learning model. Therefore the universal perturbation designed for one model may not generalize

---

[1] For any $p \geq 1$, the $\ell_p$ norm of $x$ is defined as $\|\boldsymbol{x}\|_p = (\sum_{i=1}^{d} |\boldsymbol{x}_i|^p)^{1/p}$. It can be shown that $\|\boldsymbol{x}\|_\infty = \max_i |\boldsymbol{x}_i|$. The $\ell_0$ norm of $\|\boldsymbol{x}\|_0$ is defined as the number of nonzero entries in $\boldsymbol{x}$. Rigorously speaking, $\ell_0$ is a seminorm.

to another model. Finding the universal perturbation can make attack more efficient in real time and will reveal the weakness of a particular model across all the images.

The problem of generating the universal adversarial perturbation for a model $F$ can also be formulated as an optimization problem. Instead of considering only one image, we have to consider a set of images, denoted by $D$. Both constrained and unconstrained optimization formulations can then be generalized by considering the overall loss on multiple examples. For instance, the constrained form in (2.1) can be generalized to the universal attack setting as

$$\underset{\Delta}{\operatorname{argmax}} \sum_{x \in D} g(x + \Delta) \text{ s.t. } \|\Delta\|_p \le \epsilon. \tag{2.12}$$

The optimizer of this problem will then be a small perturbation that can successfully attack as many images as possible. Similarly, FGSM or PGD attack can be derived to solve this problem. Moreover, we can also generalize the unconstrained form (2.9) to the universal attack setting. Wang et al. (2021a) improve the performance of universal attack over (2.12) by using a min–max optimization solver.

## 2.8  Adaptive white-box attack

In early days, in the research community, there are active and rolling discussions on how claiming a defense is effective against an attack, because the conclusion will differ significantly based on the action order of the attacker and defender, which is an important specification of the threat model. If the attacker makes the first move by creating adversarial examples, and later the defender comes into discern those generated adversarial examples, such as using techniques based on input filtering or data reconstruction prior to data inference, then many attacks can be alleviated or mitigated. On the other hand, if the defender makes the first move, and the attacker knows the defense in place, then many defenses were shown to be ineffective, or "broken", in the latter setting (Carlini and Wagner, 2017a; Athalye et al., 2018; Carlini et al., 2019a).

The latter setting is known as the *adaptive white-box attack* setting, which essentially assumes that the defense is totally transparent to the attacker (other than some uncontrollable randomness) when crafting adversarial attacks. This setting may be unrealistic for implementing practical attacks, but it offers honest (worst-case) assessment about the true robustness of the protected model against adversarial attacks beyond the advantage from the information asymmetry between the attacker and defender. Otherwise, it is argued that models that are robust in the first setting may give a false sense of security or robustness if they are not robust against adaptive attacks (Carlini and Wagner, 2017a; Athalye et al., 2018; Carlini et al., 2019a). One typical example is the so-called "gradient obfuscation" effect brought by defenses that confuse gradient-based attacks due to information obfuscation (e.g., overly smooth or noisy gradients on the loss landscape in the input space) as discussed by Athalye et al. (2018). However, an attacker that is aware of the defense mechanism can propose advanced methods or adopt nongradient-based attacks to render these defenses ineffective. Carlini et al. (2019a) provide many principles on evaluating adversarial robustness based on adaptive attacks.

## 2.9 Empirical comparison

Following Chen et al. (2018b); Xu et al. (2019b), Table 2.1 compares white-box attacks of targeted attacks with randomly selected classes and with different $\ell_p$ norms on three image classification tasks: MNIST, CIFAR-10, and ImageNet. A set of images from the test set with correct classification are selected to perform adversarial attacks. For each image, we report the smallest distortion leading to successful attacks. If all tested $\epsilon$ thresholds of a given attack fail, then we mark it as an unsuccessful attack. The attack success rate (ASR) reports the fraction of successful attacks for all tested images. The FGSM/I-FGSM attacks use norm projections to a specified perturbation threshold as described by Kurakin et al. (2016).[2] We provide a fine grid of $\epsilon$ thresholds for FGSM/I-FGSM attacks. For norm-penalty-based attacks such as C&W and EAD, we use the binary search strategy for tuning the coefficient $\lambda$ as proposed by Carlini and Wagner (2017b), which balances attack successfulness and distortion. For C&W attack, we use the $\ell_2$ norm penalty. For EAD attack, we use the mixed $\ell_1 + \ell_2$ norm penalty (i.e., the elastic net norm $\|x - x_0\|_2 + \beta \cdot \|x - x_0\|_1$ with $\beta = 10^{-3}$) and select the best distortion according to either the elastic net norm (EN rule) or the $\ell_1$ norm ($\ell_1$ rule). As seen from Table 2.1, all

---

[2] Note that the $\ell_1$ norm projection in (Kurakin et al., 2016) is only an approximation of the true projection function. The exact projection requires solving another optimization subproblem as described by Xu et al. (2019b). We include the empirical results here just for completeness.

**Table 2.1** Comparison of different attacks on MNIST, CIFAR10, and ImageNet (average case). ASR means attack success rate (%) of random targeted attacks. The distortion metrics are averaged over successful examples. EAD, the C&W attack, and I-FGSM-$\ell_\infty$ attain the least $\ell_1$, $\ell_2$, and $\ell_\infty$ distorted adversarial examples, respectively.

| Attack method | MNIST | | | | CIFAR-10 | | | | ImageNet | | | |
|---|---|---|---|---|---|---|---|---|---|---|---|---|
| | ASR | $\ell_1$ | $\ell_2$ | $\ell_\infty$ | ASR | $\ell_1$ | $\ell_2$ | $\ell_\infty$ | ASR | $\ell_1$ | $\ell_2$ | $\ell_\infty$ |
| C&W ($\ell_2$) | 100 | 22.46 | **1.972** | 0.514 | 100 | 13.62 | **0.392** | 0.044 | 100 | 232.2 | **0.705** | 0.03 |
| FGSM-$\ell_1$ | 39 | 53.5 | 4.186 | 0.782 | 48.8 | 51.97 | 1.48 | 0.152 | 1 | 61 | 0.187 | 0.007 |
| FGSM-$\ell_2$ | 34.6 | 39.15 | 3.284 | 0.747 | 42.8 | 39.5 | 1.157 | 0.136 | 1 | 2338 | 6.823 | 0.25 |
| FGSM-$\ell_\infty$ | 42.5 | 127.2 | 6.09 | 0.296 | 52.3 | 127.81 | 2.373 | 0.047 | 3 | 3655 | 7.102 | 0.014 |
| I-FGSM-$\ell_1$ | 100 | 32.94 | 2.606 | 0.591 | 100 | 17.53 | 0.502 | 0.055 | 77 | 526.4 | 1.609 | 0.054 |
| I-FGSM-$\ell_2$ | 100 | 30.32 | 2.41 | 0.561 | 100 | 17.12 | 0.489 | 0.054 | 100 | 774.1 | 2.358 | 0.086 |
| I-FGSM-$\ell_\infty$ | 100 | 71.39 | 3.472 | **0.227** | 100 | 33.3 | 0.68 | **0.018** | 100 | 864.2 | 2.079 | **0.01** |
| EAD (EN rule) | 100 | **17.4** | 2.001 | 0.594 | 100 | **8.18** | 0.502 | 0.097 | 100 | **69.47** | 1.563 | 0.238 |
| EAD ($\ell_1$ rule) | 100 | **14.11** | 2.211 | 0.768 | 100 | **6.066** | 0.613 | 0.17 | 100 | **40.9** | 1.598 | 0.293 |

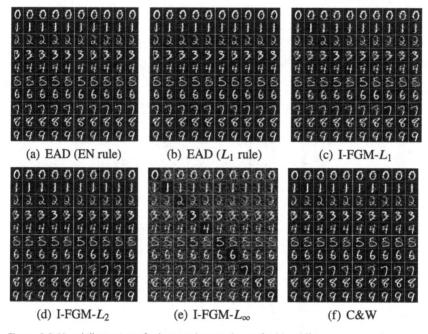

**Figure 2.3** Visual illustration of adversarial examples crafted by different attack methods on MNIST. For each method, the images displayed on the diagonal are the original examples. In each row the off-diagonal images are the corresponding adversarial examples with columns indexing target labels (from left to right: digits 0 to 9).

attacks other than FGSM can reach 100% ASR due to the use of iterative gradient optimization. Attacks tailored with different norm constraints or penalty functions can indeed find corresponding adversarial examples with small perturbations.

For visual illustration, the adversarial examples of selected benign images from the test sets are displayed in Figs. 2.3, 2.4, and 2.5. On CIFAR10 and ImageNet the adversarial examples are visually indistinguishable. On MNIST the I-FGM examples are blurrier than EAD and the C&W attack.

## 2.10  Extended reading

- Adversarial attacks beyond $\ell_p$ norms include semantically similar examples such as color space shifting (Hosseini and Poovendran, 2018) and spatial transformations (e.g., rotation) (Xiao et al., 2018; Engstrom et al., 2019b). Tsai et al. (2022) proposed composite adversarial attacks consdering multiple attack types and their attack orders.

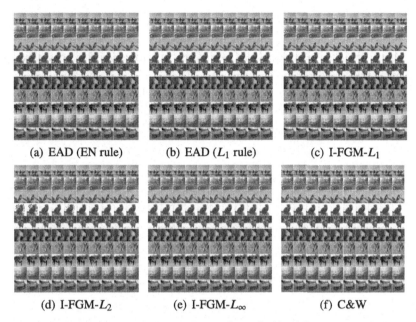

(a) EAD (EN rule)    (b) EAD ($L_1$ rule)    (c) I-FGM-$L_1$

(d) I-FGM-$L_2$    (e) I-FGM-$L_\infty$    (f) C&W

**Figure 2.4** Visual illustration of adversarial examples crafted by different attack methods on CIFAR10. For each method, the images displayed on the diagonal are the original examples. In each row the off-diagonal images are the corresponding adversarial examples with columns indexing target labels.

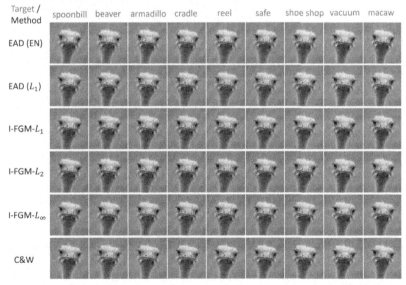

**Figure 2.5** Visual illustration of adversarial examples crafted by different attack methods on ImageNet. Each column represents a targeted class to attack, and each row represents an attack method.

- Adversarial attacks considering multiple $\ell_p$ norms simultaneously (Xu et al., 2019b; Tramer and Boneh, 2019).
- Auto-Attack: An ensemble of parameter-free adversarial attacks (Croce and Hein, 2020).
- Unrestricted adversarial examples (Brown et al., 2018).
- On and off manifold adversarial examples (Stutz et al., 2019).
- Natural adversarial examples (Hendrycks et al., 2021).

# CHAPTER 3

# Black-box adversarial attacks

In recent years, "machine learning as a service" has offered the world an effortless access to powerful machine learning tools for a wide variety of tasks. For example, commercially available services such as Google Cloud Vision API[1] and Clarifai.com[2] provide well-trained image classifiers to the public. One is able to upload and obtain the class prediction results for images at hand at a low price. However, the details of the model behind the service are unknown to an attacker/user, which means that the function/model $f$ can be viewed as a *black-box* model. A *query* is defined as an instance to upload a data input $x$ and obtain the function/model output $f(x)$. In addition to attack success rate, the number of query counts to a targeted black-box model required to launch successful adversarial attacks (e.g., finding adversarial examples) is also important to evaluate the efficiency of black-box attacks.

## 3.1 Evasion attack taxonomy

Evasion attacks can be categorized based on attackers' knowledge of the target model. Fig. 3.1 illustrates the taxonomy of different attack types.

*White-box attack* introduced in Chapter 2 assumes complete knowledge about the target model, including model architecture and model parameters. Consequently, an attacker can exploit the autodifferentiation function offered by deep learning packages, such as backpropagation (input gradient) from the model output to the model input, to craft adversarial examples. This "attack" would be most practical for model developers to perform a series of in-house robustness testing, that is, a virtual adversary or a white-hat hacker. For real attackers, requiring white-box access to the target model is often not feasible.

*Black-box attack* assumes that an attacker can only observe the model prediction of a data input (i.e., a query) and does not know any other information. The target model can be viewed as a black-box function, and thus backpropagation for input gradient is infeasible without knowing the

---

[1] https://cloud.google.com/vision.
[2] https://clarifai.com.

*Adversarial Robustness for Machine Learning*
https://doi.org/10.1016/B978-0-12-824020-5.00012-0
29

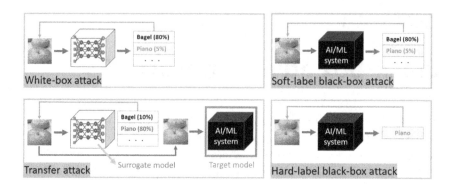

**Figure 3.1** Taxonomy and illustration of evasion attacks.

model details. In the *soft-label black-box attack* setting, an attacker can observe (parts of) class predictions and their associated confidence scores. In the *hard-label black-box attack* (decision-based) setting, an attacker can only observe the top-1 label prediction, which is the least information required to be returned to remain utility of the model. In addition to attack success rate, the query efficiency is also an important metric for performance evaluation of black-box attacks.

*Transfer attack* is a branch of black-box attack that uses adversarial examples generated from a white-box surrogate model to attack the target black-box model. The surrogate model can be either pretrained (Liu et al., 2017b) or distilled from a set of data samples with soft labels given by the target model as their training labels (Papernot et al., 2016, 2017).

Between the spectrum of white-box and black-box attacks, variations in the threat models and the attacker's capability will result in different *gray-box* attacks.

## 3.2  Soft-label black-box attack

Black-box attack algorithms often adopt either the penalty-based (e.g., Eq. (2.9)) or budget-based (e.g., Eq. (2.1)) formulation. Since the input gradient of the attacker's loss is unavailable to obtain in the black-box setting, one principal approach is performing gradient estimation using model queries and then using the estimated gradient to replace the true gradient in white-box attack algorithms, leading to the zeroth-order optimization (ZOO) based black-box attacks (Chen et al., 2017a).

Without loss of generality, it suffices to denote the target model as a classification function parameterized by $\boldsymbol{\theta}$, defined as $f_{\boldsymbol{\theta}} : [0, 1]^d \mapsto \mathbb{R}^K$, that takes a $d$-dimensional scaled data sample as its input and yields a vector of prediction scores of all $K$ classes, such as the prediction probabilities for each class. The term "soft labels" refers to the fact that an attacker can observe the prediction score of each class. We further consider the case of applying an entrywise monotonic transformation $M(f_{\boldsymbol{\theta}})$ to the output of $f_{\boldsymbol{\theta}}$ for black-box attacks, since a monotonic transformation preserves the ranking of the class predictions and can alleviate the problem of large score variation in $f_{\boldsymbol{\theta}}$ (e.g., the transformation of probability to log probability is monotonic).

Here we formulate soft-label black-box targeted attacks using penalty-based loss. The formulation can be easily adapted to untargeted attacks. Let $(\boldsymbol{x}_0, t_0)$ denote a natural image $\boldsymbol{x}_0$ and its ground-truth class label $t_0$, and let $(\boldsymbol{x}, t)$ denote the adversarial example of $\boldsymbol{x}_0$ and the target attack class label $t \neq t_0$. The problem of finding an adversarial example can be formulated as an optimization problem taking the generic form of

$$\min_{\boldsymbol{x} \in [0,1]^d} \text{Dist}(\mathbf{x}, \mathbf{x}_0) + \lambda \cdot \text{Loss}\big(\mathbf{x}, M(f_{\boldsymbol{\theta}}(\boldsymbol{x})), t\big), \qquad (3.1)$$

where $\text{Dist}(\mathbf{x}, \mathbf{x}_0)$ measures the distortion between $\mathbf{x}$ and $\mathbf{x}_0$, $\text{Loss}(\cdot)$ is an attack objective reflecting the likelihood of predicting $t = \arg\max_{k \in \{1,\dots,K\}} [M(f_{\boldsymbol{\theta}}(\boldsymbol{x}))]_k$, $\lambda \geq 0$ is a regularization coefficient, and the constraint $\mathbf{x} \in [0, 1]^d$ confines the adversarial image $\boldsymbol{x}$ to the valid scaled data space. Consider the case of additive input perturbation, $\text{Dist}(\boldsymbol{x}, \boldsymbol{x}_0)$ is often evaluated by the $\ell_p$ norm defined as $\text{Dist}(\boldsymbol{x}, \boldsymbol{x}_0) = \|\boldsymbol{x} - \boldsymbol{x}_0\|_p$, where $\delta = \boldsymbol{x} - \boldsymbol{x}_0$ is the additive perturbation to $\boldsymbol{x}_0$. The attack objective $\text{Loss}(\cdot)$ can be the training loss (e.g., cross-entropy) for classification or the margin-based C&W loss (Carlini and Wagner, 2017b), as introduced in Chapter 2. The log operation is often adopted for the entrywise monotonic transformation function $M$.

In the black-box attack setting, the attack objective in (3.1) can be viewed as a black-box function $F$. Since only the function values of $F$ are observable, unlike white-box attacks, we cannot use gradient-based approaches for solving (3.1). A fundamental tool to address this issue is the use of *zeroth-order optimization* (ZOO), which follows gradient-based (first-order) optimization rules but uses function values at two closeby points to estimate the gradient instead of using the true gradient.

*Coordinatewise gradient estimation.* As a first attempt to enable gradient-free black-box attacks, Chen et al. (2017a) use the symmetric difference quotient method (Lax and Terrell, 2014) to evaluate the gradient $\frac{\partial F(x)}{\partial x_i}$ of the $i$th component by

$$g_i = \frac{F(x + he_i) - F(x - he_i)}{2h} \approx \frac{\partial F(x)}{\partial x_i} \qquad (3.2)$$

using a small $h$, and here $e_i$ denotes the $i$th elementary basis (having one at the $i$th entry and zero elsewhere). Theoretically this estimation will get the exact gradient value when $h \to 0$, however, in practice taking very small $h$ also results in some numerical error, so one usually choose some small-enough value such as $h = 0.001$.

Note that the nature of coordinatewise gradient estimation step in (3.2) must incur an enormous amount of model queries to obtain the full gradient estimate and is hence not query-efficient. To estimate the gradient of dimension $d$, it needs $2 \cdot d$ model queries to $F$. For example, the ImageNet dataset has $d = 299 \times 299 \times 3 \approx 270,000$ input dimensions, rendering coordinatewise zeroth-order optimization query-inefficient. Therefore, to use this coordinatewise gradient estimation, Chen et al. (2017a) uses a coordinate descent algorithm to solve the attack objective (3.1), where at each iteration the coordinate descent algorithm picks a coordinate $i$, computes gradient based on (3.2), and then update the coordinate by $x_i \leftarrow x_i - \alpha g_i$, where $\alpha$ is the step size.

*Random vector based gradient estimation.* The coordinatewise gradient estimation mentioned above can be viewed as computing the derectional derivative along the direction of $e_i$. However, in standard attacks when the perturbation is bounded by small $\ell_2$ or $\ell_\infty$ norm, coordinate-wise perturbation is usually insufficient, so using coordinate gradient estimation will require a large amount of queries. Therefore, query-efficient black-box attacks such as (Tu et al., 2019) use the following gradient estimator which computes the directional derivative at a randomly sampled direction $u$:

$$g = b \cdot \frac{f(x + \beta u) - f(x)}{\beta} \cdot u, \qquad (3.3)$$

where $\beta > 0$ is a smoothing parameter, $u$ is a unit-length vector that is uniformly drawn at random from a unit Euclidean sphere, and $b$ is a tunable scaling parameter that balances the bias and variance trade-off of the gradient estimation error.

To effectively control the error in gradient estimation, we consider a more general gradient estimator, in which the gradient estimate is averaged over $q$ random directions $\{\mathbf{u}^{(j)}\}_{j=1}^{q}$, that is,

$$\bar{g} = \frac{1}{q}\sum_{j=1}^{q}g^{(j)}, \tag{3.4}$$

where $g^{(j)}$ is a gradient estimate defined in (3.3) with $\mathbf{u} = \mathbf{u}^{(j)}$. The use of multiple random directions can reduce the variance of $\bar{g}$ in (3.4) for convex loss functions (Duchi et al., 2015; Liu et al., 2018a).

Below we establish an error analysis of the averaged random gradient estimator in (3.4) for studying the influence of the parameters $b$ and $q$ on estimation error and query efficiency.

**Theorem 1.** *Let $F : \mathbb{R}^d \mapsto \mathbb{R}$ be a differentiable function with L-Lipschitz gradient $\nabla F$.[3] Then the mean squared estimation error of $\bar{g}$ in (3.4) is upper bounded by*

$$\mathbb{E}\|\bar{g} - \nabla F(\mathbf{x})\|_2^2 \le 4\left(\frac{b^2}{d^2} + \frac{b^2}{dq} + \frac{(b-d)^2}{d^2}\right)\|\nabla F(\mathbf{x})\|_2^2 + \frac{2q+1}{q}b^2\beta^2 L^2. \tag{3.5}$$

*Proof.* See Section 3.7.                                                    □

Here we highlight the important implications based on Theorem 1: (i) The error analysis holds when $F$ is *nonconvex*; (ii) In neural network implementations, the true gradient $\nabla F$ can be viewed as the numerical gradient obtained via back-propagation; (iii) For any fixed $b$, selecting a small $\beta$ (e.g., $\beta = 1/d$) can effectively reduce the last error term in (3.5), and we therefore focus on optimizing the first error term; (iv) The first error term in (3.5) exhibits the influence of $b$ and $q$ on the estimation error and is independent of $\beta$. We further elaborate on (iv) as follows. Fixing $q$ and letting $\eta(b) = \frac{b^2}{d^2} + \frac{b^2}{dq} + \frac{(b-d)^2}{d^2}$ be the coefficient of the first error term in (3.5), the optimal $b$ that minimizes $\eta(b)$ is $b^* = \frac{dq}{2q+d}$. For query efficiency, we would like to keep $q$ small, which then implies $b^* \approx q$ and $\eta(b^*) \approx 1$ when the dimension $d$ is large. On the other hand, as $q \to \infty$, $b^* \approx d/2$ and $\eta(b^*) \approx 1/2$, which yields a smaller error upper bound but is query-inefficient. We also note that by setting $b = q$ the coefficient $\eta(b) = \frac{b^2}{d^2} + \frac{b^2}{dq} + \frac{(b-d)^2}{d^2} \approx 1$ and thus is independent of the dimension $d$ and parameter $q$.

---

[3] A function $W$ is L-Lipschitz if $\|W(\mathbf{w}_1) - W(\mathbf{w}_2)\|_2 \le L\|\mathbf{w}_1 - \mathbf{w}_2\|_2$ for all $\mathbf{w}_1, \mathbf{w}_2$. For neural networks with ReLU activations, $L$ can be derived from the model weights (Szegedy et al., 2014).

*Pseudo-gradient descent.* With the estimated gradient $g$, we can extend any gradient-based white-box attack to the soft-label black-box setting, by conducting the same gradient-based attack with gradient replaced by the gradient estimator $g$. For example, we can solve (3.1) using a regular (projected) gradient descent/ascent algorithm following

$$x_{t+1} \leftarrow \Pi\big(x_t - \alpha \cdot g(x_t)\big), \tag{3.6}$$

where $t$ denotes the iteration index, $\Pi$ denotes the project operations (e.g., projection to $[0, 1]^d$), and $\alpha$ denotes the step size. The choices in gradient estimators and the type of gradient-based optimization solvers (e.g., PGD, Adam or Mementum-SGD) will lead to different black-box attack algorithms.

## 3.3 Hard-label black-box attack

Hard-label black-box attacks assume the most information-restricted setting that only the top-1 class prediction (but not the scores) is observable to an attacker. In this setting, the naive attack objective in (3.1) will be ill-defined so one cannot directly extend white-box or soft-label black-box attacks to the hard-label setting. If we replace $f_\theta(x)$ by the hard-label prediction in (3.1), the objective function will be a discrete step function; we can observe small perturbation either doesn't affect the objective function value (when the prediction label is unchanged) or result in a discrete change to the objective function value (when the prediction label is changed). Therefore, zeroth order optimization attacks used in the soft-label black-box setting cannot be easily applied. Despite the above-mentioned difficulty, it has been shown that by carefully reformulating the attack objective function, zeroth-order optimization principles can still be applied by spending extra queries to explore local loss landscapes for gradient estimation (Cheng et al., 2019a, 2020c; Chen et al., 2020a).

For a given example $x_0$, true label $t_0$, and the hard-label black-box function $f_\theta : \mathbb{R}^d \to \{1, \ldots, K\}$, we define our objective function $h : \mathbb{R}^d \to \mathbb{R}$ depending on the type of attack:

$$\textit{Untargeted attack: } h(s) = \min_{\lambda > 0} \lambda \quad \text{s.t.} \quad f_\theta\left(x_0 + \lambda \frac{s}{\|s\|}\right) \neq t_0. \tag{3.7}$$

*Targeted attack (given target t):* $h(s) = \min_{\lambda > 0} \lambda$   s.t.   $f_\theta\left(x_0 + \lambda \frac{s}{\|s\|}\right) = t.$

$$(3.8)$$

In this formulation, $s$ represents the direction of adversarial example, and $h(s)$ is the distance from $x_0$ to the nearest adversarial example along the direction $s$. The norm $\|s\|$ in the denominator makes the search vector $\frac{s}{\|s\|}$ having unit length. For untargeted attack, $h(s)$ also corresponds to the distance to the decision boundary along the direction $s$.

The main idea of this reformulation proposed in (Cheng et al., 2019a) is that instead of directly optimizing the adversarial perturbation as in (3.1), we aim to find a direction $s$ such that the worst-case perturbation will be along that direction. As $h(s)$ defined above measures the distance to the closest adversarial example along direction $s$, finding the direction of adversarial example can be formulated as the following optimization problem:

$$\min_s \ h(s). \qquad (3.9)$$

Finally, the adversarial example can be found by $x = x_0 + h(s^*)\frac{s^*}{\|s^*\|}$, where $s^*$ is the optimal solution of (3.9).

In the black-box attack setting, we are not able to obtain the gradient of $h$, but we can evaluate the function value of $h$ using the hard-label queries. For simplicity, we focus on untargeted attack here, but the same procedure can be applied to targeted attack as well.

Here we discuss how to compute $h(s)$ directly without additional information. For a given normalized $s$, this can be computed by a coarse-grained search and then a binary search. Taking untargeted attack as an example, in coarse-grained search, the algorithm queries the points $\{x_0 + \alpha s, x_0 + 2\alpha s, \dots\}$ one by one until finding an adversarial example $f(x + i\alpha s) \neq t_0$. This means that the boundary lies between $[x_0 + (i-1)\alpha s, x_0 + i\alpha s]$. We can then enter the second phase to conduct a binary search to find the solution within this region. Note that there is an upper bound of the first stage if we choose $s$ by the direction of $x - x_0$ with some $x$ from another class. This procedure is used to find the initial $s_0$ and corresponding $g(s_0)$ in our optimization algorithm. The entire procedure for computing the $h$ value is presented in Algorithm 1. Note that this procedure is query-inefficient since it may take many queries in the coarse-grained search until finding the interval contains an adversarial example. However, the procedure is guaranteed to find the closest adversarial example when the interval is small enough.

---

**Algorithm 1** Local computation of $h(s)$.

---

1: **Input:** Hard-label model $f_\theta$, original sample $x_0$, query direction $s$, previous solution $v$, increase/decrease ratio $\alpha = 0.01$, stopping tolerance $\gamma$ (maximum tolerance of computed error)

2: $s \leftarrow s/\|s\|$

3: **if** $f_\theta(x_0 + vs) = t_0$ **then**

4:     $v_{left} \leftarrow v, v_{right} \leftarrow (1 + \alpha)v$

5:     **while** $f_\theta(x_0 + v_{right}s) = t_0$ **do**

6:         $v_{right} \leftarrow (1 + \alpha)v_{right}$

7:     **end while**

8: **else**

9:     $v_{right} \leftarrow v, v_{left} \leftarrow (1 - \alpha)v$

10:     **while** $f_\theta(x_0 + v_{left}s) \neq t_0$ **do**

11:         $v_{left} \leftarrow (1 - \alpha)v_{left}$

12:     **end while**

13: **end if**

14: ## Binary Search within $[v_{left}, v_{right}]$

15: **while** $v_{right} - v_{left} > \gamma$ **do**

16:     $v_{mid} \leftarrow (v_{right} + v_{left})/2$

17:     **if** $f_\theta(x_0 + v_{mid}s) = t_0$ **then**

18:         $v_{left} \leftarrow v_{mid}$

19:     **else**

20:         $v_{right} \leftarrow v_{mid}$

21:     **end if**

22: **end while**

23: **return** $v_{right}$

---

Although it requires many samples to exactly compute the $h$ value, when integrating it in the zeroth order optimization algorithm we can usually ignore the coarse-grained search and directly enter the binary search phase. This is because the computation of $h$ values is needed for finite-difference gradient estimator (such as (3.3)), which means we already know $h(x)$ and want to compute a closeby point $h(x + \beta u)$. Therefore, the queried direction will only be a slight modification of the previous one. In this case, we first increase or decrease $v$ in the local region to find the interval that contains the nearby boundary (e.g., $f_\theta(x_0 + vs) = t_0$ and $f_\theta(x_0 + v's) \neq t_0$), then conduct a binary search to find the final value of $h$.

---

**Algorithm 2** Hard-label black-box attack (OPT attack) in (Cheng et al., 2019a).

---

1: **Input:** Hard-label model $f_\theta$, original sample $x_0$, initial $s_0$, total iteration $T$, step size $\{\eta_t\}$
2: **for** $t = 0, 1, 2, \ldots, T$ **do**
3:      Evaluate $h(s_t)$ and $h(s_t + \beta u)$ using Algorithm 1
4:      Compute the estimated gradient $\bar{g}$ using (3.3) and (3.4).
5:      Update    $s_{t+1} = s_t - \eta_t \bar{g}$
6: **end for**
7: **return** $x_0 + g(s_T)\frac{s_T}{\|s_T\|}$

---

With the local computation of $h(s)$, we can apply zeroth-order gradient descent to solve the optimization problem (3.9) in the hard-label setting. The procedure is summarized in Algorithm 2. If $g(s)$ is Lipschitz-smooth, then the number of iterations needed achieve stationary points using Algorithm 2 is given by Cheng et al. (2019a).

In the follow-up work, Cheng et al. (2020c) further improve the query efficiency of Algorithm 2 by estimating the sign value of $h(s + \alpha u) - h(s)$ instead of its exact value. The main idea is that estimating the sign will only require 1 single query (see below), which already gives sufficient information for gradient-based optimizers to progress. In the untargeted attack case the sign can be computed by

$$\text{sign}\big(h(s + \alpha u) - h(s)\big) = \begin{cases} +1, & f_\theta(x_0 + g(s)\frac{(s+\alpha u)}{\|s+\alpha u\|}) = t_0, \\ -1 & \text{otherwise.} \end{cases} \tag{3.10}$$

Essentially, for a new direction $s + \alpha u$, we test whether a point at the original distance $h(s)$ from $x_0$ in this direction lies inside or outside the decision boundary, i.e., if the produced perturbation will result in a wrong prediction by the classifier. If the produced perturbation is outside the boundary, i.e., $f_\theta(x_0 + h(s)\frac{(s+\alpha u)}{\|s+\alpha u\|}) \neq t_0$, then the new direction has a smaller distance to its decision boundary and thus gives a smaller value of $h$. It indicates that $u$ is a descent direction to minimize $h$.

The resulting attack, which is called Sign-OPT attack, follows the same procedure as in Algorithm 2 by replacing the gradient estimation in step 4 with the following sign estimator:

$$\bar{g} = \sum_{j=1}^{q} \text{sign}\big(h(s + \alpha u^{(j)}) - h(s)\big) \cdot u^{(j)}, \tag{3.11}$$

and since each sign can be computed using a single query, this gradient estimator requires siginficaintly less number of queries compared with the original gradient estimator. Intuitively, this new gradient estimator computes the gradient sign on each randomly sampled direction and then averages the results. As sign already gives sufficient information for the optimizer to progress, the algorithm enjoys similar convergence speed while being much more query efficient. The corresponding convergence analysis of zeroth order optimization using this sign estimator is also given by Cheng et al. (2020c).

## 3.4 Transfer attack

Generally speaking, transfer attack means generating adversarial examples from a source model to attack a target model. This typically corresponds to the "no-box" setting, where an attacker has no information about the target model and takes another pretrained model as a source to generate adversarial examples. Although the models can be vastly different, some adversarial examples can transfer from one model to another (Papernot et al., 2016; Liu et al., 2017b), and several attempts have been made, most empirically, to study how to generate more transferable adversarial examples. For instance, Dong et al. (2018) boosted the transferability by integrating the momentum term into the iterative process. Other techniques like data augmentations (Xie et al., 2019), exploiting gradients of skip-connection (Wu et al., 2020a), also contribute to stronger transferable attacks. A large-scale attack transferability study among 18 pretrained ImageNet models is conducted by Su et al. (2018). Instead of using pretrained surrogate models, it is also possible to construct a "meta-surrogate model" based on a set of pretrained surrogate models, where the meta-surrogate model can generate more transferable adversarial examples. This can be done with a meta-learning framework, as proposed by Qin et al. (2021).

In the soft-label black-box attack setting, Papernot et al. (2017) propose to train a substitute model using iterative model queries, perform white-box attacks on the substitute model, and leverage the transferability of adversarial examples to attack the target model. However, training a representative surrogate for a state-of-the-art classifier is challenging due to the complicated and nonlinear classification rules of the machine learning model (e.g., neural networks) and high dimensionality of the underlying dataset. The performance of black-box attacks can be severely degraded

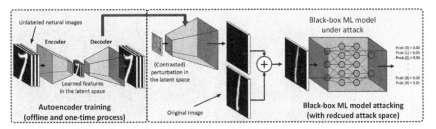

**Figure 3.2** Illustration of attack dimension reduction through a "decoder" in (Tu et al., 2019) for improving query efficiency in black-box attacks. The decoder has two modes: (i) An autoencoder (AE) trained on unlabeled natural images that are different from the attacked images and training data; (ii) a simple bilinear image resizer (BiLIN) applied channelwise to extrapolate low-dimensional feature to the original image dimension (width × height). In the latter mode, no additional training is required.

if the adversarial examples for the substitute model transfer poorly to the target model.

## 3.5  Attack dimension reduction

Different from the first-order convergence results, the convergence rate of zeroth-order gradient descent methods has an additional multiplicative dimension-dependent factor $d$. In the convex loss setting the rate is $O(\sqrt{d/T})$, sufficiently close to the optimal value, where $T$ is the number of iterations (Nesterov and Spokoiny, 2017; Liu et al., 2018a; Gao et al., 2014; Wang et al., 2018b). The same convergence rate has also been found in the nonconvex setting (Ghadimi and Lan, 2013). The dimension-dependent convergence factor $d$ suggests that vanilla black-box attacks using gradient estimations can be query inefficient when the (vectorized) image dimension $d$ is large, due to the curse of dimensionality in convergence.

To reduce the attack dimension and improve query efficiency in black-box attacks, Tu et al. (2019) propose to perform gradient estimation from a reduced dimension $d' < d$ to improve query efficiency. Specifically, as illustrated in Fig. 3.2, the additive perturbation to an image $x_0$ is actually implemented through a "decoder" $D : \mathbb{R}^{d'} \mapsto \mathbb{R}^d$ such that $x = x_0 + D(\delta')$, where $\delta' \in \mathbb{R}^{d'}$. In other words, the adversarial perturbation $\delta \in \mathbb{R}^d$ to $x_0$ is in fact generated from a dimension-reduced space with an aim of improving query efficiency due to the reduced dimension-dependent factor in the convergence analysis. The **AutoZOOM** method proposed by Tu et al. (2019), which is short for **Auto**encoder-based **Z**eroth-**O**rder **O**ptimization **M**ethod, provides two modes for such a decoder $D$:

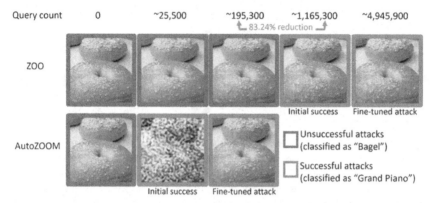

**Figure 3.3** AutoZOOM (Tu et al., 2019) significantly reduces the number of queries required to generate a successful adversarial Bagel image from the black-box Inception-v3 model.

- An autoencoder (AE) trained on unlabeled data that are different from the training data to learn reconstruction from a dimension-reduced representation. The encoder $E$ in an AE that compresses the data to a low-dimensional latent space, and the decoder $D$ reconstructs an example from its latent representation. The weights of an AE are learned to minimize the average $\ell_2$ reconstruction error. Note that training such an AE for black-box adversarial attacks is one-time and entirely offline (i.e., no model queries needed).
- A simple channelwise bilinear image resizer (BiLIN) that scales a small image to a large image via bilinear extrapolation.[4] Note that no additional training is required for BiLIN.

## 3.6 Empirical comparisons

There are two widely used criteria to evaluate the effectiveness of black-box attacks. Given a set of data samples to generate adversarial examples from, one criterion is to report the attack success rate and the average distortion given a model query budget. The other criterion is to report the attack success rate and the average query counts required to find an adversarial example with a given perturbation budget.

For soft-label black-box attacks, Fig. 3.3 displays a prediction-evasive adversarial example crafted via iterative model queries from a black-box image classifier (the Inception-v3 model Szegedy et al., 2016) trained

---

[4] See tf.image.resize_images, a TensorFlow example.

on ImageNet. The ZOO attack uses coordinatewise gradient estimation, whereas the AutoZOOM attack uses random vector-based gradient estimation. The results show that advanced gradient estimation and dimension reduction techniques can greatly improve the query efficiency while attaining visual quality in finding adversarial examples.

Next, we evaluate the following hard-label black-box attacks on three different standard datasets MNIST, CIFAR-10, and ImageNet-1K. For the black-box models, we use the convolutional neural networks provided by Carlini and Wagner (2017b) for both MNIST and CIFAR-10 and the pre-trained Resnet-50 network (He et al., 2016) for ImageNet-1K.

We compare the performance of the following untargeted attacks:

- *Sign-OPT attack* (black box) (Cheng et al., 2020c)
- *OPT attack* (black box) (Cheng et al., 2019a)
- *Boundary attack* (black box) (Brendel et al., 2018): This method starts from a large adversarial perturbation and reduces it while staying adversarial via random walk on the decision boundary.
- *Guessing Smart Attack* (black box) (Brunner et al., 2019): This attack enhances boundary attack by biased sampling using some prior.
- *C&W attack* (white box) (Carlini and Wagner, 2017b): We use C&W $\ell_2$-norm attack as a baseline for the white-box attack performance.

For each attack, we randomly sample 100 examples from validation set and generate adversarial perturbations for them. We only consider examples that are correctly predicted by the target model. To compare different methods, we mainly use *average distortion* of successful adversarial attacks as the metric. We also report the *attack success rate (ASR)* for $B$ queries for a given $\ell_2$ perturbation threshold $\epsilon$, which is the percentage of the number of examples that have achieved an adversarial perturbation below $\epsilon$ with less than $B$ queries.

Table 3.1 summarizes the attack results. Given the same query budget, Sign-OPT consistently yields higher ASR and lower $\ell_2$ distortion (the latter is comparable to the C&W white-box attack), demonstrating its attack efficiency. Particularly for ImageNet dataset on ResNet-50 model, Sign-OPT attack reaches a median distortion below 3.0 in less than $30k$ queries, whereas other attacks need more than $200k$ queries for the same.

Fig. 3.4 shows some examples of adversarial examples generated by hard-label black-box attacks. The first two rows show comparison of Sign-OPT attack (Cheng et al., 2020c) and Opt attack (Cheng et al., 2019a), respectively, on an example from MNIST dataset. These figures show adversarial examples generated at almost same number of queries for both

**Table 3.1** $\ell_2$ Untargeted attack results. Comparison of average $\ell_2$ distortion achieved using a given query budget for different attacks. ASR stands for success rate.

| | MNIST | | | CIFAR10 | | | ImageNet (ResNet-50) | | |
|---|---|---|---|---|---|---|---|---|---|
| | #Queries | Avg $\ell_2$ | ASR($\epsilon=1.5$) | #Queries | Avg $\ell_2$ | ASR($\epsilon=0.5$) | #Queries | Avg $\ell_2$ | ASR($\epsilon=3.0$) |
| Boundary attack | 4,000 | 4.24 | 1.0% | 4,000 | 3.12 | 2.3% | 4,000 | 209.63 | 0% |
| | 8,000 | 4.24 | 1.0% | 8,000 | 2.84 | 7.6% | 30,000 | 17.40 | 16.6% |
| | 14,000 | 2.13 | 16.3% | 12,000 | 0.78 | 29.2% | 160,000 | 4.62 | 41.6% |
| Guessing Smart | 4,000 | 1.74 | 41.0% | 4,000 | 0.29 | 75.0% | 4,000 | 16.69 | 12.0% |
| | 8,000 | 1.69 | 42.0% | 8,000 | 0.25 | 80.0% | 30,000 | 13.27 | 12.0% |
| | 14,000 | 1.68 | 43.0% | 12,000 | 0.24 | 80.0% | 160,000 | 12.88 | 12.0% |
| OPT attack | 4,000 | 3.65 | 3.0% | 4,000 | 0.77 | 37.0% | 4,000 | 83.85 | 2.0% |
| | 8,000 | 2.41 | 18.0% | 8,000 | 0.43 | 53.0% | 30,000 | 16.77 | 14.0% |
| | 14,000 | 1.76 | 36.0% | 12,000 | 0.33 | 61.0% | 160,000 | 4.27 | 34.0% |
| Sign-OPT attack | 4,000 | 1.54 | 46.0% | 4,000 | 0.26 | 73.0% | 4,000 | 23.19 | 8.0% |
| | 8,000 | 1.18 | 84.0% | 8,000 | 0.16 | 90.0% | 30,000 | 2.99 | 50.0% |
| | 14,000 | 1.09 | 94.0% | 12,000 | 0.13 | 95.0% | 160,000 | 1.21 | 90.0% |
| C&W (white-box) | – | 0.88 | 99.0% | – | 0.25 | 85.0% | – | 1.51 | 80.0% |

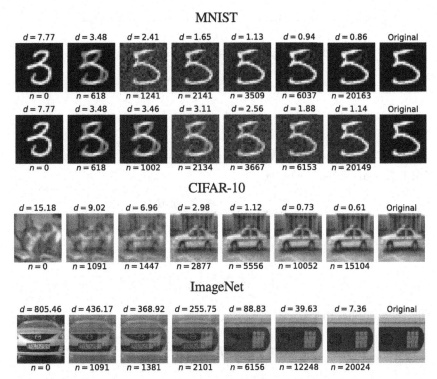

**Figure 3.4** Examples of hard-label black targeted attacks over query iterations. The first column is a randomly selected (unperturbed) image from the target class. Images in all other columns except for the last column (the original image) will give the same prediction as the first column. $\ell_2$ distortions and queries ($n$) used are shown above and below the images. First two rows: Example comparison of Sign-OPT (Cheng et al., 2020c) attack and OPT attack (Cheng et al., 2019a). Third and fourth rows: Examples of Sign-OPT attack on CIFAR-10 and ImageNet.

attacks. Sign–OPT method generates an $\ell_2$ adversarial perturbation of $0.94$ in $\sim 6k$ queries for this particular example, whereas Opt-based attack requires $\sim 35k$ for the same.

## 3.7 Proof of Theorem 1

Recall that the data dimension is $d$ and we assume $F$ to be differentiable and its gradient $\nabla F$ to be $L$-Lipschitz. Fixing $\beta$, we consider a smoothed version of $F$,

$$F_\beta(\mathbf{x}) = \mathbb{E}_{\mathbf{u}}\big[F(\mathbf{x} + \beta\mathbf{u})\big]. \tag{3.12}$$

Based on Gao et al. (2014, Lemma 4.1-a), we have the relation

$$\nabla F_\beta(\mathbf{x}) = \mathbb{E}_\mathbf{u}\left[\frac{d}{\beta}F(\mathbf{x} + \beta\mathbf{u})\mathbf{u}\right] = \frac{d}{b}\mathbb{E}_\mathbf{u}[\mathbf{g}], \tag{3.13}$$

which then yields

$$\mathbb{E}_\mathbf{u}[\mathbf{g}] = \frac{b}{d}\nabla F_\beta(\mathbf{x}), \tag{3.14}$$

where we recall that $\mathbf{g}$ is defined in (3.3). Moreover, based on Gao et al. (2014, Lemma 4.1-b), we have

$$\|\nabla F_\beta(\mathbf{x}) - \nabla F(\mathbf{x})\|_2 \le \frac{\beta dL}{2}. \tag{3.15}$$

Substituting (3.14) into (3.15), we obtain

$$\left\|\mathbb{E}[\mathbf{g}] - \frac{b}{d}\nabla F(\mathbf{x})\right\|_2 \le \frac{\beta bL}{2}.$$

This then implies that

$$\mathbb{E}[\mathbf{g}] = \frac{b}{d}\nabla F(\mathbf{x}) + \boldsymbol{\gamma}, \tag{3.16}$$

where $\|\boldsymbol{\gamma}\|_2 \le \frac{b\beta L}{2}$.

Once again, by applying Gao et al. (2014, Lemma 4.1-b), we can easily obtain that

$$\mathbb{E}_\mathbf{u}\left[\|\mathbf{g}\|_2^2\right] \le \frac{b^2 L^2 \beta^2}{2} + \frac{2b^2}{d}\|\nabla F(\mathbf{x})\|_2^2. \tag{3.17}$$

Now let us consider the averaged random gradient estimator in (3.4),

$$\overline{\mathbf{g}} = \frac{1}{q}\sum_{i=1}^{q}\mathbf{g}^{(i)} = \frac{b}{q}\sum_{i=1}^{q}\frac{F(\mathbf{x} + \beta\mathbf{u}^{(i)}) - F(\mathbf{x})}{\beta}\mathbf{u}^{(i)}.$$

Due to the properties of i.i.d. samples $\{\mathbf{u}^{(i)}\}$ and (3.16), we define

$$\boldsymbol{v} =: \mathbb{E}\left[\mathbf{g}^{(i)}\right] = \frac{b}{d}\nabla F(\mathbf{x}) + \boldsymbol{\gamma}. \tag{3.18}$$

Moreover, we have

$$\mathbb{E}\left[\|\overline{\mathbf{g}}\|_2^2\right] = \mathbb{E}\left[\left\|\frac{1}{q}\sum_{i=1}^{q}(\mathbf{g}^{(i)} - \boldsymbol{v}) + \boldsymbol{v}\right\|_2^2\right] \tag{3.19}$$

$$= \|\boldsymbol{v}\|_2^2 + \mathbb{E}\left[\left\|\frac{1}{q}\sum_{i=1}^{q}(\mathbf{g}^{(i)} - \boldsymbol{v})\right\|_2^2\right]$$

$$= \|\boldsymbol{v}\|_2^2 + \frac{1}{q}\mathbb{E}\left[\|\mathbf{g}^{(1)} - \boldsymbol{v}\|_2^2\right] \tag{3.20}$$

$$= \|\boldsymbol{v}\|_2^2 + \frac{1}{q}\mathbb{E}\left[\|\mathbf{g}^{(1)}\|_2^2\right] - \frac{1}{q}\|\boldsymbol{v}\|_2^2, \tag{3.21}$$

where we have used the fact that $\mathbb{E}[\mathbf{g}^{(i)}] = \mathbb{E}[\mathbf{g}^{(1)}] = \boldsymbol{v}$ for all $i$. The definition of $\boldsymbol{v}$ in (3.18) yields

$$\|\boldsymbol{v}\|_2^2 \leq 2\frac{b^2}{d^2}\|\nabla F(\mathbf{x})\|_2^2 + 2\|\boldsymbol{\gamma}\|_2^2$$

$$\leq 2\frac{b^2}{d^2}\|\nabla f(\mathbf{x})\|_2^2 + \frac{1}{2}b^2\beta^2 L^2. \tag{3.22}$$

From (3.17) we also obtain that for all $i$,

$$\mathbb{E}\left[\|\mathbf{g}^{(i)}\|_2^2\right] \leq \frac{b^2 L^2 \beta^2}{2} + \frac{2b^2}{d}\|\nabla F(\mathbf{x})\|_2^2. \tag{3.23}$$

Substituting (3.22) and (3.23) into (3.21), we obtain

$$\mathbb{E}\left[\|\overline{\mathbf{g}}\|_2^2\right] \leq \|\boldsymbol{v}\|_2^2 + \frac{1}{q}\mathbb{E}\left[\|\mathbf{g}^{(1)}\|_2^2\right] \tag{3.24}$$

$$\leq 2\left(\frac{b^2}{d^2} + \frac{b^2}{dq}\right)\|\nabla F(\mathbf{x})\|_2^2 + \frac{q+1}{2q}b^2 L^2 \beta^2. \tag{3.25}$$

Finally, we bound the mean squared estimation error as

$$\mathbb{E}\left[\|\overline{\mathbf{g}} - \nabla f(\mathbf{x})\|_2^2\right] \leq 2\mathbb{E}\left[\|\overline{\mathbf{g}} - \boldsymbol{v}\|_2^2\right] + 2\|\boldsymbol{v} - \nabla F(\mathbf{x})\|_2^2$$

$$\leq 2\mathbb{E}\left[\|\overline{\mathbf{g}}\|_2^2\right] + 2\|\frac{b}{d}\nabla F(\mathbf{x}) + \boldsymbol{\gamma} - \nabla F(\mathbf{x})\|_2^2$$

$$\leq 4\left(\frac{b^2}{d^2} + \frac{b^2}{dq} + \frac{(b-d)^2}{d^2}\right)\|\nabla F(\mathbf{x})\|_2^2 + \frac{2q+1}{q}b^2 L^2 \beta^2,$$
$$\tag{3.26}$$

which completes the proof.

## 3.8 Extended reading

- Survey paper on zeroth-order optimization and applications (Liu et al., 2020a).

- Garcia et al. (2021) provide detailed analysis on hard-label attacks and dimension reduction.
- Chen et al. (2020a) proposed a query-efficient hard-label attack called Hopskipjump attack.
- Black-box attacks beyond pseudo-gradient descent: natural gradient descent (Zhao et al., 2020b), bandit algorithm (Ilyas et al., 2019), genetic algorithm (Alzantot et al., 2019), alternating direction method of multipliers (Zhao et al., 2019a), random walk around the decision boundary (Brendel et al., 2018), and ray searching (Chen and Gu, 2020).
- "No-box" attack that does not assume model queries nor accessing to the training data (Li et al., 2020b).

# CHAPTER 4

# Physical adversarial attacks

Beyond digital space, adversarial examples can also be realized in physical world to evade the prediction of machine learning-based applications such as object detection, known as *physical adversarial examples*. In this chapter, we cover the attack formulation for physical adversarial examples and provide an overview of such attacks in the physical world.

## 4.1 Physical adversarial attack formulation

Physical adversarial examples are often realized as robust adversarial examples crafted from digital spaces (e.g., simulated physical environments) that remain the adversarial objective in the physical space. To bridge the gap between adversarial examples in digital and physical spaces, there are two major obstacles: (i) The digital adversarial examples cannot be precisely realized in the physical space. For example, some RGB color values in the digital space cannot be printed exactly. (ii) Digital adversarial examples may not well generalize to physical environments. For example, simple rotation or zooming in and out a printed adversarial image may make the adversarial effect in vain.

To address challenge (i), during the attack process, we can project the digital adversarial examples to the space of realizable actions in the physical space (e.g., the space of printable colors) or add an additional regularization loss in the attack loss to minimize inconsistency between the digital adversarial examples and the resulting physical versions.

To address challenge (ii), a common practice is to introduce multiple transformations during the generation process such that the resulting adversarial example will remain effective. The methodology can also be thought as learning a universal adversarial manipulation that is simultaneously effective to most of (if not all) considered transformations.

Expectation over transformation (EOT) (Athalye and Sutskever, 2018) introduces a set of data transformations denoted by $\mathcal{T}$ in generating a robust adversarial example $x$ of a data sample $x_0$ via solving the following optimization problem:

$$\underset{x \in \mathcal{X}}{\operatorname{argmin}} \ \mathbb{E}_{t \sim \mathcal{T}} \ g(t(x)) + r(x), \tag{4.1}$$

*Adversarial Robustness for Machine Learning*
https://doi.org/10.1016/B978-0-12-824020-5.00013-2

where $\mathcal{X}$ is the space of feasible physical adversarial examples, $t$ is a transformation function drawn from $\mathcal{T}$, $g$ is the attack objective loss function as introduced in Chapter 2, and $r$ is the regularizer (e.g., a penalty function on unrealizable printing colors).

The optimization objective of EOT attack can be viewed as minimizing the average loss over all data transformations in $\mathcal{T}$. Instead of minimizing the average loss, Wang et al. (2021a) proposed a MinMax attack formulation that optimizes the worst-case transformation loss through

$$\min_{x \in \mathcal{X}} \max_{w \in \mathcal{P}} \sum_{i=1}^{K} w_i \cdot g(t_i(x)) - \gamma \|w - 1/K\|_2^2 + r(x), \qquad (4.2)$$

where $K$ is the number of transformations in $\mathcal{T}$, $w$ is a nonnegative $K$-dimensional vector in the probability simplex $\mathcal{P}$ satisfying $\sum_{i=1}^{K} w_i = 1$, $t_i$ is the $i$th transformation with $w_i$ being its weighting factor, $1/K$ is a uniform vector, and $\gamma \geq 0$ is a regularization coefficient. If $w = 1/K$, then problem (4.2) reduces to the existing EOT formulation. Using the alternating one-step projected gradient descent-ascent (APGDA) algorithm for solving (4.2), it is shown by Wang et al. (2021a) that MinMax attack leads to more robust adversarial examples against multiple data transformations than EOT. MinMax attack also offers some interpretation on the difficulty level of each transformation through the associated learned weighting factor $\{w_i\}_{i=1}^{K}$ while solving the min-max optimization problem. It is also used by Xu et al. (2020c) in the design of physical adversarial T-shirts that are robust to nonrigid deformations.

## 4.2 Examples of physical adversarial attacks

Here we list some studies into crafting physical adversarial examples in different scenarios. Some of the physical adversarial examples are shown in Fig. 4.1.

- *Adversarial photo* (Kurakin et al., 2016): Demonstration that when feeding adversarial images obtained from cell-phone camera to an ImageNet Inception classifier, a large fraction of adversarial examples are classified incorrectly even when perceived through the camera.
- *Adversarial eyeglasses* (Sharif et al., 2016): Realization through printing a pair of eyeglass frames such that when worn by the attacker whose image is supplied to a face-recognition algorithm, the eyeglasses allow her to evade being recognized or to impersonate another individual.

**Figure 4.1** Examples of physical adversarial examples. Left to right: Adversarial eyeglasses (Sharif et al., 2016), adversarial T-shirt (Xu et al., 2020c), adversarial hat (Komkov and Petiushko, 2021), and adversarial make-up (Lin et al., 2021).

- *Adversarial patch* (Brown et al., 2017): A physical adversarial object such that its presence causes the classifiers to ignore the other items in the scene and report a chosen target class.
- *3D-printed adversarial object* (Athalye and Sutskever, 2018): A 3D-printed adversarial object that leads to incorrect predictions when taking its pictures from different views.
- *Adversarial stop sign* (Evtimov et al., 2017): An adversarial stop sign created by adding color patches to evade the detection of real-time object detectors.
- *Adversarial board* (Thys et al., 2019): An adversarial patch able to hide a person from a person detector when wearing it.
- *Adversarial sticker* (Li et al., 2019b): Demonstration of a carefully crafted and mainly translucent sticker over the lens of a camera that can create universal perturbations of the observed images that are inconspicuous, yet misclassify target objects as a different (targeted) class.
- *Adversarial T-shirt* (Xu et al., 2020c): A robust physical adversarial example for evading person detectors, even if it undergoes nonrigid deformation due to a moving person's pose changes.
- *Adversarial hat* (Komkov and Petiushko, 2021): Designing and printing a rectangular paper sticker on a common color printer and put it on the hat to attack Face ID systems.
- *Adversarial make-up* (Lin et al., 2021): Adversarial full-face makeup guided by generative adversarial networks to impersonate a target person and fool facial recognition systems.

## 4.3 Empirical comparison

Here we compare the performance of EOT attack (avg.) (Athalye and Sutskever, 2018) and MinMAX attack (Wang et al., 2021a). For each input sample (*ori*), we transform the image under a series of functions, e.g., flipping horizontally (*flh*) or vertically (*flv*), adjusting brightness (*bri*), performing gamma correction (*gam*) and cropping (*crop*), and group each image with its transformed variants. ASR$_{all}$ is reported to measure the attack success rate (ASR) over groups of transformed images (each group is successfully attacked signifies successfully attacking an example under all transformers). In Table 4.1, compared to EOT, MinMax leads to 9.39% averaged lift in ASR$_{all}$ over given models on CIFAR-10 by optimizing the weights for various transformations.

**Table 4.1** Comparison of average and min-max optimization on robust attack over multiple data transformations on CIFAR-10. Acc (%) represents the test accuracy of classifiers on adversarial examples. Table adopted from Wang et al. (2021a).

| Model | Opt. | Acc$_{ori}$ | Acc$_{flh}$ | Acc$_{flv}$ | Acc$_{bri}$ | Acc$_{gam}$ | Acc$_{crop}$ | ASR$_{all}$ | Lift (↑) |
|---|---|---|---|---|---|---|---|---|---|
| A | *avg.* | 10.80 | 21.93 | 14.75 | 11.52 | 10.66 | 20.03 | 55.88 | – |
|   | min max | 12.14 | 18.05 | 13.61 | 13.52 | 11.99 | 16.78 | **60.03** | **7.43%** |
| B | *avg.* | 5.49 | 11.56 | 9.51 | 5.43 | 5.75 | 15.89 | 72.21 | – |
|   | min max | 6.22 | 8.61 | 9.74 | 6.35 | 6.42 | 11.99 | **77.43** | **7.23%** |
| C | *avg.* | 7.66 | 21.88 | 15.50 | 8.15 | 7.87 | 15.36 | 56.51 | – |
|   | min max | 8.51 | 14.75 | 13.88 | 9.16 | 8.58 | 13.35 | **63.58** | **12.51%** |
| D | *avg.* | 8.00 | 20.47 | 13.46 | 7.73 | 8.52 | 15.90 | 61.13 | – |
|   | min max | 9.19 | 13.18 | 12.72 | 8.79 | 9.18 | 13.11 | **67.49** | **10.40%** |

## 4.4 Extending reading

- Unadversarial examples by realizing input perturbations to design robust objects that are explicitly optimized to be confidently detected or classified (Salman et al., 2020a).

# CHAPTER 5

# Training-time adversarial attacks

Aforementioned attacks in this part focus on evasion attacks targeting on an already trained and fixed model at the testing/deployment phase. Here we shift our focus to training-phase attacks. Training-phase attacks assume the ability to modify the training data to achieve malicious attempts on the resulting model when trained on the manipulated datasets, which can be realized through noisy data collection such as crowdsourcing. Specifically, the memorization effect of deep learning models (Zhang et al., 2017; Carlini et al., 2019b) can be leveraged as vulnerabilities. We note that sometimes the term "data poisoning" entails both poisoning and backdoor attacks though their attack objectives are different. In this chapter, (data) poisoning attack has a specific goal of degrading the generalization of a target model, such that the model trained on the poisoned training dataset will fail to generalize well on the clean testing dataset (e.g., having high training accuracy but low testing accuracy). On the other hand, a backdoored model tends to behave like a normal (nonbackdoored) model when the embedded trigger patter is absent; when the trigger is present, the backdoored model will give a designed output by the adversary regardless of the actual contents of any data inputs.

## 5.1 Poisoning attack

Poisoning attack aims to design a poisoned dataset $D_{poison}$ such that models trained on $D_{poison}$ will fail to generalize on a standard test set $D_{test}$. The poisoned dataset $D_{poison}$ can be created by modifying the original training dataset $D_{train}$, such as label flipping, data addition/deletion, and feature modification. The rationale is training on $D_{poison}$ will land on a "bad" local minimum of model parameters in the loss landscape. Take classification task as an example, letting $f_\theta$ be the classifier trained on a poisoned dataset, which gives the most-likely class prediction. Data poisoning aims to lead the classifier to give a wrong prediction on most of test data samples (but the model still has relatively good accuracy on the training dataset) such that $f_\theta(x_{test}) \neq y_{test}$, where $(x_{test}, y_{test}) \sim D_{test}$.

In general, a poisoning attack can be realized by adding a poisoned dataset $D_{poison}$ to the existing training dataset $D_{train}$ and by solving the fol-

*Adversarial Robustness for Machine Learning*
https://doi.org/10.1016/B978-0-12-824020-5.00014-4

lowing bilevel optimization problem:

$$\underset{D_{\text{poison}}}{\text{Maximize}}\; \mathcal{L}_{\text{attack}}(D'; \theta^*) \text{ such that } \theta^* \in \underset{\theta}{\arg\min}\; \mathcal{L}_{\text{train}}(D_{\text{train}} \cup D_{\text{poison}}; \theta),$$

$$(5.1)$$

where $\mathcal{L}_{\text{attack}}$ is the attacker's designed objective function (higher is better for the attacker), $D'$ is an untrained (hold-out) dataset for attack performance evaluation, and $\theta^*$ is the model parameters obtained by minimizing a standard training loss function $\mathcal{L}_{\text{train}}$ on the augmented poisoned dataset denoted by $D_{\text{train}} \cup D_{\text{poison}}$. The attacker's objective function can be as simple as the training loss; for example, $\mathcal{L}_{\text{attack}}$ can be the cross entropy loss.

To control the amount of data modification and reduce the overall accuracy on $D_{\text{test}}$ (i.e., test accuracy), poisoning attack often assumes the knowledge of target model and its training method (Jagielski et al., 2018). Liu et al. (2020b) propose black-box poisoning with additional conditions on the training loss function. Targeted poisoning attack aims at manipulating the prediction of a subset of data samples in $D_{\text{test}}$, which can be accomplished by clean–label poisoning (small perturbations to a subset of $D_{\text{train}}$ while keeping their labels intact) (Shafahi et al., 2018; Zhu et al., 2019b) or gradient-matching poisoning (Geiping et al., 2021).

## 5.2 Backdoor attack

Backdoor attack is also known as Trojan attack. The central idea is to embed a universal trigger $\Delta$ to a subset of data samples in $D_{\text{train}}$ with a modified target label $t$ (Gu et al., 2019). Examples of trigger patterns are a small patch in images and a specific text string in sentences. Typically, backdoor attack only assumes access to the training data and does not assume the knowledge of the model and its training. The model $f_\theta$ trained on the tampered data is called a backdoored (Trojan) model. Its attack objective has two folds: (i) High standard accuracy in the absence of trigger – the backdoored model should behave like a normal model (same model trained on untampered data), i.e., $f_\theta(x_{\text{test}}) = y_{\text{test}}$; (ii) High attack success rate in the presence of trigger – the backdoored model will predict any data input with the trigger as the target label $t$, i.e., $f_\theta(x_{\text{test}} + \Delta) = t$. Therefore backdoor attack is stealthy and insidious. The trigger pattern can also be made input-aware and dynamic (Nguyen and Tran, 2020).

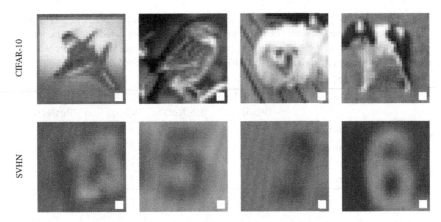

**Figure 5.1** Examples of backdoored images on CIFAR-10 and SVHN. The triggers are white blocks located at the right-bottom area of each image, and their associated data labels are changed to a target class label.

## 5.3 Empirical comparison

We follow the procedures in (Gu et al., 2019) to implement backdoor attacks and obtain two independently backdoored models trained on the same manipulated training data (models I and II). The trigger pattern is placed at the right–bottom of the poisoned images as shown in Fig. 5.1. Specifically, 10% of the training data are backdoored by inserting the trigger and changing the original correct labels to the target label(s). Here we investigate two kinds of backdoor attacks: (a) single-target attack that sets the target label $t$ to a specific label (we choose $t =$ class 1); and (b) all-targets attack where the target label $t$ is set to the original label $i$ plus 1 and then modulo 9, i.e., $T = i + 1(\mathrm{mod}\ 9)$.

Their performance on clean (untriggered) and triggered data samples are given in Table 5.1. The backdoored models have similar performance on clean data as untampered models but will indeed misclassify a majority of triggered samples. Comparing to single-target attack, all-targets attack is more difficult and has a higher attack failure rate, since the target labels vary with the original labels.

## 5.4 Case study: distributed backdoor attacks on federated learning

Federated learning (FL) has been recently proposed to address the problems for training machine learning models without direct access to diverse train-

**Table 5.1** Error rate of backdoored models. The error rate of clean/backdoored samples means standard-test-error/attack-failure-rate, respectively. The results are evaluated on 5000 nonoverlapping clean/triggered images selected from the test set. For reference, the test errors of clean images on untampered models are 12% for CIFAR-10 (VGG) and 4% for SVHN (ResNet).

| Backdoor attacks | | Single-target attack | | All-targets attack | |
|---|---|---|---|---|---|
| Dataset | | CIFAR-10 (VGG) | SVHN (ResNet) | CIFAR-10 (VGG) | SVHN (ResNet) |
| Model I | Clean images | 15% | 5.4% | 14.2% | 6.1% |
| | Triggered images | 0.07% | 0.22% | 12.9% | 8.3% |
| Model II | Clean images | 13% | 7.7% | 19% | 7.5% |
| | Triggered images | 2% | 0.17% | 13.6% | 9.2% |

ing data, especially for privacy–sensitive tasks (Smith et al., 2017; McMahan et al., 2017; Zhao et al., 2018). Utilizing local training data of participants (i.e., parties), FL helps train a shared global model with improved performance. There have been prominent applications and ever-growing trends in deploying FL in practice, such as loan status prediction, health situation assessment (e.g., potential cancer risk assessment), and next–word prediction while typing (Hard et al., 2018; Yang et al., 2018, 2019a).

Although FL is capable of aggregating dispersed (and often restricted) information provided by different parties to train a better model, its distributed learning methodology and inherently heterogeneous (i.e., non-i.i.d.) data distribution across different parties may unintentionally provide a venue to new attacks. In particular, the fact of limiting access to individual party data due to privacy concerns or regulation constraints may facilitate backdoor attacks on the shared model trained with FL.

Backdoor attacks on FL have been studied in (Bagdasaryan et al., 2018; Bhagoji et al., 2019). However, these attacks do not fully exploit the distributed learning methodology of FL, as they embed the *same* global trigger pattern to all adversarial parties. This attacking scheme is referred to as the *centralized* backdoor attack. Leveraging the power of FL in aggregating dispersed information from local parties to train a shared model, Xie et al. (2020) propose *distributed* backdoor attack (DBA) against FL. Given the same global trigger pattern as the centralized attack, DBA decomposes it into local patterns and embed them to different adversarial parties respectively. A schematic comparison between the centralized and distributed backdoor attacks is illustrated in Fig. 5.2.

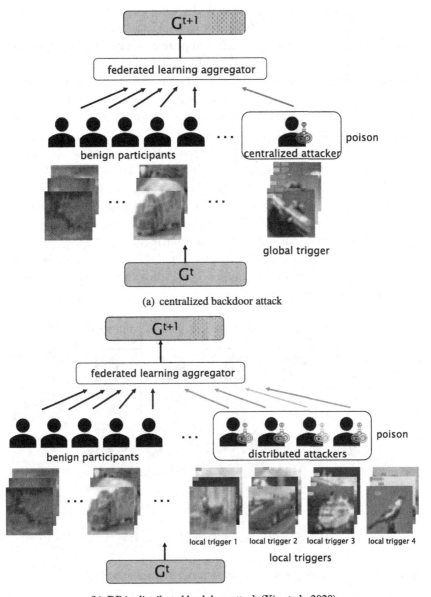

(a) centralized backdoor attack

(b) DBA: distributed backdoor attack (Xie et al., 2020)

**Figure 5.2** Overview of centralized and distributed backdoor attacks on FL. The aggregator in FL at round $t + 1$ combines information from local parties (benign and adversarial) in the previous round $t$ and updates the shared model. When implementing backdoor attacks, centralized attacker uses a global trigger, whereas distributed attacker uses a local trigger, which is part of the global one.

Centralized backdoor attack embeds the same global trigger for all local attackers[1] (Bagdasaryan et al., 2018). For example, the attacker in Fig. 5.2(a) embeds the training data with the selected patterns highlighted by four colors, which altogether constitute a complete global pattern as the backdoor trigger. In DBA, as illustrated in Fig. 5.2(b), all attackers only use parts of the global trigger to poison their local models, whereas the ultimate adversarial goal is still the same as centralized attack: using the global trigger to attack the shared model. For example, the attacker with the orange (gray in print version) sign poisons a subset of his training data *only* using the trigger pattern located at the orange (gray in print version) area. Similar attacking methodology applies to green (mid gray in print version), yellow (light gray in print version), and blue (dark gray in print version) signs. We define each DBA attacker's trigger as the *local trigger* and the combined whole trigger as the *global trigger*. DBA can also be realized on irregular shape triggers, such as decomposing the logo "ICLR" into "I", "C", "L", "R" as local triggers on three image datasets and decomposing the physical pattern glasses into four parts as shown in Fig. 5.3.

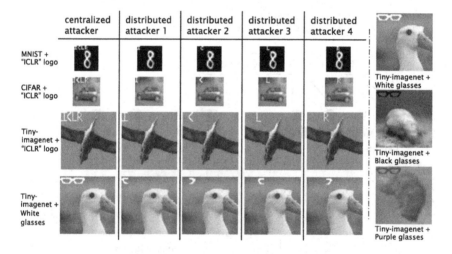

**Figure 5.3** Examples of irregular shape triggers in image datasets in (Xie et al., 2020).

Keeping similar amount of total injected triggers (e.g., modified pixels) for both centralized attack and DBA, it was shown by Xie et al. (2020)

---

[1] Although only one centralized attacker and one adversarial party are shown in Fig. 5.2, in practice, centralized backdoor attack can poison multiple parties with the same global trigger, as discussed by Bagdasaryan et al. (2018).

that although none of the adversarial party has ever been poisoned by the global trigger under DBA, DBA indeed outperforms centralized attack significantly when evaluated with the global trigger. Moreover, DBA achieves higher attack success rate, faster convergence, and better resiliency in single-shot and multiple-shot attack scenarios. It is also demonstrated that DBA is more stealthy and can successfully evade two robust FL approaches.

## 5.5  Extended reading

- Mehra et al. (2021a) study the robustness of randomized smoothing defenses (see Chapter 14) at test time in the presence of data poisoning attacks.
- Mehra et al. (2021b) use poisoning attack to study the performance of unsupervised domain adaptation algorithms.
- Zawad et al. (2021) study the effect of data heterogeneity on affecting the robustness of federated learning against backdoor attacks.
- Detailed survey on backdoor and poisoning attacks can be found in (Goldblum et al., 2022).
- Zhao et al. (2020a) propose to use mode connectivity in the loss landscape of neural networks to sanitize backdoored models with limited clean data by mitigating their adversarial effects while maintaining clean accuracy.

# CHAPTER 6

# Adversarial attacks beyond image classification

## 6.1 Data modality and task objectives

For classification tasks on data modalities that can be presented in real-valued continuous vectors, such as images (pixel values), text embeddings, audio signals, time series, and real-valued tabular data, the methodology of the aforementioned adversarial attacks can be adopted in a principled manner by specifying the corresponding attack loss function and threat model, and then solving the formulated objective using continuous optimization tools such as gradient-based methods.

For classification tasks on noncontinuous data modalities, such as text tokens (e.g., words and characters), graphs, and malwares, the attack objective is similar, but the solver needs to use discrete optimization tools such as genetic algorithms, evolutionary algorithms, relaxation to continuous optimization methods due to the fact that the feasible action space of an attacker will be discrete in nature, such as adding, removing, or editing certain words in a sentence to change the sentiment.

For tasks beyond classification, such as regression, reconstruction, text summarization, generation, etc., the rule of thumb is to define the appropriate threat models and attackers' capabilities for making meaningful analysis of adversarial robustness for the corresponding machine learning models. After the attack objective is formulated, a proper solver will be used to execute the adversarial attack depending on the data modality.

In what follows, we introduce some examples for data modalities and tasks beyond image classification.

## 6.2 Audio adversarial example

Carlini and Wagner (2018) propose an optimization-based attack for generating audio adversarial examples for automatic speech recognition systems. Given an audio waveform $x$, the task is to construct another audio waveform $x' = x + \delta$ such that $x$ and $x'$ sound similar but their output transcription differs. To cater to the audio domain, they use decibels

59

($dB$) as the distortion metric, defined as $dB_x(\delta) = dB(\delta) - dB(x)$, where $dB(x) = 20 \cdot \max_i \log_{10}(x_i)$. The optimal audio adversarial perturbation $\delta^*$ with a target transcription $t$ can be found by solving the following constrained objective function:

$$\underset{\delta}{\text{minimize}} \ \|\delta\|_2^2 + \lambda \cdot \mathcal{L}(x + \delta, t)$$

$$\text{such that } dB_x(\delta) \leq \epsilon, \tag{6.1}$$

where $\mathcal{L}$ can be the connectionist temporal classification (CTC) loss or other improved loss functions proposed by Carlini and Wagner (2018), and $\lambda$ is its regularization coefficient. Similarly, adversarial examples for time series data can be formulated by using the task-specific loss function and appropriate similarity/distortion metric.

## 6.3  Feature identification

Chen et al. (2018c) investigate the robustness of sparse regression models with strongly correlated covariates to adversarially designed measurement noises. Specifically, they consider the family of ordered weighted $\ell_1$ (OWL) regularized regression methods (Bogdan et al., 2013; Zeng and Figueiredo, 2014a) and study the case of OSCAR (octagonal shrinkage clustering algorithm for regression) in the adversarial setting. It is worth mentioning that OSCAR is in fact a particular case of the OWL regularizer (Zeng and Figueiredo, 2014b). OSCAR is known to be more effective in identifying feature groups (i.e., strongly correlated covariates) than other feature selection methods such as LASSO (Tibshirani, 1996).

Under a norm-bounded threat model, they formulate the process of finding a maximally disruptive noise for OWL-regularized regression as an optimization problem and illustrate the steps toward finding such a noise in the case of OSCAR. Experimental results demonstrate that the regression performance of grouping strongly correlated features can be severely degraded under the studied adversarial setting, even when the noise budget is significantly smaller than the ground-truth signals.

## 6.4  Graph neural network

Graph structured data play a crucial role in many AI applications. It is an important and versatile representation to model a wide variety of datasets from many domains, such as molecules, social networks, or interlinked documents with citations. Graph neural networks (GNNs) on graph structured data have shown outstanding results in various applications (Kipf and Welling, 2016). The input data for GNN applications are usually given in the format of a graph (with edges and nodes) and each node can be associated with a $d$-dimensional feature vector. Therefore, to evaluate the robustness of GNN models, one can consider perturbations to node features and/or edges.

First, we briefly discuss the perturbations on node features. If node features are in a continuous domain, perturbing node features can be easily done by a gradient-based optimizer, similar to the attacks in computer vision introduced in the previous sections. For discrete node features, one can also adopt existing attacks in the literature. For instance, if node features are text, we can borrow attacks from the text domain to attack such GNN models.

On the other hand, attacks on edges cannot be easily done. Conventional (first-order) continuous optimization methods do not directly apply to attacks using edge manipulations (which are called *topology attacks* by Xu et al. (2019a)) due to the discrete nature of graphs. Xu et al. (2019a) close this gap by studying the problem of generating topology attacks via convex relaxation so that gradient-based adversarial attacks become plausible for GNNs. Evaluated on node classification tasks using GNNs, their gradient-based topology attacks outperform current state-of-the-art attacks subject to an edge perturbation budget. Moreover, by leveraging the proposed gradient-based attack, they propose the first optimization-based adversarial training technique for GNNs, yielding significantly improved robustness against gradient-based and greedy topology attacks. Other than optimization-based approaches, different methods are proposed for adversarial attacks on graph neural networks, such as the use of greedy search (Zügner et al., 2018), reinforcement learning (Dai et al., 2018), and meta learning (Zügner and Günnemann, 2019).

## 6.5 Natural language processing

Natural Language Processing (NLP) has been widely used in many important domains, and the robustness of NLP models is also crucial to mission-critical applications. For instance, when applying machine translation model to real-time machine translation, it is important to make sure the correctness of translation against small input perturbations. Another potentially important area is the evasion attacks to fake news detection (or spam detection) models; if there exists semantic-preserved perturbations to fool the fake news detection models, malicious users can leverage those perturbations to create fake news while being able to bypass the detection models. Beyond security concerns, adversarial robustness of text models has also been deeply studied recently as finding adversarial examples could be the first step for model debugging.

There are two main challenges when conducting attacks to nature language processing (NLP) models. First, as inputs of NLP are discrete, finding adversarial examples usually leads to a discrete optimization problem instead of the continuous one in computer vision attacks. Second, the "semantic invariance" perturbation in NLP is harder to define than in the computer vision cases. In the image domain, a slight change on each pixel value usually would not be perceptible by human, but this is not true in NLP as changing a word in a sentence may significantly change the semantic meaning of the whole sentence. Therefore adversarial attacks in the NLP domain need to consider these two factors. For handling discrete inputs, we usually seak to discrete optimization algorithms. To construct a semantic-invariance perturbation set, we often resort to either word embedding or contextualized word embeddings. In the following, we briefly introduce several NLP attacks developed for sentence classification and sequence-to-sequence translation. There are many NLP attacks beyond these two applications that are not covered in this book, such as question answering, dialogue systems and semantic parsing.

## Sentence classification

Most of the NLP attacks focused on sentence classification, as this is one of the most simple but representative tasks. Earlier attacks to text classification usually define the perturbation set by constraining the number of words or characters changed in the sentence. However, as discussed above, it is possible to change the meaning of the whole sentence by only replacing one word (or character). Therefore more recent attacks usually try to constrain the replaced words to enforce the semantic invariance. In NLP, word embeddings have been developed to represent the semantic meaning of each word by a latent vector, and there are several well-trained word embeddings such as Word2Vec (Mikolov et al., 2013) and Glove (Pennington et al., 2014). Alzantot et al. (2018) used distances in the word embedding space to construct a set of synonyms and used them to define the perturbation set: each word is only allowed to be replaced by its synonyms. More recently, due to the popularity of large-scale pretrained language models such as BERT (Devlin et al., 2018), many works start to use these language models to define the perturbation set (Li et al., 2020a). More specifically, as BERT provides the probability of the words at each position given the context words (e.g., all the other words in the same sentence), we can assume that those top possible words preserve the "natureness" of the sentence, and combining with synonyms, this can lead to more natural adversarial examples that preserve semantics.

With the perturbation set defined, another challenge for NLP attacks is to find the adversarial examples that maximize the task-specific loss (or other criterion) within the perturbation set. As the input space and perturbation set are discrete, this leads to a discrete optimization problem, which is usually harder to solve than continuous ones. Several discrete search algorithms have been proposed for NLP attacks. For example, evolutionary algorithms and reinforcement learning have been used to search for adversarial examples in the perturbation space (Alzantot et al., 2018; Li et al., 2016). To make the attacks faster, some other works consider simple greedy approaches. For example, Yang et al. (2020e) proposed a greedy attack that iteratively replaces words in the original sentence. At each iteration, they first mask each word in the input sentence and select the best position to attack based on the attack loss function (classification loss), and then go through the synonyms for the selected position to find the best word replacement (also to maximize the classification loss). However, greedy approaches typically do not have theoretical guarantee and may lead to suboptimal solutions.

Lei et al. (2019) formulate the attacks with discrete input on a set function as an optimization task. They prove that this set function is submodular for two types of popular neural network text classifiers under simplifying assumption: the first is a word-level convolutional neural network (CNN) without dropout or softmax layers, and the second is a recurrent neural network (RNN) with one-dimensional hidden units and arbitrary time steps. This finding guarantees a $1 - 1/e$ approximation factor for attacks that use the greedy algorithm. Meanwhile, they also show how to use the gradient of the attacked classifier to guide the greedy search.

With the proposed optimization scheme, they show significantly improved attack performance over most baselines. Meanwhile, they also propose a joint sentence and word paraphrasing technique to simultaneously ensure retention of the semantics and syntax of the text, known as the *paraphrasing attack* (Lei et al., 2019). Interestingly, they also found that in their experiments, under almost all circumstances, model retraining via augmenting the adversarial examples with correct labels can improve the generalization of the model and make it less susceptible to attack.

Fig. 6.1 shows the text adversarial examples generated by the paraphrasing attack (Lei et al., 2019) for sentiment analysis and fake-news detection using neural networks.

---

Task: Sentiment Analysis. Classifier: LSTM. Original: 100% Positive. ADV label: 100% Negative.

---

I suppose I should write a review here since my little Noodle-oo is currently serving as their spokes dog in the photos. We both love Scooby Do's. They treat my little butt-faced dog like a prince and are receptive to correcting anything about the cut that I perceive as being weird. Like that funny poofy pompadour. Mohawk it out, yo. Done. In like five seconds my little man was looking fabulous and bad ass. Not something easily accomplished with a prancing pup that literally chases butterflies through tall grasses. (He ended up looking like a little lamb as the cut grew out too. So adorable.) The shampoo they use here is also amazing. Noodles usually smells like tacos (a combination of beef stank and corn chips) but after getting back from the Do's, he smelled like Christmas morning! Sugar and spice and everything nice instead of frogs and snails and puppy dog tails. He's got some gender identity issues to deal with. ~~The pricing is also cheaper than some of the big name conglomerates out there~~ The price is cheaper than some of the big names below. I'm talking to you Petsmart! I've taken my other pup to Smelly Dog before, but unless I need dog sitting play time after the cut, I'll go with Scooby's. They genuinely seem to like my little Noodle monster.

---

Task: Fake-News Detection. Classifier: LSTM. Original label: 100% Fake. ADV label: 77% Real

---

~~Man~~ Guy punctuates high-speed chase with stop at In-N-Out Burger drive-thru Print [Ed.— ~~Well, that's~~ Okay, that 's a new one.] ~~A~~ One man is in custody after leading police on a bizarre chase into the east Valley on Wednesday night. Phoenix police ~~began~~ has begun following the suspect in Phoenix and the pursuit ~~continued~~ into the east Valley, but it took a bizarre turn when the suspect stopped at an In-N-Out Burger restaurant's ~~drive-thru~~ drive-through near Priest and Ray Roads in Chandler. The suspect appeared to order food, but then drove away and got out of his pickup truck near Rock Wren Way and Ray Road. He ~~then ran into a backyard~~ ran to the backyard and tried to ~~get into a house through the back door~~ get in the home.

---

**Figure 6.1** Examples of generated adversarial examples using the paraphrasing attack proposed by Lei et al. (2019). The color red (gray in print version) denotes sentence-level paraphrasing, and blue (dark gray in print version) denotes word-level paraphrasing.

## Sequence-to-sequence translation

Beyond text classification, Cheng et al. (2020d) study the much more challenging problem of crafting adversarial examples for sequence-to-sequence (seq2seq) models (Sutskever et al., 2014) whose inputs are discrete text strings and outputs have an almost infinite number of possibilities. They propose an effective adversarial attack framework called *Seq2Sick* to address the challenges caused by the discrete input space, a projected gradient method combined with group lasso and gradient regularization. To handle the almost infinite output space, they design some novel loss functions to conduct nonoverlapping attack and targeted keyword attack. When applying their attack algorithm to machine translation and text summarization tasks, by changing less than three words, they can make seq2seq model to produce desired outputs with high success rates. They also use an external sentiment classifier to verify the property of preserving semantic meanings for the generated adversarial examples. Table 6.1 shows some such examples.

**Table 6.1** Text summarization adversarial examples using nonoverlapping method proposed by Cheng et al. (2020d). Surprisingly, it is possible to make the output sequence completely different by changing only one or few words in the input sequence. Red (gray in print version) color indicates changed words.

| | |
|---|---|
| Source input seq | among asia's leaders, prime minister mahathir mohamad was notable as a man with a bold vision: a physical and social transformation that would push this nation into the forefront of world affairs. |
| Adv input seq | among lynn's leaders, prime minister mahathir mohamad was notable as a man with a bold vision: a physical and social transformation that would push this nation into the forefront of world affairs. |
| Source output seq | asia's leaders are a man of the world |
| Adv output seq | **a vision for the world** |
| Source input seq | under nato threat to end his punishing offensive against ethnic albanian separatists in kosovo, president slobodan milosevic of yugoslavia has ordered most units of his army back to their barracks and may well avoid an attack by the alliance, military observers and diplomats say |
| Adv input seq | under nato threat to end his punishing offensive against ethnic albanian separatists in kosovo, president slobodan milosevic of yugoslavia has jean-sebastien most units of his army back to their barracks and may well avoid an attack by the alliance, military observers and diplomats say. |
| Source output seq | milosevic orders army back to barracks |
| Adv output seq | **nato may not attack kosovo** |
| Source input seq | flooding on the yangtze river remains serious although water levels on parts of the river decreased today, according to the state headquarters of flood control and drought relief. |
| Adv input seq | flooding that the yangtze river becomes serious although water levels on parts of the river decreased today, according to the state headquarters of flood control and drought relief. |
| Source output seq | floods on yangtze river continue |
| Adv output seq | **flooding in water recedes in river** |

## 6.6 Deep reinforcement learning

Deep reinforcement learning (DRL) models are shown to possess many advantages in optimizing robot learning systems, such as autonomous navigation and continuous robot arm control. Yang et al. (2020b) propose timing-based adversarial strategies against a DRL-based navigation system by jamming in physical noise patterns on the selected time frames. To study the vulnerability of learning-based navigation systems, they propose two adversarial agent models: one refers to online learning, and another one is based on evolutionary learning. Under white-box and black-box adversarial settings, their experimental results show that the adversarial timing attacks can lead to a significant performance drop of the target DRL model. Yang et al. (2022) studies different types of obervational interference to Q-learning based DRL models and show that incoporating them into neural network architecture design and training can lead to improved robustness.

## 6.7 Image captioning

Image captioning is an example of deep learning on mixed data modalities (texts and images). The model input is an image, and the model output is some caption describing the content in the image. Image captioning adopts an encoder–decoder framework consisting of two principal components, a convolutional neural network (CNN) for image feature extraction and a recurrent neural network (RNN) for language caption generation.

Chen et al. (2018a) propose *Show-and-Fool*, a novel algorithm for crafting adversarial examples in neural image captioning. The proposed algorithm provides two evaluation approaches, which check whether neural image captioning systems can be misled to output some randomly chosen or targeted captions or keywords. Their experiments show that their algorithm can successfully craft visually similar adversarial examples with randomly targeted captions or keywords, and the adversarial examples can be made highly transferable to other image captioning systems.

As an illustration, Fig. 6.2 shows adversarial examples crafted by Show-and-Fool using the targeted caption method. The adversarial perturbations are visually imperceptible but can successfully mislead the Show-and-Tell (Vinyals et al., 2015) neural image captioning model to generate the targeted captions. Interestingly and perhaps surprisingly, their results pinpoint the Achilles heel of the language and vision models used in the tested image captioning systems. Moreover, the adversarial examples in neural image captioning highlight the inconsistency in visual language grounding be-

Original Top-3 inferred captions:
1. A red stop sign sitting on the side of a road.
2. A stop sign on the corner of a street.
3. A red stop sign sitting on the side of a street.

Adversarial Top-3 captions:
1. A brown teddy bear laying on top of a bed.
2. A brown teddy bear sitting on top of a bed.
3. A large brown teddy bear laying on top of a bed.

Original Top-3 inferred captions:
1. A man holding a tennis racquet on a tennis court.
2. A man holding a tennis racquet on top of a tennis court.
3. A man holding a tennis racquet on a court.

Adversarial Top-3 captions:
1. A woman brushing her teeth in a bathroom.
2. A woman brushing her teeth in the bathroom.
3. A woman brushing her teeth in front of a bathroom mirror.

Figure 6.2 Adversarial examples crafted by Show-and-Fool (Chen et al., 2018a) using the targeted caption method. The target captioning model is Show-and-Tell (Vinyals et al., 2015), the original images are selected from the MSCOCO validation set, and the targeted captions are randomly selected from the top-1 inferred caption of other validation images.

tween humans and machines, suggesting a possible weakness of current machine vision and perception machinery.

## 6.8 Weight perturbation

Beyond perturbations on the data inputs, the need for studying the sensitivity of neural networks to weight perturbations is also intensifying owing to several practical motivations. For instance, in model compression the robustness to weight quantization is crucial for designing energy-efficient hardware accelerator (Stutz et al., 2020) and for reducing memory storage while retaining model performance (Hubara et al., 2017; Weng et al., 2020). The notion of weight perturbation sensitivity is also used as a property to reflect the generalization gap at local minima (Keskar et al., 2017; Neyshabur et al., 2017). Intuitively, the "sharpness" of a local minimum can be measured by the increase of loss function under a norm-bounded perturbation, and a sharp local minimum is usually less generalizable since the model will encounter siginificant performance loss when testing samples are slightly different from training. Motivated by these observations, a family of sharpness aware minimization has been introduced in the literature Foret et al. (2020). Instead of minimizing the standard training loss, they proposed to train neural networks with the following bi-level objective function:

$$\min_{\theta} \frac{1}{n} \sum_{i=1}^{n} \max_{\|\theta - \theta'\| \leq \epsilon} \mathcal{L}(f_{\theta'}(x_i), y_i),$$

where $\theta'$ is the norm-bounded perturbed weight. Since sharp minimums have higher loss under perturbation, minimizing the above objective will converge to a flatter minimum, and the flatness–loss tradeoff is controlled by the constant $\epsilon$. It has been shown in (Chen et al., 2022) that sharpness aware minimization can significantly improve the (clean) accuracy of Vision Transformer models since those models typically tend to overfit the training data. Several improvements have also been made to improve the performance and the speed of sharpness-aware minimization (Zhuang et al., 2022; Liu et al., 2022).

In adversarial robustness and security, weight sensitivity can be leveraged as a vulnerability for fault injection and causing erroneous prediction (Liu et al., 2017a; Zhao et al., 2019b). It has also been shown that weight perturbation, when combined with adversarial training, can improve adversarial robustness (Wu et al., 2020b). However, theoretical characterization of its impacts on generalization and robustness of neural networks remains elusive. Tsai et al. (2021a) bridge this gap by developing a novel theoretical framework for understanding the generalization gap (through Rademacher complexity) and the robustness (through classification margin) of neural networks against norm-bounded weight perturbations. Specifically, they consider the multiclass classification problem setup and multilayer feed-forward neural networks with nonnegative monotonic activation functions. Their analysis offers fundamental insights into how weight perturbation affects the generalization gap and the pairwise class margin. Moreover, based on their analysis, they propose a theory-driven loss function for training generalizable and robust neural networks against norm-bounded weight perturbations. Their results offer fundamental insights for characterizing the generalization and robustness of neural networks against weight perturbations. The adversarial robustness of joint perturbations to input and weight spaces is studied in (Tsai et al., 2021b).

Weng et al. (2020) study the problem of weight quantization through the lens of weight perturbations and certified robustness. They demonstrate significant improvements on the generalization ability of quantized networks through their robustness-aware quantization scheme.

## 6.9 Extended reading

- Qin et al. (2019) propose advanced and more robust audio adversarial examples for automatic speech recognition, including realization of physical attacks.
- Xu et al. (2020a) propose advanced robust training algorithms for graph neural networks.
- Survey of graph adversarial attacks (Sun et al., 2018).
- Survey of text adversarial attacks (Li et al., 2018a; Zhang et al., 2020b).

# PART 3

# Robustness verification

# CHAPTER 7

# Overview of neural network verification

## 7.1 Robustness verification versus adversarial attack

To introduce the concept of robustness verification, we will first mathematically define the notion of adversarial robustness and discuss the relationship between robustness verification and attack.

We consider a classification model $F : \mathbb{R}^d \to \{1, \ldots, K\}$, where $K$ is the number of classes. For simplicity, we consider the most simple $\ell_p$ norm threat model, where an adversarial example aims to change the prediction with minimum $\ell_p$ norm perturbation. In this case, for an input example $x_0$, the *minimum adversarial perturbation* can be mathematically defined as

$$\epsilon^* = \min_{\delta} \|\delta\|_p \quad \text{s.t.} \quad F(x_0 + \delta) \neq F(x_0). \tag{7.1}$$

The value of $\epsilon^*$ defines the distance to the closest decision boundary and also gives a "safe region", which guarantees that the prediction remains unchanged within $\mathcal{B}_{x_0}(\epsilon^*) := \{x \mid \|x - x_0\| < \epsilon^*\}$. This is also the shortest distance from $x_0$ to the decision boundary of the model $F$, as illustrated in Fig. 7.1.

Unfortunately, computing $\epsilon^*$ is NP-complete even for a simple ReLU network (Katz et al., 2017). Therefore we can only expect an efficient way for computing upper or lower bounds of $\epsilon^*$.

*Adversarial attacks* are developed for finding a feasible solution $\bar{\delta}$ of (7.1), which corresponds to a counterexample for the robustness property. The norm of $\bar{\delta}$ can then serve as an *upper bound of $\epsilon^*$, denoted by $\bar{\epsilon}$*. For neural networks, several attacking algorithms have been proposed (see Chapter 2), including L-BFGS (Szegedy et al., 2014), FGSM (Goodfellow et al., 2015), I-FGSM (Kurakin et al., 2016), C&W (Carlini and Wagner, 2017b), and PGD attack (Madry et al., 2018). All of them try to solve (7.1) or its reformulations by a gradient-based optimizer. However, due to the non-convexity of neural networks, attacks may not converge to the minimal adversarial perturbation, so the robustness measurement computed by an attack may not represent the true adversarial robustness. There are many examples that a model was considered "robust" under standard attack but

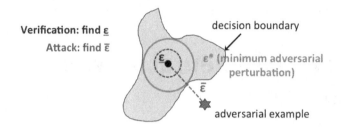

**Figure 7.1** Illustration of adversarial robustness, attack and verification.

later on was broken by more carefully designed attacks (Athalye et al., 2018; Carlini and Wagner, 2017a; Carlini et al., 2019a).

*Robustness verification.* In comparison, robustness verification methods aim to give a reliable measurement of robustness. Finding the exact value of $\epsilon^*$ is regarded as *sound and complete verification*, which requires exponential computational complexity. For instance, several branch-and-bound algorithms were developed to split the problem into an exponential number of sub-regions and solve each of them separately. They usually only scale to less than 100 neurons and couldn't handle most of the practically used neural networks.

To address the computational issue, algorithms for *sound but incomplete* neural network verification has become increasingly important. Those verification algorithms aim to compute a lower bound $\underline{\epsilon} \leq \epsilon^*$ of minimum adversarial perturbation. This guarantees that no adversarial example exists within an $\underline{\epsilon}$-ball around $x$ no matter which attack is used. Fig. 7.1 illustrates the relationships between sound verification, attack, and minimum adversarial perturbation. The word "soundness" comes from the formal verification community, since with $\underline{\epsilon}$ available, we can provably state that some points are $\epsilon$-robust (when $\epsilon \leq \underline{\epsilon}$), which is the property of soundness. However, when $\epsilon > \underline{\epsilon}$ we do not know whether it is robust, so the verification is "incomplete".

In addition to viewing robustness verification as finding the lower bound $\underline{\epsilon} \leq \epsilon^*$, we can also formulate it as the following problem:

Decide whether there exists $x' \in \{x \mid \|x - x_0\| \leq \epsilon\}$ such that $F(x_0) \neq F(x')$.

$$(7.2)$$

If we can answer this decision problem exactly, then a binary search can immediately give an accurate $\epsilon^*$ value. Instead of solving this decision problem exactly, sound (but incomplete) verification algorithms will answer the question with yes if the robustness of the point can be verified within $\epsilon$ perturbation, but will not give a certified answer for the rest of the points.

## 7.2 Formulations of robustness verification

In this section we briefly show how to formulate robustness verification problems mathematically and discuss the challengings of solving it.

We first consider a binary classification neural network, where the output layer only has one neuron $f(x)$ and the label prediction is sign$(f(x))$. In this case, if we denote the perturbation set as $S_\epsilon(x_0) := \{x \mid \|x - x_0\|_p \leq \epsilon\}$ and assume the original example $x_0$ is predicted as $+1$, then problem (7.2) is equivalent to solving

$$\min f(x) \quad \text{s.t.} \quad x \in S_\epsilon(x_0). \tag{7.3}$$

When the solution of (7.3) is negative, there exists a perturbation that can change the prediction from positive to negative, so the model is not robust on $x_0$; otherwise if the solution of (7.3) is positive, then the model is provably robust on $x_0$. A sound but incomplete verification will produce a lower bound of (7.3); when the lower bound is positive, the model is provably robust on $x_0$; otherwise if the lower bound is negative, the robustness is not certified.

Therefore, we can see that robustness verification is equivalent to solving an optimization problem. To gain more intuition why this optimization problem is difficult when $f(x)$ is a neural network, let's further expand the function $f(x)$. For simplicity, let us assume that $f(x)$ is an $L$-layer feedforward network:

$$f(x) := z^{(L)} = W^{(L)}x^{(L)} + b^{(L)}, \quad x^{(l)} = \sigma^{(l)}(W^{(l)}x^{(l)} + b^{(l)}), \quad l \in [L], \tag{7.4}$$

where $x^{(0)} = x$ is the input, $W^{(l)}$ and $b^{(l)}$ are the weight matrix and bias vector of the $l$th layer, $\sigma^{(l)}$ is a (nonlinear) activation function, and $z^{(L)}$ in the binary classification case will be a single output neuron corresponding to the value of $f(x)$. With these definitions, the optimization problem (7.3) can be further expanded as

$$\min_{x^{(0)} \in S_\epsilon} z^{(L)} \quad \text{s.t.} \quad z^{(l)} = W^{(l)}x^{(l)} + b^{(l)}, \tag{7.5}$$

$$x^{(l+1)} = \sigma^{(l)}(z^{(l)}), \tag{7.6}$$

$$l \in [L]. \tag{7.7}$$

In this minimization problem, constraint (7.5) is just a linear equality constraint, but constraint (7.6) is a non-linear and non-convex constraint when $\sigma^{(l)}$ is a nonlinear function such as ReLU. Therefore, it is theoretically difficult to solve this optimization problem exactly. The idea in sound but incomplete verification aims to relax constraint (7.6) to make the problem tractable while being able to compute a lower bound of the solution. We will discuss how to achieve a lower bound and the exact solution of this problem in the next two chapters, corresponding to algorithms for incomplete and complete verifications.

Before delving into the actual verification algorithms, we will first discuss the generalized form of (7.3). In fact, neural network verification can be used to verify many other properties in addition to adversarial robustness. Given a neural network $f : \mathbb{R}^d \to \mathbb{R}^K$ that maps input to output neurons, verification aims to find a lower bound or exact solution of an affine function within an input region $S$:

$$\min \langle c, f(\boldsymbol{x}) \rangle \text{ s.t. } \boldsymbol{x} \in S, \tag{7.8}$$

where $c$ is called a linear specification, which corresponds to the property we want to verify. In the setting of binary classification, as in formulation (7.3), $f(x)$ is just a single value and we can set $c = 1$ for verification. For multi-class classification problem, by setting $c$ as a vector with 1 on the positive class and $-1$ on the opposite class (e.g., class $t$), the sign of the solution of (7.8) indicates whether there exists any adversarial example predicted as class $t$. If we verify there exists no adversarial example for each class $t$, then the robustness can be certified. In addition to robustness verification, this framework is also used to guarantee safety in many real-time control systems, such as aircraft controls (Julian et al., 2019; Katz et al., 2017).

## 7.3 Applications of neural network verification

As mentioned before, neural network verification can verify not only robustness, but also other safety specifications as long as the specification can be written as an affine function locally. Here we introduce some important applications for neural network verification.

### Safety-critical control systems

Verification has been used in many control systems. Among them, the safety verification problem of next-generation airborne collision avoidance system for unmanned aircraft (ACAS Xu) has been used as the benchmark for this field (Katz et al., 2017; Julian et al., 2019), and several other practical systems are also considered in the previous verification work such as a LiDAR object detection system (Sun et al., 2019a), a perception network for automated driving (Cheng, 2019), and a fuel injecting system (Wong et al., 2020b). Taking the ACAS Xu system as an example, it contains 45 neural networks with hundreds of neurons, and the goal is to verify whether these networks satisfy some predefined safety specifications for collision avoidance.

## Natural language processing

The robustness of natural language models have become an important problem in natural language processing. It has been shown that semantic preserved perturbations (e.g., replacing a word by its synonym) can alter the model's prediction in many NLP tasks. Certified defense methods have been applied in (Jia et al., 2019; Huang et al., 2019) by using neural network verification methods and extending to the discrete perturbation setting.

## Machine learning interpretability

Neural network verification is also an important tool for understanding the model's behavior. For instance, many feature-based explanations (Hsieh et al., 2020) are based on the sensitivity of models – how much perturbation to a feature can change the model's prediction – which can be easily answered by verification tools. Also, verification methods can be used to find an important set of features as well as identifying unimportant features that are provably having no effect on the model.

## 7.4  Extended reading

- A survey on neural network verification in (Liu et al., 2019a) gives an overview on both incomplete and complete verifications.
- The International Verification of Neural Network Competition (VNN-Comp) that takes place each year has been a place for teams demonstrating state-of-the-art tools on neural network verification on various problems.

# CHAPTER 8

# Incomplete neural network verification

As mentioned in the previous section, solving the complete neural network verification problem is challenging and time-consuming, and ealier works that focused on complete verification usually do not scale to problems beyond a hundred neurons. Further, it has been shown that complete verification for ReLU networks is NP-complete (Katz et al., 2017). Motivated by the fundamental limit and practical difficulties, incomplete verification algorithms were rised since 2018, where they aim to provide sound verification for large neural networks, with the trade-off that they can only certify some but not all instances. These verifiers are often efficient and can be easily parallelized with GPU. Interestingly, these incomplete verifiers later become powerful tools even for complete verification, as will be shown in the next section.

## 8.1 A convex relaxation framework

We first introduce the convex relaxation framework, which covers most of the existing incomplete neural network verification methods. As mentioned in the last chapter, neural network verification can be formulated as an optimization problem. For simplicity, let us assume that $f(x)$ is an $L$-layer feedforward network:

$$f(x) := z^{(L)} = W^{(L)}x^{(L)} + b^{(L)}, \quad x^{(l)} = \sigma^{(l)}(W^{(l)}x^{(l)} + b^{(l)}), \quad l \in [L], \quad (8.1)$$

where $x^{(0)} = x$ is the input, $W^{(l)}$ and $b^{(l)}$ are the weight matrix and bias vector of the $l$th layer, and $\sigma^{(l)}$ is a (nonlinear) activation function. Instead of passing a single $x$ to the network, neural network verification aims to propagate an input region $S$ and verify some properties of output neurons. This can be written as the following optimization problem:

$$\min_{x^{(0)} \in S} c^T x^{(L)} \text{ s.t. } z^{(l)} = W^{(l)}x^{(l)} + b^{(l)},$$

$$x^{(l+1)} = \sigma^{(l)}(z^{(l)}), \quad (\mathcal{O})$$

$$l \in [L],$$

*Adversarial Robustness for Machine Learning*
https://doi.org/10.1016/B978-0-12-824020-5.00018-1
79

where $c$ corresponds to the specification as defined in (7.8). Unfortunately, solving ($\mathcal{O}$) is intractable due to the nonconvex constraints; it is thus natural to conduct convex relaxation on the feasible set. Specifically, we relax each $x^{(l+1)} = \sigma^{(l)}(z^{(l)})$ by convex inequality constraints, leading to the following convex relaxation:

$$\min_{x^{(0)} \in S} c^T x^{(L)} \quad \text{s.t.} \quad z^{(l)} = W^{(l)} x^{(l)} + b^{(l)},$$
$$\underline{\sigma}^{(l)}(z^{(l)}) \leq x^{(l+1)} \leq \bar{\sigma}^{(l)}(z^{(l)}), \qquad (\mathcal{C})$$
$$\underline{z}^{(l)} \leq x^{(l)} \leq \bar{z}_l,$$
$$l \in [L],$$

where $\underline{\sigma}^{(l)}(z)$ ($\bar{\sigma}^{(l)}(z)$) is convex (concave) and satisfies $\underline{\sigma}^{(l)}(z) \leq \sigma^{(l)}(z) \leq \bar{\sigma}^{(l)}(z)$ for $\underline{z}^{(l)} \leq z \leq \bar{z}^{(l)}$. The preactivation upper and lower bounds $\bar{z}^{(l)}$ and $\underline{z}^{(l)}$ correspond to some precomputed upper and lower bounds for each $z$. In general, we can set $\underline{z}^{(l)} = -\infty$ and $\bar{z}^{(l)} = \infty$ for all $l$, but tighter ranges of $\underline{z}^{(l)}$ and $\bar{z}^{(l)}$ can achieve tighter solutions. A typical approach is to solve ($\mathcal{C}$) recursively to obtain the tightest $\underline{z}^{(l)}$ and $\bar{z}^{(l)}$.

In the following, we will introduce a family of linear relaxation–based methods, which can be viewed as particular cases of ($\mathcal{C}$) when the nonlinear activation functions are bounded by linear upper and lower bounds.

## 8.2 Linear bound propagation methods

Linear bound propagation is a simple yet effective method for sound but incomplete verification. Note that there were several papers proposing different versions of linear bound propagation methods, such as (Wong and Kolter, 2017; Weng et al., 2018a; Zhang et al., 2018; Singh et al., 2018a, 2019b) (see Fig. 8.1). However, since they lead to similar algorithms with slightly different choices of upper/lower bounds, we will mainly focus on introducing the CROWN algorithm (Zhang et al., 2018) in this section and then talk about the relationship between CROWN and other algorithms.

The key idea is to use linear functions to bound the values of each particular neuron in any intermediate and final layer. The main difficulty for obtaining a linear bound is the nonlinear activations. If there are no nonlinear activations, then clearly any $z^{(l)}$ can be written as a linear function to the input. Then for any output neuron $f(x)$, we can write it as $f(x) = a^T x$, where $a$ is the slope, and in this case, verification is equivalent to

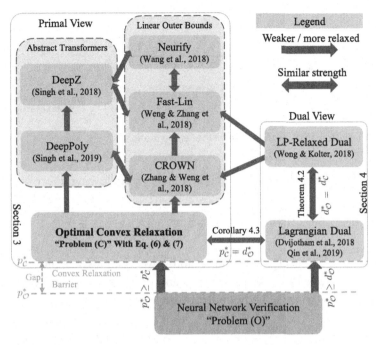

**Figure 8.1** Illustration of the convex relaxation methods and convex relaxation barrier from (Salman et al., 2019b), where they showed almost all the incomplete verification algorithms can be formulated based on a convex relaxation framework and summarized the relationships between different incomplete verifiers.

finding

$$\max_{x' \in S} a^T x'.$$

For example, when $S$ is an $\ell_\infty$ ball with radius $\epsilon$ centered at $x_0$, the worst-case output will be $\epsilon \|a\|_1 + a^T x_0$.

What if we have some nonlinear activations such as ReLU? The main idea of linear bound propagation methods is forming linear upper and lower bounds $\bar{\sigma}$ and $\underline{\sigma}$ for the activation function. Consider a ReLU function, and for simplicity, we assume the current preactivation lower and upper bounds $z \in [l, u]$, and we aim to bound $\mathrm{ReLU}(z) = \max(z, 0)$ by linear functions. We can consider three cases illustrated in Fig. 8.2. If $l \geq 0$, then we know that $z$ is always positive, and thus $\mathrm{ReLU}(z) = z$ will be linear. If $u \leq 0$, then we know that $z$ is always negative, and thus $\mathrm{ReLU}(z) = 0$ will also be linear. The third case $l < 0 < u$ is the most tricky, where ReLU is truly nonlinear, and we need to find linear upper and lower bounds. We call these "unstable neurons".

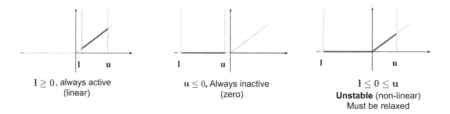

**Figure 8.2** Illustration of the three cases of the ReLU activations.

For these unstable neurons, we can derive the following linear bounds:

$$\underline{\sigma}^{(l)}(z) := \alpha^{(l)} z, \quad \overline{\sigma}^{(l)}(z) := \frac{\overline{z}^{(l)}}{\overline{z}^{(l)} - \underline{z}^{(l)}}(z - \underline{z}^{(l)}) \qquad (8.2)$$

with some $\alpha^{(l)} \in [0, 1]$. The upper and lower bounds are illustrated in Fig. 8.3. We can easily verify that for any $\alpha^{(l)} \in [0, 1]$, the output value of ReLU activation will be bounded by these two functions:

$$\underline{\sigma}^{(l)}(z) \leq \max(z, 0) \leq \overline{\sigma}^{(l)}(z) \quad \forall z \in [\underline{z}^{(l)}, \overline{z}^{(l)}].$$

Interestingly, there could be multiple choices for the lower bounds. Some common choices are: using the same slope of upper and lower bounds; using 0 slope for the lower bound; using some heuristics to adaptively choose the slope. More recently, it has been shown that one can choose the lower bound to optimize the final verification performance, as will be discussed in the end of this section.

With the linear upper and lower bounds for the ReLU function, we can then bound the output of a ReLU layer, where the constants are determined by slope of the linear functions used in (8.2):

**Lemma 1** (ReLU relaxation in CROWN). *Given* $w, v \in \mathbb{R}^d$, $u \leq v \leq l$ *(elementwise), we have*

$$w^\top ReLU(v) \geq w^\top \mathcal{D}v + b',$$

*where* $\mathcal{D}$ *is a diagonal matrix containing free variables only when* $u_j > 0 > l_j$ *and* $w_j \geq 0$, *whereas its remaining values and constant* $b'$ *are determined by* $l, u, w$.

With linear upper and lower bounds for each neuron, we can linearize the whole neural network step by step, where at each step, we form linear upper and lower bounds for neurons at layer $l$. This results in an efficient

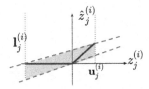

**Figure 8.3** Illustration of forming a linear upper and lower bound of an unstable neuron.

back-substitution procedure to derive a linear lower bound of NN output with respect to $x$.

**Lemma 2** (Linear Relaxation Bound). *Given an L-layer ReLU NN $f(x)$ : $\mathbb{R}^{d_0} \to \mathbb{R}$ with weights $W_i$, biases $\mathbf{b}^i$, and input constraint $x \in S$, we have*

$$\min_{x \in S} f(x) \geq \min_{x \in S} a_{\text{CROWN}}^{\top} x + c_{\text{CROWN}},$$

*where $a_{\text{CROWN}}$ and $c_{\text{CROWN}}$ can be computed using $W_i$, $\mathbf{b}^i$, $l_i$, $u_i$ in polynomial time. The detailed procedure can be found in several papers such as (Weng et al., 2018a; Zhang et al., 2018; Singh et al., 2019b).*

When $S$ is an $\ell_p$ norm ball, minimization over the linear function can be easily solved using Hölder's inequality. The main benefit of CROWN is its efficiency: CROWN can be efficiently implemented on machine learning accelerators such as GPUs (Xu et al., 2020b) and TPUs (Zhang et al., 2020a), and it can be a few magnitudes faster than a linear programming (LP) verifier, which is hard to parallelize on GPUs. CROWN was generalized to general architectures, whereas we only demonstrate it for feedforward ReLU networks for simplicity. Additionally, Xu et al. (2021) showed that it is possible to optimize the slope of the lower bound $\alpha$ using gradient ascent to further tighten the bound (sometimes referred to as $\alpha$-CROWN).

Fast-Lin (Weng et al., 2018a) and Neurify (Wang et al., 2018a) assigned $\alpha^{(l)} = \frac{\bar{z}^{(l)}}{\bar{z}^{(l)} - \underline{z}^{(l)}}$, which is strictly looser than Crown but enjoys slight computational benefit. DeepZ (Singh et al., 2018a) and DeepPoly (Singh et al., 2019b) are discovered from the formal verification community using the abstract interpretation approach but can also be covered in this framework.

## The optimal layerwise convex relaxation

Although the discussions have been focused on the robustness verification of ReLU networks, the above-mentioned linear bound propagation

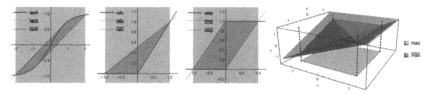

**Figure 8.4** Optimal convex relaxations for common nonlinearities. For tanh, the relaxation contains two linear segments and parts of the tanh function. For ReLU and the step function, the optimal relaxations are written as 3 and 4 linear constraints, respectively. For $z = \max(x, y)$, the light orange (light gray in print version) shadow indicates the preactivation bounds for $x$ and $y$, and the optimal convex relaxation is lower bounded by the max function itself. More details can be found in (Salman et al., 2019b).

methods can be easily extended to any network with general activation functions. The only requirement is to form a linear upper and lower bound for the activation function given the pre-activation bounds. More details can be found in (Zhang et al., 2018).

If we go beyond linear upper and lower bounds and use general convex functions instead, we can design the optimal convex relaxation $\underline{\sigma}$ and $\bar{\sigma}$ by the following convex envelop within $[\underline{z}, \bar{z}]$. For instance, the optimal lower bound is

$$\underline{\sigma}_{\mathrm{opt}}(z) := \sup_{(\alpha, \gamma) \in \mathcal{A}} \alpha^\top z + \gamma, \quad \mathcal{A} = \{(\alpha, \gamma) : \alpha^\top z' + \gamma \le \sigma(z'), \forall z' \in [\underline{z}, \bar{z}]\}.$$

This gives the tightest bound achieved by convex relaxation framework *for general activation functions* as shown in Fig. 8.4. With the optimal convex relaxation, one can get the tightest result but with significantly increased time complexity. For instance, for ReLU activation, Fig. 8.4 showed that the optimal convex relaxation is one linaer upper bound and the union of two linear lower bounds. Although this can still be expressed in a simple form, from the bound propagation perspective this will lead to exponentially growing number of linear bounds, which has to be solved by a linear programming solver. Therefore, in practice linear bound propagation methods are still the most popular choice for incomplete verification. It has been also discussed in (Salman et al., 2019b) regarding the gap between the optimal convex relaxation versus linear bound propagation. For some ReLU networks, they form two linear lower bounds for each ReLU activation and solve the resulting problem by linear programming. They demonstrated that the gap between the optimal convex relaxation and linear bound propagation could be reasonable in some realistic cases, but there is still some gap between the optimal convex relaxation and the exact verification problem, also known as the *"convex relaxation barrier"*, as illustrated in Fig. 8.4 (the orange (light gray in print version) gap between $(\mathcal{O})$ and $(\mathcal{C})$).

## 8.3 Convex relaxation in the dual space

Another way to solve the robustness verification problem $(\mathcal{C})$ is to solve its dual problem. Its Lagrangian dual can be written as

$$g_{\mathcal{C}}(\mu^{[L]}, \underline{\lambda}^{[L]}, \overline{\lambda}^{[L]}) := \min_{x^{[L+1]}, z^{[L]}} \quad c^\top x^{(L)} + \sum_{l=0}^{L-1} \mu^{(l)\top} (z^{(l)} - W^{(l)} x^{(l)} - \mathbf{b}^{(l)})$$

$$- \sum_{l=0}^{L-1} \underline{\lambda}^{(l)\top} (x^{(l+1)} - \underline{\sigma}^{(l)}(z^{(l)})) + \sum_{l=0}^{L-1} \overline{\lambda}^{(l)\top} (x^{(l+1)} - \overline{\sigma}^{(l)}(z^{(l)})). \tag{8.3}$$

By weak duality

$$d_{\mathcal{C}}^* := \max_{\mu^{[L]}, \underline{\lambda}^{[L]} \geq 0, \overline{\lambda}^{[L]} \geq 0} g_{\mathcal{C}}(\mu^{[L]}, \underline{\lambda}^{[L]}, \overline{\lambda}^{[L]}) \leq p_{\mathcal{C}}^*, \tag{8.4}$$

but in fact Salman et al. (2019b) showed strong duality under mild conditions, which means the equality can hold in most cases.

Based on this primal-dual relationship, another way to find the lower bound of the primal objective is to find a dual solution. When the relaxed bounds $\underline{\sigma}$ and $\overline{\sigma}$ are linear, the dual objective (8.4) can be further simplified. Wong and Kolter (2018) proposed to solve this dual form with the following choices of the linear relaxation functions:

$$\underline{\sigma}^{(l)}(z(l)) := \alpha^{(l)} z(l), \quad \overline{\sigma}^{(l)}(z(l)) := \frac{\overline{z}^{(l)}}{\overline{z}^{(l)} - \underline{z}^{(l)}} (z(l) - \underline{z}^{(l)}),$$

and $0 \leq \alpha^{(l)} \leq 1$ represents the slope of the lower bound. This is equivalent to the choices of linear relaxations introduced in Fig. 8.3. When $\alpha^{(l)} = \frac{\overline{z}^{(l)}}{\overline{z}^{(l)} - \underline{z}^{(l)}}$, the greedy algorithm also recovers Fast-Lin (Weng et al., 2018a), which explains the arrow from Wong and Kolter (2018) to Weng et al. (2018a) in Fig. 8.1. Several other relationships between dual algorithms and primal algorithms can be analyzed similarly, as discussed in (Salman et al., 2019b).

## 8.4 Recent progresses in linear relaxation-based methods

We briefly discuss several other improvements on the above mentioned linear relaxation-based incomplete verification methods:

- Adaptive linear bound selections: As shown in the previous sections, the linear relaxation bound for each neuron in (8.2) is controlled by $\alpha$, and some heuristic ways for choosing $\alpha$ have been discussed in CROWN. Interestingly, it is possible to automatically obtain an optimized $\alpha$ by optimizing the bound tightness. More specifically, for a set of given $\alpha$, the final verification can be presented in Lemma 2, and we can thus try to formulate $\alpha$ in $a^T_{\text{CROWN}}$ as learnable parameters and optimize for $\alpha$ to get tighter bounds. More details can be found in (Xu et al., 2021).

- Breaking the convex relaxation barrier: The framework mentioned above assumes convex upper and lower bounds for each single neuron. However, it has been observed that forming a convex relaxation for a group of neurons leads to tighter results, then relaxing each neuron independently. However, how to group more relevant neurons is still an open research topic. See more discussions in (Tjandraatmadja et al., 2020).

- Automatic bound propagation: Existing verification methods often focus on feed-forward ReLU networks. Only few work tried to extend existing verification methods to other models: Ko et al. (2019) extended Crown to recurrent neural networks; and Shi et al. (2020) extended Crown to the Transformer architecture. Unfortunately, each of these requires re-deriving and implementing the verification algorithm for each network architecture, which is hard even for a senior machine learning researcher. Instead of extending the proposed algorithm to each network architecture one-by-one, Xu et al. (2020a) developed an **automatic** verification framework where the mechanism is similar to auto-differentiation for back-propagation in Tensorflow/Pytorch. Users only need to write the model in Pytorch or Tensorflow, and the tool will automatically conduct verification and output the measurement without any additional human effort. This is done by representing the target function $f$ as a given computational graph, where each edge corresponds to a *basic operation* such as addition, multiplication, ReLU, softmax, sigmoid. Nodes in this graph can be divided into input nodes, output nodes, intermediate nodes and constant nodes, and the graph is supposed to be a Directed Acyclic Graph (DAG). Linear bound propagation algorithms mentioned in this section can then be easily generalized to the computational graph – each relaxation is done on an edge (operation) instead of a neural network layer. With this framework, verification can be automatically done for any given computational graph, as long as we have the propagation rule for basic operations. The overall usage is similar to how gradient is computed by auto-differentiation.

## 8.5 Extended reading

- We refer the readers to (Salman et al., 2019b) on detailed discussions about various incomplete verification algorithms.
- For linear relaxation-based methods, we encourage the readers to read (Wong and Kolter, 2017), who focused on using those bounds for certified robust training.
- Beyond verification for input perturbations, similar methodology can be applied to verifying weight perturbations in neural networks (Weng et al., 2020).
- A probabilistic framework for robustness certification based on additive noises following a given distributional characterization is proposed in (Weng et al., 2019).
- A robustness certification framework optimized for convolutional neural networks (CNN-Cert) is proposed in (Boopathy et al., 2019).

# CHAPTER 9

# Complete neural network verification

Complete verification is a hard problem due to the nonlinearity of deep neural networks. Even for a simple ReLU network, Katz et al. (2017) showed that complete verification is NP-complete. Therefore earlier works that formulate complete verification as Mixed Integer Programming (MIP) usually failed to handle networks beyond 100 neurons. However, significant progress has been made in the past few years and nowadays good verification tools can already handle some larger networks beyond 1 million parameters. In this chapter, we will discuss the main techniques used in the current complete verifiers.

## 9.1 Mixed integer programming

For ReLU networks, the complete verification problem can be formulated into the mixed integer programming (MIP) problem. The key insight is using binary variables to indicate the activation pattern of ReLU functions. Following the notation used in the previous sections, for a feed-forward network $f$ we can formulate the neural network verification problem (7.8) into the following MIP problem:

$$
\begin{aligned}
&\min \; c^T f \quad \text{s.t.} \;\; i \in [L], \; j \in [n_i]; \\
&z^{(i)} = W^{(i)} \hat{z}^{(i-1)} + b^{(i)}; \;\; f = z^{(L)}; \;\; \hat{z}^{(0)} = x \in \mathcal{C}; \\
&\hat{z}_j^{(i)} \geq z_j^{(i)}; \;\; \hat{z}^{(i)} j \leq u_j^{(i)} s_j^{(i)}; \;\; \hat{z}_j^{(i)} \leq z_j^{(i)} - l_j^{(i)}(1 - s_j^{(i)}); \\
&\hat{z}_j^{(i)} \geq 0; \;\; z_j^{(i)} \in [l_j^{(i)}, u_j^{(i)}]; \;\; s_j^{(i)} \in \{0, 1\};
\end{aligned}
\tag{9.1}
$$

where $s_j^{(i)}$ indicates the two statuses of ReLU: (1) *inactive*: when $s_j^{(i)} = 0$, constraints on $z_j^{(i)}$ simplify to $\hat{z}_j^{(i)} = 0$; or (2) *active*: when $s_j^{(i)} = 1$, we have $\hat{z}_j^{(i)} = z_j^{(i)}$. Here $l_j^{(i)}$ and $u_j^{(i)}$ are precomputed intermediate lower and upper bounds on preactivation $z_j^{(i)}$ such that $l_j^{(i)} \leq z_j^{(i)}(x) \leq u_j^{(i)}$ for $x \in \mathcal{C}$. Note that (9.1) requires exponential time to solve exactly due to the integer variable $s_i^{(j)}$ (activation pattern of each ReLU), but meanwhile there exists software packages such as Gurobi, which can handle small-scale instances relatively

*Adversarial Robustness for Machine Learning*
https://doi.org/10.1016/B978-0-12-824020-5.00019-3
89

well. For example, for problems with tens of neurons, it is still possible to directly apply Gurobi to conduct complete verification. Unfortunately, the complexity of this problem can increase exponentially with the number of ReLU neurons, so it can take hours to run even on a small network, unless the network is trained with a strong regularization such as a certified dense (Wong and Kolter, 2018; Xiao et al., 2019b).

## 9.2 Branch and bound

To speed up complete verification, most of the modern algorithms adopt the Branch-and-Bound (BaB) method (Bunel et al., 2018). Note that BaB is also a crucial component in off-the-shelf MIP solvers, and by developing a specialized BaB procedure for verification can improve the efficiency. BaB-based verification framework is a recursive process consisting of two main steps, branching and bounding. For *branching*, BaB-based methods will divide the bounded input domain $\mathcal{C}$ into subdomains $\{\mathcal{C}_i | \mathcal{C} = \bigcup_i \mathcal{C}_i\}$, each of these domains corresponds to a new independent verification problem. For instance, we can split a ReLU unit $\hat{z}^{(k)} = \text{ReLU}(z^{(k)})$ to negative and positive cases as $\mathcal{C}_0 = \{x \mid z^{(k)} \geq 0\}$ and $\mathcal{C}_1 = \{x \mid z^{(k)} < 0\}$ for a ReLU-based network, where each of these domains are the set of input that satisfies a certain constraint. For each subdomain $\mathcal{C}_i$, BaB-based methods perform *bounding* to obtain a relaxed but sound lower bound $\underline{f}_{\mathcal{C}_i}$. A tightened global lower bound over $\mathcal{C}$ can then be obtained by taking the minimum values of the subdomain lower bounds from all the subdomains: $\underline{f} = \min_i \underline{f}_{\mathcal{C}_i}$.

Based on this splitting approach, BaB will be performed recursively to tighten the approximated global lower bound. This can be implemented into a tree structure, where each node corresponds to a subdomain $C$. Starting from the root note where $C$ is the entire input domain (e.g., an $\ell_p$ ball around some data point $x_0$), BaB splits the node(domain) based on the sign of one ReLU neuron. After the split, we will create two children for a node, each of them consists a subdomain, and compute the lower bound for the subdomain. This is done until either (i) the global lower bound $\underline{f}$ becomes larger than 0 and thus the property is proven or (ii) a violation (e.g., identification of an adversarial example) is located in a subdomain to disprove the property.

*Soundness of BaB.* We say that the verification process is sound if we can always trust the "yes" (the property is successfully verified) answer given by the verifier. When a BaB-based verification process outputs "yes", it means all the leaf nodes output "yes". Therefore, we can easily see that if the bounding method used for each subdomain $C_i$ is sound, then the whole BaB-based verifier will also be sound.

*Completeness of BaB.* In a BaB-based verifier, it will keep splitting nodes until all the nodes are proved or disapproved. To guarantee the completeness of the procedure, we have to ensure that the bounding method will become a complete verifier for each subdomain after splitting all the ReLU neurons. This is true when applying the LP-based bounding method or linear bound propagation methods to each subdomain.

*Bounding with Linear Programming (LP).* For neural network verification, a classical bounding method used in BaB-based verification is the *Linear Programming bounding procedure*. Specifically, one can transform the original verification problem into a linear programming problem. This is done by relaxing each ReLU activation function $\hat{z} = \max(z, 0)$ into linear constraints. If the ReLU neuron has been splitted, then it has already been replaced by a linear constraint (either $z \leq 0, \hat{z} = 0$ or $z > 0, \hat{z} = z$). For each unsplitted neurons, it can be relaxed into the following three constraints:

$$\hat{z} \geq 0 \tag{9.2}$$

$$\hat{z} \geq z \tag{9.3}$$

$$\hat{z} \leq \frac{u}{u-l}(z-l), \tag{9.4}$$

where $u, l$ are the lower and upper bound of $z$, which can be computed by a simple forward bound propagation or using the linear propagation-based method mentioned in the previous section. Eq (9.4) is known as the "triangle relaxation" for ReLU neurons, since it essentially bounds the ReLU by a convex triangle region. After doing this for all the unsplitted neurons, the verification problem will become a linear programming problem and can thus be solved by off-the-shelf LP solvers. Using the above mentioned LP-based bounding method with BaB can lead to a complete verifier, since when all the ReLU neurons are splitted, there will be no relaxation to the original problem, and the LP will get the exact solution of the verification problem for the given subdomain.

*Branching in BaB.* Since the branching step determines the shape of the search tree, the main challenge is to efficiently choose a good leaf to split, which can significantly reduce the total number of branches and running time. For example, (Bunel et al., 2018) includes a simple branching heuristic, which assigns each ReLU node a score to estimate the improvement for tightening $f$ by splitting it, and splits the node with the highest score.

Different implementations usually use slightly different branching heuristics.

## 9.3  Branch-and-bound with linear bound propagation

Although linear programming (LP) can provide tight bounds for each subdomain when conducting BaB, they are usually time consuming to solve and cannot fully exploit the parallelization provided by GPUs or TPUs. Therefore many recent works applied incomplete verification solvers mentioned in the previous chapter to efficiently rule out some regions and provide guidance to BaB (Bunel et al., 2020a; Xu et al., 2021). In particular, Xu et al. (2021) combines BaB with a linear propagation-based incomplete verifier CROWN to conduct complete verification.

The main challenge of using linear propagation-based incomplete verifiers to BaB is to combine the split constraint ($z \geq 0$ or $z < 0$ for a neuron $z$) into the linear propagation procedure. One simple way to do that is to just use it as a pre-activation bound for each neuron ($l, u$ in (9.4)), but this is insufficient as the pre-activation constraint does not eliminate all the inputs outside the domain. Therefore, algorithms such as (Xu et al., 2021) incorporates the split constraints using Lagragian multipliers. More specifically, linear propagation methods lead to the following minimization problem for verification:

$$\min_{x \in C} f(x) \geq \min_{x \in C} w^T D z,$$

where $z$ is the values of some layer of neural network and $D$ is the diagonal matrix derived from bounding each neurons (see Lemma 1 in Chapter 8). The split constraint can then be added into this formulation as

$$\min_{x \in C} f(x) \geq \min_{x \in C} w^T D z, \quad Sz \leq 0, \tag{9.5}$$

where $S$ is a diagonal matrix with $+1, -1, 0$ on the diagonal, indicating the split constraints (postive, negative or no split). Optimizing (9.5) will then lead to the optimal solution within the constraint set. To deal with the constraint minimization problem, a standard approach is to transform it into an unconstrained problem with Lagrangian multipliers:

$$\min_{x \in C} f(x) \geq \max_{\beta \geq 0} \min_{x \in C} w^T D z + \beta S z, \tag{9.6}$$

where $\beta$ are the multipliers. We can thus merge the two linear terms in the objective together, which reduced to the linear propagation method, with the only change being introducing a few Lagrange multipliers ($\beta$) where we need to use another gradient ascent on $\beta$ to find the optimal value.

The main advantage of using linear propagation-based method in complete verification is that those methods are highly parallelizable, which can make the overall procedure efficient when running on GPU.

## 9.4 Empirical comparison

To give a full comparison between existing complete verification methods, we show the experimental results reported in a recent paper by Wang et al. (2021c). They evaluate verification algorithms using the benchmark containing three CIFAR-10 models (Base, Wide, and Deep) with 100 examples each. Each data example is associated with an $\ell_\infty$ norm perturbation budget $\epsilon$ and a target label for verification (referred to as a *property* to verify). The comparison includes the following methods:

- BaBSR (Bunel et al., 2020b), a basic BaB- and LP-based verifier;
- MIPplanet (Ehlers, 2017), a customized MIP solver for NN verification, where unstable ReLU neurons are randomly selected for splitting;
- ERAN (Singh et al., 2018a,b, 2019a,b), an abstract interpretation-based verifier, which performs well on this benchmark in VNN-COMP 2020;
- GNN-Online Lu and Kumar (2020), a BaB- and LP-based verifiers using a learned Graph Neural Network (GNN) to guide the ReLU splits;
- BDD+ BaBSR (Bunel et al., 2020a), a verification framework based on Lagrangian decomposition on GPUs (BDD+) with BaBSR branching strategy;
- OVAL (BDD+ GNN) (Bunel et al., 2020a; Lu and Kumar, 2020), a strong verifier in VNN-COMP 2020 using BDD+ with GNN guiding the ReLU splits; A.set BaBSR;
- Big-M+A.set BaBSR (De Palma et al., 2021a), which are dual-space verifiers on GPUs with a tighter linear relaxation than triangle LP relaxations;
- Fast-and-Complete (Xu et al., 2021), which uses CROWN on GPUs as the incomplete verifier in BaB without neuron split constraints;
- BaDNB (BDD+ FSB) (De Palma et al., 2021b), a complete verifier using BDD+ on GPUs with FSB branching strategy. $\beta$-CROWN BaB can use either BaBSR or FSB branching heuristic, and we include both in the evaluation.

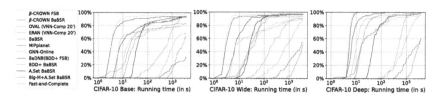

**Figure 9.1** Percentage of solved properties with growing running time. $\beta$-CROWN FSB (light green (light gray in print version)) and $\beta$-CROWN BaBSR (dark green (dark gray in print version)) clearly lead in all three settings and solve over 90% properties within 10 seconds.

The experiments are run on a machine with a single NVIDIA RTX 3090 GPU (24 GB GPU memory), an AMD Ryzen 9 5950X CPU and 64 GB memory. All methods use a 1-hour timeout threshold. Fig. 9.1 plots the percentage of solved properties over time. $\beta$-CROWN FSB achieves the fastest average running time compared to all other baselines with minimal timeouts and also clearly leads on the cactus plot. When using a weaker branching heuristic, $\beta$-CROWN BaBSR still outperforms all baselines.

# CHAPTER 10

# Verification against semantic perturbations

Whereas current verification methods mainly focus on the $\ell_p$-norm threat model of the input instances, robustness verification against semantic adversarial attacks inducing large $\ell_p$-norm perturbations, such as color shifting and lighting adjustment, are beyond their capacity. To bridge this gap, in this chapter, we introduce the *Semantify-NN* framework proposed by Mohapatra et al. (2020), a model-agnostic and generic robustness verification approach against semantic perturbations for neural networks. By simply inserting the proposed *semantic perturbation layers* (SP-layers) to the input layer of any given model, *Semantify-NN* is model-agnostic, and any $\ell_p$-norm based verification tools can be used to verify the model robustness against semantic perturbations. We will illustrate the principles of designing the SP-layers and provide examples including semantic perturbations to image classification in the space of hue, saturation, lightness, brightness, contrast, and rotation. In addition, we discuss an efficient refinement technique to further improve the semantic certificate.

## 10.1 Semantic adversarial example

Beyond the $\ell_p$-norm bounded threat model, some works have shown the possibility of generating *semantic adversarial examples* based on semantic perturbation techniques such as color shifting, lighting adjustment, and rotation (Hosseini and Poovendran, 2018; Liu et al., 2019b; Bhattad et al., 2019; Joshi et al., 2019; Fawzi and Frossard, 2015; Engstrom et al., 2017). We refer the readers to Fig. 10.1 for the illustration of some semantic perturbations for images. Notably, although semantically similar, these semantic adversarial attacks essentially consider threat models different from $\ell_p$-norm bounded attacks in the RGB (red, green, and blue) space. Therefore semantic adversarial examples usually incur large $\ell_p$-norm perturbations to the original data sample and thus exceed the verification capacity of $\ell_p$-norm-based verification methods.

In general, semantic adversarial attacks craft adversarial examples by tuning a set of parameters governing semantic manipulations of data sam-

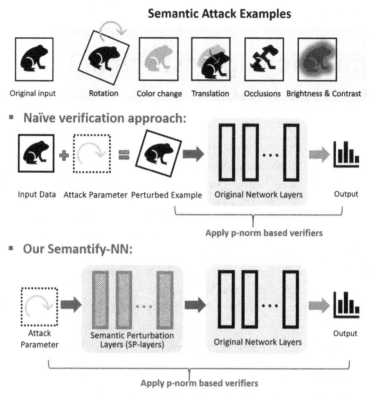

**Figure 10.1** Schematic illustration of the *Semantify-NN* robustness verification framework in (Mohapatra et al., 2020). Given a semantic attack threat model, Semantify-NN designs the corresponding semantic perturbation layers (SP-layers) and inserts them to the input layer of the original network for verification. With SP-layers, Semantify-NN can use any $\ell_p$-norm-based verification method for verifying semantic perturbations.

ples, which are either explicitly specified (e.g., rotation angle) or implicitly learned (e.g., latent representations of generative models). Hosseini and Poovendran (2018) use the HSV (hue, saturation, and value) representation of the RGB color space to find semantic adversarial examples for natural images. To encourage visual similarity, the authors propose to fix the value, minimize the changes in saturation, and fully utilize the hue changes to find semantic adversarial examples. Liu et al. (2019b) present a physically based differentiable renderer allowing propagating pixel-level gradients to the parametric space of lightness and geometry. Bhattad et al. (2019) introduce texture and colorization to induce semantic perturbation with a large $\ell_p$ norm perturbation to the raw pixel space while remaining visual imperceptibility. Joshi et al. (2019) train an adversarial network composed of an encoder and a generator conditioned on attributes to find semantic adversarial examples. Fawzi and Frossard (2015) and Engstrom et al. (2017) show that simple operations such as image rotation or object translation can result in a notable misclassification rate.

We note that for the semantic perturbations that are *continuously parameterized* (such as hue, saturation, lightness, brightness, contrast, and rotations), it is *not* possible to enumerate all possible values even if we only perturb one single parameter (e.g., rotation angle). The reason is that these parameters take *real values* in the continuous space, and hence it is not possible to finitely enumerate all possible values, unlike its discrete parameterized counterpart (e.g., translations and occlusions have finite enumerations). Taking the rotation angle for example, an attacker can try to do a grid search by sweeping rotation angle $\theta$ from $0°$ to $90°$ with a uniform grid of $10^6$ samples. However, if the attacks are not successful at $\theta = 30°$ and $30.00009°$, then it is possible that there exists some $\theta'$ that could "fool" the classifier where $30° < \theta' < 30.00009°$. This is indeed the motivation and necessity to have the robustness verification algorithm for semantic perturbations as discussed in this chapter – with a proper semantic robustness verification algorithm, we aim to deliver a robustness *guarantee* that neural networks will have a consistent prediction on the given image for any $\theta < a$, where $a$ is the semantic robustness certificate of the image.

## 10.2 Semantic perturbation layer

To bridge this gap and with an endeavor to render robustness verification methods more inclusive, Mohapatra et al. (2020) propose *Semantify-NN*, a model-agnostic and generic robustness verification against semantic perturbations. Semantify-NN is model-agnostic because it can apply to any given trained model by simply inserting the designed *semantic perturbation layers* (SP-layers). It is also generic since after adding SP-layers, we can apply any $\ell_p$-norm-based verification tools for certifying semantic perturbations. In other words, the proposed SP-layers work as a carefully designed converter that transforms semantic threat models to $\ell_p$-norm threat models.

Let $\mathcal{A}$ be a general threat model. For an input data sample $x$, we define an associated space of perturbed images $x'$, denoted as the *Attack Space* $\Omega_{\mathcal{A}}(x)$, which is equipped with a distance function $d_{\mathcal{A}}$ to measure the magnitude of the perturbation. The robustness certification problem under the threat model $\mathcal{A}$ is formulated as follows: given a trained $K$-class neural network function $f$ and an input data sample $x$, we aim to find the largest $\delta$ such that

$$\min_{x' \in \Omega_\mathcal{A}(x), d_\mathcal{A}(x',x) \leq \delta} \left( \min_{j \neq c} f_c(x') - f_j(x') \right) > 0, \quad\quad (10.1)$$

where $f_j$ denotes the confidence (or logit) of the $j$th class, $j \in \{1, 2, \ldots, K\}$, and $c$ is the predicted class of unperturbed input data $x$.

We consider semantic threat models that target semantically meaningful attacks, which are usually beyond the coverage of conventional $\ell_p$-norm bounded threat models in the pixel space. For an attack space $\Omega_\mathcal{A}^k$, there exists a function $g : X \times (I_1 \times I_2 \times \cdots \times I_k) \to X$ such that

$$\Omega_\mathcal{A}^k(x) = \{g(x, \epsilon_1, \ldots, \epsilon_k) \mid \epsilon_i \in I_i\}, \quad\quad (10.2)$$
$$d_\mathcal{A}(g(x, \epsilon_1, \ldots, \epsilon_k), x) = ||(\epsilon_1, \ldots, \epsilon_k)||_p,$$

where $X$ is the pixel space (the raw image), $I_i$ is the set of feasible semantic operations, and $\|\cdot\|_p$ denotes the $\ell_p$ norm. The parameters $\epsilon_i$ specify semantic operations selected from $I_i$. For example, $\epsilon_i$ can describe some human-interpretable characteristic of an image, such as translations shift, rotation angle, etc. For convenience, we define $\epsilon^k = (\epsilon_1, \epsilon_2, \ldots, \epsilon_k)$ and $I^k = I_1 \times \ldots \times I_k$, where $k$ denotes the dimension of the semantic attack. In other words, we show that it is possible to define an explicit function $g$ for all the semantic perturbations considered in this work, including translations, occlusions, color space transformations, and rotations, and we then measure the $\ell_p$ norm of the semantic perturbations on the space of semantic features $\epsilon^k$ rather than the raw pixel space. Notice that the conventional $\ell_p$ norm perturbations on the raw RGB pixels are a particular case under this definition: by letting $I_i$ equal to a bounded real set (i.e., $x_i' - x_i$, all possible difference between $i$th pixel) and $k$ the dimension of input vector $x$, we recover $d_\mathcal{A} = \|x' - x\|_p$.

Based on the definition above, semantic attacks can be divided into two categories: discretely parameterized perturbations (i.e., $I_k$ is a discrete set) including translation and occlusions, and continuously parameterized perturbations (i.e., $I_k$ is a continuous set) including color changes, brightness, contrast, and spatial transformations (e.g., rotations).

### Discretely parameterized semantic perturbation

**Translation:** Translation is a two-dimensional semantic attack with the parameters being the relative position of left-uppermost pixel of perturbed image to the original image. Therefore $I_1 = \{0, 1, \ldots, r\}$ and $I_2 =$

$\{0, 1, \ldots, h\}$, where $r$ and $h$ are the dimensions of width and height of our input image $x$. Note that any padding methods can be applied including padding with the black pixels or boundary pixels, etc.

*Occlusion.* Similarly to translation, occlusion attack can be expressed by three-dimensional attack parameters: the coordinates of the left-uppermost pixel of the occlusion patch and the occlusion patch size.[1] Note that for discretely parameterized semantic perturbations, provided with sufficient computation resources, we could simply exhaustively enumerate all the possible perturbed images. At the scale of our considered image dimensions, we find that exhaustive enumeration can be accomplished within a reasonable computation time and the generated images can be used for direct verification. In this case the SP-layers are reduced to enumeration operations given a discretely parameterized semantic attack threat model. Nonetheless, the computation complexity of exhaustive enumeration grows combinatorially when considering a joint attack threat model consisting of multiple types of discretely parameterized semantic attacks.

### Continuously parameterized semantic perturbation

Most of the semantic perturbations fall under the framework where the parameters are continuous values, i.e., $I^k \subset \mathbb{R}^k$. Mohapatra et al. (2020) propose the idea of adding *semantic perturbation layers* (SP-layers) to the input layer of any given neural network model for efficient robustness verification, as illustrated in Fig. 10.1. By letting $g_x(\epsilon^k) = g(x, \epsilon^k)$ the verification problem for neural network $f$ formulated in (10.1) becomes

$$\min_{\epsilon^k \in I^k, d_{\mathcal{A}}(g_x(\epsilon^k), x) \leq \delta} \left( \min_{j \neq c} f_c(g_x(\epsilon^k)) - f_j(g_x(\epsilon^k)) \right) > 0. \qquad (10.3)$$

If we consider the new network as $f^{sem} = f \circ g_x$, then we have the following problem:

$$\min_{\epsilon^k \in I^k, ||\epsilon^k||_p \leq \delta} \left( \min_{j \neq c} f_c^{sem}(\epsilon^k) - f_j^{sem}(\epsilon^k) \right) > 0, \qquad (10.4)$$

which has a similar form to $\ell_p$-norm perturbations but now on the semantic space $I^k$. The proposed SP-layers allow us to explicitly define the dimensionality of our perturbations and put explicit dependence between

---

[1] We use a squared patch, but it can be rectangular in general.

the manner and the effect of the semantic perturbation on different pixels of the image. In other words, we can view our proposed SP-layers as a parameterized input transformation function from the semantic space to RGB space, and $g(x, \epsilon^k)$ is the perturbed input in the RGB space, which is a function of perturbations in the semantic space. Our key idea is to express $g$ in terms of commonly used activation functions, and thus $g$ is in the form of neural network and can be easily incorporated into the original neural network classifier $f$. Note that $g$ can be arbitrarily complicated to allow for general transformations for SP-layers; nevertheless, it does not result in any difficulties to apply the conventional $\ell_p$-norm-based methods such as (Zhang et al., 2018; Wang et al., 2018a; Singh et al., 2018a; Boopathy et al., 2019; Weng et al., 2018a), as Semantify-NN only requires the activation functions to have custom linear bounds and do not need them to be continuous or differentiable. Below we specify the explicit form of SP-layers corresponding to five different semantic perturbations using (i) hue, (ii) saturation, (iii) lightness, (iv) brightness and contrast, and (v) rotation.

*Color space transformation.* We consider color transformations parameterized by the hue, saturation, and lightness (HSL space). Unlike RGB values, HSL form a more intuitive basis for understanding the effect of the color transformation as it is semantically meaningful. For each of the basis, we can define the following functions for $g$:

- *Hue* This dimension corresponds to the position of a color on the color wheel. Two colors with the same hue are generally considered as different shades of a color, like blue and light blue. The hue is represented on the scale 0–360°, which we have rescaled to the range $[0, 6]$ for convenience. Therefore we have $g(R, G, B, \epsilon_h) = (d \cdot \phi_R^h(h') + m, d \cdot \phi_G^h(h') + m, d \cdot \phi_B^h(h') + m)$, where $d = (1 - |2l - 1|)s$, $m = l - \frac{d}{2}$, and $h' = (h + \epsilon_h) \bmod 6$ are functions of $R$, $G$, $B$ independent of $\epsilon_h$, and

$$(\phi_R^h(h'), \phi_G^h(h'), \phi_B^h(h')) = \begin{cases} (1, V, 0), & 0 \le h' \le 1, \\ (V, 1, 0), & 1 \le h' \le 2, \\ (0, 1, V), & 2 \le h' \le 3, \\ (0, V, 1), & 3 \le h' \le 4, \\ (V, 0, 1), & 4 \le h' \le 5, \\ (1, 0, V), & 5 \le h' \le 6, \end{cases}$$

where $V = (1 - |(h' \bmod 2) - 1|)$.

For $0 \leq h' \leq 6$, the above can be reduced to the following in the ReLU form ($\sigma_i(x) = \text{ReLU}(x - i)$) and hence can be seen as one hidden layer with ReLU activation connecting from hue space to original RGB space:

$$\phi_R^h(h') = 1 + \sigma_2(h') + \sigma_4(h') - (\sigma_5(h') + \sigma_1(h')),$$
$$\phi_G^h(h') = \sigma_0(h') + \sigma_4(h') - (\sigma_1(h') + \sigma_3(h')), \qquad (10.5)$$
$$\phi_B^h(h') = \sigma_2(h') + \sigma_6(h') - (\sigma_5(h') + \sigma_3(h')).$$

- *Saturation* This corresponds to the colorfulness of the picture. At saturation 0, we get grey-scale images, whereas at a saturation of 1, we see the colors pretty distinctly. We have $g(R, G, B, \epsilon_s) = (d_R \cdot \phi^s(s') + l, d_G \cdot \phi^s(s') + l, d_B \cdot \phi^s(s') + l)$, where $s' = s + \epsilon_s$, $d_R = \frac{R-l}{s}$, $d_G = \frac{G-l}{s}$, and $d_B = \frac{B-l}{s}$ are functions of $R, G, B$ independent of $\epsilon_s$, and

$$\phi^s(s') = \min(\max(s', 0), 1) = \sigma_0(s') - \sigma_1(s'). \qquad (10.6)$$

- *Lightness* This property corresponds to the perceived brightness of the image, where a lightness of 1 gives us white, and a lightness of 0 gives us black images. In this case, $g(R, G, B, \epsilon_l) = (d_R \cdot \phi_1^l(l') + \phi_2^l(l'), d_G \cdot \phi_1^l(l') + \phi_2^l(l'), d_B \cdot \phi_1^l(l') + \phi_2^l(l'))$, where $l' = l + \epsilon_l$, $d_R = \frac{R-l}{1-|2l-1|}$, $d_G = \frac{G-l}{1-|2l-1|}$, and $d_B = \frac{B-l}{1-|2l-1|}$ are functions of $R, G, B$ independent of $\epsilon_l$, and

$$\phi_1^l(l') = 1 - |2 \cdot \min(\max(l', 0), 1) - 1|$$
$$= -\sigma_0(2 \cdot l') - \sigma_2(2 \cdot l') + 2 \cdot \sigma_1(2 \cdot l') + 1, \qquad (10.7)$$
$$\phi_2^l(l') = \min(\max(l', 0), 1) = \sigma_0(l') - \sigma_1(l').$$

*Brightness and contrast.* We also use the similar technique as HSL color space for multiparameter transformations such as brightness and contrast: the attack parameters are $\epsilon_b$ for brightness perturbation and $\epsilon_c$ for contrast perturbation, and we have

$$g(x, \epsilon_b, \epsilon_c) = \min(\max((1 + \epsilon_c) \cdot x + \epsilon_b, 0), 1) \qquad (10.8)$$
$$= \sigma_0((1 + \epsilon_c) \cdot x + \epsilon_b) - \sigma_1((1 + \epsilon_c) \cdot x + \epsilon_b).$$

Therefore $g$ can be expressed as one additional ReLU layer before the original network model, which is the proposed SP Layers in Fig. 10.1.

*Rotation.* We have a one-dimensional semantic attack parameterized by the rotation angle $\theta$, and we consider rotations at the center of the image with the boundaries being extended to the area outside the image. We use the following interpolation to get the values $x'_{i,j}$ of output pixel at position $(i,j)$ after rotation by $\theta$. Let $i' = i\cos\theta - j\sin\theta$ and $j' = j\cos\theta + i\sin\theta$. Then

$$x'_{i,j} = \frac{\sum_{k,l} x_{k,l} \cdot \max(0, 1 - \sqrt{(k-i')^2 + (l-j')^2})}{\sum_{k,l} \max(0, 1 - \sqrt{(k-i')^2 + (l-j')^2})}, \tag{10.9}$$

where $k$ and $l$ range over all possible values. For individual pixels at position $(k, l)$ of the original image, the scaling factor for its influence on the output pixel at position $(i, j)$ is given by the following function:

$$m_{(k,l),(i,j)}(\theta) = \frac{\max(0, 1 - \sqrt{(k-i')^2 + (l-j')^2})}{\sum_{k',l'} \max(0, 1 - \sqrt{(k'-i')^2 + (l'-j')^2})}, \tag{10.10}$$

which is highly nonlinear. It is 0 for most $\theta$, and for a very small range of $\theta$, it takes nonzero values, which can go up to 1. Thus it makes naive verification infeasible. One idea is to use *Explicit Input Splitting* to split the input the range of $\theta$ into smaller parts and certify all parts, which will give a tighter bound since in smaller ranges the bounds are tighter. However, the required number of splits in *Explicit Input Splitting* may become too large, making it computationally infeasible. To balance this trade-off, Mohapatra et al. (2020) propose a new refinement technique named as *implicit input splitting* in the following section, which has light computational overhead and helps substantial boost in verification performance.

## 10.3 Input space refinement for semantify-NN

To better handle highly nonlinear functions that might arise from the general activation functions in the SP-layers, Mohapatra et al. (2020) propose two types of input-level refinement strategies. For linear-relaxation–based verification methods, they prove that given an image $x$, if we can verify that a set $S$ of perturbed images $x'$ is correctly classified for a threat model using one certification cycle, then we can verify that every perturbed image $x'$ in the convex hull of $S$ is also correctly classified, where the convex hull in the pixel space.

Here one certification cycle means one pass through the certification algorithm sharing the same linear relaxation values. Although $\ell_p$-norm balls are convex regions in pixel space, other threat models (especially, semantic perturbations) usually do not have this property. This in turn poses a big challenge for semantic verification. We remark that for some nonconvex attack spaces embedded in high-dimensional pixel spaces, the convex hull of the attack space associated with an image can contain images belonging to a different class. Thus we cannot certify large intervals of perturbations using a single certification cycle of linear relaxation-based verifiers.

*Explicit input splitting.* As we cannot certify large ranges of perturbation simultaneously, input-splitting is essential for verifying semantic perturbations. It reduces the gap between the linear bounds on activation functions and yields tighter bounds. We observe that

$$\min_{\epsilon^k \in (I_1^k \cup I_2^k), h(\epsilon^k) \leq \delta} \min_{j \neq c} f_c^{sem}(\epsilon^k) - f_j^{sem}(\epsilon^k)$$

$$= \min_{l \in \{1,2\}} \min_{\epsilon^k \in I_l^k, h(\epsilon^k) \leq \delta} \min_{j \neq c} f_c^{sem}(\epsilon^k) - f_j^{sem}(\epsilon^k).$$

If $\min_{\epsilon^k \in I_l^k, h(\epsilon^k) \leq \delta}(\min_j f_c^{sem}(\epsilon^k) - f_j^{sem}(\epsilon^k)) > 0$ for both parameter dimensions $l = \{1, 2\}$, then we have $\min_{\epsilon^k \in I_1^k \cup I_2^k, h(\epsilon^k) \leq \delta}(\min_j f_c^{sem}(\epsilon^k) - f_j^{sem}(\epsilon^k)) > 0$. As a result, we can split the original interval into smaller parts and certify each of them separately to certify the larger interval. The drawback of this procedure is that the computation time scales linearly with the number of divisions as one has to run the certification for every part. However, for the color space experiments, it is found that a few partitions are already sufficient for tight certificate.

*Implicit input splitting.* As a motivating example, in Fig. 10.2(a), we give the form of the activation function for rotation. Even in a small range of rotation angle $\theta$ (2°), the function is quite nonlinear, resulting in very loose linear bounds. As a result, we find that we are unable to get good verification results for datasets like MNIST and CIFAR-10 without increasing the number of partitions to very large values ($\approx 40,000$). This makes verification methods computationally infeasible. We aim at reducing the cost in *explicit splitting* by combining the intermediate bounds used by linear relaxation methods such as (Raghunathan et al., 2018; Zhang et al., 2018) to compute the suitable relaxation for the layerwise nonlinear activations. The idea is to use the shared linear bounds among all subproblems, and hence we only need to construct the matrices (Def. 3.3 and Cor. 3.7 in Weng et al., 2018a) $\mathbf{A}^{(k)}$, $\mathbf{T}^{(k)}$, $\mathbf{H}^{(k)}$ once for all $S$-subproblems instead of having different matrices for each subproblem. This helps to reduce the cost significantly from a factor of $S$ to 1 when $S$ is large (which is usually the case to get good refinement).

For implementation, we split the original problem into $S$-subproblems. To derive bounds on the output of a neuron at any given layer $l$, we cal-

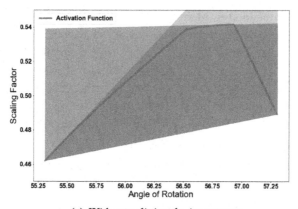

(a) Without splitting the input range

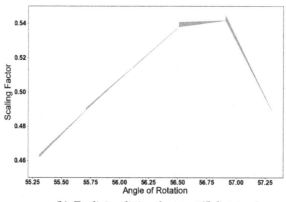

(b) Explicit splitting the input (5 divisions)

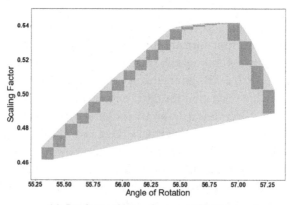

(c) Implicit splitting the input (20 divisions)

**Figure 10.2** Bounds for activation function of SP layer in rotation.

culate the preactivation range for every subproblem. Then we merge the intervals of each neuron among all the subproblems (e.g., set $\boldsymbol{u}_r = \max_i \boldsymbol{u}_{r,\text{sub}i}$ and $\boldsymbol{l}_r = \min_i \boldsymbol{l}_{r,\text{sub}i}$ in Weng et al. (2018a)) to construct the linear relaxation, $\mathbf{A}^{(k)}, \mathbf{T}^{(k)}, \mathbf{H}^{(k)}$ for the postactivation output of layer $l$. Continuing this procedure till the last layer gives the bounds on the output of the whole neural network.

Fig. 10.3 illustrates the difference between explicit and implicit input space splittings. Recall that in Fig. 10.2(a), we give the form of the activation function for rotation. Even in a small range of rotation angle $\theta$ (2°), we see that the function is quite nonlinear resulting in very loose linear bounds. Splitting the images explicitly into five parts and running them separately (i.e., explicit splitting as shown in Fig. 10.2(b)) give us a much tighter approximation. However, explicit splitting results in a high computation time as the time scales linearly with the number of splits. To efficiently approximate this function, we can instead make the splits to get explicit bounds on each subinterval and then run them through certification simultaneously (i.e., implicit splitting as shown in Fig. 10.2(c)). As we observe in Fig. 10.2(c), splitting into 20 implicit parts gives a very good approximation with very little overhead (the number of certification cycles used is still the same).

## 10.4 Empirical comparison

Following Mohapatra et al. (2020), we conduct extensive experiments for all the continuously parametrized semantic attack threat models presented in this chapter. The verification of discretely parameterized semantic perturbations can be straightforward using enumeration. We apply Semantify-NN to $\ell_p$-norm verification algorithms proposed by Zhang et al. (2018) and Boopathy et al. (2019) to certify multilayer perceptron (MLP) models and convolutional neural network (CNN) models.

- *Baselines.* We calculate the upper and lower bounds for possible value ranges of each pixel $x_i$ of the original image given perturbation magnitude in the semantic space. Then we use an $\ell_\infty$-norm-based verifier to perform bisection on the perturbation magnitude and report its value. We show that directly converting the perturbation range from semantic space to original RGB space and then applying $\ell_p$-norm-based verifiers give very poor results in all tables. We also give a weighted-$\epsilon$ version, where we allow for different levels of perturbation for different pixels.

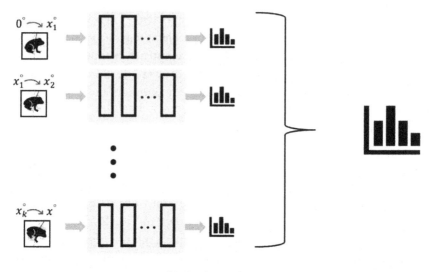

(a) Explicit splitting

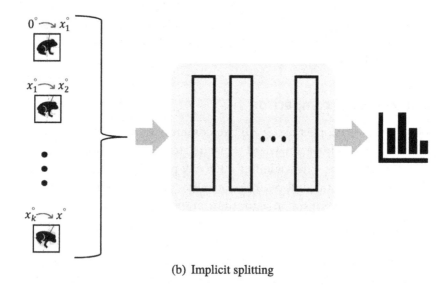

(b) Implicit splitting

**Figure 10.3** Illustration of refinement techniques.

- *Attack.* We use a grid–search attack with the granularity of the order of the size of the subintervals after input splitting. Although this is not the optimal attack value, it is indeed an upper bound for the mininum adversarial perturbation. Increasing the granularity would only result in a tighter upper bound and does not affect the lower bound (the certificate we deliver).

- *Semantify-NN*: We implement both SP-layers (SPL) and with refinement (SPL+Refine).

The SP-layers are added as fully connected layers for MLPs and as modified convolution blocks for CNN models (we allow the filter weights and biases to be different for different neurons). We evaluate Semantify-NN and other methods on MLP and CNN models trained on the MNIST, CIFAR-10 and GTSRB (German Traffic Sign Benchmark) datasets. We use the released MNIST and CIFAR models, and their standard test accuracy of MNIST/CIFAR models are 98–99%/60–70%. We train the GTSRB models from scratch to have 94–95% test accuracies. All CNNs (LeNet) use 3-by-3 convolutions and two max pooling layers and along with filter size specified in the description for two convolution layers each. LeNet uses a similar architecture to LeNet-5 (LeCun et al., 1998), with the no-pooling version applying the same convolutions over larger inputs. We also have two kinds of adversarially trained models. The models (denoted as sem adv in the table) are trained using data augmentation where we add perturbed images (according to the corresponding threat model) to the training data. The models denoted as $\ell_\infty$ adv are trained using the $\ell_\infty$ norm adversarial training method (Madry et al., 2018). We evaluate all methods on 200 random test images and random targeted attacks. We train all models for 50 epochs and tune hyperparameters to optimize validation accuracy.

*Experiment (I): HSL space perturbations.* Table 10.1 demonstrates that using $\ell_p$-norm-based verification results in extremely loose bounds because of the mismatch in the dimensionality of the semantic attack and dimensionality of the induced $\ell_p$-norm attack. Explicitly introducing this dimensionality constraint by augmenting the neural networks with our proposed SP-layers gives a significant increase in the maximum certifiable lower bound, resulting in 4–50× larger bounds. However, there is still an apparent gap between the Semantify-NN's certified lower bound and attack upper bound. Notably, we observe that adding input-space refinements helps us to further tighten the bounds, yielding an extra 1.5–5× improvement. This corroborates the importance of input splitting for the certification against semantic attacks. The transformations for HSL space attacks are fairly linear, so the gap between our certified lower bound and attack upper bound becomes quite small.

Table 10.1 Evaluation of averaged bounds on HSL space perturbation. SPL denotes our proposed SP-layers. SPL + Refine refers to certificate obtained after using explicit splitting. Grid search on parameter space is used for attack. The results demonstrate the significance of using SPL layers for certification.

| Network | Certified Bounds | | | | Ours Improvement (vs. Weighted) | | Attack |
|---|---|---|---|---|---|---|---|
| | Naive | Weighted | SPL | SPL + Refine | w/o refine | w/ refine | Grid |
| **Experiment (I)-A: Hue** | | | | | | | |
| CIFAR, MLP 6 × 2048 | 0.00316 | 0.028 | 0.347 | 0.974 | 11.39x | 51.00x | 1.456 |
| CIFAR, CNN 5 × 10 | 0.0067 | 0.046 | 0.395 | 1.794 | 7.58x | 38.00x | 1.964 |
| GTSRB, MLP 4 × 256 | 0.01477 | 0.091 | 0.771 | 2.310 | 8.47x | 22.31x | 2.388 |
| GTSRB MLP 4 × 256 sem adv | 0.01512 | 0.092 | 0.785 | 2.407 | 8.53x | 26.16x | 2.474 |
| **Experiment (I)-B: Saturation** | | | | | | | |
| CIFAR, MLP 6 × 2048 | 0.00167 | 0.004 | 0.101 | 0.314 | 24.25x | 77.50x | 0.342 |
| CIFAR, CNN 5 × 10 | 0.00348 | 0.019 | 0.169 | 0.389 | 7.89x | 19.47x | 0.404 |
| GTSRB, MLP 4 × 256 | 0.00951 | 0.020 | 0.38 | 0.435 | 19.00x | 21.75x | 0.444 |
| GTSRB MLP 4 × 256 sem adv | 0.00968 | 0.020 | 0.431 | 0.458 | 21.55x | 22.90x | 0.467 |
| **Experiment (I)-C: Lightness** | | | | | | | |
| CIFAR, MLP 6 × 2048 | 0.00043 | 0.001 | 0.047 | 0.244 | 46.00x | 243.00x | 0.263 |
| CIFAR, CNN 5 × 10 | 0.00096 | 0.002 | 0.080 | 0.273 | 39.00x | 135.50x | 0.303 |
| GTSRB, MLP 4 × 256 | 0.0025 | 0.005 | 0.134 | 0.332 | 26.80x | 66.40x | 0.365 |
| GTSRB MLP 4 × 256 sem adv | 0.00268 | 0.005 | 0.148 | 0.362 | 29.80x | 72.40x | 0.398 |

**Table 10.2** Evaluation of averaged bounds on rotation space perturbation. SPL denotes our proposed SP-layers. The certified bounds obtained from SPL+Refine are close to the upper bounds from grid attack.

| Network | Certified Bounds (degrees) | | | | Attack (degrees) |
|---|---|---|---|---|---|
| | Number of Implicit Splits | | | SPL + Refine | Grid Attack |
| | 1 implicit No explicit | 5 implicit No explicit | 10 implicit No explicit | 100 implicit + explicit intervals of 0.5° | |
| **Experiment (II): Rotations** | | | | | |
| MNIST, MLP 2 × 1024 | 0.627 | 1.505 | 2.515 | 46.24 | 51.42 |
| MNIST, MLP 2 × 1024 $l_\infty$ adv | 1.376 | 2.253 | 2.866 | 45.49 | 46.02 |
| MNIST, CNN LeNet | 0.171 | 0.397 | 0.652 | 43.33 | 48.00 |
| CIFAR, MLP 5 × 2048 | 0.006 | 0.016 | 0.033 | 14.81 | 37.53 |
| CIFAR, CNN 5 × 10 | 0.008 | 0.021 | 0.042 | 10.65 | 30.81 |
| GTSRB, MLP 4 × 256 | 0.041 | 0.104 | 0.206 | 31.53 | 33.43 |

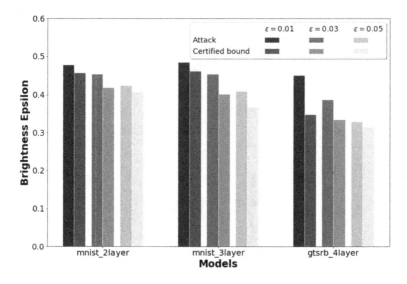

**Figure 10.4** Semantic certification for brightness and contrast.

*Experiment (II): Rotation.* Table 10.2 shows the results of rotation space verification. Rotation induces a highly nonlinear transformation on the pixel space, so we use this to illustrate the use of refinement for certifying such functions. As the transforms are very nonlinear, the linear bounds used by our SP-layers are very loose, yielding very small robustness certification. In this case, explicit input splitting is not a computationally appealing approach as there are a huge amount of intervals to be certified. Table 10.2 shows how using implicit splits can increase the size of certifiable intervals to the point where the total number of intervals needed is manageably big. At this point, we use explicit splitting to get tight bounds. For the results in *SPL + Refine*, we use intervals of size 0.5 at a time with 100 implicit splits for each interval.

*Experiment (III): Brightness and contrast.* For multidimensional semantic attacks (here a combination attack using both brightness and contrast), we can consider any $\ell_p$ norm of the parameters to be our distance function. In Fig. 10.4, we show the results for average lower bound for brightness perturbations while fixing the maximum perturbation for contrast parameter $\epsilon$ to be 0.01, 0.03, and 0.05.

# PART 4

# Adversarial defense

# CHAPTER 11

# Overview of adversarial defense

Many techniques have been proposed to improve the robustness of deep neural networks. In this chapter, we focus on methods that try to make neural networks robust against adversarial examples generated by an evasion attack. A defense algorithm can be designed in many different forms. Some defense algorithms modify the training stage of machine learning models to obtain a more robust model, whereas some other algorithms postprocess the model by adding some particular components to improve its robustness. We give an overview of existing techniques and discuss some of the more promising defense approaches in the next few chapters.

## 11.1 Empirical defense versus certified defense

After the discovering of adversarial examples by Szegedy et al. (2014), many works have been proposed to empirically improve the robustness of neural network models. However, evaluating these defense methods remains tricky. Many earlier works evaluated defense methods only by some simple off-the-shelf attack methods such as FGSM (Goodfellow et al., 2015) or PGD (Kurakin et al., 2017; Madry et al., 2018) attack. However, attack methods provide no formal guarantee on the true adversarial robustness of a defensive model – even if a model is safe evaluated on existing attacks, it is still possible that there still exists a small perturbation to fool the machine learning model, whereas existing attack methods cannot find it. Therefore, without careful empirical evaluations, it is very possible that the defense method is safe against some standard attack methods (e.g., FGSM and PGD) but vulnerable to some other attacks (e.g., attacks particularly developed for attacking the defense model). This may lead to a false sense of security, which indeed happens frequently in the literature. For example, Athalye et al. (2018) showed that most of the defense methods proposed in ICLR 2018, although showing strong defense performance against off-the-shelf attacks, are actually vulnerable under stronger and carefully designed attacks.

To overcome this issue, one approach is to keep improving the attack methods, both in terms of attack performance and their diversity. For example, AutoAttack (Croce and Hein, 2020) gathered a set of diverse and strong attack methods to test the robustness of defensive models. Furthermore, some work also tried to come up with principled way to conduct attack when facing different attack mechanisms (Athalye et al., 2018; Tramer et al., 2020). This is also known as adaptive attack. We will introduce some of the adaptive attack techniques when introducing each particular defense mechanism.

On the other hand, another way to tackle this issue is to study "certified defense" methods. For certified defense, in addition to empirical evaluation of the robustness, we also need to provide a verifiable robustness bound for each example − for each example $x$, we say the model is certifiably robust on $x$ if $x$ can be predicted correctly and it can be formally verified that any perturbation within the perturbation set cannot change the model's prediction. Certified robust accuracy on a dataset or a data distribution is then defined as the ratio of the examples that can be certifiably robust classified by the model. Certified robust accuracy is a lower bound of robust accuracy, since there could exist examples that can be robustly classified but cannot be easily verified. Certified robust accuracy can usually be computed by some verification methods discussed in the previous sections, and in some particular cases a defense method will have the most suitable verification method for computing certified robust accuracy. In comparison, the "empirical robust accuracy" computed by conducting attacks to the defensive model can only give an upper bound of true robust accuracy, since attack methods fail to find an adversarial example; does not imply that an adversarial example does not exist.

Although certified defense methods are much safer and more reliable, currently they also encounter a serious drawback that existing certified methods lead to very poor certified robust accuracy. For instance, on CIFAR-10 classification with 8/255 $\ell_\infty$ ball perturbation, a standard deep learning model can achieve over 90% clean accuracy; a good empirical defense model can often achieve over 80% clean accuracy and over 60% empirical robust accuracy; however, the best certified defense methods can only achieve around 50% accuracy and around 40% certified robust accuracy. Therefore there are pros and cons of empirical defense versus certified defense, and we will introduce both of them in the following sections.

## 11.2 Overview of empirical defenses

In the following, we will categorize some popular defense methods into the following categories, including adversarial training, randomization, detection, filtering/projection, discrete components, and adversarial detection. Among them, adversarial training, randomization and detection has demonstrated more promising results in the literature, so we will introduce those methods in detail in the following chapters.

*Adversarial training.* To combat adversarial examples, a natural idea is to add adversarial examples in the training set. This leads to the most widely used defense methods known as adversarial training. Even in one of the first papers talking about adversarial examples, Goodfellow et al. (2015) already tried to train the model on adversarial examples generated by Fast Gradient Sign Method (FGSM). Later on, Kurakin et al. (2017) suggested using a multistep FGSM to further improve adversarial robustness. However, these earlier works often generate adversarial examples periodically, and the robustness improvements are not stable. Instead, Madry et al. (2018) showed that adversarial training can be formulated as a min-max optimization problem: given the current neural network model, an attacker generates adversarial examples to maximize the classification loss, and the learner aims to update the model to minimize the classification loss on those adversarial examples. With this clean min-max formulation, the adversarial examples can be generated on-the-fly. In ICLR 2018, many defense methods were proposed including this min-max adversarial training method. When Athalye et al. (2018) tried to develop stronger attacks to evaluate the defense methods published in ICLR 2018, they showed that adversarial training is the only approach that still performs well under stronger attacks, whereas many other methods have almost 0% accuracy under stronger attacks. After that, adversarial training becomes widely used, and many variations of adversarial training have been developed. We will introduce them in Chapter 12.

*Randomization.* Another effective defense method is to add some randomized components into the model. Intuitively, randomness in the model can make it harder for the attacker to create a fixed attack to fool the model. Therefore randomization has been proposed as heuristics to improve the robustness empirically (Xie et al., 2017; Dhillon et al., 2018; Liu et al., 2018c, 2019d). Although some earlier developed randomization methods are based on heuristics, several theoretical explanations have been developed, showing that randomness can truly boost the robustness of neural networks (Lecuyer et al., 2019; Liu et al., 2020c). We will give more details in Chapter 13.

*Detection.* The task of making a classifier robust can be more challenging as the input space is very high dimensional, and it is difficult to make classifier correct in all the input region. Therefore another natural way to combat adversarial examples is developing a method to detect "abnormal" examples where the classifiers would not need to make predictions on those examples. To detect adversarial examples, methods have been developed including simple methods that measure the distance between adversarial example and natural images (Lee et al., 2018) and some more complicated methods that detect adversarial examples by feature attribution (Yang et al., 2020d). We will introduce several representative methods in Chapter 15. However, an important problem is how to evaluate the performance of a detection model – it is possible that an attacker can leverage the information about the detecting model to improve their successful rate by trying to bypass the detectors. Therefore it is important to try to evaluate the whole model, jointly including both detector and classifier, when conducting experiments on detecting models.

*Filtering and projection.* It is commonly believed that adversarial examples fall outside the natural image manifold, for which DNNs are poorly trained. This leads to a natural line of defense methods to project the adversarial examples back to the natural image manifold, or in another words, filter out the "unnatural noises" added into the example. To capture the natural image manifold, most of the approaches in this category adopt some kind of generative models (e.g., some version of autoencoder or generative adversarial networks). Since generative models are trained on natural examples, adversarial examples will be projected to the manifold learned by the generative model. Furthermore, "projecting" the adversarial examples onto the range of the generative model can have the desirable effect of reducing the adversarial perturbation.

Meng and Chen (2017) trained an autoencoder to capture the natural image manifold. An autoencoder is a type of neural network that consists of two major parts, the encoder that maps the input to a low-dimensional space and the decoder that recovers the input from the low-dimensional embedding. The autoencoder is usually trained on the reconstruction loss with respect to the input. Therefore the high-dimensional data are summarized by the low-dimensional embedding through the training process. In MagNet, one autoencoder is chosen at random attesting time to filter the input samples, and thus adversarial perturbation could potentially be removed through this encoding and decoding process. Instead of using autoencoders, Samangouei et al. (2018) proposed to train a generative adversarial network (GAN) to capture the natural image manifold and then use it in the inference stage to filter out unnatural noise in the image. Unfortunately, both MegNet and Defense-GAN are shown to be nonrobust when the attacker can jointly attack the filtering step and the classifier (Athalye and Sutskever, 2018).

More recently, Li et al. (2018b) proposed a different defense framework, termed *ER-Classifier*, which combines the process of filtering and classification in a single joint framework. In fact, any deep classifier can be viewed as a combination of these two parts, an encoder part to extract useful features from the input data and a classifier part to perform classification based on the extracted features. Both the encoder and the classifier are neural networks. ER-Classifier is similar to a regular deep classifier, which first projects the input to a low-dimensional space with an encoder $G$ and then performs classification based on the low-dimensional embedding with a classifier $C$. The main different is that at the training stage, the low-dimensional embedding of ER-Classifier is stabilized with a discriminator $D$ by minimizing the dispersion between the distribution of the embedding and the distribution of a selected prior. The goal of the discriminator is separating the true code sampled from a prior and the "fake" code produced by the encoder, whereas the encoder will try to produce generated code that is similar to the true one. The result of this competition is that the distribution of the embedding space will be pushed toward the prior distribution. Therefore it is expected that this regularization process can help remove the effects of any adversarial distortion and push the adversarial examples back to the natural data manifold. Another difference is that the embedding space dimension is much smaller for the ER-classifier, when compared with a general deep classifier, making it easier for the training process to converge. In this framework the projection is used as a regularization to improve robustness, and the method can be used jointly with other defense (e.g., adversarial training) to further improve the performance.

*Discrete components.* Since most of the attack algorithms, such as PGD and C&W attacks, rely on the gradient computation, several defense methods try to introduce some discrete and nondifferentiable components into the neural network model to make it harder for gradient-based attacks. For instance, Papernot and McDaniel (2018) and Dubey et al. (2019) adopt a nearest-neighbor finding component in the neural network to project images to the nearest neighbors in the database, which creates difficulty in conducting attacks. Further, some nondifferential activation functions have been proposed by Xiao et al. (2019a). Moreover, it has been shown that voting-based ensembles can improve robustness against adversarial examples (Khatri et al., 2020). However, due to the difficulties of conducting attacks on the defense components, it is harder to reach a conclusion whether a discrete component can truly make models more robust or there exist non-gradient-based attack methods to break these defenses.

# CHAPTER 12

# Adversarial training

As the ultimate goal of defenses is to make models robust against adversarial examples, a very natural idea is to add adversarial examples into the training dataset. This idea, also known as adversarial training, has been implemented in many earlier papers such as (Goodfellow et al., 2015; Kurakin et al., 2017), where they usually generate adversarial examples periodically (e.g., after every few training epochs). However, as the model evolves quickly during the optimization procedure, those adversarial examples usually fail to capture the vulnerable points of the latest model, leading to instability and poor performance on robust accuracy (i.e., accuracy against adversarial examples at test time). Later on Madry et al. (2018) showed that adversarial training can be formulated as solving a min-max optimization problem. This simple but insightful formulation enables generating adversarial examples on-the-fly, which significantly improves the robustness of the model. As a result, adversarial training becomes one of the most widely used defense methods.

In this chapter, we will first introduce the min-max formulation of adversarial training in Section 12.1, and then discuss several improvements over vanilla AT in Section 12.2 and 12.3.

## 12.1 Formulating adversarial training as bilevel optimization

In standard training, the goal is to learn the model parameters $\theta$ to minimize the empirical loss, defined as the average loss on all the training examples. The objective of standard training can thus be formulated as solving the following empirical risk minimization problem:

$$\arg\min_{\theta} E_{(x,y)\in\mathcal{D}} L(f_\theta(x), y), \tag{12.1}$$

where $E$ denotes expectation, $(x, y) \in \mathcal{D}$ denotes a pair of dample sample and its label randomly drawn from a distribution $\mathcal{D}$, $L$ is a supervised loss function, and $f_\theta(x)$ is the model's prediction on $x$.

In adversarial training, we consider that there may be an attacker trying to find the adversarial example with the maximal loss within an $\ell_p$ ball of

*Adversarial Robustness for Machine Learning*
https://doi.org/10.1016/B978-0-12-824020-5.00023-5
119

each example. Therefore, instead of minimizing the regular loss function $L(\cdot, \cdot)$, we want to minimize the loss on the worst-case perturbed example around each natural example. It is thus natural to replace the loss in (12.1) by the maximal loss around each example, which can be written as

$$\arg\min_{\theta} E_{(x,y)\in\mathcal{D}} \max_{x'\in B(x)} L(f_\theta(x'), y), \qquad (12.2)$$

where $B(x)$ is the perturbation set around the natural example $x$. For instance, under a commonly used $\ell_\infty$ perturbation set, $B(x)$ is the $\epsilon$-bounded $\ell_\infty$ ball around $x$, so the objective can be written as

$$\arg\min_{\theta} E_{(x,y)\in\mathcal{D}} \max_{x'\in\|x'-x\|_\infty\le\epsilon} L(f_\theta(x'), y). \qquad (12.3)$$

This formulation is proposed by Madry et al. (2018). This is also called a bilevel optimization as there are two levels (min and max) in the objective. Bilevel optimization problems can often be solved by the alternating minimization procedure: at each update, solve the inner maximization problem to obtain $x'$ and then conduct an outer update on the model parameter $\theta$ based on $x'$.

In alternating minimization, the inner maximization can be viewed as finding an adversarial example of a given input data point $x$ within the perturbation set $B(x)$. In Eq. (12.3), as the inner problem is a constrained maximization task, a natural idea is to solve it by a projected gradient descent (PGD) algorithm, similar to the PGD algorithm when we conduct adversarial attack. In the PGD algorithm, we start from $x_0 = x$ and conduct the following iterative updates:

$$x_t \leftarrow \text{Proj}_{B(x)}(x_{t-1} + \alpha \cdot \text{sign}(\nabla_x L(f_\theta(x_{t-1}), y))), \qquad (12.4)$$

where the operator Proj projects the input vector into the constraint set $B(x)$, in this case the $\ell_\infty$ ball around $x$. This can be done by clipping each input dimension by

$$\text{Proj}(u)_i = \min(x_i + \epsilon, \max(x_i - \epsilon, u_i))$$

for a given vector $u$. If we run the inner maximization for $k$ iterations, then we set $x'$ as the output of the $k$th PGD step and use it to conduct the parameter update of $\theta$. Ideally, a larger $k$ will lead to better results but also consumes more time. If we run PGD for $k$ iterations, then the computational time of the whole adversarial training process will be roughly $k$ times more than the standard training, which makes adversarial training slow. We will discuss some ways to overcome this problem in the next section.

After obtaining $x'$, we will run one update to solve the outer minimization problem to obtain a better parameter $\theta$. This can be done by computing the gradient of $\theta$ with respect to $x'$ ($\nabla_\theta L(f_\theta(x'), y)$) and then pass this gradient to the update rule optimizers (e.g., (SGD or Adam) for the parameter update. The overall PGD-based adversarial training algorithm can be found in Algorithm 3.

---

**Algorithm 3** PGD-based adversarial training (Madry et al., 2018).

---

1: **Input:** Initial model parameter $\theta_0$, number of PGD steps $k$
2: **for** $t = 0, 1, 2, \ldots$ **do**
3:     Sample $(x, y)$ from training data $\mathcal{D}$
4:     Let $x_0 = x$
5:     **for** $t' = 0, \ldots, k-1$ **do**
6:         $x_{t'+1} \leftarrow \text{Proj}_{B(x)}(x_{t'} + \alpha \cdot \text{sign}(\nabla_x L(f_\theta(x_{t'}), y)))$
7:     **end for**
8:     Update $\theta$ by $\theta \leftarrow \theta - \eta \nabla_\theta L(f_\theta(x_k), y)$
9: **end for**

---

## 12.2 Faster adversarial training

As mentioned in the previous section, PGD-based adversarial training requires $k$ inner steps, which will increase the training time by $k$ times over standard training. To reduce this overhead, several methods have been developed to achieve a better tradeoff between the robust accuracy and training speed.

Recall that in adversarial training the model update requires gradient of loss function with respect to $\theta$, whereas the PGD updates rely on the gradient of the same loss function with respect to $x$. These two gradients, denoted as $\nabla_\theta L(f_\theta(x), y)$ and $\nabla_x L(f_\theta(x), y)$, compute the gradient of the same function, but with respect to different variables. In neural networks, gradient is usually computed by back-propagation, and these two gradients can actually share the whole back-propagation process – after computing $\nabla_\theta L(f_\theta(x), y)$, only one additional linear projection step can compute $\nabla_x L(f_\theta(x), y)$. This means that computing both $\nabla_\theta L(f_\theta(x), y)$ and $\nabla_x L(f_\theta(x), y)$ together will have the same cost as computing each of them individually. Motivated by this observation, we can make additional updates during inner PGD steps. In the original adversarial training, each PGD step computes $\nabla_x L(f_\theta(x), y)$ and only using it to update $x$. However, as we can also obtain $\nabla_\theta L(f_\theta(x), y)$ with almost zero cost, we can also update $\theta$ at each PGD iteration. These simultaneous updates of $\theta$ and $x$ will speedup the convergence since we make more updates to $\theta$. At each time, when we find a perturbation (with one PGD step), we immediately update $\theta$ to make it performs better on this adversarial example. The resulting algorithm, also known as Free Adversarial Training proposed by Shafahi et al. (2019), thus requires less inner steps to converge to a competitive robust model as standard adversarial training. The algorithm of Free Adversarial Training is described in Algorithm 4.

---

**Algorithm 4** Free adversarial training (Shafahi et al., 2019).

---
1: **Input:**  Initial model parameter $\theta_0$, number of PGD steps $m$
2: **for** $t = 0, 1, 2, \ldots$ **do**
3:      Sample $(x, y)$ from training data $\mathcal{D}$
4:      Let $x_0 = x$
5:      **for** $t' = 0, \ldots, m - 1$ **do**
6:          $x_{t'+1} \leftarrow \text{Proj}_{B(x)}(x_{t'} + \alpha \cdot \text{sign}(\nabla_x L(f_\theta(x_{t'}), y)))$
7:          Update $\theta$ by $\theta \leftarrow \theta - \eta \nabla_\theta L(f_\theta(x_{t'}), y)$
8:      **end for**
9: **end for**

---

Several other algorithms also exploited the back-propagation process to speed up adversarial training. See, for instance, (Zhang et al., 2019a). However, more recently, it has been shown that a proper implementation of PGD-based adversarial training with only a single step ($k = 1$) can already achieve good performance. The main trick is that instead of initializing the PGD iterate $x_0$ from $x$, we should initialize it from $x$ plus a random noise. Wong et al. (2020a) showed that if we initialize PGD attack from $x$ plus a random vector sampled from Gaussian, adversarial training with a single step can outperform many strong baselines (e.g., FreeAdvTrain). This algorithm with 1-step PGD inner iteration and random initialization is known as Fast Adversarial Training. By further controlling the PGD steps we can then control the tradeoff between speed and robust accuracy.

## 12.3 Improvements on adversarial training

In theory, robust error can be bounded by two factors: one corresponds to the error on the natural input data, and another corresponds to how much the prediction can be changed when perturbing an input within an $\epsilon$ ball. Inspired by this observation, Zhang et al. (2019b) modify the bilevel objective function of adversarial training as follows:

$$\min_{\theta} E_{(x,y)\in \mathcal{D}} L(f_{\theta}(x), y) + \lambda \max_{x' \in B(x)} L'(f_{\theta}(x'), f_{\theta}(x)), \qquad (12.5)$$

where $L$ and $L'$ are two loss functions. In this formulation, we assume both loss functions are cross-entropy loss, so the first term is the standard training loss defined on the clean data, and the second term measures the difference between the prediction of clean example $(f(x))$ and the perturbed example $(f(x'))$; $\lambda$ is a positive constant that controls the balance between two terms. By decomposing the clean and robust loss it becomes easier to control the robustness and accuracy tradeoff (with a properly chosen $\lambda$). This formulation, also known as *TRADES*, is shown to achieve better performance than adversarial training and was the winner of the NeurIPS 2018 defense challenge.

Later on, several improvements have been made over TRADES. In particular, many papers found that one has to weight each sample differently to obtain the best performance. There are several motivations behind this. First, we should treat misclassified samples differently from correctly classified ones. For misclassified samples, as the classifier already predicts the wrong label, it is not useful to make the model robust on those points. Second, some examples are intrinsically hard to classify (e.g., examples that are close to decision boundary), so forcing them to be robust will result in poor performance. For instance, in Fig. 12.1, we showed a linear classifier, where the true margin between two classes are 2.5, and there does not exist a classifier that can robustly classify all the samples with $\epsilon = 3$. If we train the classifier with $\epsilon = 3$, then the result will be a poor classifier as shown in Fig. 12.1(c).

As a result, many formulations have been developed to conduct adversarial training with nonuniform weights among samples. For instance, Wang et al. (2019d) proposed a weighted version of TRADES, where they weight the samples by the correctness of each prediction. More specifically, let $p_y(x, \theta) := (f_{\theta}(x'))_y$ be the normalized prediction probability for label $y$ — it is the softmax output of the model between $[0, 1]$. Then we can consider a weighted version of the TRADES objective as

$$\min_{\theta} E_{(x,y)\in \mathcal{D}} L(f_{\theta}(x), y) + \lambda \max_{x' \in B(x)} L(f_{\theta}(x'), f_{\theta}(x))(1 - p_y(x, \theta)), \qquad (12.6)$$

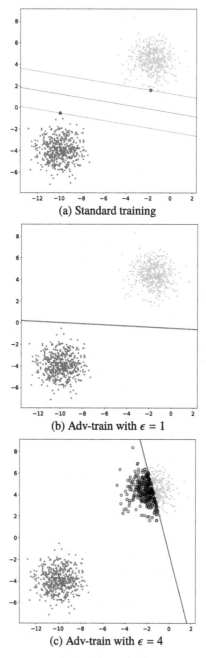

(a) Standard training

(b) Adv-train with $\epsilon = 1$

(c) Adv-train with $\epsilon = 4$

**Figure 12.1** Different training methods on a linearly separable binary classification dataset with 1.75 margin for both classes. Adversarial training with small $\epsilon$ works fine, but for a large $\epsilon$ beyond the true margin, adversarial training would ruin the classifier's classification performance.

where the second term is weighted by $1 - p_y(x, \theta)$, which is close to 0 if the sample is correctly classified and to 1 if it is (more) misclassified. This encourages the network to make more progress to the misclassified data points.

Based on a similar idea, we can also have adaptive $\epsilon$ for each sample. A sample that is misclassified should have smaller $\epsilon$ since it is not important (or not possible) to make it robust, whereas a corrected classified should be assigned with larger $\epsilon$. Several methods have been proposed in this direction, including (Ding et al., 2018; Balaji et al., 2019; Cheng et al., 2020b).

## 12.4 Extended reading

- Wang et al. (2019d) developed algorithmic convergence analysis for adversarial training.
- Zhang et al. (2022) proposed distributed training algorithms for scaling up adversarial training.
- Cheng et al. (2021) proposed a self-progressing robust training method.

# CHAPTER 13

# Randomization-based defense

Randomized components are expected to make the attacker harder to succeed, so several earlier defensive methods add randomized components to a neural network to make it more robust. However, later on a stronger attack based on expectation over transformations (EoT) (Athalye and Sutskever, 2018; Athalye et al., 2018) is developed for evaluating the robustness of randomized models (see Chapter 4 for details on EoT attacks), and some naive ways for adding randomness may not really improve robustness under the EoT attacks. Nevertheless, later works have demonstrated that some types of randomness can improve robustness, and surprisingly, it has been shown that a randomized component can theoretically improve the robustness of a model, and further, the robustness of such randomized models can be certifiable. In this section, we first discuss some earlier attempts in introducing randomness and how to properly evaluate the robustness of randomized models. Then we discuss two kinds of randomness, adding to either the first layer or all the layers, where they can theoretically improve the robustness.

## 13.1 Earlier attempts and the EoT attack

Adversarial perturbation can be viewed as a special type of additive noise, and various methods have been proposed to improve the robustness of DNNs by incorporating random components into the model. For instance, Xie et al. (2017) introduced a simple preprocessing method to randomize the input of neural networks, hoping to remove the potential adversarial perturbation. During the testing phase, the input is randomly resized into several different sizes, and then around each of the resized inputs, zeros are randomly padded. The authors demonstrated that this simple method can be applied to large-scale datasets, such as Imagenet. Similarly, Zantedeschi et al. (2017) showed that by using a modified ReLU activation layer (called BReLU) and adding noise to the origin input to augment the training data, the learned model will gain some stability to adversarial examples. On the other hand, Dhillon et al. (2018) introduce randomness into the evaluation of a neural network to defend against adversarial examples. Their method randomly drops some neurons of each layer to 0 with probability

*Adversarial Robustness for Machine Learning*
https://doi.org/10.1016/B978-0-12-824020-5.00024-7
127

proportional to their absolute value. That is, their method essentially applies dropout at each layer, where instead of dropping with uniform probability, nodes are dropped according to a weighted distribution. Values that are retained are scaled up (as is done in dropout) to retain accuracy.

Despite those defense methods demonstrated good performance against regular attack methods (such as FGSM or PGD attacks), it has been shown that under a more carefully designed attack, those simple randomization methods may not work. The main trick is that when conducting an attack, we have to consider the randomness in the model. Let $f_{\theta,\tau}$ be the randomized model with a randomized component $\tau$ sampled from some distribution. In the original PGD attack, each step will compute the gradient on a particular random $\tau$, which encounters high variance and may encounter difficulties to converge to a good solution. Therefore, instead of taking $\nabla_x f_{\theta,\tau}(x)$ with one particular $\tau$, we need to take several samples and use the average to estimate the gradient. More specifically, each iteration will take the following form of gradient estimation:

$$\frac{1}{R}\sum_{i=1}^{R}\nabla_x f_{\theta,\tau_i}(x), \tag{13.1}$$

where $\tau_1,\ldots,\tau_R$ are sampled from the distribution of $\tau$. Therefore, even though PGD takes more time at each iteration, it can obtain a much stronger adversarial example against the randomized model $f_{\theta,\tau}$, by performing parameter update using the averaged gradient. It has been shown by Athalye et al. (2018) that under this stronger attack, these previously introduced simple randomized defense models will fail.

## 13.2  Adding randomness to each layer

Liu et al. (2018c) demonstrated a simple strategy that can make randomized defense achieve similar robustness performance as adversarial training, even under stronger EoT attacks. In this method, they define a "noise layer" to introduce randomness to both the input and the hidden layer output. In this "noise layer", randomly generated Gaussian noise is added to the input:

$$x \leftarrow x + \varepsilon, \quad \varepsilon \sim \mathcal{N}(0,\sigma^2 I),$$

where $\sigma$ is a hyperparameter. Larger values of $\sigma$ lead to better robustness but worse prediction accuracy, whereas smaller values of $\sigma$ result in

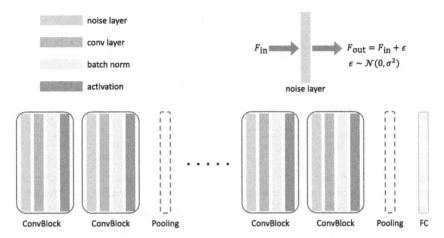

**Figure 13.1** In random self-ensemble (RSE) the noise layer is added into the beginning of each convolution block for computer vision applications.

better prediction accuracy but deteriorated robustness. One can then add this noise layer into any place of the neural networks. For example, Liu et al. (2018c) add the noise layer into the beginning of each convolution block. This method, called the random self-ensemble (RSE), is illustrated in Fig. 13.1.

In RSE, a noise layer is added in both training and testing time. In the training phase, gradient for the parameter update is computed as $\nabla_\theta f_{\theta,\tau}(x)$ for each sample $x$, and $f_{\theta,\tau}$ is a classical convolutional neural network with noise layer added. The noise is generated randomly for each stochastic gradient descent update. In the testing phase, instead of a single prediction, we need to compute the expected prediction value over the random variable $\tau$:

$$E_\tau[f_{\theta,\tau}(x)]. \tag{13.2}$$

As computing the real expected prediction requires huge amount of samples, we can approximate it by sampling only $R$ random noises and compute the average prediction. Usually, the prediction is already stable when $R \approx 10$:

$$p = \sum_{j=1}^{R} f_{\epsilon_j}(w, x), \text{ and predict } \hat{y} = \arg\max_k p_k. \tag{13.3}$$

It has been demonstrated that under a proper EoT attack, this method is only slightly worse than the plain adversarial training method discussed

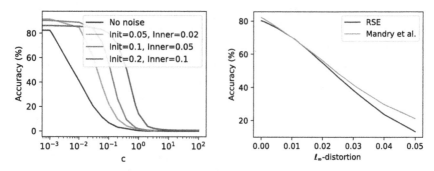

**Figure 13.2** *Left*: the effect of noise level on robustness and generalization ability. Clearly, random noise can improve the robustness of the model. *Right*: comparing RSE with adversarial defense method of Madry et al. (2018).

in the previous chapter. Some experimental results are shown in Fig. 13.2. This surprising finding leads to several later investigations on why randomized ensemble can improve adversarial robustness.

But why can the robustness be improved when adding randomness? Wang et al. (2019a) and Liu et al. (2020c) provide a nice interpretation via the neural ordinal differential equation framework. Traditional neural networks are usually stacked with multiple layers; recent work (Chen et al., 2018d) shows that we can model it in the continuous limit. This means that there is no notion of discrete layers, and hidden features are changed smoothly. Mathematically, it has the following form:

$$h_t = h_s + \int_s^t f(h_\tau, \tau; w)d\tau, \tag{13.4}$$

where $t > s$ are two different layers, but unlike the traditional discrete notion of layer, here we assume the index of the layer $(t, s)$ are continuous variables. $h_t$ is the hidden features at layer $t$. The $f$ function characterizes how to transform from one layer to another layer, which corresponds to the residual block parameterized by $w$. This formula is exactly the continuous limit of the original Residual Network (ResNet) architecture proposed in (He et al., 2016) structure

$$h_{n+1} = h_n + f(h_n; w_n), \tag{13.5}$$

where the layer index $n = 1, 2, \ldots, N$ is discrete.

Notice that the original neural ODE model does not contain any randomness in hidden features $h_t$. Thus it is not ready to model a variety of random neural networks (such as dropout). To address this limitation, Liu et al. (2020c) proposed to augment the original neural ODE model (13.4) with two kinds of stochastic terms: one is the diffusion term (to model Gaussian noise), and the other is jump term (to model Bernoulli noise); formally,

$$h_t = h_s + \underbrace{\int_s^t f(h_\tau, \tau; w)d\tau}_{\text{drift term}} + \underbrace{\int_s^t G(h_\tau, \tau)dB_\tau}_{\text{diffusion term}}$$

$$+ \underbrace{\int_s^t J(h_\tau, \tau) \odot Z_{N_\tau} dN_\tau}_{\text{jump term}} .$$

(13.6)

Compared with neural ODE model in (13.4) that only contains deterministic component (drift term), we add two extra terms in (13.6) to model different nature of randomness, diffusion and jump terms. The diffusion term consists of Brownian motion $B_t$ and its coefficient $G$ (optionally) parameterized by unknown variables $v$. Inside the jump term, the deterministic function $J(h_\tau, \tau)$ controls the jump size, the random variables $Z_{N_\tau} \sim \text{Bernoulli}(\pm 1, p)$ control the direction; and $N_\tau \sim \text{Poisson}(\lambda\tau)$ is a Poisson counting process controlling the "frequency" of jumps.

To explain the supervior robustness performance of RSE, we just need the diffusion term. The $dB_t$ term is also know as the Brownian motion, which can be viewed as i.i.d. Gaussian random variables with distribution $\mathcal{N}(0, dt)$. This is thus a small Gaussian random variable added to the hidden state, similar to the Gaussian noise in RSE but at the continuous limit.

The behavior of model's prediction, in the Neural ODE case, can be viewed as how the initial value ($h_0$) affects the final value ($h_t$) in the the differentiable equation like (13.4). The solution of the ODE system is usually more sensitive to the initial point, however, it has been shown that the diffusion term in (13.6) can lead to the "converged" solution under certain input perturbation. More specifically, it can be shown that under certain condition, the Neural SDE system (13.6) has a converged value of $\lim_{t \to \infty} h_t$, which means the prediction will be stable with respect to input perturbation, when there's infinite depth. More details can be found in (Liu et al., 2020c).

In addition to adding randomness into each convolution block, another method (Liu et al., 2019d) introduced a new min-max formulation to combine adversarial training with Bayesian neural networks (BNNs). All weights in a Bayesian neural network are represented by probability distributions over possible values, rather than having a single fixed value. The proposed framework, called Adv–BNN, combines adversarial training with randomness and is shown to have significant improvement over previous approaches including RSE and Madry's adversarial training.

## 13.3 Certified defense with randomized smoothing

In the previous section, we have shown that adding randomized components in neural network can improve adversarial robustness, with a theoretical justification by explaining the behavior of neural networks under a neural SDE framework. However, as this analysis often requires taking limits to infinite numbers of layers, it is difficult to actually compute the actual robustness of those networks in practice.

Surprisingly, it has been shown that by properly adding randomness into the input layer of neural networks, the robustness of such randomized network can be certifiable. That is, for those networks, we will be able to obtain a robust radius $r$ for each point $x$, where it is guaranteed that with high probability, any perturbation within those robust radius cannot change the prediction of neural networks. This technique is called randomized smoothing, first proposed by Lecuyer et al. (2019), and then the bounds are significantly improved in (Cohen et al., 2019; Li et al., 2019a).

In randomized smoothing, we consider a classification model $f$ that maps inputs in $\mathbb{R}^d$ to classes $\mathcal{Y}$. Randomized smoothing is a method for constructing a "smoothed" classifier $g$ from $f$. For input $x$, the smoothed classifier $g$ returns whichever class the base classifier $f$ is most likely to return when $x$ is perturbed with a Gaussian random noise. This can be mathematically defined as

$$g(x) = \arg\max_{y \in \mathcal{Y}} P(f(x + \epsilon) = y), \tag{13.7}$$

$$\text{where } \epsilon \sim \mathcal{N}(0, \sigma^2 I), \tag{13.8}$$

where $\sigma$ is the standard deviation of an isotropic Gaussian distribution controlling the noise added to the classifier. $P(\cdot)$ is the probability for the event. Note that this is equivalent to adding the noise layer introduced in RSE into the input of neural network, whereas all the intermediate layers are unperturbed.

Why adding noise to the input layer can improve robustness? The first paper proposing randomized smoothing established robustness guarantees by connecting randomized smoothing with differential privacy (Lecuyer

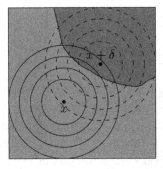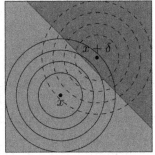

**Figure 13.3** Illustration of randomized smoothing in (Cohen et al., 2019). The concentric circles are the density contours of Gaussian random noise added to the input, and the color denotes the binary prediction yielded by the classifier. The ratio of blue (mid gray in print version) and red (dark gray in print version) around $x$ and $x + \delta$ correspond to the predicted probability of blue class versus red class in smoothed classifier, and we can observe that the change of this ratio can be bounded when perturbing $x$ to $x + \delta$.

et al., 2019). Differential privacy adds randomness so that different inputs cannot be distinguished by only looking at the output, which is equivalent to saying "any nearby input yields the same or similar prediction", and this is exactly the definition of robustness here.

However, later on Cohen et al. (2019) established a simpler way to obtain a better certifiable robustness bound. The intuition can be illustrated in Fig. 13.3. Assume that $f$ is the base classifier with binary prediction, each point in the figure corresponds to an input (assuming 2D) of $x$, and the concentric circles are the density contours of Gaussian random noise added to $x$ or $x+\delta$. We define $p_A(x)$ as the probability that $f(x+\epsilon) = A$ and $p_B(x)$ as the probability that $f(x+\epsilon) = B$. They then correspond to the ratio of blue (mid gray in print version) and red (dark gray in print version) colors in the solid concentric circles around $x$. After adding the perturbation $\delta$, we have another point $x + \delta$, and we can similarly define $p_A(x + \delta)$ and $p_B(x + \delta)$ based on the dashed concentric circles.

Assume that the smoothed classifier predicts correctly on $x$, which implies $p_A(x) > p_B(x)$ and there exists a positive gap $p_A(x) - p_B(x) > 0$. We then want to show that when $\|\delta\|$ is small enough, there's still a positive gap between $p_A(x + \delta) - p_B(x + \delta)$. Note that the actual value of $p_A(x + \delta) - p_B(x + \delta)$ depends on the model itself, which corresponds to the placement of the blue and red color in the space. However, it is hard to track the actual placement of red/blue, so to establish a bound on robustness, we are then interested in the "worst" placements of red and blue regions (the "worst" classifier) that will minimize $p_A(x + \delta) - p_B(x + \delta)$. In another words, assuming that $p_A(x)$ and $p_B(x)$ are fixed, we want to find

$$\min_f p_A(x+\delta) - p_B(x+\delta) \quad \text{s.t.} \quad p_A(x) = p_A, \ p_B(x) = p_B. \tag{13.9}$$

Interestingly, if the noise is Gaussian, then there is a very simple way to obtain the worst-case $f$ for (13.9). Intuitively, when we paint a certain point $z$ with red color (corresponding to class $B$), its contribution to the overall $p_B$ will be enlarged by the ratio $P(N(x+\delta, \sigma^2) = z)/P(N(x, \sigma^2) = z)$ when $x$ is perturbed to $x + \delta$. Therefore the worst-case placements of the colors will be assign red points according to the decreasing order of $P(N(x+\delta, \sigma^2) = z)/P(N(x, \sigma^2) = z)$ until utilized all the mass of red. This is true for any distribution, but for general distribution, it may be hard to calculate an explicit form of this. However, things become simple when we add Gaussian random noise. From Fig. 13.3, $p_B(x)$ is the Gaussian centered at $x$, and $p_B(x+\delta)$ is another Gaussian centered at $x+\delta$, and if we compute the ratio, then we will see that

$$\frac{P(N(x+\delta, \sigma^2) = z)}{P(N(x, \sigma^2) = z)} = \frac{e^{-\|z-(x+\delta)\|^2/\sigma^2}}{e^{-\|z-x\|^2/\sigma^2}} = Ce^{-((z-x)^T\delta)/\sigma^2}, \tag{13.10}$$

where $C$ is a constant irrelevant to $z$. Therefore the worst-case $f$ can be illustrated in the right panel of Fig. 13.3, where we place all the red mass to the top-right corner, and the boundary is a hyperplane orthogonal to the perturbation $\delta$. As a Gaussian distribution, when projecting to the 1D space, is still a Gaussian distribution, if we consider the 1-D space pointing from $x$ to $x+\delta$, then the boundary will be the point for which the probability mass of the right-hand side is equal to $P_B(x)$. Therefore the cutting point will be $\Phi^{-1}(p_B)$, where $\Phi^{-1}$ is the inverse of standard Gaussian CDF.

By the argument above we can establish the certified robustness bound for randomized smoothed model in the binary case, as follows.

**Theorem 2** (Cohen et al., 2019). *For binary classification problem with two classes $A$, $B$, suppose $p_A \in (\frac{1}{2}, 1]$. Then $g(x+\delta) = c_A$ for all $\|\delta\|_2 < \sigma \Phi^{-1}(p_A)$.*

In practice, we cannot really compute $p_A$ as it requires infinite amount of samples, but we can sample $m$ points to estimate $p_A$ (ratio of points predicted as class $A$) and then use some statistical bounds (e.g., Chernoff bounds) to obtain a high probability lower bound of $p_A$, denoted as $\underline{p_A}$, and then apply Theorem 2 with all $p_A$ replaced by $\underline{p_A}$ to obtain the certified robustness.

It is easy to use a similar way to establish guarantees for multiclass classification models. Assume that there are $K$ classes in total and the smoothed classifier predicts class $A$. Then for any other class $B$, we can establish a similar guarantee as follows.

**Theorem 3** (Cohen et al., 2019). *For multiclass classification problem with $K$ classes, suppose that for any pair of classes $A$, $B$, we have bounds $\underline{p_A}$, $\overline{p_B}$ satisfying*

$$P(g(x) = A) \geq \underline{p_A} \geq \overline{p_B} \geq \max_{c \neq A} P(g(x) = C).$$

*Then $g(x + \delta) = A$ for any $\|\delta\|_2 < R$, where*

$$R = \frac{\sigma}{2}(\Phi^{-1}(\underline{p_A}) - \Phi^{-1}(\overline{p_B})).$$

When applying randomized smoothing to a pretrained model, we need to choose the parameter $\sigma$ that corresponds to the noise level. Usually, a smaller $\sigma$ leads to more accurate prediction as the prediction is closer to the original model $f$, but to a weaker certified robust radius. On the other hand, adding a very large $\sigma$ will destroy the original prediction while having more robustness.

Note that the ability to be easily applied to any pretrained model is a strength of randomized smoothing. However, as most of the pretrained models will have significantly degraded performance when adding random noise, this often leads to poor robustness guarantees. A better choice is to also add random perturbation in the training stage, so the model is "aware of" the random input noise in the training stage and can perform properly when applying randomized smoothing. This is also very similar to the RSE technique described in the previous subsection, where random noise is added in both training and testing stages. Further, Salman et al. (2019a) showed that conducting adversarial training in the training phase can also improve the certified robustness through randomized smoothing.

The above-mentioned randomized smoothing technique is mostly designed for Gaussian noise. We can see in the analysis that the symmetry of Gaussian noise is very helpful. However, the natural of Gaussian noise only helps to establish the guarantees for $\ell_2$ robustness, and if one is interested in bounding the perturbation with another norm (e.g., $\ell_1$ or $\ell_\infty$ norm), then bounding the other $\ell_p$ norm based on the $\ell_2$ robust radius will lead to very loose bounds. Therefore there have been many works trying to extend randomized smoothing to other norms or discuss the difficulty when certifying for some particular norms (Blum et al., 2020; Yang et al., 2020c; Dvijotham et al., 2020).

## 13.4  Extended reading

- Higher-order randomized smoothing: (Mohapatra et al., 2020).
- Data poisoning attack on randomized smoothing: (Mehra et al., 2021a).
- Randmoized denoizing for certifying pre-trained classifiers: (Salman et al., 2020b).
- Randmoized defense based on hierarchical random switching: (Wang et al., 2019e).

# CHAPTER 14

# Certified robustness training

In the end of the last chapter, we have shown a way to compute the "certified radius" when conducting randomized smoothing, where it is guaranteed (with high probability) that any perturbation within such radius will not change the prediction. In this chapter, we introduce another way to establish the certified robustness guarantees for neural networks without using randomized techniques, and the resulting robustness guarantees are deterministic (with 100% probability).

The main idea of this technique, also known as certified robust training, is based on incomplete neural network verification methods introduced in Part 3. Note that for any given neural network, we can apply any verification techniques introduced in Part 3 to obtain a certified robust radius for each point. Therefore, even without conducting any form of specialized training, we can obtain a certified robust loss or error for any neural network based on the verification methods. However, as complete verification methods are time-consuming to run on larger models (with exponential time complexity), and incomplete verification methods usually give us very loose bounds, applying verification on a standard neural network model can give very low certified robustness. To resolve this issue, we will show that it is possible to define a loss function based on the certified robustness obtained by incomplete verification. When training a model to minimize this loss function, it will achieve reasonably well certified robustness, at least for some standard classification tasks.

## 14.1 A framework for certified robust training

For training a robust model, we care about the robust error defined as

$$E_{(x,y)} \max_{x' \in B(x)} I(f(x'), y), \tag{14.1}$$

where $I(f(x'), y)$ returns 1 if the (top-1) prediction $f(x')$ does not match the groundtruth label $y$, and we consider the worst-case perturbation within a perturbation set, so any instance $(x, y)$ is considered correct only if it is predicted correctly and any perturbation within the perturbation set cannot

*Adversarial Robustness for Machine Learning*
https://doi.org/10.1016/B978-0-12-824020-5.00025-9

change its prediction. However, it is impossible to compute the exact robust error for general neural network, so there are two ways to evaluate this value. The first way is to conduct an adversarial attack to find adversarial example $x'$, which is equivalent to finding a nonoptimal solution for the inner maximization problem, and the resulting value (error under attack) will be a lower bound of the real robust error. However, this lower bound can be far from the exact robust error, which sometimes gives a false sense of security. On the other hand, in this chapter, we care about "certified robust error", where we use some verification method to obtain upper and lower bounds of the prediction value of $f(x')$ for $x' \in B(x)$. Using this value, we can establish an *upper bound* of robust error, where we consider a sample to be robustly correct only if it is predicted correctly and it can be verified that within $B(x)$ that the (top-1) prediction never changes. For many security-sensitive applications, when we want to prove that the prediction is definitely correct within a certain region, this is much more important than errors under attacks. Further, as we discussed previously, some models are robust against certain attacks but vulnerable to others, so error under attack may not be a reliable measurement to robustness and can deliver biased evaluation of security. Therefore, for certified defense, we will focus on improving the certified robust error instead of error under attacks.

As it is impossible to directly minimize the 0/1 error in (14.1), a commonly used technique is defining a loss function as a surrogate for robust error and learning a model to minimize an upper bound of this robust loss. For example, we can define the robust cross-entropy loss as

$$E_{(x,y)} \max_{x' \in B(x)} \ell_{CE}(f(x'), y). \tag{14.2}$$

Computing the upper bound of the CE loss is based on any neural network verification technique. Note that neural network verification typically bounds $c^T f(x)$ for any $x \in B(x)$, where $c$ is a specification vector. To ensure that the logit of target label $i$ is larger than another label $j$, we can set $c_i = 1$, $c_j = -1$, and all other elements of $c$ to be zeros. To consider all the labels, we then define a set of $L$ specifications:

$$C_{i,j} = \begin{cases} 1 & \text{if } j = y, i \neq y \text{ (output of ground truth class)} \\ -1 & \text{if } i = j, i \neq y \text{ (output of other classes, negated)} \\ 0 & \text{otherwise (note that the } y\text{th row contains all 0).} \end{cases} \tag{14.3}$$

Each element in vector $m := Cf(x)$ gives us margins between class $y$ and all other classes. We define the lower bound of $Cf(x)$ for all $x \in B(x)$ as $\underline{m}(x, \epsilon)$, which is a very important quantity: when all elements of $\underline{m}(x, \epsilon) > 0$, $x$ is verifiably robust for any perturbation within $B(x)$. The bound $\underline{m}(x, \epsilon)$ can be obtained by an incomplete neural network verification algorithm, such as convex adversarial polytope, interval bound propagation (IBP), or CROWN, as introduced in Part 3. Based on this formulation, Wong and Kolter (2017) showed that for the cross-entropy (CE) loss,

$$\max_{x \in B(x)} L(f(x); y; \theta) \leq L(f(-\underline{m}(x, \epsilon); y; \theta)). \tag{14.4}$$

Therefore we can solve the upper bound in (14.4) to minimize a tractible upper bound of the inner maximization problem in (14.2). Note that to make this training work, the verification algorithm used to obtain $\underline{m}(x_k, \epsilon)$ has to be *differentiable*. In certified robust training, at each iteration when a batch of samples are selected, we first conduct verification to form $\underline{m}(x_k, \epsilon)$ for every $x_k$ in the batch and then perform back-propagation to compute the gradient $\nabla_\theta L(f(-\underline{m}(x_k, \epsilon); y; \theta))$ to conduct parameter updates. In what follows, we will introduce several effective verification methods that can be used for certified robust training under this framework.

## 14.2 Existing algorithms and their performances

There are two popular verification algorithms that have been successfully adopted in certified robust training: interval bound propagation (IBP) and linear relaxation-based training. Among them, IBP produces very loose bound but lead to surprisingly good results in certified training; linear relaxation methods provide much tighter bounds than IBP but often lead to unstable training. Therefore some recent methods also tried to combine these two bounds. We will discuss these approaches below.

### Interval bound propagation (IBP)

Interval bound propagation uses a simple bound propagation rule. The idea is to obtain an upper and lower bound of each neuron layer-by-layer in forward propagation. For the input layer, we set $x_L \leq x \leq x_U$ elementwise. We then propagate the bound for each neuron to the next layer. When passing through the linear layer $z^{(l)} = Wh^{(l-1)} + b^{(l)}$, assume $\bar{h}^{(l-1)}, \underline{h}^{(l-1)}$ are the (element-wise) upper and lower bounds of $h^{(l-1)}$, we can obtain the upper and lower bounds for $z^{(l)}$ by

$$\bar{z}^{(l)} = W^{(l)} \frac{\bar{h}^{(l-1)} + \underline{h}^{(l-1)}}{2} + |W^{(l)}| \frac{\bar{h}^{(l-1)} - \underline{h}^{(l-1)}}{2} + b^{(l)},$$

$$\underline{z}^{(l)} = W^{(l)} \frac{\bar{h}^{(l-1)} + \underline{h}^{(l-1)}}{2} - |W^{(l)}| \frac{\bar{h}^{(l-1)} - \underline{h}^{(l-1)}}{2} + b^{(l)},$$

where $|W^{(l)}|$ takes an elementwise absolute value. Note that $\bar{h}^{(0)} = x_U$ and $\underline{h}^{(0)} = x_L$. For an elementwise activation function (such as ReLU), we straightforwardly propagate the upper and lower bound through the activation function:

$$\bar{h}^{(l)} = \sigma(\bar{z}^{(l)}) \qquad \underline{h}^{(l)} = \sigma(\underline{z}^{(l)}).$$

Note that as a verification method, IBP gets much looser bounds than linear relaxation-based methods, since they only maintain the upper and lower bound for each neuron on each layer, without forming a linear approximation to the input. However, surprisingly, Gowal et al. (2018) found that training with IBP can achieve good certified robustness.

When conducting IBP-based training in a naive way, the performance is usually very bad since the bounds computed by IBP are very loose, especially at the initial point, which makes training very unstable. There are thus several important techniques used to stabilize IBP-based certified training. First, Gowal et al. (2018) proposed to use a mixture of robust cross-entropy loss with natural cross-entropy loss as the objective to stabilize training. Further, since training with IBP usually suffers from very bad initial loss, a commonly used technique called $\epsilon$-scheduling has been used in IBP training. The main idea is to initialize $\epsilon$ (the perturbation tolerance) as 0 or very small initially, and gradually increase $\epsilon$ over iterations. However, the $\epsilon$-scheduling also leads to significant longer training epochs. For example, to achieve state-of-the-art IBP performance, we need thousands of warmup and final training epochs. To resolve this issue, Shi et al. (2021) proposed several regularization methods including batch normalization and a penalty to control the number of inactive neurons to stabilize IBP training. With their training recipes, IBP can achieve competitive results only with around two hundred training epochs on several publich benchmark models and datasets.

## Linear relaxation-based training

Based on the formulation of (14.4), it is natural to apply a tighter bound derived by linear relaxation based-methods as $\underline{m}(x, \epsilon)$. As linear relaxation-based methods obtain linear upper and lower bounds for output neurons with respect to inputs, when plugging-in the function into $\underline{m}$, the whole loss function will be differentiable. Surprisingly, although those bounds are much tighter than IBP, when conducting certified training, it leads to much worse performance than IBP. Zhang et al. (2020a) observed that linear relaxation-based training usually leads to small norms of the model parameters, thus forcing many neurons to be inactive. A conjecture is that since linear relaxation-based methods have much tighter bounds when neurons are either inactive or active, they tend to over-regularize the network to enforce most of neurons to be inactive. However, it remains to be a open question on why this phenomenon happens more common in linear relaxation-based training than in IBP training.

However, linear relaxation-based training is still useful for certified defense. In particular, Zhang et al. (2020a) developed a Crown-IBP training method that combines the linear relaxation-based method with IBP. As mentioned before, the problem of IBP training is that the bounds tend to be very bad near initialization, which makes training extremely unstable. Crown-IBP uses CROWN training (a linear relaxation-based method) at the initial phase and then gradually switches the training objective to IBP. More specifically, Crown-IBP considers the following training objective:

$$\min_{\theta} E_{(x,y)}\big[\kappa L(x; y; \theta) + (1 - \kappa)L(-((1 - \beta)\underline{m}_{\text{IBP}}(x, \epsilon)$$
$$+ \beta \underline{m}_{\text{CROWN-IBP}}(x, \epsilon)); y; \theta)\big],$$

where $\underline{m}$ is a combination of two bounds such that $\underline{m}_{\text{CROWN-IBP}}$ conducts IBP in the forward bounding pass and CROWN bound propagation in a backward bounding pass. By setting $\beta$ to be close to 1 in the beginning and gradually reduced to 0, the Crown-IBP training methods take the advantage of CROWN (linear relaxation-based methods) in the initial training phase but do not over-regularize the neurons. More details can be found in (Zhang et al., 2020a).

## 14.3 Empirical comparison

We present the comparison of existing certified training approaches on MNIST and CIFAR-10 datasets. For simplicity, we focus on the $\ell_\infty$ certified robust training with several commonly used settings of $\epsilon$. Experimental results are presented in Table 14.1. Note that for IBP training, we mainly

**Table 14.1** A comparison of IBP, Crown-IBP, and Improved IBP on MNIST and CIFAR-10 datasets.

| Dataset | $\epsilon$ | Training Method | Standard error | Certified error |
|---------|------------|-----------------|----------------|-----------------|
| MNIST | 0.4 | IBP | 1.66 | 15.01 |
| MNIST | 0.4 | Crown–IBP | 2.17 | 12.06 |
| MNIST | 0.4 | Improved IBP | 2.2 | 10.82 |
| CIFAR-10 | 8/255 | IBP | 58.72 | 69.88 |
| CIFAR-10 | 8/255 | CROWN-IBP | 53.73 | 66.62 |
| CIFAR-10 | 8/255 | Improved IBP | 51.06 | 65.05 |

refer to the training recipe proposed in (Gowal et al., 2018); for Crown-IBP, we used the results from (Zhang et al., 2020a) and (Xu et al., 2020b), and for improved IBP, we consider IBP with the tricks proposed by Shi et al. (2021). For both datasets, we use the seven-layer CNN model used commonly in those papers. We can observe that current methods already achieve reasonably good performance on MNIST datasets; since each pixel value is normalized to be [0, 1], a perturbation of $\epsilon = 0.4$ is already very large, and certified training can obtain models with almost 10% data correctly and robustly classified on MNIST. However, the performance of CIFAR-10 is still not ideal, so many recent works still try to improve the certified robustness accuracy on CIFAR-10 and larger-scale datasets.

## 14.4 Extended reading

- Fast certified robustness training: (Boopathy et al., 2021).

# CHAPTER 15

# Adversary detection

Another type of defense methods against evasion attacks, which we call *adversary detection*, aims to detect the existence of adversarial examples, rather than trying to classify them into the correct classes. The main assumption behind these methods is that the adversarial examples came from a different distribution compared with natural samples, so they could be detected with carefully designed detectors. In addition to evasion attacks, similar methodology can be applied to detect other types of adversarial attacks. In this section, we first discuss adversarial detection to testing time adversarial attacks. We then discuss detection methods against other attack scenarios.

## 15.1 Detecting adversarial inputs

A straightforward way toward adversarial example detection is to build a simple binary classifier separating the adversarial examples apart from the clean data. However, these methods usually suffer from lack of generalization to unforeseen attacks. Therefore an effective detection method is usually based on some characteristics of adversarial attacks instead of purely classifying an existing attack. In the following, we will introduce several popular detection methods.

*Density estimation.* A common observation is that adversarial examples often lie outside the natural image manifold, and many detection methods are based on these characteristics. In particular, Feinman et al. (2017) proposed to use kernel density estimation to measure how far a sample is from the provided data manifold. Letting $X = \{x_1, \ldots, x_n\}$ be training samples stored in the database, we can assume that the training data distribution is a mixture of Gaussians centered at those points, denoted as $p_X(x)$. Therefore, for a testing instance $x$, the density can be estimated as

$$p_X(x) = \frac{1}{n} \sum_{i=1}^{n} K_\sigma(x_i, x),$$

where $K_\sigma(\cdot, \cdot)$ is a kernel function. A commonly used kernel function is the Gaussian kernel, where $K_\sigma(x_i, x) = e^{-\frac{\|x_i - x\|^2}{2\sigma^2}}$. The KD-detection method proposed in (Feinman et al., 2017) fits the density function on each label. If

*Adversarial Robustness for Machine Learning*
https://doi.org/10.1016/B978-0-12-824020-5.00026-0

an incoming example $x$ is predicted as label $y$, we use the density estimation based on the samples from class $y$. Once $p_X(x)$ is computed, we can then get the statistics of KD estimation of natural examples versus adversarial examples to determine the threshold for detecting adversarial examples.

Many other algorithms also fall into this kernel density estimation framework. For example, Ma et al. (2018) observed that the local intrinsic dimension (LID) of hidden layer outputs differ between adversarial examples and natural examples, so they conduct density estimations on hidden layer features (instead of input layers) to detect adversarial examples. It is also observed in many works that an ensemble of several different layers can significantly boost the performance of adversarial detection in computer vision tasks, so most of the existing detectors are based on not only one, but on several hidden layer features. In another work, Lee et al. (2018) generated the class of conditional Gaussian distributions with respect to hidden layer output of the DNN under Gaussian discriminant analysis, which results in a confidence score based on the Mahalanobis distance (MAHA), followed by a logistic regression model on the confidence scores to detect adversarial examples. A joint statistical test pooling information from multiple layers is proposed by Raghuram et al. (2020) to detect adversarial examples.

*Feature attribution methods for adversarial detection.* In addition to density estimation based on hidden layer features, many works identify some other important features that can distinguish adversarial examples from natural examples. Here we will discuss an interesting finding that adversarial examples can be detected by feature attribution methods (Yang et al., 2020d).

Assume that the model is a function $f : \mathbb{R}^d \to [0, 1]^K$ and a feature attribution method $\phi$ maps an input image $x \in \mathbb{R}^d$ to a $d$-dimensional vector $\phi(x) \in \mathbb{R}^d$, where each element in $\phi(x)$ corresponds to how important the feature contributes to the model prediction. There are many feature attribution methods developed in the literature. For instance, the widely used leave-one-out (LOO) feature attribution method (Zeiler and Fergus, 2014; Li et al., 2016) measures the importance of each feature by the change of model output when removing the feature (e.g., setting it as 0). Mathematically, the LOO method designs $\phi$ as

$$\phi(x)_i = f(x)_c - f(x_{(i)})_c,$$

where $c$ is the target class we are interested in, and $x_{(i)}$ means $x$ with feature $i$ removed.

Interestingly, Yang et al. (2020d) observed that adversarial examples have very different feature attribution maps from natural examples. As shown in Fig. 15.1, we observe that the feature attribution map for adversarial examples is much more spread than for natural examples, where for each plot we have the original example (top left figure) and the adversarial example generated by PGD attack (bottom left figure), and generate feature attribution map (e.g., using leave-one-out) of each figure. The pixel value distribution of each feature attribution map is then compared in the histogram on the bottom panel, showing very different patterns between original example and adversarial example. One hypothesis is that classifiers are very confident about the prediction based on certain feature when facing natural examples, but in adversarial examples, since we add noise to the input, the feature attributions become more spread since there is no particular pixel in the image leading to this false prediction. Similar behavior is also observed when applying other feature attribution maps, such as integrated gradient (IG) or other gradient-based feature attribution methods.

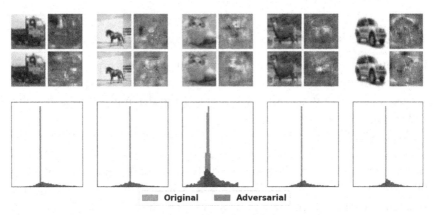

Original    Adversarial

Figure 15.1 Feature attibution analysis in (Yang et al., 2020d). The first row shows the original CIFAR-10 examples and their corresponding feature attributions. The second row shows the adversarial examples and their corresponding feature attributions. The third row plots the histograms of the original and adversarial feature attributions. We can easily observe that adversarial examples have very different feature attribution maps from natural examples.

Motivated by this observation, we can measure the statistical dispersion in the feature attribution map to detect adversarial examples. In particular, Yang et al. (2020d) adopted several statistical measurements, including standard deviation, median absolute deviation (the median of absolute differences between entries and their median), and interquartile range (the difference between the 75th and 25th percentiles among all entries of feature attribution values). These values can serve as a good detection score for adversarial versus natural examples, as shown in Fig. 15.2. Using these scores and ensemble feature attribution maps on multiple layers, the ML-LOO detection algorithm proposed by Yang et al. (2020d) achieved very good performance on adversarial detection, compared with purely density-based methods.

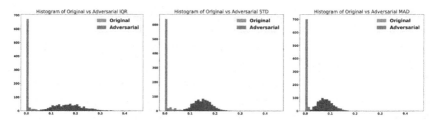

**Figure 15.2** The dispersion scores (standard deviation, median absolute deviation, and interquartile range) for adversarial examples versus natural examples presented in (Yang et al., 2020d).

## 15.2 Detecting adversarial audio inputs

In general, detecting adversarial examples can be a challenging task. Many detection methods have been shown to be weakened or bypassed by advanced adversarial attacks that are aware of the defenses in place (Carlini and Wagner, 2017a).

However, in some data domains, we can leverage specific domain knowledge and data characteristics to detect adversarial inputs. In particular, for audio data inputs, Yang et al. (2019c) reveal the importance of using the temporal dependency in audio data to gain discriminate power against adversarial examples. Testing the automatic speech recognition (ASR) tasks and three recent audio adversarial attacks, they find that (i) input transformation developed from image adversarial defense provides limited robustness improvement and is subtle to advanced attacks and (ii) temporal dependency can be exploited to gain discriminative power against audio adversarial examples and is resistant to the considered adaptive attacks.

For (i), Yang et al. (2019c) show that four implemented transformation techniques on audio inputs, including waveform quantization, temporal smoothing, down-sampling, and autoencoder reformation, provide limited robustness improvement against the adaptive white-box attack proposed by Athalye et al. (2018), which aims to circumvent the gradient obfuscation issue incurred by input transformations.

For (ii), Yang et al. (2019c) propose a temporal dependency (TD) based detection method. Due to the fact that audio sequence has explicit temporal dependency (e.g., correlations in consecutive waveform segments), they explore if such temporal dependency will be affected by adversarial perturbations.

*Methodology.* The pipeline of the temporal dependency-based method is shown in Fig. 15.3. Given an audio sequence, they propose to select the first $k$ portions of it (i.e., the prefix of length $k$) as input for ASR to obtain transcribed results as $S_k$. Moreover, they will also insert the whole sequence into ASR and select the prefix of length $k$ of the transcribed result as $S_{\{whole,k\}}$, which has the same length as $S_k$. We will then compare the consistency between $S_k$ and $S_{\{whole,k\}}$ in terms of temporal dependency distance. Here the word error rate (WER) is adopted as the distance metric (Levenshtein, 1966). For normal/benign audio instance, $S_k$ and $S_{\{whole,k\}}$ should be similar since the ASR model is consistent for different sections of a given sequence due to its temporal dependency. However, for audio adversarial examples, since the added perturbation aims to alter the ASR output toward the targeted transcription, it may fail to preserve the temporal information of the original sequence. Therefore, due to the loss of temporal dependency, $S_k$ and $S_{\{whole,k\}}$ in this case will not be able to produce consistent results. Based on such a hypothesis, they leverage the prefix of length $k$ of the transcribed results and the transcribed $k$ portion to potentially recognize adversarial inputs.

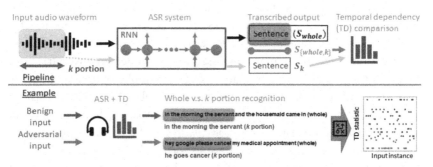

**Figure 15.3** Pipeline and example of the proposed temporal dependency (TD) based method for discriminating audio adversarial examples in (Yang et al., 2019c).

*Numerical experiments.* Two attacks are considered for evaluation on the speech-to-text task.

*Commander Song attack against speech-to-text translation (Commander).* Commander Song (Yuan et al., 2018) is a speech-to-text targeted attack, which can attack an audio extracted from a popular song. The adversarial audio can even be played over the air with its adversarial characteristics. The Kaldi speech recognition platform is used for analysis.

*Optimization based attack against speech-to-text translation (Opt).* The targeted speech-to-text attack proposed by Carlini and Wagner (2018) uses connectionist temporal classification (CTC) loss in a speech recognition system as an objective function and solves the task of adversarial attack as an optimization problem. The DeepSpeech speech-to-text transcription network is used for analysis, which is a biRNN-based model with beam search to decode text.

For detection methods, the standard evaluation metric is the area under curve (AUC) score, aiming to evaluate the detection efficiency. The proposed TD method focuses on how many adversarial instances are captured (true positive) without affecting benign instances (false positive). Therefore we follow the standard criteria and report AUC for TD. For the proposed TD method, we compare the temporal dependency based on WER, character error rate (CER), and the longest common prefix (LCP). LCP is a commonly used metric to evaluate the similarity between two strings. Given strings $b_1$ and $b_2$, the corresponding LCP is defined as $\max_{b_1[:k]=b_2[:k]} k$, where $[:k]$ represents the prefix of length $k$ of a translated sentence.

In Commander Song attack, Yang et al. (2019c) directly examine whether the generated adversarial audio is consistent with its prefix of length $k$ or not. Using TD method with $k = \frac{1}{2}$, all the generated adversarial samples showed inconsistency and thus were successfully detected. In Opt attack, as a baseline, Yang et al. (2019c) also directly train a one-layer LSTM with 64 hidden feature dimensions based on the collected adversarial and benign audio instances for classification. Some examples of translated results for benign and adversarial audios are shown in Table 15.1. They consider three types of adversarial targets: short − *hey google*; medium − *this is an adversarial example*; and long − *hey google please cancel my medical appointment*. The AUC score for these detection results for $k = 1/2$ in Table 15.2.

We can see that by using WER as the detection metric the temporal dependency-based method can achieve AUC as high as 0.936 on Common Voice and 0.93 on LIBRIS. Yang et al. (2019c) also explored different values of $k$ and observed that the results do not vary too much. When $k = 4/5$, the AUC score based on CER can reach 0.969, which shows that such temporal dependency-based method is indeed promising in terms of distinguishing adversarial instances. Notably, these results suggest that the

Table 15.1  Examples of the temporal dependency-based detection method.

| Type | Transcribed results |
|---|---|
| Original | then good bye said the rats and they went home |
| the first half of Original | then good bye said the raps |
| Adversarial (short) | hey google |
| First half of Adversarial | he is |
| Adversarial (medium) | this is an adversarial example |
| First half of Adversarial | these on adequate |
| Adversarial (long) | hey google please cancel my medical appointment |
| First half of Adversarial | he goes cancer |

Table 15.2  AUC results of the proposed temporal dependency method.

| Dataset | LSTM | TD (WER) | TD (CER) | TD (LCP ratio) |
|---|---|---|---|---|
| Common Voice | 0.712 | **0.936** | 0.916 | 0.859 |
| LIBRIS | 0.645 | 0.930 | **0.933** | 0.806 |

temporal dependency-based method would suggest an easy-to-implement but effective method for characterizing adversarial audio attacks.

## 15.3  Detecting Trojan models

Wang et al. (2020d) study the problem of the Trojan network (TrojanNet) detection in the data-scarce regime, where only the weights of a trained DNN are accessed by the detector. We refer to Chapter 5 for details regarding backdoor attacks. Wang et al. (2020d) propose a data-limited TrojanNet detector (TND), when only a few data samples are available for TrojanNet detection. They show that an effective data-limited TND can be established by exploring connections between Trojan attack and prediction-evasion adversarial attacks including per-sample attack and all-sample universal attack. In addition, they propose a data-free TND, which can detect a Trojan-Net without accessing any data samples for convolutional neural networks. Wang et al. (2020d) show that such a TND can be built by leveraging the internal response of hidden neurons, which exhibits the Trojan behavior even at random noise inputs. Their work offers a practical tool for Trojan-Net detection and addresses the challenge of *How to detect a TrojanNet when having access to training/testing data samples is restricted or not allowed?* This is a practical scenario because it is a common practice for machine learning to leverage a pretrained but potentially untrusted neural networks in downstream applications such as transfer learning or finetuing.

Take image classifiers as an example. For backdoored models, since arbitrary images can be misclassified as the same target label by TrojanNet when these inputs consisting of the Trojan trigger are used in data poisoning, Wang et al. (2020d) hypothesize that there exists a *shortcut* in TrojanNet, leading to *input-agnostic* misclassification. Their approach is motivated by exploiting the existing *shortcut* for the detection of TrojanNets.

*Trojan perturbation.* Given a neural network model, let $f \in \mathbb{R}^K$ be the mapping from the input space to the logits of $K$ classes. Let $f_y$ denote the logits value corresponding to class $y$. The final prediction is then given by $\mathrm{argmax}_y f_y$. Let $r \in \mathbb{R}^d$ be the mapping from the input space to neuron's representation defined by the output of the penultimate layer (namely, prior to the fully connected block of the model). Given a clean data $\mathbf{x} \in \mathbb{R}^n$, the poisoned data through *Trojan perturbation* $\boldsymbol{\delta}$ is then formulated as

$$\hat{\mathbf{x}}(\mathbf{m}, \boldsymbol{\delta}) = (1 - \mathbf{m}) \cdot \mathbf{x} + \mathbf{m} \cdot \boldsymbol{\delta}, \tag{15.1}$$

where $\boldsymbol{\delta} \in \mathbb{R}^n$ denotes pixelwise perturbations, $\mathbf{m} \in \{0, 1\}^n$ is a binary mask to encode the position where a Trojan stamp is placed, and $\cdot$ denotes the elementwise product. In trigger-driven Trojan attacks (Gu et al., 2017; Chen et al., 2017b; Yao et al., 2019), the poisoned training data $\hat{\mathbf{x}}(\mathbf{m}, \boldsymbol{\delta})$ is mislabeled to a target class to enforce a backdoor during model training. In clean-label Trojan attacks (Shafahi et al., 2018; Zhu et al., 2019a), the variables $(\mathbf{m}, \boldsymbol{\delta})$ are designed to misalign the feature representation $r(\hat{\mathbf{x}}(\mathbf{m}, \boldsymbol{\delta}))$ with $r(\mathbf{x})$ but without perturbing the label of the poisoned training data. We call this model a TrojanNet if it is trained over poisoned training data given by (15.1).

*Data-limited TrojanNet detector (DL-TND):* Wang et al. (2020d) address the problem of TrojanNet detection with the prior knowledge on model weights and a few clean test images, at least one sample per class. Let $\mathcal{D}_k$ denote the set of data within the (predicted) class $k$, and let $\mathcal{D}_{k-}$ denote the set of data with prediction labels different from $k$. Wang et al. (2020d) propose to design a detector by exploring how the per-image adversarial perturbation is coupled with the universal perturbation due to the presence of backdoor in TrojanNets. The rationale behind that is the per-image and universal perturbations would maintain a strong similarity while perturbing images toward the Trojan target class due to the existence of a Trojan shortcut. The framework is illustrated in Fig. 15.4(a).

*Untargeted universal perturbation.* Given images $\{\mathbf{x}_i \in \mathcal{D}_{k-}\}$, the goal is to find a *universal perturbation* tuple $\mathbf{u}^{(k)} = (\mathbf{m}^{(k)}, \boldsymbol{\delta}^{(k)})$ such that the predictions

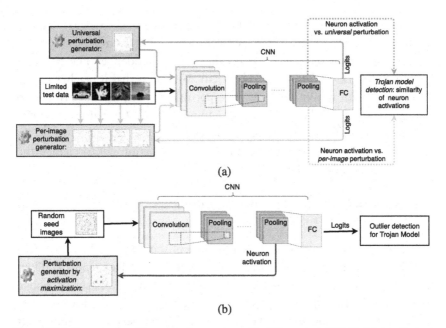

(a)

(b)

**Figure 15.4** Frameworks of two detectors proposed in (Wang et al., 2020d): (a) data-limited TrojanNet detector (DL-TND); (b) data-free TrojanNet detector (DF-TND).

of these images in $\mathcal{D}_{k-}$ are *altered* given the current model. However, we require $\mathbf{u}^{(k)}$ not to alter the prediction of images belonging to class $k$, namely, $\{\mathbf{x}_i \in \mathcal{D}_k\}$. Spurred by that, the design of $\mathbf{u}^{(k)} = (\mathbf{m}^{(k)}, \boldsymbol{\delta}^{(k)})$ can be cast as the following optimization problem:

$$\begin{aligned} \underset{\mathbf{m},\boldsymbol{\delta}}{\text{minimize}} \quad & \ell_{\text{atk}}(\hat{\mathbf{x}}(\mathbf{m}, \boldsymbol{\delta}); \mathcal{D}_{k-}) + \bar{\ell}_{\text{atk}}(\hat{\mathbf{x}}(\mathbf{m}, \boldsymbol{\delta}); \mathcal{D}_k) + \lambda \|\mathbf{m}\|_1 \\ \text{subject to} \quad & \{\boldsymbol{\delta}, \mathbf{m}\} \in \mathcal{C}, \end{aligned} \tag{15.2}$$

where $\hat{\mathbf{x}}(\mathbf{m}, \boldsymbol{\delta})$ was defined in (15.1), $\lambda \geq 0$ is a regularization parameter that strikes a balance between the loss term $\ell_{\text{uatk}} + \bar{\ell}_{\text{atk}}$ and the sparsity of the trigger pattern $\|\mathbf{m}\|_1$, and $\mathcal{C} = \{0 \leq \boldsymbol{\delta} \leq 255, \mathbf{m} \in \{0, 1\}^n\}$ is the constraint set of optimization variables $\mathbf{m}$ and $\boldsymbol{\delta}$, where $[0,255]$ is the range of the RGB pixel values.

We next elaborate on the loss terms $\ell_{\text{atk}}$ and $\bar{\ell}_{\text{atk}}$ in problem (15.2). First, the loss $\ell_{\text{atk}}$ enforces to alter the prediction labels of images in $\mathcal{D}_{k-}$, and is defined as the C&W *untargeted* attack loss (Carlini and Wagner, 2017a)

$$\ell_{\text{atk}}(\hat{\mathbf{x}}(\mathbf{m}, \boldsymbol{\delta}); \mathcal{D}_{k-}) = \sum_{\mathbf{x}_i \in \mathcal{D}_{k-}} \max\{f_{y_i}(\hat{\mathbf{x}}_i(\mathbf{m}, \boldsymbol{\delta})) - \max_{t \neq y_i} f_t(\hat{\mathbf{x}}_i(\mathbf{m}, \boldsymbol{\delta})), -\tau\}, \tag{15.3}$$

where $y_i$ denotes the prediction label of $\mathbf{x}_i$ (recall that $f_t(\hat{\mathbf{x}}_i(\mathbf{m}, \boldsymbol{\delta}))$ denotes the logit value of the class $t$ with respect to the input $\hat{\mathbf{x}}_i(\mathbf{m}, \boldsymbol{\delta})$), and $\tau \geq 0$ is a given constant that characterizes the attack confidence. The rationale behind $\max\{f_{y_i}(\hat{\mathbf{x}}_i(\mathbf{m}, \boldsymbol{\delta})) - \max_{t \neq y_i} f_t(\hat{\mathbf{x}}_i(\mathbf{m}, \boldsymbol{\delta})), -\tau\}$ is that it reaches a negative value (with minimum $-\tau$) if the perturbed input $\hat{\mathbf{x}}_i(\mathbf{m}, \boldsymbol{\delta})$ is able to change the original label $y_i$. Thus the minimization of $\ell_{\text{atk}}$ enforces the ensemble of successful label change of images in $\mathcal{D}_{k-}$. Second, the loss $\bar{\ell}_{\text{atk}}$ in (15.2) is proposed to enforce the universal perturbation *not* to change the prediction of images in $\mathcal{D}_k$. This yields

$$\bar{\ell}_{\text{atk}}(\hat{\mathbf{x}}(\mathbf{m}, \boldsymbol{\delta}); \mathcal{D}_k) = \sum_{\mathbf{x}_i \in \mathcal{D}_k} \max\{\max_{t \neq k} f_t(\hat{\mathbf{x}}_i(\mathbf{m}, \boldsymbol{\delta})) - f_{y_i}(\hat{\mathbf{x}}_i(\mathbf{m}, \boldsymbol{\delta})), -\tau\}, \quad (15.4)$$

where recall that $y_i = k$ for $\mathbf{x}_i \in \mathcal{D}_k$. We present the rationale behind (15.3) and (15.4) as follows. Suppose that $k$ is a target label of Trojan attack. Then the presence of backdoor would enforce the perturbed images of non-$k$ class in (15.3) toward being predicted as the target label $k$. However, the universal perturbation (performed like a Trojan trigger) would not affect images within the target class $k$, as characterized by (15.4).

*Targeted per-image perturbation.* If a label $k$ is the target label specified by the Trojan adversary, then we hypothesize that perturbing each image in $\mathcal{D}_{k-}$ toward the target class $k$ could go through the similar Trojan shortcut as the universal adversarial examples found in (15.2). Spurred by that, we generate the following targeted per-image adversarial perturbation for $\mathbf{x}_i \in \mathcal{D}_k$:

$$\underset{\mathbf{m}, \boldsymbol{\delta}}{\text{minimize}} \quad \ell'_{\text{atk}}(\hat{\mathbf{x}}(\mathbf{m}, \boldsymbol{\delta}); \mathbf{x}_i) + \lambda \|\mathbf{m}\|_1 \quad \text{subject to} \quad \{\boldsymbol{\delta}, \mathbf{m}\} \in \mathcal{C}, \quad (15.5)$$

where $\ell'_{\text{atk}}(\hat{\mathbf{x}}(\mathbf{m}, \boldsymbol{\delta}); \mathbf{x}_i)$ is the targeted C&W attack loss (Carlini and Wagner, 2017a)

$$\ell'_{\text{atk}}(\hat{\mathbf{x}}(\mathbf{m}, \boldsymbol{\delta}); \mathbf{x}_i) = \sum_{\mathbf{x}_i \in \mathcal{D}_{k-}} \max\{\max_{t \neq k} f_t(\hat{\mathbf{x}}_i(\mathbf{m}, \boldsymbol{\delta})) - f_k(\hat{\mathbf{x}}_i(\mathbf{m}, \boldsymbol{\delta})), -\tau\}. \quad (15.6)$$

For each pair of label $k$ and data $\mathbf{x}_i$, we can obtain a per-image perturbation tuple $\mathbf{s}^{(k,i)} = (\mathbf{m}^{(k,i)}, \boldsymbol{\delta}^{(k,i)})$.

For solving both problems of universal perturbation generation (15.2) and per-image perturbation generation (15.5), the promotion of $\lambda$ enforces a sparse perturbation mask $\mathbf{m}$. This is desired when the Trojan trigger is of small size. When the Trojan trigger might not be sparse, multiple values of $\lambda$ can also be used to generate different sets of adversarial perturbations. The proposed TrojanNet detector will then be conducted to examine every set of adversarial perturbations.

*DL-TND detection rule.* Let $\hat{\mathbf{x}}_i(\mathbf{u}^{(k)})$ and $\hat{\mathbf{x}}_i(\mathbf{s}^{(k,i)})$ denote the adversarial example of $\mathbf{x}_i$ under the universal perturbation $\mathbf{u}^{(k)}$ and the imagewise perturbation $\mathbf{s}^{(k,i)}$, respectively. If $k$ is the target label of the Trojan attack, then based on our similarity hypothesis, $\mathbf{u}^{(k)}$ and $\mathbf{s}^{(k,i)}$ would share a strong similarity in fooling the decision of the CNN model due to the presence of backdoor. We evaluate such a similarity from the neuron representation against $\hat{\mathbf{x}}_i(\mathbf{u}^{(k)})$ and $\hat{\mathbf{x}}_i(\mathbf{s}^{(k,i)})$, given by $v_i^{(k)} = \cos\left(r(\hat{\mathbf{x}}_i(\mathbf{u}^{(k)})), r(\hat{\mathbf{x}}_i(\mathbf{s}^{(k,i)}))\right)$, where $\cos(\cdot, \cdot)$ represents cosine similarity. Here recall that $r$ denotes the mapping from the input image to the neuron representation in CNN. For any $\mathbf{x}_i \in D_{k-}$, we form the vector of similarity scores $\mathbf{v}_{\text{sim}}^{(k)} = \{v_i^{(k)}\}_i$.

Given the similarity scores $\mathbf{v}_{\text{sim}}^{(k)}$ for each label $k$, we detect whether or not the model is a TrojanNet (and thus $k$ is the target class) by calculating the so-called detection index $I^{(k)}$, given by the $q\%$-percentile of $\mathbf{v}_{\text{sim}}^{(k)}$. The decision for TrojanNet is then made by $I^{(k)} \geq T_1$ for a given threshold $T_1$, and accordingly $k$ is the target label. We can also employ the median absolute deviation (MAD) method to $\mathbf{v}_{\text{sim}}^{(k)}$ to mitigate the manual specification of $T_1$.

*Data-free TrojanNet detector (DF-TND).* The framework of data-free TrojanNet detector is summarized in Fig. 15.4(b). It was previously shown by Cheng et al. (2020a) and Wang et al. (2019b) that a TrojanNet exhibits an unexpectedly high neuron activation at certain coordinates. That is because the TrojanNet produces robust representation toward the input-agnostic misclassification induced by the backdoor. Given a clean data $\mathbf{x}$, let $r_i(\mathbf{x})$ denote the $i$th coordinate of the neuron activation vector. Motivated by (Engstrom et al., 2019a; Fong et al., 2019; Wang et al., 2020d), we study whether or not an inverted image that maximizes neuron activation is able to reveal the characteristics of the Trojan signature from model weights. We formulate the inverted image as $\hat{\mathbf{x}}(\mathbf{m}, \boldsymbol{\delta})$ in (15.1), parameterized by the pixel-level perturbations $\boldsymbol{\delta}$ and the binary mask $\mathbf{m}$ with respect to $\mathbf{x}$. To find $\hat{\mathbf{x}}(\mathbf{m}, \boldsymbol{\delta})$, we solve the problem of activation maximization

$$\underset{\mathbf{m}, \boldsymbol{\delta}, \mathbf{w}}{\text{maximize}} \quad \sum_{i=1}^{d} \left[ w_i r_i(\hat{\mathbf{x}}(\mathbf{m}, \boldsymbol{\delta})) \right] - \lambda \|\mathbf{m}\|_1$$
$$\text{subject to} \quad \{\boldsymbol{\delta}, \mathbf{m}\} \in \mathcal{C}, 0 \leq \mathbf{w} \leq \mathbf{1}, \mathbf{1}^T \mathbf{w} = 1, \tag{15.7}$$

where the notations follow (15.2) except the newly introduced variables $\mathbf{w}$, which adjust the importance of neuron coordinates. Note that if $\mathbf{w} = 1/d$, then the first loss term in (15.7) becomes the average of coordinatewise neuron activation. However, since the Trojan-relevant coordinates are expected to make larger impacts, the corresponding variables $w_i$ are desired for more penalization. In this sense the introduction of self-adjusted variables $\mathbf{w}$ helps us to avoid the manual selection of neuron coordinates that are most relevant to the backdoor.

*DF-TND detection rule.* Let the vector tuple $\mathbf{p}^{(i)} = (\mathbf{m}^{(i)}, \boldsymbol{\delta}^{(i)})$ be a solution of problem (15.7) given at a random input $\mathbf{x}_i$ for $i \in \{1, 2, \ldots, N\}$. Here $N$ denotes the number of random images used in TrojanNet detection. We then detect if a model is TrojanNet by investigating the change of logits outputs with respect to $\mathbf{x}_i$ and $\hat{\mathbf{x}}_i(\mathbf{p}^{(i)})$, respectively. For each label $k \in [K]$, we obtain

$$L_k = \frac{1}{N} \sum_i^N [f_k(\hat{\mathbf{x}}_i(\mathbf{p}^{(i)})) - f_k(\mathbf{x}_i)]. \tag{15.8}$$

The decision of TrojanNet with the target label $k$ is then made according to $L_k \geq T_2$ for a given threshold $T_2$.

*Numerical experiments.* As reported by Wang et al. (2020d), the neural network models include VGG16 (Simonyan and Zisserman, 2014), ResNet-50 (He et al., 2016), and AlexNet (Krizhevsky et al., 2012). Datasets include CIFAR-10 (Krizhevsky et al., 2009), GTSRB (Stallkamp et al., 2012), and Restricted ImageNet (R-ImgNet) (restricting ImageNet (Deng et al., 2009) to 9 classes). Wang et al. (2020d) trained 85 TrojanNets and 85 clean networks. The backdoor process includes different trigger patterns and poisoning data ratios. DL-TND is compared with the baseline Neural Cleanse (NC) (Wang et al., 2019b) for detecting TrojanNets.

To build DL-TND, Wang et al. (2020d) use 5 validation data points for each class of CIFAR-10 and R-ImgNet, and 2 validation data points for each class of GTSRB. They set $I^{(k)}$ to quantile-0.25, median, and quantile-0.75 and vary $T_1$. Let the true positive rate be the detection success rate for TrojanNets, and let the false negative rate be the detection error rate for cleanNets. Then the area under the curve (AUC) of receiver operating characteristics (ROC) can be used to measure the performance of the detection. Table 15.3 shows the AUC values, where "Total" refers to the collection of all models from different datasets. The results show that DL-TND can perform well across different datasets and model architectures. Moreover, fixing $I^{(k)}$ as the median, $T_1 = 0.54 \sim 0.896$ could provide a detection success rate over 76.5% for TrojanNets and a detection success rate over 82% for cleanNets.

**Table 15.3** AUC values for TrojanNet detection and target label detection, given in the format $(\cdot, \cdot)$. The detection index for each class is selected as quantile $Q = 0.25$, $Q = 0.5$, and $Q = 0.75$ of the similarity scores.

|  | CIFAR-10 | GTSRB | R-ImgNet | Total |
|---|---|---|---|---|
| $Q = 0.25$ | $(1, 1)$ | $(0.99, 0.99)$ | $(1, 1)$ | $(1, 0.99)$ |
| $Q = 0.5$ | $(1, 0.99)$ | $(1, 1)$ | $(1, 1)$ | $(1, 0.99)$ |
| $Q = 0.75$ | $(1, 0.98)$ | $(1, 1)$ | $(0.99, 0.97)$ | $(0.99, 0.98)$ |

**Table 15.4** Comparisons between DL-TND (Wang et al., 2020d) and NC (Wang et al., 2019b) on TrojanNets and cleanNets using $T_1 = 0.7$. The results are reported in the format (number of correctly detected models)/(total number of models).

|  |  | DL-TND (clean) | DL-TND (Trojan) | NC (clean) | NC (Trojan) |
|---|---|---|---|---|---|
| CIFAR-10 | ResNet-50 | 20/20 | 20/20 | 11/20 | 13/20 |
|  | VGG16 | 10/10 | 9/10 | 5/10 | 6/10 |
|  | AlexNet | 10/10 | 10/10 | 6/10 | 7/10 |
| GTSRB | ResNet-50 | 12/12 | 12/12 | 10/12 | 6/12 |
|  | VGG16 | 9/9 | 9/9 | 6/9 | 7/9 |
|  | AlexNet | 9/9 | 8/9 | 5/9 | 5/9 |
| ImageNet | ResNet-50 | 5/5 | 5/5 | 4/5 | 1/5 |
|  | VGG16 | 5/5 | 4/5 | 3/5 | 2/5 |
|  | AlexNet | 4/5 | 5/5 | 4/5 | 1/5 |
| Total |  | **84/85** | **82/85** | **54/85** | **48/85** |

Table 15.4 shows the comparisons of DL-TND to Neural Cleanse (NC) (Wang et al., 2019b) on TrojanNets and cleanNets ($T_1 = 0.7$). The results for DF-TND can be found in (Wang et al., 2020d).

Finally, after detecting a trained model has backdoors, we can apply the model sanitization technique proposed by Zhao et al. (2020a), which uses limited clean dataset to mitigate the Trojan effects while maintaining high clean accuracy.

## 15.4 Extended reading

- Yang et al. (2020a) study how self-attention U-Net can enhance the characterization of adversarial audio examples.

# CHAPTER 16

# Adversarial robustness of beyond neural network models

Adversarial robustness of neural network models have been extensively studied, and up to this chapter we were mainly discussing attack, defense and verification for neural networks. Many other continuous machine learning models, such as support vector machines (SVM) or logistic regression models, can be viewed as a special kind of neural networks, so that most of the techniques developed for neural networks can be immediately applied. However, there are many other important machine learning models that involve some "discrete" components, and the studies on neural networks cannot be directly extended to those models. For example, K-nearest neighbor (KNN) is a very important fundamental machine learning model, where prediction is made based on one or few closest samples in the training dataset. The decision boundary of KNN can be visualized as in Fig. 16.1, which is nonsmooth and nondifferentiable. Also, a decision tree or decision forest (an ensemble of multiple decision trees) makes discrete decisions based on some cut-offs of feature values, so its decision function is discrete rather than continuous. Due to the discrete properties of those models, we need different ways for attack, verification, and defense.

In this chapter, we discuss how to evaluate and improve the robustness of two important discrete nonneural network models: K-nearest-neighbor (KNN) classifiers and decision tree ensembles, including gradient boosting decision tree (GBDT) and random forest (RF) models. In general, we will show that measuring the robustness of these models can be formulated as optimization problems, similar to neural networks, despite the fact that those optimization problems involve discrete variables. We will then show that attacking those models is equivalent to finding a primal feasible solution to the optimization problem, whereas robustness verification is equivalent to finding a dual solution to give a lower bound of those optimization problems. We will also discuss how to enhance the robustness of those discrete models.

Before going to detail, we would like to emphasize that there are several good reasons to study the robustness of those discrete machine learning models, as listed below:

*Adversarial Robustness for Machine Learning*
https://doi.org/10.1016/B978-0-12-824020-5.00027-2

1. Although neural networks are good at extracting informative features from images/audio/text, there are many other applications where neural networks may not outperform other classical machine learning models. In particular, the gradient boosting decision tree (GBDT) model is more widely used than neural networks in many data mining tasks. Many Kaggle data mining competitions are won by GBDT models, and GBDT is still widely used in ranking systems in industry. Hence it is important to understand how to measure and improve the robustness of these discrete models.

2. Discrete structures may be more robust than neural networks since the discrete operations are less sensitive to small perturbations. Several practical defense approaches have combined nearest-neighbor classifier with neural networks (Papernot and McDaniel, 2018; Dubey et al., 2019; Sitawarin and Wagner, 2019). Studying the robustness of discrete models is thus essential for understanding whether they can provide improved robustness.

## 16.1 Evaluating the robustness of K-nearest-neighbor models

Nearest-neighbor (NN) classifiers predict the label of a testing instance by one or $K$ closest samples in the database. Assume that there are $C$ labels in total. We use $\{(x_1, y_1), \ldots, (x_n, y_n)\}$ to denote the database where each $x_i$ is a $d$-dimensional vector, and $y_i \in \{1, \ldots, C\}$ is the corresponding label. A $K$-NN classifier $f : \mathbb{R}^d \to \{1, \ldots, C\}$ maps a test instance to a predicted label. Given a test instance $z \in \mathbb{R}^d$, the classifier first identifies the $K$-nearest neighbors $\{x_{\pi(1)}, \ldots, x_{\pi(K)}\}$ based on the Euclidean distance $\|x_i - z\|$ and then predicts the final label by majority voting among $\{y_{\pi(1)}, \ldots, y_{\pi(K)}\}$.

Given a test sample $z$, assume that it is correctly classified as class-1 by the NN model. An adversarial perturbation is defined as $\delta \in \mathbb{R}^d$ such that $f(z + \delta) \neq 1$. Robustness evaluation aims to find the minimum-norm adversarial perturbation

$$\delta^* = \arg\min_{\delta} \|\delta\| \quad \text{s.t.} \quad f(z + \delta) \neq 1, \tag{16.1}$$

and we define $\epsilon^* = \|\delta^*\|$ as the norm of this perturbation. In many cases it is challenging to obtain the optimal solution of (16.1), so we will discuss algorithms for attack and verification. Attack algorithms aim to find a feasible (but may be subpotimal) solution $\delta$ for (16.1), which serves as an

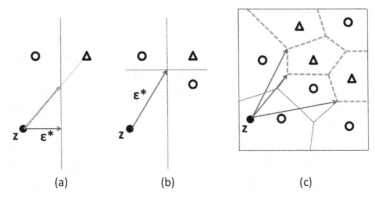

Figure 16.1 Illustration of the minimum adversarial perturbation for 1-NN model. The goal is to perturb $z$ to be classified as triangle class instead of the circle class; (a) shows the optimal perturbation ($\epsilon^*$) with two training points (circle and triangle); (b) shows the optimal perturbation when there are three training points; (c) shows that the optimal perturbation can be computed by evaluating the distance from $z$ to each Voronoi cell of triangle instances.

adversarial example. A verification algorithm aims to find a lower bound $r$ on the minimal perturbation such that

$$f(z + \delta) = 1 \quad \forall \|\delta\| \leq r.$$

Clearly, by definition the maximum lower bound $r^*$ will match the minimum perturbation norm $\epsilon^*$ if both attack and verification are optimal. When $r < r^*$, we say the verification algorithm is sound but incomplete (more discussions about complete versus incomplete verification can be found in Chapter 7.

For simplicity, we will mainly focus on the $\ell_2$ norm with 1-NN model (only looking at the closest sample in the database) and then generalize to $K > 1$ later.

First, let's consider some simple examples to gain intuition what would be the optimal adversarial example for the 1-NN model. In Fig. 16.1(a), we have two points (a circle and a triangle) in the database. For the testing sample $z$, it is predicted as a circle, and we would like to know the minimum perturbation to change the prediction (nearest neighbor becomes a triangle). A naive way is to find the perturbation on the direction pointing to the triangle, but in fact we cannot find the minimum perturbation on that direction. When there are only one circle and one triangle, the minimum perturbation will be pointing from $z$ to the bisection hyperplane between two training samples (blue (dark gray in print version) $\epsilon^*$

in Fig. 16.1(a)). However, when there are more than two samples, it becomes insufficient to check the projection to each bisection hyperplane. For example, in Fig. 16.1(b), there are two circles and one triangle, and the optimal perturbation ($\epsilon^*$ in blue (dark gray in print version)) is pointing to the intersection of two bisection hyperplanes (two dash lines). If we check the perturbation from $z$ to all the intersections of bisection hyperplanes, then we will be able to find the minimum adversarial perturbation. However, as the number of intersections of bisections grows exponentially to the number of training samples, it becomes computationally intractable to conduct an exhausted search.

In fact, the decision boundary of a 1–NN model can be captured by the Voronoi diagram (see Fig. 16.1(c)). In the Voronoi diagram, each training instance $x_i$ forms a cell, and the decision boundary of the cell is captured by the convex boundary formed by bisections between $x_i$ and its neighbors. We can thus obtain the minimum adversarial perturbation by computing the distances from $z$ to all the cells with $y_i \neq 1$. However, to compute the distance, we need to check all the faces (captured by one bisection hyperplane) and angles (intersections of more than one bisection hyperplanes) of the cell.

For the two-dimensional space ($d = 2$), it has been shown by Aurenhammer and Klein (1999) that each cell can only have finite faces and angles and there exists a polynomial-time algorithm for computing a Voronoi diagram. In general, for $d$–dimensional problems with $n$ points, Voronoi diagram computation requires $O(n \log n + n^{\frac{d}{2}})$ time, which works for low-dimensional problems. However, the time complexity grows exponentially with dimension $d$, so in general, it is hard to use this algorithm unless $d$ is very small.

## A primal-dual quadratic programming formulation

Computing minimum adversarial perturbations for ReLU networks is NP-hard (Katz et al., 2017). Also, as discussed in the previous section, we can connect it to the Voronoi diagram computation, but the solver will require exponential time in dimensionality. So is it NP-hard to compute the minimum adversarial perturbation for 1–NN? Surprisingly, the answer is no, and we will describe an efficient algorithm for doing that.

For a given instance $z$, if we want to perturb it so that $z + \delta$ is closer to $x_j$ with $y_j \neq 1$ than to all class-1 instances, then the problem of finding the minimum perturbation can be formulated as

$$\epsilon^{(j)} = \min_{\delta} \frac{1}{2}\delta^T\delta \quad \text{s.t. } \|z + \delta - x_j\|^2 \leq \|z + \delta - x_i\|^2 \quad \forall i, y_i = 1. \quad (16.2)$$

Note that this formulation was proposed by (Wang et al., 2019c; Yang et al., 2020f). (Wang et al., 2019c) further shows that (16.2) can be solved in polynomial time as follows.

Each constraint in the formulation can be rewritten as

$$\delta^T(x_j - x_i) + \frac{\|z - x_i\|^2 - \|z - x_j\|^2}{2} \geq 0.$$

Therefore (16.2) becomes

$$\epsilon^{(j)} = \min_{\delta: A\delta + b \geq 0} \{\frac{1}{2}\delta^T\delta\} := P^{(j)}(\delta), \quad (16.3)$$

where $A \in \mathbb{R}^{n \times d}$ and $b \in \mathbb{R}^n$ with $y_i = 1$, $a_i = (x_j - x_i)$, and $b_i = \frac{\|z-x_i\|^2 - \|z-x_j\|^2}{2}$ for each row $i$ (**0** otherwise). By solving the quadratic programming (QP) problem (16.3) for each $\{j : y_j \neq 1\}$, the final minimum adversarial perturbation norm is $\epsilon^* = \min_{j:y_j \neq 1} \sqrt{2\epsilon^{(j)}}$. It has been shown that convex quadratic programming can be solved in polynomial time (Kozlov et al., 1980), so this formulation leads to a *polynomial-time algorithm* for finding $\epsilon^*$. However, naively solving this will still be too expensive as the number of constraint grows quadratically. We will thus introduce the dual problems below, which not only give an efficient way for computing robustness of 1-NN model, but also provide ways to compute a certifiable robustness bound for 1-NN robustness verification.

## Dual quadratic programming problems

We also introduce the dual form of each QP as it is more efficient to solve in practice and will lead to a family of verification algorithms for adversarial robustness. The dual problem of (16.3) can be written as

$$\max_{\lambda \geq 0} \left\{ -\frac{1}{2}\lambda^T A A^T \lambda - \lambda^T b \right\} := D^{(j)}(\lambda), \quad (16.4)$$

where $\lambda \in \mathbb{R}^{n^+}$ are the corresponding dual variables. This follows the standard derivation of dual QP problems (e.g., almost identical to the primal and dual problems of support vector machines). The primal-dual relationship connects primal and dual variables by $\delta = A^T\lambda$. Based on weak duality, we have $D^{(j)}(\lambda) \leq P^{(j)}(\delta)$ for any dual feasible solution $\lambda$ and primal feasible solution $\delta$. Furthermore, based on Slater's condition, we can show that (16.3) satisfies strong duality, so $D^{(j)}(\lambda^*) = P^{(j)}(\delta^*)$, where $\lambda^*$ and $\delta^*$ are optimal solutions for the primal and dual problems, respectively, if $x_j^- \neq x_i^+$ for all $i \in [n^+]$.[1] Based on strong duality, we have

$$\frac{1}{2}(\epsilon^*)^2 = \min_{j \in [n^-]} \{P^{(j)}(\delta^*)\}$$

$$= \min_{j \in [n^-]} \{\max_{\lambda \geq 0} D^{(j)}(\lambda)\}$$

$$\geq \min_{j \in [n^-]} \{D^{(j)}(\lambda^{(j)})\} \text{ with feasible } \lambda^{(j)}, \tag{16.5}$$

so a set of feasible solutions $\{\lambda^{(j)}\}_{j \in [n^-]}$ leads to a lower bound of the minimum adversarial perturbation. In summary, we conclude the primal–dual relationship between 1-NN attack and verification:

- A primal feasible solution of $P^{(j)}$ is a successful attack and gives us an upper bound of $\epsilon^*$. Therefore we can solve a subset of QPs and select the minimum. Usually, $x_j^-$ closer to $z$ will lead to a smaller adversarial perturbation, so in practice we can sort $x_j^-$ by the distance to $z$, solve the subproblems one by one, and stop at any time. It will give a valid adversarial perturbation. After solving all the subproblems, the result will reach the minimum, i.e., the minimum adversarial perturbation norm $\epsilon^*$.

- A set of dual feasible solutions $\{\lambda^{(j)}\}_{j \in [n^-]}$ will lead to a lower bound of $\epsilon^*$ according to (16.5). Thus any heuristic method for setting up a set of dual feasible solutions will give us a lower bound, which can be used for robustness verification. If all the dual problems are solved exactly, then we will derive the tightest (maximum) lower bound, which is also $\epsilon^*$.

## Robustness verification for 1-NN models

Here we give an example of how to quickly set up dual variables to give a nontrivial lower bound of the minimum adversarial perturbation without solving any subproblem exactly. For a dual problem $D^{(j)}$, consider only having one variable $\lambda_i^{(j)}$ to be the optimization variable and fixing all the remaining variables zero; then the optimal closed-form solution for this

---

[1] If the precondition holds, then any point in a small ball around the center $\delta = x_j^- - z$ will be a feasible solution, which implies strong duality by Slater's condition.

simplified dual QP problem is

$$\lambda_i^{(j)} = \max\left(0, -\frac{b_i}{\|a_i\|^2}\right),$$

$$D^{(j)}([0, \ldots, 0, \lambda_i^{(j)}, 0, \ldots, 0]) = \frac{\max(-b_i, 0)^2}{2\|a_i\|^2}.$$

(16.6)

Since $b_i = (\|z - x_i^+\|^2 - \|z - x_j^-\|^2)/2$ and $a_i = x_j^- - x_i^+$ can be easily computed, we can use (16.5) to obtain a guaranteed lower bound $\epsilon^*$ by:

$$\min_{j \in [n^-]} \max_{i \in [n^+]} \frac{\max(\|z - x_j^-\|^2 - \|z - x_i^+\|^2, 0)}{2\|x_j^- - x_i^+\|}.$$

(16.7)

In addition, the certified bound in the above formulation has an interesting geometrical meaning. The inner value captures the distance between $z$ and the bisection between $x_i^+$ and $x_j^-$. Perturbing $z$ to this bisection is the smallest perturbation to make it closer to $x_j^-$ than $x_i^+$. If we want to perturb $z$ so that the nearest neighbor is $x_j^-$, then we need to make sure $z$ is closer to $x_j^-$ than any data point with positive label, so we take the max operation among all the distances to bisections. And to make $z$ being classified as the negative label, we only need to make it to be closer to one of the $x_j^-$ than positive samples, so we take the min outside. In general, we can also get improved lower bounds by optimizing more coordinates rather than one variable for each subproblem, which could lead to tighter bound but may require additional computation.

## Efficient algorithms for computing 1-NN robustness

To compute the exact robustness of a 1-NN classifier, we need to solve all the primal problems (16.3), or equivalently, the corresponding dual problems (16.4). Although they are polynomial time solvable, in practice a naive algorithm is still too slow since there are $O(n)$ quadratic problems involved and each has $O(n)$ dual variables. Typically solving each QP takes $O(n^2)$, so roughly $O(n^3)$ time is required. This is too expensive when $n$ is large.

To resolve this problem, Wang et al. (2019c) developed a method to efficiently solve the $O(n)$ subproblems. The main idea is to remove unnecessary variables and unnecessary subproblems by exploiting the primal-dual relationships. Intuitively, the final solution is the minimum among all the subproblem solutions, so if we know that the lower bound of the solution of a subproblem is larger than the current solution, then the subproblem can be removed. As shown in the previous two sections, based on duality, *any* dual solution can give a lower bound of primal solution, so we can remove the subproblem when we found a dual solution with objective function value larger than the current minimum. Therefore, we can solve all the subproblems simultaneously and progressively remove subproblems.

On the other hand, for each subproblem, we can also try to remove unnecessary dual variables (corresponding to primal constraints). As each constraint corresponds to another point $x_i$ where we hope the point after perturbation $(z + \delta)$ is closer to the target point $x_j$ than to $x_i$, intuitively, if the point is far away, then we can remove the constraint. This can be also done by a screening algorithm derived from the primal dual relationship, and the interested readers can check more details in (Wang et al., 2019c). In general, how to efficiently compute the minimum adversarial perturbation is still an unresolved problem.

## Extending beyond 1-NN

Next, we extend the above-mentioned robustness evaluation approach to $K$-NN models with $K > 1$. Consider the binary classification case, we let $\mathbb{S}^+ = \{x_1^+, \dots, x_{n^+}^+\}$ be the set of samples with the same label with $z$ and $\mathbb{S}^- = \{x_1^-, \dots, x_{n^-}^-\}$ be the set of samples with opposite label to $z$. We assume $K$ is an odd number to avoid the tie in $K$-NN voting and both $n^+, n^-$ are large enough. We can list all the possible combinations of $(\mathbb{I}, \mathbb{J})$ with $\mathbb{I} \subseteq [n^+]$, $\mathbb{J} \subseteq [n^-]$, $|\mathbb{I}| = (K-1)/2$, and $|\mathbb{J}| = (K+1)/2$, and then solve the following QP problem to force $z + \delta$ to be closer to $x_j^-$ for all $j \in [\mathbb{J}]$ than to all instances in $\mathbb{S}^+$ except $x_i^+$ for all $i \in [\mathbb{I}]$:

$$
\epsilon^{(\mathbb{I}, \mathbb{J})} = \min_{\delta} \frac{1}{2} \delta^T \delta
$$
$$
\text{s.t. } \|z + \delta - x_j^-\|^2 \leq \|z + \delta - x_i^+\|^2 \qquad (16.8)
$$
$$
\forall i \in [n^+] - \mathbb{I}, \ \forall j \in \mathbb{J}.
$$

Then the norm of the minimum adversarial perturbation can be computed by $\epsilon^* = \min_{(\mathbb{I}, \mathbb{J})} \sqrt{2\epsilon^{(\mathbb{I}, \mathbb{J})}}$. There will be exponential number of QPs in totat, so it is usually impossible to compute the minimum adversarial perturbation by iterating all QPs. However, we can still obtain upper and lower bounds corresponding to attack and verification. For an upper bound (attack), we can just choose a small number of $(\mathbb{I}, \mathbb{J})$ tuples and only solve these QPs. The quality of the bound will rely on how good is the selected subset of QPs.

For a lower bound (verification), by extending (16.7) to the $K > 1$ case we have the following lemma.

**Lemma 3.** *For a K-NN model with odd K, we have the following lower bound for the minimum adversarial perturbation:*

$$\epsilon^* \geq s\,\text{th}\min_{j\in[n^-]}\left(s\,\text{th}\max_{i\in[n^+]}\sqrt{2\epsilon^{(i,j)}}\right), \tag{16.9}$$

*where $s = (K+1)/2$ is a positive integer, "$s$ th min" and "$s$ th max" select the sth minimum value and the sth maximum value, respectively, and*

$$\epsilon^{(i,j)} = \frac{\max(\|z - x_j^-\|^2 - \|z - x_i^+\|^2, 0)^2}{8\|x_j^- - x_i^+\|^2}.$$

This is a simple extension of the 1-NN case. Note that the lower bound (16.9) can be efficiently computed. It requires $O(n^2 d)$ time to compute all $\epsilon^{(i,j)}$, and then the top-$s$ selection can be done in linear time, so the overall complexity is just $O(n^2 d)$, which is independent of $K$.

## Robustness of KNN vs neural network on simple problems

Using the above-mentioned algorithms implemented by Wang et al. (2019c), we are able to 1) efficiently compute the exact robustness of 1-NN models for a reasonable number of examples (e.g., for MNIST dataset, Wang et al. (2019c) showed that we can conduct evaluation in few seconds) and 2) for K-NN models, compute the certified robustness (verification) efficiently using Lemma 3.

With these algorithms, we can then compare the robustness between K-NN models and neural networks. We compare *certified robust errors*, defined as the fractions with lower bounds less than the given threshold (if an instance is wrongly classified, then the lower bound is 0), of 1-NN, a simple convolutional network (ConvNet), and a strong $\ell_2$ certified defense network (RandSmooth) (Cohen et al., 2019) in Fig. 16.2 (see Chapter 13 for more details on randomized smoothing). The results show that 1-NN can achieve better certified robust errors than neural networks on these two datasets. This is partially because the proposed verification algorithm provides very tight certified regions for NN classifiers. Note that this is not saying that K-NN is more robust than neural networks on more complex datasets such as CIFAR and ImageNet. However, this is showing K-NN could obtain better certified robust errors on some simpler tasks.

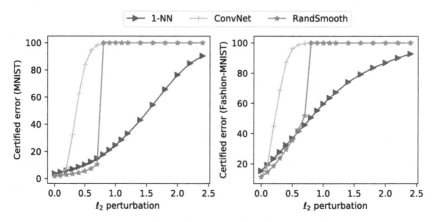

**Figure 16.2** Comparing certified (robust) errors of 1-NN, ConvNet (a simple convolutional network), and RandSmooth (a defense neural network via random smoothing proposed by Cohen et al. (2019)). For RandSmooth, we choose the noise standard deviation $\sigma = 0.2$. 1-NN is more robust on these two datasets.

## 16.2 Defenses with nearest-neighbor classifiers

We have shown how to compute the robustness of K-NN, but can we use these techniques to improve the robustness of K-NN? The answer is affirmative.

Note that in the original K-NN models defined in the Euclidean space, we measure the distance between two points by $\|x - x'\|_2$. However, we can generalize the distance measurement to a family of Mahalanobis distances as follows:

$$d_M(x, x') = (x - x')^\top M(x - x'), \qquad (16.10)$$

where $M \in \mathbb{R}^{D \times D}$ is a positive semidefinite matrix. We can then try to learn a positive semidefinite matrix $M$ to minimize the certified robust training error.

For a classifier $f$ on an instance $(x, y)$, following the previous sections, we can define the *minimal adversarial perturbation* as

$$\underset{\delta}{\arg\min} \ \|\delta\| \ \text{ s.t. } f(x + \delta) \neq y, \qquad (16.11)$$

which is the smallest perturbation that could lead to "misclassification". Note that if $(x, y)$ is not correctly classified, the minimal adversarial perturbation is the zero vector $\mathbf{0}$. Let $\delta^*(x, y)$ denote the optimal solution, and let $\epsilon^*(x, y) = \|\delta^*(x, y)\|$ be the optimal value. Since the Mahalanobis $K$-NN classifier is parameterized by a positive semidefinite matrix $M$ and the training set $\mathbb{S}$, we further let the optimal solution $\delta_{\mathbb{S}}^*(x, y; M)$ and the optimal value $\epsilon_{\mathbb{S}}^*(x, y; M)$ explicitly indicate their dependence on $M$ and $\mathbb{S}$.

To learn an $M$ that leads to robust $K$-NN, Wang et al. (2020c) define the objective function as

$$\min_{G \in \mathbb{R}^{D \times D}} \frac{1}{N} \sum_{i=1}^{N} \ell \left( \epsilon_{\mathbb{S}-\{(x_i, y_i)\}}^*(x_i, y_i; M) \right) \quad \text{s.t. } M = G^\top G, \qquad (16.12)$$

where $\ell : \mathbb{R} \to \mathbb{R}$ is a nonincreasing function, e.g., the hinge loss $[1 - \epsilon]_+$, exponential loss $\exp(-\epsilon)$, logistic loss $\log(1 + \exp(-\epsilon))$, or "negative" loss $-\epsilon$. The constraint $M = G^\top G$ is used to enforce the positive semidefiniteness of the $M$ matrix, otherwise the Mahalanobis distance defined by $M$ will not be a valid distance metric. Also, the minimal adversarial perturbation is defined on the training set excluding $(x_i, y_i)$ itself, since otherwise a 1-nearest neighbor classifier with any distance measurement will have 100% accuracy. Therefore, the above objectie can be viewed as minimizing the "leave-one-out" certified robust error.

As mentioned in the previous section, computing the exact $\epsilon_{\mathbb{S}}^*(x, y; M)$ is too expensive and becomes impossible when $K > 1$. Therefore we focus on improving the *certified robust error*. Let $\underline{\epsilon}^*(x, y)$ be a lower bound of the norm of the minimal adversarial perturbation $\epsilon^*(x, y)$, which can be computed by extending our $K$-NN certified bound derived in Lemma 3 to the Mahalanobis distance setting. Since the derivation is quite simple, we directly show the results below. The detailed proof can be found in (Wang et al., 2020c).

**Theorem 4** (Robustness verification for Mahalanobis $K$-NN). *Given a Mahalanobis $K$-NN classifier parameterized by a neighbor parameter $K$, a training dataset $\mathbb{S}$, and a positive semidefinite matrix $M$, for any instance $(x_{test}, y_{test})$, we have*

$$\epsilon^*(x_{test}, y_{test}; M) \geq k \operatorname{th\,min}_{j:y_j \neq y_{test}} \ k \operatorname{th\,max}_{i:y_i = y_{test}} \ \tilde{\epsilon}(x_i, x_j, x_{test}; M), \qquad (16.13)$$

*where $k \operatorname{th\,max}$ and $k \operatorname{th\,min}$ select the $k$th maximum and $k$th minimum, respectively, with $k = (K + 1)/2$, and*

$$\tilde{\epsilon}(x^+, x^-, x; M) = \frac{d_M(x, x^-) - d_M(x, x^+)}{2\sqrt{(x^+ - x^-)^\top M^\top M(x^+ - x^-)}}. \qquad (16.14)$$

Note that Theorem 4 is a generalization of Lemma 3 to the Mahalanobis distance setting.

By replacing the $\epsilon^*$ in (16.12) with the lower bound derived in Theorem 4 we get a trainable objective function for adversarially robust metric learning:

$$\min_{G \in \mathbb{R}^{D \times D}} \frac{1}{N} \sum_{t=1}^{N} \ell \left( \underset{j: y_j \neq y_t}{k\, \text{th} \min} \, k \underset{i: i \neq t, y_i = y_t}{\text{th} \max} \tilde{\epsilon}(x_t, x_j, x_i; M) \right) \quad \text{s.t. } M = G^{\top} G.$$

$$(16.15)$$

Although Eq. (16.15) is trainable since $\tilde{\epsilon}$ is a function of $M$, for large datasets, it is time-consuming to run the inner min-max procedure. Furthermore, since what we really care is the generalization performance of the learned metric instead of the leave-one-out robust training error, it is unnecessary to compute the exact solution. Therefore, instead of computing the $k$th max and $k$th min exactly, Wang et al. (2020c) proposed to sample positive and negative instances from the neighborhood of each training instance, which leads to the following formulation:

$$\min_{G \in \mathbb{R}^{D \times D}} \frac{1}{N} \sum_{i=1}^{N} \ell \left( \tilde{\epsilon} \left( \text{randnear}_M^+(x_i), \text{randnear}_M^-(x_i), x_i; M \right) \right) \quad \text{s.t. } M = G^{\top} G,$$

$$(16.16)$$

where $\text{randnear}_M^+(\cdot)$ denotes a sampling procedure for an instance in the same class within $x_i$'s neighborhood, and $\text{randnear}_M^-(\cdot)$ denotes a sampling procedure for an instance in a different class, also within a neighborhood of $x_i$, and the distances are measured by the Mahalanobis distance $d_M$. Wang et al. (2020c) showed that sampling instances from a fixed number of nearest instances is sufficient. As a result, the optimization formulation (16.16) approximately minimizes the certified robust error and significantly improves computational efficiency.

The overall training algorithm is as follows. At every iteration, $G$ is updated with the gradient of the loss function, whereas the calculations of $\text{randnear}_M^+(\cdot)$ and $\text{randnear}_M^-(\cdot)$ do not contribute to the gradient for efficient and stable computation. The algorithm is called *adversarially robust metric learning* (ARML).

Clearly, ARML can significantly improve the robustness of KNN models. In Table 16.1, we show that in 1-NN, when the exact robustness can be computed by the method mentioned in the previous section, ARML

**Table 16.1** Certified robust errors of Mahalanobis 1-NN. The best (minimum) certified robust errors among all methods are in bold. Note that the certified robust errors of 1-NN are also the optimal empirical robust errors (attack errors), and these robust errors at the radius 0 are also the clean errors.

|  | $\ell_2$-radius | 0.000 | 0.500 | 1.000 | 1.500 | 2.000 | 2.500 |
|---|---|---|---|---|---|---|---|
| | Euclidean | 0.033 | 0.112 | 0.274 | 0.521 | 0.788 | 0.945 |
| | NCA | 0.025 | 0.140 | 0.452 | 0.839 | 0.977 | 1.000 |
| MNIST | LMNN | 0.032 | 0.641 | 0.999 | 1.000 | 1.000 | 1.000 |
| | ITML | 0.073 | 0.571 | 0.928 | 1.000 | 1.000 | 1.000 |
| | LFDA | 0.152 | 1.000 | 1.000 | 1.000 | 1.000 | 1.000 |
| | ARML (Ours) | **0.024** | **0.089** | **0.222** | **0.455** | **0.757** | **0.924** |
|  | $\ell_2$-radius | 0.000 | 0.500 | 1.000 | 1.500 | 2.000 | 2.500 |
| | Euclidean | 0.145 | 0.381 | 0.606 | 0.790 | 0.879 | 0.943 |
| Fashion-MNIST | NCA | **0.116** | 0.538 | 0.834 | 0.950 | 0.998 | 1.000 |
| | LMNN | 0.142 | 0.756 | 0.991 | 1.000 | 1.000 | 1.000 |
| | ITML | 0.163 | 0.672 | 0.929 | 0.998 | 1.000 | 1.000 |
| | LFDA | 0.211 | 1.000 | 1.000 | 1.000 | 1.000 | 1.000 |
| | ARML (Ours) | 0.127 | **0.348** | **0.568** | **0.763** | **0.859** | **0.928** |
|  | $\ell_2$-radius | 0.000 | 0.100 | 0.200 | 0.300 | 0.400 | 0.500 |
| | Euclidean | 0.320 | 0.513 | 0.677 | 0.800 | 0.854 | 0.880 |
| | NCA | **0.130** | 0.252 | 0.404 | 0.584 | 0.733 | 0.836 |
| Splice | LMNN | 0.190 | 0.345 | 0.533 | 0.697 | 0.814 | 0.874 |
| | ITML | 0.306 | 0.488 | 0.679 | 0.809 | 0.862 | 0.882 |
| | LFDA | 0.264 | 0.434 | 0.605 | 0.760 | 0.845 | 0.872 |
| | ARML (Ours) | **0.130** | **0.233** | **0.370** | **0.526** | **0.652** | **0.758** |
|  | $\ell_2$-radius | 0.000 | 0.100 | 0.200 | 0.300 | 0.400 | 0.500 |
| | Euclidean | 0.032 | 0.119 | 0.347 | 0.606 | 0.829 | 0.969 |
| | NCA | 0.034 | 0.202 | 0.586 | 0.911 | 0.997 | 1.000 |
| Pendigits | LMNN | 0.029 | 0.183 | 0.570 | 0.912 | 0.995 | 0.999 |
| | ITML | 0.049 | 0.308 | 0.794 | 0.991 | 1.000 | 1.000 |
| | LFDA | 0.042 | 0.236 | 0.603 | 0.912 | 0.998 | 1.000 |
| | ARML (Ours) | **0.028** | **0.115** | **0.344** | **0.598** | **0.823** | **0.967** |
|  | $\ell_2$-radius | 0.000 | 0.150 | 0.300 | 0.450 | 0.600 | 0.750 |
| | Euclidean | 0.108 | 0.642 | 0.864 | 0.905 | 0.928 | 0.951 |
| | NCA | 0.103 | 0.710 | 0.885 | 0.915 | 0.940 | 0.963 |
| Satimage | LMNN | **0.092** | 0.665 | 0.871 | 0.912 | 0.944 | 0.969 |
| | ITML | 0.127 | 0.807 | 0.979 | 1.000 | 1.000 | 1.000 |
| | LFDA | 0.125 | 0.836 | 0.919 | 0.956 | 0.992 | 1.000 |
| | ARML (Ours) | 0.095 | **0.605** | **0.839** | **0.899** | **0.920** | **0.946** |

*continued on next page*

**Table 16.1** (*continued*)

|  | $\ell_2$-radius | 0.000 | 0.500 | 1.000 | 1.500 | 2.000 | 2.500 |
|---|---|---|---|---|---|---|---|
|  | Euclidean | 0.045 | 0.224 | 0.585 | 0.864 | **0.970** | **0.999** |
|  | NCA | 0.056 | 0.384 | 0.888 | 0.987 | 1.000 | 1.000 |
| USPS | LMNN | 0.046 | 0.825 | 1.000 | 1.000 | 1.000 | 1.000 |
|  | ITML | 0.060 | 0.720 | 0.999 | 1.000 | 1.000 | 1.000 |
|  | LFDA | 0.098 | 1.000 | 1.000 | 1.000 | 1.000 | 1.000 |
|  | ARML | **0.043** | **0.204** | **0.565** | **0.857** | **0.970** | **0.999** |

can consistently improve the robustness over 1-NN model with the original Euclidean norm. Note that in addition to Euclidean (original Euclidean space 1-NN model) and ARML (adversarially robust metric learning), in the comparison, we also include some traditional metric learning baselines including NCA (Goldberger et al., 2004), LMNN (Weinberger and Saul, 2009), ITML (Davis et al., 2007), and LFDA (Sugiyama, 2007). Note that those methods try to learn a better $M$ metric to improve the classification performance. We can observe that the ARML algorithm can consistently achieve the best robustness.

On the other hand, when running KNN with $K > 1$, as mentioned in the previous section, it becomes computational infeasible to compute the exact robustness score. However, we can still compute certified robustness of KNN models using Theorem 4, and Table 16.2 demonstrates that ARML can consistently improve the certified error. For more empirical results, we refer the readers to (Wang et al., 2020c), who also compare the certified robustness of ARML with neural networks on some simple datasets such as MNIST and FashionMNIST.

## 16.3 Evaluating the robustness of decision tree ensembles

Next, we discuss the adversarial robustness of decision-tree based classifiers, including several widely used ensemble tree models such as random forest (RF) and gradient boosting decision tree (GBDT) models. These models have shown significant performance, outperforming neural networks on many data mining tasks.

### Robustness of a single decision tree

First, we discuss the case when there is a single decision tree. We assume that the decision tree has $n$ nodes and the root node is indexed as 0. For a given example $x = [x_1, \ldots, x_d]$ with $d$ features, starting from the root node,

**Table 16.2** Certified robust errors (left) and empirical robust errors (right) of Mahalanobis $K$-NN. The best (minimum) robust errors among all methods are in bold. The empirical robust errors at the radius 0 are also the clean errors.

| | | Certified robust errors | | | | | | Empirical robust errors | | | | | |
|---|---|---|---|---|---|---|---|---|---|---|---|---|---|
| | $\ell_2$-radius | 0.000 | 0.500 | 1.000 | 1.500 | 2.000 | 2.500 | 0.000 | 0.500 | 1.000 | 1.500 | 2.000 | 2.500 |
| MNIST | Euclidean | 0.038 | 0.134 | 0.360 | 0.618 | 0.814 | 0.975 | 0.031 | 0.063 | 0.104 | 0.155 | 0.204 | 0.262 |
| | NCA | **0.030** | 0.175 | 0.528 | 0.870 | 0.986 | 1.000 | **0.027** | 0.063 | 0.120 | 0.216 | 0.330 | 0.535 |
| | LMNN | 0.040 | 0.669 | 1.000 | 1.000 | 1.000 | 1.000 | 0.036 | 0.121 | 0.336 | 0.775 | 0.972 | 1.000 |
| | ITML | 0.106 | 0.731 | 0.943 | 1.000 | 1.000 | 1.000 | 0.084 | 0.218 | 0.355 | 0.510 | 0.669 | 0.844 |
| | LFDA | 0.237 | 1.000 | 1.000 | 1.000 | 1.000 | 1.000 | 0.215 | 1.000 | 1.000 | 1.000 | 1.000 | 1.000 |
| | ARML | 0.034 | **0.101** | **0.276** | **0.537** | **0.760** | **0.951** | 0.032 | **0.055** | **0.077** | **0.109** | **0.160** | **0.213** |
| | $\ell_2$-radius | 0.000 | 0.500 | 1.000 | 1.500 | 2.000 | 2.500 | 0.000 | 0.500 | 1.000 | 1.500 | 2.000 | 2.500 |
| Fashion-MNIST | Euclidean | 0.160 | 0.420 | 0.650 | 0.800 | 0.895 | 0.946 | 0.143 | 0.227 | 0.298 | 0.360 | 0.420 | 0.489 |
| | NCA | **0.144** | 0.557 | 0.832 | 0.946 | 1.000 | 1.000 | **0.121** | 0.232 | 0.343 | 0.483 | 0.624 | 0.780 |
| | LMNN | 0.158 | 0.792 | 0.991 | 1.000 | 1.000 | 1.000 | 0.140 | 0.364 | 0.572 | 0.846 | 0.983 | 0.999 |
| | ITML | 0.236 | 0.784 | 0.949 | 1.000 | 1.000 | 1.000 | 0.209 | 0.460 | 0.692 | 0.892 | 0.978 | 1.000 |
| | LFDA | 0.291 | 1.000 | 1.000 | 1.000 | 1.000 | 1.000 | 0.263 | 0.870 | 0.951 | 0.975 | 0.988 | 0.995 |
| | ARML | 0.152 | **0.371** | **0.589** | **0.755** | **0.856** | **0.924** | 0.134 | **0.202** | **0.274** | **0.344** | **0.403** | **0.487** |
| | $\ell_2$-radius | 0.000 | 0.500 | 1.000 | 1.500 | 2.000 | 2.500 | 0.000 | 0.500 | 1.000 | 1.500 | 2.000 | 2.500 |
| Splice | Euclidean | 0.333 | 0.558 | 0.826 | 0.965 | 0.988 | 0.996 | 0.306 | 0.431 | 0.526 | 0.608 | 0.676 | 0.743 |
| | NCA | **0.103** | **0.209** | 0.415 | 0.659 | 0.824 | 0.921 | **0.103** | **0.173** | 0.274 | 0.414 | 0.570 | 0.684 |
| | LMNN | 0.149 | 0.332 | 0.630 | 0.851 | 0.969 | 0.994 | 0.149 | 0.241 | 0.357 | 0.492 | 0.621 | 0.722 |
| | ITML | 0.279 | 0.571 | 0.843 | 0.974 | 0.995 | 0.997 | 0.279 | 0.423 | 0.525 | 0.603 | 0.675 | 0.751 |
| | LFDA | 0.242 | 0.471 | 0.705 | 0.906 | 0.987 | 0.997 | 0.242 | 0.371 | 0.466 | 0.553 | 0.637 | 0.737 |
| | ARML | 0.128 | 0.221 | **0.345** | **0.509** | **0.666** | **0.819** | 0.128 | 0.196 | **0.273** | **0.380** | **0.497** | **0.639** |

*continued on next page*

**Table 16.2** (*continued*)

| | | Certified robust errors | | | | | | Empirical robust errors | | | | | |
|---|---|---|---|---|---|---|---|---|---|---|---|---|---|
| **Pendigits** | $\ell_2$-radius | 0.000 | 0.100 | 0.200 | 0.300 | 0.400 | 0.500 | 0.000 | 0.100 | 0.200 | 0.300 | 0.400 | 0.500 |
| | Euclidean | 0.039 | 0.126 | 0.316 | 0.577 | 0.784 | 0.937 | 0.036 | 0.085 | 0.155 | 0.248 | 0.371 | 0.528 |
| | NCA | 0.038 | 0.196 | 0.607 | 0.884 | 0.997 | 1.000 | 0.038 | 0.103 | 0.246 | 0.428 | 0.637 | 0.804 |
| | LMNN | 0.034 | 0.180 | 0.568 | 0.898 | 0.993 | 0.999 | **0.030** | 0.096 | 0.246 | 0.462 | 0.681 | 0.862 |
| | ITML | 0.060 | 0.334 | 0.773 | 0.987 | 1.000 | 1.000 | 0.060 | 0.149 | 0.343 | 0.616 | 0.814 | 0.926 |
| | LFDA | 0.047 | 0.228 | 0.595 | 0.904 | 1.000 | 1.000 | 0.043 | 0.104 | 0.248 | 0.490 | 0.705 | 0.842 |
| | ARML | **0.035** | **0.114** | **0.308** | **0.568** | **0.780** | **0.937** | 0.034 | **0.078** | **0.138** | **0.235** | **0.368** | **0.516** |
| **Satimage** | $\ell_2$-radius | 0.000 | 0.150 | 0.300 | 0.450 | 0.600 | 0.750 | 0.000 | 0.150 | 0.300 | 0.450 | 0.600 | 0.750 |
| | Euclidean | **0.101** | 0.579 | 0.842 | 0.899 | 0.927 | 0.948 | 0.091 | 0.237 | 0.482 | 0.682 | **0.816** | 0.897 |
| | NCA | 0.117 | 0.670 | 0.886 | 0.915 | 0.936 | 0.961 | 0.101 | 0.297 | 0.564 | 0.746 | 0.876 | 0.931 |
| | LMNN | 0.105 | 0.613 | 0.855 | 0.914 | 0.944 | 0.961 | **0.090** | 0.269 | 0.548 | 0.737 | 0.855 | 0.910 |
| | ITML | 0.130 | 0.768 | 0.959 | 1.000 | 1.000 | 1.000 | 0.109 | 0.411 | 0.757 | 0.939 | 0.990 | 1.000 |
| | LFDA | 0.128 | 0.779 | 0.904 | 0.958 | 0.995 | 1.000 | 0.112 | 0.389 | 0.673 | 0.860 | 0.950 | 0.986 |
| | ARML | 0.103 | **0.540** | **0.824** | **0.898** | **0.920** | **0.943** | 0.092 | **0.228** | **0.464** | **0.668** | 0.817 | **0.896** |
| **USPS** | $\ell_2$-radius | 0.000 | 0.500 | 1.000 | 1.500 | 2.000 | 2.500 | 0.000 | 0.500 | 1.000 | 1.500 | 2.000 | 2.500 |
| | Euclidean | 0.063 | 0.239 | 0.586 | 0.888 | 0.977 | 1.000 | 0.058 | 0.125 | 0.211 | 0.365 | 0.612 | **0.751** |
| | NCA | 0.072 | 0.367 | 0.903 | 0.986 | 1.000 | 1.000 | 0.063 | 0.158 | 0.365 | 0.686 | 0.899 | 0.980 |
| | LMNN | 0.062 | 0.856 | 1.000 | 1.000 | 1.000 | 1.000 | 0.055 | 0.359 | 0.890 | 0.999 | 1.000 | 1.000 |
| | ITML | 0.082 | 0.696 | 0.999 | 1.000 | 1.000 | 1.000 | 0.072 | 0.273 | 0.708 | 0.987 | 1.000 | 1.000 |
| | LFDA | 0.134 | 1.000 | 1.000 | 1.000 | 1.000 | 1.000 | 0.118 | 0.996 | 1.000 | 1.000 | 1.000 | 1.000 |
| | ARML | **0.057** | **0.203** | **0.527** | **0.867** | **0.971** | **0.997** | **0.053** | **0.118** | **0.209** | **0.344** | **0.572** | 0.785 |

$x$ traverses the decision tree model until reaching a leaf node. Each internal node, say node $i$, has two children and a univariate feature-threshold pair $(t_i, \eta_i)$ to determine the traversal direction: $x$ will be passed to the left child if $x_{t_i} \leq \eta_i$ and to the right child otherwise. Each leaf node has a value $v_i$ corresponding to the predicted class label for a classification tree or a real value for a regression tree.

Similar to the previous sections, we first discuss how to compute the minimum adversarial perturbation that can change the decision of a given test sample. More specifically, for a given tree-based model $f$, a test sample $x$, and the corresponding label $y_0$, the goal is to find

$$r^* = \min_{\delta} \|\delta\|_{\infty} \quad \text{s.t.} \quad f(x + \delta) \neq y_0. \tag{16.17}$$

If $f$ is a single decision tree, there is a simple linear-time algorithm for computing $r^*$. The main idea is to compute a $d$-dimensional box for each leaf node such that any example in this box will fall into this leaf. Mathematically, the box of node $i$ is defined as the Cartesian product $B^i = (l_1^i, r_1^i] \times \cdots \times (l_d^i, r_d^i]$ of $d$ intervals on the real line. By definition the root node has the box $[-\infty, \infty] \times \cdots \times [-\infty, \infty]$, and given the box of an internal node $i$, its children's boxes can be obtained by changing only one interval of the box based on the split condition $(t_i, \eta_i)$. More specifically, if $p$, $q$ are left and right child nodes of node $i$, respectively, then we set their boxes $B^p = (l_1^p, r_1^p] \times \cdots \times (l_d^p, r_d^p]$ and $B^q = (l_1^q, r_1^q] \times \cdots \times (l_d^q, r_d^q]$ by

$$(l_t^p, r_t^p] = \begin{cases} (l_t^i, r_t^i] & \text{if } t \neq t_i, \\ (l_t^i, \min\{r_t^i, \eta_i\}] & \text{if } t = t_i, \end{cases} \quad (l_t^q, r_t^q] = \begin{cases} (l_t^i, r_t^i] & \text{if } t \neq t_i, \\ (\max\{l_t^i, \eta_i\}, r_t^i] & \text{if } t = t_i. \end{cases} \tag{16.18}$$

After computing the boxes for internal nodes, we can also obtain the boxes for leaf nodes using (16.18). Therefore computing the boxes for all the leaf nodes of a decision tree can be done by a traversal (either depth-first or breadth-first) of the tree with time complexity $O(nd)$.

This technique can be easily generalized to the $\ell_p$ norm perturbations with $p < \infty$. In particular, to certify whether there exist any misclassified points under perturbation $\|\delta\|_p \leq \epsilon$, we can enumerate boxes for all $n$ leaf nodes and check the minimum distance from $x_0$ to each box. The following proposition shows that the $\ell_p$ norm distance between a point and a box can be computed in $O(d)$ time, and thus the complete robustness verification problem for a single tree can be solved in $O(dn)$ time.

**Theorem 5.** *Given a box $B = (l_1, r_1] \times \cdots \times (l_d, r_d]$ and a point $\mathbf{x} \in \mathbb{R}^d$, the minimum $\ell_p$ distance $(p \in [0, \infty])$ from $x$ to $B$ is $\|z - x\|_p$, where*

$$
z_i = \begin{cases} x_i, & l_i \le x_i \le u_i, \\ l_i, & x_i < l_i, \\ u_i, & x_i > u_i. \end{cases} \tag{16.19}
$$

We can use this theorem to compute the minimum $\ell_p$ norm perturbation to move the test sample $x$ to the box. The minimum $\ell_p$ norm adversarial perturbation can then be easily computed by enumerating the possibilities to move $x$ to each leaf node with an opposite label.

## Robustness of ensemble decision stumps

A decision stump is a decision tree with only one root node and two leaf nodes. We assume that there are $T$ decision stumps and the $i$th decision stump gives the prediction

$$
f^i(x) = \begin{cases} w_l^i & \text{if } x_{t_i} < \eta^i, \\ w_r^i & \text{if } x_{t_i} \ge \eta^i. \end{cases}
$$

An ensemble of decision stumps has been widely used in boosting models when using decision stump as the base classifier, such as Adaboost (Freund and Schapire, 1997).

The robustness of ensemble decision stumps have been studied by Wang et al. (2020e) and Andriushchenko and Hein (2019). We have shown in the previous subsection that the robustness evaluation can be done in linear time for any $\ell_p$ norms, but interestingly, the complexity will varies for different $p$ when considering robustness evaluation of ensemble decision stumps.

The prediction of a decision stump ensemble $F(x) = \sum_i f^i(x)$ can be decomposed into each feature in the following way. For each feature $j$, letting $j_1, \ldots, j_{T_j}$ be the decision stumps using feature $j$, we can collect all the thresholds $[\eta^{j_1}, \ldots, \eta^{j_{T_j}}]$. Without loss of generality, assume that $\eta^{j_1} \le \cdots \le \eta^{j_{T_j}}$. Then the prediction values assigned in each interval can be denoted as

$$
g^j(x_j) = v^{j_t} \quad \text{if } \eta^{j_t} < x_j \le \eta^{j_{t+1}}, \tag{16.20}
$$

where

$$
v^{j_t} = w_l^{j_1} + \cdots + w_l^{j_t} + w_r^{j_{t+1}} + \cdots + w_r^{j_{T_j}},
$$

and $x_j$ is the value of sample $x$ on feature $j$. The overall prediction can be written as the sum over the predicted values of each feature,

$$F(x) = \sum_{j=1}^{d} g^j(x_j),  \tag{16.21}$$

and the final prediction is given by $y = \text{sgn}(F(x))$.

$\ell_\infty$ *and* $\ell_0$ *norm robustness evaluation.* For $\ell_\infty$ norm robustness evaluation, we try to study whether there exists a perturbation $\delta$ within an $\epsilon$-$\ell_\infty$ ball around a certain input $x$ that can change the prediction. As the prediction can be decomposed into each dimension, we just need to investigate within $\epsilon$ perturbation what is the worst-case perturbation for each dimension. This can be trivially evaluated with a linear scan, so the evaluation can be done in linear time. Mathematically, for each feature $j$, we want to know *the maximum decrease of prediction value by changing this feature,* which can be computed as

$$c^j = \min_{t:(\eta^{jt-1},\eta^{jt}]\cap[x_j-\epsilon,x_j+\epsilon]\neq\emptyset} v^{jt} - g^j(x_j).  \tag{16.22}$$

Then the minimum prediction that can be achieved within the $\epsilon$ $\ell_\infty$ ball will be $\sum_j c^j$.

On the other hand, when considering the $\ell_0$ norm ball perturbation set, it is equivalent to saying that we can perturb at most $\epsilon$ features (assuming that $\epsilon$ is an integer), and the perturbation on each feature is not constrained. Therefore, the optimal perturbation will be choosing the features with the bottom-$\epsilon$ lowest $c^j$ values to perturb, so the computation can be done also in linear time.

**Other $\ell_p$ norm robustness evaluation**

The difficulty of $\ell_p$ norm robustness verification is that the perturbations on each feature are correlated, so we cannot separate all the features as in (Andriushchenko and Hein, 2019) for the $\ell_\infty$ norm case. In the following, we prove that the complete $\ell_p$ norm verification is NP-complete by showing a reduction from Knapsack to $\ell_p$ norm ensemble stump verification. This shows that $\ell_p$ norm verification can belong to a different complexity class compared to the $\ell_\infty$ norm case.

**Theorem 6.** *Solving $\ell_p$ norm robustness verification (with soundness and completeness) for an ensemble decision stumps is NP-complete when $p \in (0, \infty)$.*

As computing the exact robustness is NP-Complete, Wang et al. (2020e) proposed several ways to find an upper bound for robustness verification, based on the connection between $\ell_p$ norm robustness evaluation and the Kanpsack problem. More details can be found in (Wang et al., 2020e).

## Robustness of ensemble decision trees

Now we discuss the robustness verification for tree (instead of decision stump) ensembles. Assuming that the tree ensemble has $K$ decision trees, we use $S^{(k)}$ to denote the set of leaf nodes of tree $k$ and $m^{(k)}(x)$ to denote the function that maps the input example $x$ to the leaf node of tree $k$ according to the traversal rule of the tree. Given an input example $x$, the tree ensemble will pass $x$ to each of these $K$ trees independently and reach $K$ leaf nodes $i^{(k)} = m^{(k)}(x)$ for $k = 1, \ldots, K$. Each leaf node will assign a prediction value $v_{i^{(k)}}$. For simplicity, we start with the binary classification case, with original label of $x$ being $y_0 = -1$ and the goal (for adversary) is to turn the label into $+1$. For binary classification, the prediction of the tree ensemble is computed by $\mathrm{sign}(\sum_{k=1}^{K} v_{i^{(k)}})$, which covers both GBDTs and random forests, two widely used tree ensemble models. Since $x$ is assumed to have label $y_0 = -1$, we know $\mathrm{sign}(\sum_k v_{i^{(k)}}) < 0$ for $x$, and our task is to verify whether the sign of the sum can be flipped within $\mathrm{Ball}(x, \epsilon)$.

We consider the decision problem of robustness verification to verify whether there exists an adversarial perturbation within a small region. A naive analysis will need to check all the points in $\mathrm{Ball}(x, \epsilon)$, which is uncountably infinite. To reduce the search space to a finite one, the main idea is to represent the space by all the possible choices of leaf nodes of these $K$ trees. More specifically, we let $C = \{(i^{(1)}, \ldots, i^{(K)}) \mid i^{(k)} \in S^{(k)} \; \forall k = 1, \ldots, L\}$ to be all the possible tuples of leaf nodes, and let $C(x) = [m^{(1)}(x), \ldots, m^{(K)}(x)]$ be the function that maps $x$ to the corresponding leaf nodes. Therefore a tuple $C$ directly determines the model prediction $\sum v_C := \sum_k v_{i^{(k)}}$, and the good thing is that this space only have finite (although exponentially many) of choices.

Now we define a valid tuple for robustness verification.

**Definition 1.** *A tuple* $C = (i^{(1)}, \ldots, i^{(K)})$ *is called valid if there exists* $x' \in \mathrm{Ball}(x, \epsilon)$ *such that* $C = C(x')$.

The decision problem of robustness verification can then be written as

*Does there exist a valid tuple* $C$ *such that* $\sum v_C > 0$?

Next, we show how to model the set of valid tuples. We have two observations. First, if a tuple contains any node $i$ where the box $i$ is out of the range from $x$ $(\inf_{x' \in B^i}\{\|x - x'\|_\infty\} > \epsilon)$, then it is invalid. Second, since the box corresponding to each leaf node captures all the possible points fall into the node, there exists $x$ such that $C = C(x)$ if and only if the intersection of all these boxes are nonempty. This can be written as $B^{i^{(1)}} \cap \cdots \cap B^{i^{(K)}} \neq \emptyset$.

Based on these observations, we can represent the set of valid tuples as cliques in a graph $G = (V, E)$, where each node is a valid leaf node $V := \{i | B^i \cap \text{Ball}(x, \epsilon) \neq \emptyset\}$, and each edge indicates that two end nodes have non-empty intersection $E := \{(i, j) | B^i \cap B^j \neq \emptyset\}$. The graph will then be a $K$-partite graph since there cannot be any edge between nodes from the same tree, and thus maximum cliques in this graph will have $K$ nodes. We denote each part of the $K$-partite graph as $V_k$. Here a "part" means a disjoint and independent set in the $K$-partite graph. The following lemma shows that intersections of boxes have very nice properties.

**Lemma 4.** *For boxes $B^1, \ldots, B^K$, if $B^i \cap B^j \neq \emptyset$ for all $i, j \in [K]$, let $\bar{B} = B^1 \cap B^2 \cap \cdots \cap B^K$ be their intersection. Then $\bar{B}$ is also a box, and $\bar{B} \neq \emptyset$.*

Details of the proof can be found in Chen et al. (2019b). Therefore, each $K$-clique (fully connected subgraph with $K$ nodes) in $G$ can be viewed as a set of leaf nodes that has nonempty intersection with each other and also has nonempty intersection with $\text{Ball}(x, \epsilon)$, so the intersection of those $K$ boxes and $\text{Ball}(x, \epsilon)$ will be a nonempty box, which implies that each $K$-clique corresponds to a valid tuple of leaf nodes.

**Lemma 5.** *A tuple $C = (i^{(1)}, \ldots, i^{(K)})$ is valid if and only if nodes $i^{(1)}, \ldots, i^{(K)}$ form a $K$-clique (maximum clique) in graph $G$ constructed above.*

Therefore the robustness verification problem can be formulated as

$$\text{Is there a maximum clique } C \text{ in } G \text{ such that } \sum v_C > 0? \qquad (16.23)$$

This reformulation indicates that the tree ensemble verification problem can be solved by an efficient maximum clique enumeration algorithm. Unfortunately, it has been shown that enumerating all the maximum cliques is NP-complete and takes $O(3^{\frac{m}{3}})$ time, which is time consuming, and therefore an efficient alternative is proposed by Chen et al. (2019b), which we will briefly mention below.

**An efficient multilevel algorithm for robustness verification of decision trees**

Fig. 16.3 illustrates the multilevel algorithm proposed by Chen et al. (2019b). There are four trees, and each tree has four leaf nodes. A node is

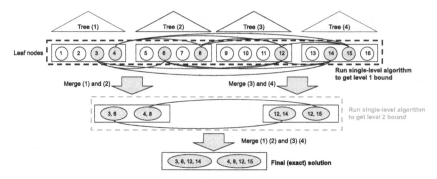

**Figure 16.3** The multilevel verification algorithm proposed in Chen et al. (2019b). Lines between leaf node $i$ on tree $t_1$ and leaf node $j$ on $t_2$ indicate that their $\ell_\infty$ feature boxes intersect (i.e., there exists an input such that tree 1 predicts $v_i$ and tree 2 predicts $v_j$).

colored if it has nonempty intersection with $\text{Ball}(x, \epsilon)$; uncolored nodes are discarded. To answer question (16.23), we need to compute the maximum $\sum v_C$ among all $K$-cliques, denoted by $v^*$. As mentioned before, for robustness verification, we only need to compute an upper bound of $v^*$ to get a lower bound of minimal adversarial perturbation. In the following, we will first discuss algorithms for computing an upper bound at the top level and then show how our multiscale algorithm iteratively refines this bound until reaching the exact solution $v^*$.

## Bounds for a single level

For each single level, Chen et al. (2019b) proposed a simple approach to compute an upper bound of the maximimum clique value. This is done by assuming the graph is fully connected between any two parts (two independent sets) of the level. By making this assumption, we will only increase the maximum clique value as we are introducing strictly more edges. With this assumption, the maximum sum of node values is the sum of the maximum value of each part (independent set). In Fig. 16.3, if we focus on one of the layers, this can be simply computed by finding the maximum value in each group and sum them up.

Another slightly better approach is exploiting the edge information but only between trees $t$ and $t + 1$. If we search over all the length-$K$ paths $[i^{(1)}, \ldots, i^{(K)}]$ from the first to the last part and define the value of a path to be $\sum_k v_{i^{(k)}}$, then the maximum-valued path will be a valid upper bound. This can be computed in linear time using dynamic programming by running from the first part to the last part and keep track of the current maximum value on each node in the current part. This dynamic programming algorithm costs slightly more time but can get a much tighter upper bound.

### Merging $T$ independent sets

To refine the relatively loose single-level bound, the multilevel algorithm partitions the graph into $K/T$ subgraphs, each with $T$ independent sets. Within each subgraph, we find all the $T$-cliques and use a new "pseudo-node" to represent each $T$-clique. $T$-cliques in a subgraph can be enumerated efficiently if we choose $T$ to be a relatively small number (e.g., 2 or 3 in the experiments).

Next, we need to form the graph at the next level by merging nodes in the previous level. By Lemma 4 we know that the intersection of $T$ boxes will still be a box, so each $T$-clique is still a box and can be represented as a pseudo-node in the level-2 graph. Also, because each pseudo-node is still a box, we can easily form edges between pseudo-nodes to indicate the nonempty overlapping between them, and this will be a $(K/T)$-partite boxicity graph since no edge can be formed for the cliques within the same subgraph. Thus we get the level-2 graph. With the level-2 graph, we can again run the single-level algorithm to compute an upper bound on $v^*$ to get a lower bound of $r^*$, but differently from the level-1 graph, now we already considered all the within-subgraph edges, so the bounds will be much tighter.

### The overall multilevel framework

We can run the algorithm level-by-level, and at each level the single-level algorithm will output a valid upper bound for verification. As we go to the next level, since the interconnections between the merged parts will be considered, the bounds will also get tighter. In the final level, the pseudo-nodes will correspond to the $K$-cliques in the original graph, and the maximum value will be the exact solution for the max clique problem. Therefore the algorithm can be viewed as an anytime algorithm that refines the upper bound level-by-level until reaching the maximum value.

## Training robust tree ensembles

Similar to neural networks, to enhance the robustness of tree ensembles, we can consider both empirical defense and certified defense. For both of them, the goal is to train a tree to minimize the robust loss defined as

$$\min_{f} E_{(x,y)\sim D} \max_{x'\in B(x,\epsilon)} \ell(f(x), y), \tag{16.24}$$

where for simplicity, we assume that $B(x, \epsilon)$ is the $\ell_\infty$ ball $B(x, \epsilon) = \{x' : \|x' - x\|_\infty \leq \epsilon\}$. In decision tree training, a commonly used technique is the top-down approach, where at each step, we determine how to split the node or, equivalently, how to pick the feature and threshold on a leaf node by minimizing the objective function. Therefore, to train the robust trees, we need to determine the best split of the node based on the robust loss (16.24) instead of the regular loss ((16.24) without the inner max). Since the training of decision trees is often complicated and there exists multiple training methods, we omit the detailed training algorithms here. Instead, we will just describe the algorithms conceptually and direct the interested readers to corresponding papers.

To minimize the adversarial loss, we can consider both the upper bound or the lower bound (similarly to adversarial training versus certified training in robust neural network learning). Chen et al. (2019a) proposed the first robust tree training algorithm based on a lower bound of robust loss. Conceptually, when determining how to split a node, a simple but effective way is testing all the possible split features and thresholds, computing the (robust) loss of each choice, and then choosing the best one. The naive procedure to compute the objective for all the splits requires $O(N^2 D)$ time, as there are $D$ features, each with $N$ thresholds, and the objective function involves $N$ samples. However, there exists an efficient way to test all the thresholds for a single feature. With the original nonrobust loss, since after ordering the thresholds from left to right, when knowing the objective function for a particular threshold, we can update it to the objective function value for the next threshold in $O(1)$ time. This leads to $O(ND)$ time complexity for each split. However, when considering the robust loss, since each sample can be either $+\epsilon$ or $-\epsilon$ depending on the worst-case scenario, it becomes nontrivial to update the objective function from a threshold to the next one in $O(1)$ time. To overcome this challenge, Chen et al. (2019a) only considers a particular assignment for the perturbation instead of the worst-case one, leading to an algorithm minimizing the lower bound of robust loss in each split.

On the other hand, it is also possible to do the split based on the upper bound of robust error computed by robust verification methods mentioned above. In particular, Andriushchenko and Hein (2019) applied their verification method, and Wang et al. (2020e) generalized the work to $\ell_p$ norm certified training. With their methods, it is possible to train a certified robust tree ensemble and outperform certified robust neural network in some simpler datasets (such as MNIST). Although it is not realistic to use tree-based methods for large image classification problems such as ImageNet, tree-based models are used in many data mining tasks and have been the main component for reranking in the retrieval systems, so it is still important to train a robust tree for those problems.

# CHAPTER 17

# Adversarial robustness in meta-learning and contrastive learning

A popular trend in machine learning is an extension of the methodology of single-task learning to fast adaptation or general representation learning, such as meta-learning, which quickly adapts the current metamodel to solve a new task in few-shot scenarios, and contrastive learning, which obtains general representations using self-supervision for efficient finetuning on specific tasks. In this chapter, we take a close look at these two machine learning paradigms and study their adversarial robustness in the downstream tasks, based on the results of (Wang et al., 2021b) and (Fan et al., 2021).

## 17.1 Fast adversarial robustness adaptation in model-agnostic meta-learning

Meta-learning, which can offer fast generalization adaptation to unseen tasks (Thrun and Pratt, 2012; Novak and Gowin, 1984), has widely been studied from model- and metric-based methods (Santoro et al., 2016; Munkhdalai and Yu, 2017; Koch et al., 2015; Snell et al., 2017) to optimization-based methods (Ravi and Larochelle, 2016; Finn et al., 2017; Nichol et al., 2018). In particular, model-agnostic meta-learning (MAML) (Finn et al., 2017) is one of the most intriguing bilevel optimization-based meta-learning methods designed for fast-adapted few-shot learning; that is, the learnt metamodel can rapidly be generalized to unforeseen tasks with only a small amount of data. It has successfully been applied to use cases such as object detection (Wang et al., 2020a), medical image analysis (Maicas et al., 2018), and language modeling (Huang et al., 2018).

Tackling the problem of adversarial robustness in MAML is more challenging than that of the standard model training, since MAML contains a bileveled learning procedure in which the meta–update step (outer loop) optimizes a task-agnostic initialization of model parameters, whereas the fine-tuning step (inner loop) learns a task-specific model instantiation updated from the common initialization. Thus it remains elusive *when*

*Adversarial Robustness for Machine Learning*
https://doi.org/10.1016/B978-0-12-824020-5.00028-4

(namely, at which learning stage) and *how* robust regularization should be promoted to strike a graceful balance between generalization/robustness and computation efficiency. Note that neither the standard MAML (Finn et al., 2017) nor the standard robust training (Madry et al., 2018; Zhang et al., 2019b) is as easy as normal training. Besides the algorithmic design in robust MAML, it is also important to draw in-depth explanation and analysis on *why* adversarial robustness can efficiently be gained in MAML. Wang et al. (2021b) study the problem of adversarial robustness in MAML (Yin et al., 2018; Goldblum et al., 2019) and make affirmative answers to the above questions on *when*, *how*, and *why*.

*MAML framework.* MAML attempts to learn an initialization of model parameters (namely, a metamodel) so that a new few-shot task can quickly and easily be tackled by fine-tuning this metamodel over a small amount of labeled data. The characteristic signature of MAML is its *bilevel* learning procedure, where the fine-tuning stage forms a task-specific *inner loop*, whereas the metamodel is updated at the *outer loop* by minimizing the validation error of fine-tuned models over cumulative tasks. Formally, consider $N$ few-shot learning tasks $\{\mathcal{T}_i\}_{i=1}^N$, each of which has a fine-tuning data set $\mathcal{D}_i$ and a validation set $\mathcal{D}_i'$, where $\mathcal{D}_i$ is used in the *fine-tuning* stage, and $\mathcal{D}_i'$ is used in the *meta-update* stage. Here the superscript (') is preserved to indicate operations/parameters at the meta-update stage. MAML is then formulated as the following bilevel optimization problem (Finn et al., 2017):

$$\begin{aligned} \text{minimize}_{\mathbf{w}} \quad & \tfrac{1}{N}\sum_{i=1}^N \ell_i'(\mathbf{w}_i'; \mathcal{D}_i') \\ \text{subject to} \quad & \mathbf{w}_i' = \underset{\mathbf{w}_i}{\arg\min}\, \ell_i(\mathbf{w}_i; \mathcal{D}_i, \mathbf{w}) \; \forall i \in [N], \end{aligned} \tag{17.1}$$

where $\mathbf{w}$ denotes the metamodel to be designed, $\mathbf{w}_i'$ is the $\mathcal{T}_i$-specific fine-tuned model, $\ell_i'(\mathbf{w}_i'; \mathcal{D}_i')$ represents the validation error using the fine-tuned model, $\ell_i(\mathbf{w}_i; \mathcal{D}_i, \mathbf{w})$ denotes the training error when fine-tuning the task-specific model parameters $\mathbf{w}_i$ using the task-agnostic initialization $\mathbf{w}$, and for ease of notation, $[K]$ represents the integer set $\{1, 2, \dots, K\}$. In (17.1) the objective function and the constraint correspond to the meta-update e and fine-tuning stages, respectively. The bilevel optimization problem is challenging because each constraint calls an inner optimization oracle, which is typically instantiated into a $K$-step gradient descent (GD) based solver:

$$\mathbf{w}_i^{(k)} = \mathbf{w}_i^{(k-1)} - \alpha \nabla_{\mathbf{w}_i} \ell_i(\mathbf{w}_i^{(k-1)}; \mathcal{D}_i, \mathbf{w}), \; k \in [K], \text{ with } \mathbf{w}_i^{(0)} = \mathbf{w}.$$

We note that even with the above-simplified fine-tuning step, updating the metamodel $\mathbf{w}$ still requires the second-order derivatives of the objective function of (17.1) with respect to $\mathbf{w}$.

Recall that the min-max optimization–based adversarial training (AT) is known as one of the most powerful defense methods to obtain a robust model against adversarial attacks (see Chapter 12). We summarize AT and its variants through the following robustness-regularized optimization problem:

$$\underset{\mathbf{w}}{\text{minimize}} \quad \lambda \mathbb{E}_{(\mathbf{x},y)\in\mathcal{D}}\left[\ell(\mathbf{w};\mathbf{x},y)\right] + \underbrace{\mathbb{E}_{(\mathbf{x},y)\in\mathcal{D}}[\underset{\|\delta\|_{\infty}\leq\epsilon}{\text{maximize}}\, g(\mathbf{w};\mathbf{x}+\delta,y)],}_{\mathcal{R}(\mathbf{w};\mathcal{D})}$$

$$(17.2)$$

where $\ell(\mathbf{w};\mathbf{x},y)$ denotes the prediction loss evaluated at the point $\mathbf{x}$ with label $y$, $\lambda \geq 0$ is a regularization parameter, $\delta$ denotes the input perturbation variable within the $\ell_{\infty}$-norm ball of radius $\epsilon$, $g$ represents the robust loss evaluated at the model $\mathbf{w}$ at the perturbed example $\mathbf{x}+\delta$ given the true label $y$, and for ease of notation, $\mathcal{R}(\mathbf{w};\mathcal{D})$ denotes the robust regularization function for model $\mathbf{w}$ under the data set $\mathcal{D}$. In the rest of this section, we consider two specifications of $\mathcal{R}$: (a) *AT regularization* (Madry et al., 2018), where we set $g=\ell$ and $\lambda = 0$; and (b) *TRADES regularization* (Zhang et al., 2019b), where we define $g$ as the cross-entropy between the distribution of prediction probabilities at the perturbed example $(\mathbf{x}+\delta)$ and that at the original sample $\mathbf{x}$.

*Robustness-promoting MAML.* Integrating MAML with AT is a natural solution to enhance adversarial robustness of a metamodel in few-shot learning. However, this seemingly simple scheme is in fact far from trivial, and there exist three critical roadblocks as elaborated below.

First, it remains elusive at which stage (fine-tuning or meta-update) robustness can most effectively be gained for MAML. Based on (17.1) and (17.2), we can cast this problem as a unified optimization problem that augments the MAML loss with robust regularization under two degrees of freedom characterized by two hyper-parameters $\gamma_{\text{out}} \geq 0$ and $\gamma_{\text{in}} \geq 0$:

$$\underset{\mathbf{w}}{\text{minimize}} \quad \frac{1}{N}\sum_{i=1}^{N}[\ell_i'(\mathbf{w}_i';\mathcal{D}_i') + \gamma_{\text{out}}\mathcal{R}_i(\mathbf{w}_i';\mathcal{D}_i')]$$
$$\text{subject to} \quad \mathbf{w}_i' = \underset{\mathbf{w}_i}{\text{argmin}}[\ell_i(\mathbf{w}_i;\mathcal{D}_i,\mathbf{w}) + \gamma_{\text{in}}\mathcal{R}_i(\mathbf{w}_i;\mathcal{D}_i)]\ \forall i \in [N]. \quad (17.3)$$

Here $\mathcal{R}_i$ denotes the task-specific robustness regularizer, and the choice of $(\gamma_{\text{in}}, \gamma_{\text{out}})$ determines the specific scenario of robustness-promoting

MAML. Clearly, the direct application is to set $\gamma_{\text{in}} > 0$ and $\gamma_{\text{out}} > 0$, that is, both fine-tuning and meta-update steps would be carried out using robust training, which calls additional loops to generate adversarial examples. Thus this would make computation most intensive. Spurred by that, we ask: *Is it possible to achieve a robust metamodel by incorporating robust regularization into only either meta-update or fine-tuning step (corresponding to $\gamma_{\text{in}} = 0$ or $\gamma_{\text{out}} = 0$)?*

Second, both MAML in (17.1) and AT in (17.2) are challenging bilevel optimization problems, which need to call inner optimization routines for fine-tuning and attack generation, respectively. Thus we ask whether or not the computationally light alternatives of inner solvers, e.g., partial fine-tuning (Raghu et al., 2019) and fast attack generation (Wong et al., 2020a), can promise adversarial robustness in few-shot learning.

Third, it has been shown that adversarial robustness can benefit from semisupervised learning by leveraging (unlabeled) data augmentation (Carmon et al., 2019; Stanforth et al., 2019). Spurred by that, we further ask: *Is it possible to generalize robustness-promoting MAML to the setup of semisupervised learning for improved accuracy-robustness tradeoff?*

## When and how to incorporate robust regularization in MAML?

Based on (17.3), we focus on two robustness-promoting meta-training protocols proposed by Wang et al. (2021b): (a) R–MAML$_{\text{both}}$, where robustness regularization is applied to *both* fine-tuning and meta-update steps with $\gamma_{\text{in}}, \gamma_{\text{out}} > 0$, and (b) R–MAML$_{\text{out}}$, where robust regularization applied to *meta-update only*, i.e., $\gamma_{\text{in}} = 0$ and $\gamma_{\text{out}} > 0$. Compared to R–MAML$_{\text{both}}$, R–MAML$_{\text{out}}$ is more user-friendly since it allows the use of *standard* fine-tuning over the learnt robust metamodel when tackling unseen few-shot test tasks (known as meta-testing). In what follows, we will show that even if R–MAML$_{\text{out}}$ does not use robust regularization in fine-tuning, it is sufficient to warrant the transferability of robustness of the metamodel to downstream fine-tuning tasks.

*All you need is robust meta-update during meta-training.* To study this claim, we solve problem (17.3) using R–MAML$_{\text{both}}$ and R–MAML$_{\text{out}}$ in the 5-way 1-shot learning setup, where one data sample at each of five randomly selected MiniImagenet classes (Ravi and Larochelle, 2016) constructs a learning task. Throughout this section, we specify $\mathcal{R}_i$ in (17.3) as the AT regularization, which calls a 10-step projected gradient descent (PGD) attack generation method with $\epsilon = 2/255$ in its inner maximization subroutine given by (17.2).

We find that the metamodel acquired by R-MAML$_{out}$ yields *nearly the same robust accuracy* (RA) as R-MAML$_{both}$ against various PGD attacks generated at the testing phase using different perturbation sizes $\epsilon = \{0, 2, \ldots, 10\}/255$ as shown in Fig. 17.1. Unless specified otherwise, we evaluate the performance of the meta-learning schemes over 2400 random unseen 5-way 1-shot test tasks. We also note that RA under $\epsilon = 0$ becomes the standard accuracy (SA) evaluated using benign (unperturbed) test examples. It is clear from Fig. 17.1 that both R-MAML$_{out}$ and R-MAML$_{both}$ can yield significantly better RA than MAML with slightly worse SA. It is also expected that RA decreases as the attack power $\epsilon$ increases.

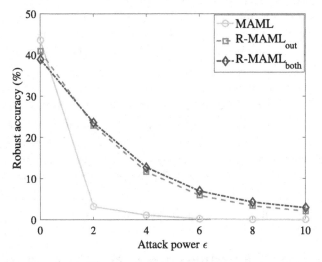

**Figure 17.1** RA of metamodels trained by standard MAML, R-MAML$_{both}$, and R-MAML$_{out}$ versus PGD attacks of different perturbation sizes during meta-testing. Results show that robustness-regularized meta-update with standard fine-tuning (namely, R-MAML$_{out}$) has already been effective in promotion of robustness.

*Robust meta-update provides robustness adaptation without additional adversarial fine-tuning at meta-testing.* Meta-testing includes only the fine-tuning stage. Therefore we need to explore if standard fine-tuning is sufficient to maintain the robustness. Suppose that R-MAML$_{out}$ is adopted as the meta-training method to solve problem (17.3); we then ask if robustness-regularized meta-testing strategy can improve the robustness of fine-tuned model at downstream tasks. Surprisingly, we find that making an additional effort to adversarially fine-tune the metamodel (trained by R-MAML$_{out}$) during testing does *not* provide an obvious robustness improvement over the standard fine-tuning scheme during testing (Table 17.1). This consis-

**Table 17.1** Comparison of different strategies in meta-testing on R-MAML$_{out}$: (a) standard fine-tuning (S-FT), (b) adversarial fine-tuning (A-FT).

|     | S-FT  | A-FT  |
| --- | ----- | ----- |
| SA  | 40.9% | 39.6% |
| RA  | 22.9% | 23.5% |

tently implies that robust meta–update (R-MAML$_{out}$) is sufficient to render intrinsic robustness in its learnt metamodel regardless of fine-tuning strategies used at meta-testing.

**Summary:** In Wang et al. (2021b), as inspired by Wong et al. (2020a), they find that the application of the fast sign gradient method (FGSM) to R-MAML$_{out}$ provides the most graceful tradeoff between the computation cost and the standard and robust accuracies. Moreover, they find that with the help of unlabeled data, R-MAML$_{out}$-TRADES improves the accuracy-robustness tradeoff over its supervised counterpart R-MAML$_{out}$ using either AT or TRADES regularization. Finally, they propose a general but efficient robustness-regularized meta-learning framework, which allows the use of unlabeled data augmentation, fast (one-step) adversarial example generation during meta-updating and partial model training during fine-tuning (only fine-tuning the classifier's head).

## 17.2 Adversarial robustness preservation for contrastive learning: from pretraining to finetuning

Contrastive learning (CL) can learn generalizable feature representations and achieve state-of-the-art performance of downstream tasks by fine-tuning a *linear* classifier on top of it. Early approaches for unsupervised representation learning leverages handcrafted tasks, like prediction rotation (Gidaris et al., 2018), solving the Jigsaw puzzle (Noroozi and Favaro, 2016; Carlucci et al., 2019), and geometry prediction (Gan et al., 2018) and Selfie (Trinh et al., 2019). Recently, contrastive learning (CL) (Chen et al., 2018e; Wang and Isola, 2020; Chen et al., 2020e; van den Oord et al., 2018; He et al., 2020; Chen et al., 2020d) and its variants (Grill et al., 2020; Tian et al., 2020; Purushwalkam and Gupta, 2020; Chen and He, 2020) have demonstrated superior abilities in learning generalizable features in an unsupervised manner. The main idea behind CL is to self-create positive samples of the same image from aggressive viewpoints and then acquire data representations by maximizing agreement between positives while contrasting with negatives. However, as adversarial robustness becomes vital in image classification, it remains unclear whether or not CL is able to preserve robustness to downstream tasks. The main challenge is that in the "self-supervised pretraining + supervised finetuning" paradigm, adversarial robustness is easily forgotten due to a learning task mismatch from pretraining to finetuning. We call such challenge "cross-task robustness transferability". To address the above problem, Fan et al. (2021) show that: (i) the design of contrastive views matters: high-frequency components of images are beneficial to improving model robustness; and (ii) augmenting CL with pseudo-supervision stimulus (e.g., resorting to feature clustering) helps preserve robustness without forgetting. They further propose ADVCL, a novel adversarial contrastive pretraining framework, to enhance cross-task robustness transferability without loss of model accuracy and finetuning efficiency. We will introduce this framework in this section.

Fan et al. (2021) focus on the study of accomplishing robustness enhancement using CL without losing its finetuning efficiency, e.g., via a standard linear finetuner. Some relevant works such as (Jiang et al., 2020; Kim et al., 2020) integrate adversarial training with CL. However, the achieved adversarial robustness at downstream tasks largely relies on the use of advanced finetuning techniques, either adversarial full finetuning (Jiang et al., 2020) or adversarial linear finetuning (Kim et al., 2020). Fan et al. (2021) find that self-supervised learning (including the state-of-the-art CL) suffers a new robustness challenge called "cross-task robustness transferability", which was largely overlooked in the previous work; that is, there exists a task mismatch from pretraining to finetuning (e.g., from CL to supervised classification) so that adversarial robustness is not able to transfer across tasks even if pretraining datasets and finetuning datasets are drawn from the same distribution. Different from supervised/semi-supervised learning, this is a characteristic behavior of self-supervision when being adapted to robust learning. As shown in Fig. 17.2, their ADVCLwork advances CL in the adversarial context, and the proposed method outperforms all state-of-the-art baseline methods, leading to a substantial improvement in both robust accuracy and standard accuracy using either the lightweight standard linear finetuning or end-to-end adversarial full finetuning.

In what follows, we elaborate on the *formulation of SimCLR* (Chen et al., 2018e), one of the most commonly used CL frameworks, which this paper focuses on. To be concrete, let $\mathcal{X} = \{x_1, x_2, \ldots, x_n\}$ denote an *unlabeled*

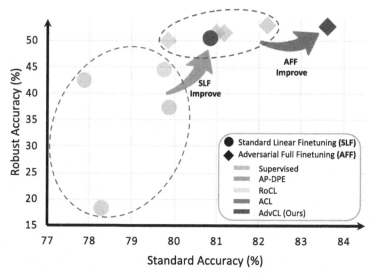

**Figure 17.2** Summary of performance for various robust pretraining methods on CIFAR-10. The covered baseline methods include AP-DPE (Chen et al., 2020c), RoCL (Kim et al., 2020), ACL (Jiang et al., 2020), and supervised adversarial training (AT) (Madry et al., 2018). Upper-right indicates better performance with respect to standard accuracy and robust accuracy (under PGD attack with 20 steps and $8/255$ $\ell_\infty$-norm perturbation strength). Different colors represent different pretraining methods, and different shapes represent different finetuning settings. Circles indicate *Standard Linear Finetuning* (SLF), and Diamonds indicates *Adversarial Full Finetuning* (AFF). The method proposed by Fan et al. (2021) (ADVCL, red circle/diamond (dark gray in print version)) has the best performance across finetuning settings.

*source* dataset; SimCLR offers a learned *feature encoder* $f_\theta$ to generate expressive deep representations of the data. To train $f_\theta$, each input $x \in \mathcal{X}$ will be transformed into two *views* $(\tau_1(x), \tau_2(x))$ and label them as a positive pair. Here transformation operations $\tau_1$ and $\tau_2$ are randomly sampled from a predefined transformation set $\mathcal{T}$, which includes, e.g., random cropping and resizing, color jittering, rotation, and cutout. The positive pair is then fed in the feature encoder $f_\theta$ with a projection head $g$ to acquire projected features, i.e., $z_i = g \circ f_\theta(\tau_i(x))$ for $j \in \{1, 2\}$. *NT-Xent loss* (i.e., the normalized temperature–scaled cross–entropy loss) is then applied to optimizing $f_\theta$, where the distance of projected positive features $(z_1, z_2)$ is minimized for each input $x$. SimCLR follows the *"self-supervised pretraining + supervised finetuning"* paradigm, that is, once $f_\theta$ is trained, a downstream supervised classification task can be handled by just finetuning a linear classifier $\phi$ over the fixed encoder $f_\theta$, leading to the eventual classification network $\phi \circ f_\theta$.

*Robust pretraining + linear finetuning.* We aim to develop robustness enhancement solutions by fully exploiting and exploring the power of CL at the pretraining phase, so that the resulting robust feature representations can seamlessly be used to generate robust predictions of downstream tasks using just a lightweight finetuning scheme. With the aid of adversarial training (AT), we formulate the *"robust pretraining + linear finetuning"* problem as follows:

$$\text{Pretraining: } \min_{\theta} \mathbb{E}_{x \in \mathcal{X}} \max_{\|\delta\|_{\infty} \leq \epsilon} \ell_{\text{pre}}(x + \delta, x; \theta), \qquad (17.4)$$

$$\text{Finetuning: } \min_{\theta_c} \mathbb{E}_{(x,y) \in \mathcal{D}} \ell_{\text{CE}}(\phi_{\theta_c} \circ f_{\theta}(x), y), \qquad (17.5)$$

where $\ell_{\text{pre}}$ denotes a properly designed robustness- and generalization-aware CL loss given as a function of the adversarial example $(x + \delta)$, original example $x$, and feature encoder parameters $\theta$. In (17.4), $\phi_{\theta_c} \circ f_{\theta}$ denotes the classifier by equipping the linear prediction head $\phi_{\theta_c}$ (with parameters $\theta_c$ to be designed) on top of the fixed feature encoder $f_{\theta}$, and $\ell_{\text{CE}}$ denotes the supervised CE loss over the target dataset $\mathcal{D}$. Note that besides the standard linear finetuning (17.5), we can also modify (17.5) using the worst-case CE loss for adversarial linear/full finetuning (Jiang et al., 2020; Kim et al., 2020). We do not consider standard full finetuning since tuning the full network weights with standard cross-entropy loss is not possible for the model to preserve robustness (Chen et al., 2020c).

ADVCL *framework.* The ADVCL framework proposed by Fan et al. (2021) includes two main components, robustness-aware view selection and pseudo-supervision stimulus generation. In particular, they advance the view selection mechanism by taking into account proper frequency-based data transformations that are beneficial to robust representation learning and pretraining generalization ability. Furthermore, they propose to design and integrate proper supervision stimulus into ADVCL to improve the cross-task robustness transferability since robust representations learned from self-supervision may lack the class-discriminative ability required for robust predictions on downstream tasks. An overview of ADVCL is provided in Fig. 17.3. In contrast to standard CL, Fan et al. (2021) propose two additional contrastive views, the adversarial and frequency views.

*Multiview CL loss.* Prior to defining new views, we first review the NT-Xent loss and its multiview version used in CL. The contrastive loss with

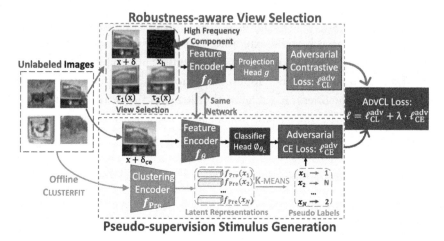

**Figure 17.3** The overall pipeline of ADVCL in (Fan et al., 2021). It mainly has two ingredients, robustness-aware view selection (orange (mid gray in print version) box) and pseudo-supervision stimulus generation (blue (gray in print version)box). The view selection mechanism is advanced by high-frequency components, and the supervision stimulus is created by generating pseudo-labels for each image through CLUSTERFIT. The pseudo-label (in yellow (light gray in print version) color) can be created in an offline manner and will not increase the computation overhead.

respect to a positive pair $(\tau_1(x), \tau_2(x))$ of each (unlabeled) data $x$ is given by

$$\ell_{\mathrm{CL}}(\tau_1(x), \tau_2(x)) = -\sum_{i=1}^{2} \sum_{j \in \mathcal{P}(i)} \log \frac{\exp\left(\mathrm{sim}(z_i, z_j)/t\right)}{\sum\limits_{k \in \mathcal{N}(i)} \exp\left(\mathrm{sim}(z_i, z_k)/t\right)}, \qquad (17.6)$$

where recall that $z_i = g \circ f(\tau_i(x))$ is the projected feature under the $i$th view, $\mathcal{P}(i)$ is the set of positive views except $i$ (e.g., $\mathcal{P}(i) = \{2\}$ if $i = 1$), $\mathcal{N}(i)$ denotes the set of augmented batch data except the point $\tau_i(x)$, the cardinality of $\mathcal{N}(i)$ is $(2b - 1)$ (for a data batch of size $b$ under two views), $\mathrm{sim}(z_{i1}, z_{i2})$ denotes the cosine similarity between representations from two views of the same data, exp denotes exponential function, $\mathrm{sim}(\cdot, \cdot)$ is the cosine similarity between two points, and $t > 0$ is a temperature parameter. The two-view CL objective can be further extend to the *multiview contrastive loss* (Khosla et al., 2020):

$$\ell_{\mathrm{CL}}(\tau_1(x), \tau_2(x), \ldots, \tau_m(x)) = -\sum_{i=1}^{m} \sum_{j \in \mathcal{P}(i)} \log \frac{\exp\left(\mathrm{sim}(z_i, z_j)/t\right)}{\sum\limits_{k \in \mathcal{N}(i)} \exp\left(\mathrm{sim}(z_i, z_k)/t\right)},$$

$$(17.7)$$

where $\mathcal{P}(i) = [m]/\{i\}$ denotes the $m$ positive views except $i$, $[m]$ denotes the integer set $\{1, 2, \ldots, m\}$, and $\mathcal{N}(i)$, with cardinality $(bm - 1)$, denotes the set of $m$-view augmented $b$ batch samples except the point $\tau_i(x)$.

*Contrastive view from adversarial example.* The methods proposed by Jiang et al. (2020), Kim et al. (2020), and Gowal et al. (2021) can be explained based on (17.6): an adversarial perturbation $\delta$ with respect to each view of a sample $x$ is generated by maximizing the contrastive loss:

$$\delta_1^*, \delta_2^* = \underset{\|\delta_i\|_\infty \leq \epsilon}{\operatorname{argmax}} \ell_{\mathrm{CL}}(\tau_1(x) + \delta_1, \tau_2(x) + \delta_2). \tag{17.8}$$

A solution to problem (17.8) eventually yields a *paired* perturbation view $(\tau_1(x) + \delta_1^*, \tau_2(x) + \delta_2^*)$. However, the definition of adversarial view (17.8) used by Jiang et al. (2020), Kim et al. (2020), and Gowal et al. (2021) may not be proper. First, standard CL commonly uses *aggressive* data transformation that treats small portions of images as positive samples of the full image (Purushwalkam and Gupta, 2020). Despite its benefit to promoting generalization, crafting perturbations over such aggressive data transformations may not be suitable for defending adversarial attacks applied to *full* images in the adversarial context. Thus a new adversarial view built upon $x$ rather than $\tau_i(x)$ is desired. Second, the contrastive loss (17.6) is only restricted to two views of the same data. As will be evident later, the multiview contrastive loss is also needed when taking into account multiple robustness-promoting views. Spurred by above, we define the *adversarial view* over $x$ without modifying the existing data augmentations $(\tau_1(x), \tau_2(x))$. This leads to the following adversarial perturbation generator by maximizing a three-view contrastive loss

$$\delta^* = \underset{\|\delta\| \leq \epsilon}{\operatorname{argmax}} \ell_{\mathrm{CL}}(\tau_1(x), \tau_2(x), x + \delta), \tag{17.9}$$

where $x + \delta^*$ is regarded as the third view of $x$.

*Contrastive view from high-frequency component.* Next, we use the high-frequency component (HFC) of data as another additional contrastive view. The rationale arises from the facts that 1) learning over HFC of data is a main cause of achieving superior generalization ability (Wang et al., 2020b) and 2) an adversary typically concentrates on HFC when manipulating an example to fool model decision (Wang et al., 2020f). Let $\mathcal{F}$ and $\mathcal{F}^{-1}$ denote the Fourier transformation and its inverse. An input image $x$ can then be decomposed into its HFC $x_{\mathrm{h}}$ and low-frequency component (LFC) $x_{\mathrm{l}}$:

$$x_{\mathrm{h}} = \mathcal{F}^{-1}(q_{\mathrm{h}}), \quad x_{\mathrm{l}} = \mathcal{F}^{-1}(q_{\mathrm{l}}), \quad [q_{\mathrm{h}}, q_{\mathrm{l}}] = \mathcal{F}(x). \tag{17.10}$$

In (17.10) the distinction between $q_h$ and $q_l$ is made by a hard thresholding operation. Let $q(i, j)$ denote the $(i, j)$th element of $\mathcal{F}(x)$, and let $c = (c_1, c_2)$ denote the centroid of the frequency spectrum. The components $q_l$ and $q_h$ in (17.10) are then generated by filtering out values according to the distance from $c$: $q_h(i, j) = \mathbb{1}_{[d((i,j),(c_1,c_2)) \geq r]} \cdot q(i, j)$, and $q_l(i, j) = \mathbb{1}_{[d((i,j),(c_1,c_2)) \leq r]} \cdot q(i, j)$, where $d(\cdot, \cdot)$ is the Euclidean distance between two spatial coordinates, $r$ is a predefined distance threshold ($r = 8$ in all our experiments), and $\mathbb{1}_{[\cdot]} \in \{0, 1\}$ is an indicator function, which equals to 1 if the condition within $[\cdot]$ is met and 0 otherwise.

*Robustness-aware contrastive learning objective.* By incorporating the adversarial perturbation $\delta$ and disentangling HFC $x_h$ from the original data $x$ we obtain a four-view contrastive loss (17.7) defined over $(\tau_1(x), \tau_2(x), x + \delta, x_h)$:

$$\ell_{CL}^{adv}(\theta; \mathcal{X}) := \mathbb{E}_{x \in \mathcal{X}} \max_{\|\delta\|_\infty \leq \epsilon} \ell_{CL}(\tau_1(x), \tau_2(x), x + \delta, x_h; \theta), \qquad (17.11)$$

where recall that $\mathcal{X}$ denotes the unlabeled dataset, $\epsilon > 0$ is a perturbation tolerance during training, and for clarity, the four-view contrastive loss (17.7) is explicitly expressed as a function of model parameters $\theta$. The eventual learning objective ADVCL will be built upon (17.11).

*Supervision stimulus generation: ADVCL empowered by CLUSTERFIT.* On top of (17.11), we further improve the robustness transferability of learned representations by generating a proper supervision stimulus. The rationale is that robust representation could lack the class-discriminative power required by robust classification as the former is acquired by optimizing an unsupervised contrastive loss, whereas the latter is achieved by a supervised cross-entropy CE loss. However, there is no knowledge about supervised data during pretraining. To improve cross-task robustness transferability without calling for supervision, we take advantage of CLUSTERFIT (Yan et al., 2020), a pseudo–label generation method used in representation learning.

To be more concrete, let $f_{pre}$ denote a pretrained representation network that can generate latent features of unlabeled data. Note that $f_{pre}$ can be set available beforehand and trained over either supervised or unsupervised dataset $\mathcal{D}_{pre}$, e.g., ImageNet using CL in experiments. Given (normalized) pretrained data representations $\{f_{pre}(x)\}_{x \in \mathcal{X}}$, CLUSTERFIT uses *K-means clustering* to find $K$ data clusters of $\mathcal{X}$ and maps a *cluster index* $c$ to a *pseudo-label*, resulting in the pseudo-labeled dataset $\{(x, c) \in \hat{\mathcal{X}}\}$. By integrating CLUSTERFIT with (17.11) the eventual training objective of ADVCL is then formed by

$$\min_{\theta} \ell_{CL}^{adv}(\theta; \mathcal{X}) + \lambda \min_{\theta, \theta_c} \underbrace{\mathbb{E}_{(x,c) \in \hat{\mathcal{X}}} \max_{\|\delta_{ce}\|_{\infty} \leq \epsilon} \ell_{CE}(\phi_{\theta_c} \circ f_{\theta}(x + \delta_{ce}), c)}_{\text{Pseudo-classification enabled AT regularization}}, \quad (17.12)$$

where $\hat{\mathcal{X}}$ denotes the pseudo-labeled dataset of $\mathcal{X}$, $\phi_{\theta_c}$ denotes a prediction head over $f_{\theta}$, and $\lambda > 0$ is a regularization parameter that strikes a balance between adversarial contrastive training and pseudo-label stimulated AT. When the number of clusters $K$ is not known a priori, we extend (17.12) to an *ensemble version* over $n$ choices of cluster numbers $\{K_1, \ldots, K_n\}$. Here each cluster number $K_i$ is paired with a unique linear classifier $\phi_i$ to obtain the supervised prediction $\phi_i \circ f$ (using cluster labels). The ensemble CE loss, given by the average of $n$ individual losses, is then used in (17.12). The experiments by Fan et al. (2021) show that the ensemble version usually leads to better generalization ability.

*Empirical comparison.* Following Fan et al. (2021), we consider three robustness evaluation metrics: (1) Auto-attack accuracy (**AA**), namely, classification accuracy over adversarially perturbed images via auto-attacks; (2) Robust accuracy (**RA**), namely, classification accuracy over adversarially perturbed images via PGD attacks; and (3) Standard accuracy (**SA**), namely, standard classification accuracy over benign images without perturbations. We use ResNet-18 for the encoder architecture of $f_{\theta}$ in CL. Unless specified otherwise, we use five-step $\ell_{\infty}$ projected gradient descent (PGD) with $\epsilon = 8/255$ to generate perturbations during pretraining and use auto-attack and 20-step $\ell_{\infty}$ PGD with $\epsilon = 8/255$ to generate perturbations in computing AA and RA at test time. We will compare ADVCL with the CL-based adversarial pretraining *baselines*, ACL (Jiang et al., 2020), RoCL (Kim et al., 2020), (non-CL) self-supervised adversarial learning baseline AP-DPE (Chen et al., 2020c), and the supervised AT baseline (Madry et al., 2018).

*Overall performance from pretraining to finetuning (across tasks).* In Table 17.2, we evaluate the robustness of a classifier (ResNet-18) finetuned over robust representations learned by different supervised/self-supervised pretraining approaches over CIFAR-10 and CIFAR-100. We focus on two representative finetuning schemes, the simplest standard linear finetuning (SLF) and the end-to-end adversarial full finetuning (AFF). As we can see, the proposed ADVCL method yields a substantial improvement over almost all baseline methods. Moreover, ADVCL simultaneously improves robustness and standard accuracy.

**Table 17.2** Cross-task performance of AdvCL (in dark gray color), compared with supervised (in white color) and self-supervised (in light gray color) baselines, in terms of AA, RA, and SA on CIFAR-10 with ResNet-18. The pretrained models are evaluated under the standard linear finetuning (SLF) setting and the adversarial full finetuning (AFF) setting. The top performance is highlighted in **bold**.

| Pretraining Method | Finetuning Method | CIFAR-10 | | | CIFAR-100 | | |
|---|---|---|---|---|---|---|---|
| | | AA (%) | RA (%) | SA (%) | AA (%) | RA (%) | SA (%) |
| Supervised | Standard linear finetuning (**SLF**) | 42.22 | 44.4 | 79.77 | 19.53 | 23.41 | **50.53** |
| AP-DPE (Chen et al., 2020c) | | 16.07 | 18.22 | 78.30 | 4.17 | 6.23 | 47.91 |
| RoCL (Kim et al., 2020) | | 28.38 | 39.54 | 79.90 | 8.66 | 18.79 | 49.53 |
| ACL (Jiang et al., 2020) | | 39.13 | 42.87 | 77.88 | 16.33 | 20.97 | 47.51 |
| AdvCL (Fan et al., 2021) | | **42.57** | **50.45** | **80.85** | **19.78** | **27.67** | 48.34 |
| Supervised | Adversarial full finetuning (**AFF**) | 46.19 | 49.89 | 79.86 | 21.61 | 25.86 | 52.22 |
| AP-DPE (Chen et al., 2020c) | | 48.13 | 51.52 | 81.19 | 22.53 | 26.89 | 55.27 |
| RoCL (Kim et al., 2020) | | 47.88 | 51.35 | 81.01 | 22.38 | 27.49 | 55.10 |
| ACL (Jiang et al., 2020) | | 49.27 | **52.82** | 82.19 | 23.63 | **29.38** | 56.61 |
| AdvCL (Fan et al., 2021) | | **49.77** | 52.77 | **83.62** | **24.72** | 28.73 | **56.77** |

**Table 17.3** Cross-dataset performance of ADVCL (dark gray color), compared with supervised (white color) and self-supervised (light gray) baselines in AA, RA, SA on STL-10 with ResNet-18.

| Method | Fine-tuning | CIFAR-10 → STL-10 | | | CIFAR-100 → STL-10 | | |
|---|---|---|---|---|---|---|---|
| | | AA (%) | RA (%) | SA (%) | AA (%) | RA (%) | SA (%) |
| Supervised | SLF | 22.26 | 30.45 | 54.70 | 19.54 | 23.63 | **51.11** |
| RoCL (Kim et al., 2020) | | 18.65 | 28.18 | 54.56 | 12.39 | 21.93 | 47.86 |
| ACL (Jiang et al., 2020) | | 25.29 | 31.80 | 55.81 | **21.75** | 26.32 | 45.91 |
| AdvCL (Fan et al., 2021) | | **25.74** | **35.80** | **63.73** | 20.86 | **30.35** | 50.71 |
| Supervised | AFF | 33.10 | 36.7 | 62.78 | 29.18 | 32.43 | 55.85 |
| RoCL (Kim et al., 2020) | | 29.40 | 34.65 | 61.75 | 27.55 | 31.38 | 57.83 |
| ACL (Jiang et al., 2020) | | 32.50 | 35.93 | 62.65 | 28.68 | 32.41 | 57.16 |
| AdvCL (Fan et al., 2021) | | **34.70** | **37.78** | **63.52** | **30.51** | **33.70** | **61.56** |

**Table 17.4** Performance (RA and SA) of ADVCL (in dark gray color) and baseline approaches on CIFAR-10 under different linear finetuning strategies, SLF and adversarial linear finetuning (ALF).

| Method | SLF | | ALF | |
|---|---|---|---|---|
| | RA (%) | SA (%) | RA (%) | SA (%) |
| Supervised | 44.40 | 79.77 | 46.75 | 79.06 |
| RoCL (Kim et al., 2020) | 39.54 | 79.90 | 43.11 | 77.33 |
| ACL (Jiang et al., 2020) | 42.87 | 77.88 | 45.40 | 77.71 |
| AdvCL (Fan et al., 2021) | **50.45** | **80.85** | **52.01** | **79.39** |

*Robustness transferability across datasets.* In Table 17.3, we next evaluate the robustness transferability across different datasets, where $A \rightarrow B$ denotes the transferability from pretraining on dataset $A$ to finetuning on another dataset $B$ ($\neq A$) of representations learned by ADVCL. Here the pretraining setup is consistent with Table 17.2. We observe that ADVCL yields better robustness and standard accuracy than almost all baseline approaches under both SLF and AFF finetuning settings. In the case of CIFAR–100 → STL-10, although ADVCL yields 0.89% AA drop compared to ACL (Jiang et al., 2020), it yields a much better SA with 4.8% improvement.

*Linear finetuning types.* We also study the robustness difference when different linear finetuning strategies: *Standard* linear finetuning (SLF) and

*Adversarial* linear finetuning (ALF) are applied. Table 17.4 shows the performance of models trained with different pretraining methods. As we can see, our ADVCL achieves the best performance under both linear fine-tuning settings and outperforms baseline approaches in a large margin. We also note that the performance gap between SLF and ALF induced by our proposal ADVCL is much smaller than in other approaches, and ADVCL with SLF achieves much better performance than baseline approaches with ALF. This indicates that the representations learned by ADVCL is already sufficient to yield satisfactory robustness.

PART 5

# Applications beyond attack and defense

# CHAPTER 18

# Model reprogramming

Model reprogramming aims to repurpose a pretrained machine learning model to solve a problem in a new domain without changing the pretrained model parameters. The application was inspired by adversarial machine learning in the sense that a trained model can be repurposed to solve a new task that is not intentionally designed/expected by the model developer. The original paper (Elsayed et al., 2019) calls this technique "adversarial reprogramming" due to induced implications on model security and resource misuse. The authors show that we can learn a universal input transformation function (e.g., a trainable universal input perturbation) to reprogram a pretrained ImageNet model (without changing the model weights) for solving MNIST/CIFAR-10 image classification and simple vision-based counting tasks with high accuracy. Later on, it was found that model reprogramming is a powerful tool for efficient machine learning in a resource-limited setting, including limitations on data and development cost (Tsai et al., 2020; Yang et al., 2021b). We will use the terms "model reprogramming" and "adversarial reprogramming" (AR) interchangeably, though in the following context the technique is not for adversarial purposes, but rather for efficient cross-domain learning in resource-limited settings.

To facilitate the discussion, in this chapter, we use the mathematical notations given in Table 18.1.

## 18.1 Reprogramming voice models for time series classification

Machine learning for time series data has rich applications in a variety of domains, ranging from medical diagnosis (e.g., physiological signals such as electrocardiogram (ECG)), finance/weather forecasting, to industrial measurements (e.g., sensors and Internet of Things (IoT)). One common practical challenge that prevents time series learning tasks from using modern large-scale deep learning models is data scarcity. Although many efforts have been made to advance transfer learning and model adaptation for time series classification, a principled approach is lacking, and its performance may not be comparable to conventional statistical learning benchmarks.

*Adversarial Robustness for Machine Learning*
https://doi.org/10.1016/B978-0-12-824020-5.00030-2

**Table 18.1** Mathematical notation for reprogramming.

| Symbol | Meaning |
|---|---|
| $\mathcal{S}$ / $\mathcal{T}$ | source/target domain |
| $\mathcal{X}_{\mathcal{S}}$ / $\mathcal{X}_{\mathcal{T}}$ | the space of source/target data samples |
| $\mathcal{Y}_{\mathcal{S}}$ / $\mathcal{Y}_{\mathcal{T}}$ | the space of source/target data labels |
| $\mathcal{D}_{\mathcal{S}} \subseteq \mathcal{X}_{\mathcal{S}} \times \mathcal{Y}_{\mathcal{S}}$ / $\mathcal{D}_{\mathcal{T}} \subseteq \mathcal{X}_{\mathcal{T}} \times \mathcal{Y}_{\mathcal{T}}$ | source/target data distribution |
| $(x, y) \sim \mathcal{D}$ | data sample $x$ and one-hot coded label $y$ drawn from $\mathcal{D}$ |
| $K$ | number of source labels |
| $f_{\mathcal{S}} : \mathbb{R}^d \mapsto [0, 1]^K$ | pretrained $K$-way source classification model |
| $\eta : \mathbb{R}^K \mapsto [0, 1]^K$ | softmax function in neural network, and $\sum_{k=1}^{K} [\eta(\cdot)]_k = 1$ |
| $z(\cdot) \in \mathbb{R}^K$ | logit (presoftmax) representation, and $f(x) = \eta(z(x))$ |
| $\ell(x, y) \triangleq \|f(x) - y\|_2$ | risk function of $(x, y)$ based on classifier $f$ |
| $\mathbb{E}_{\mathcal{D}}[\ell(x, y)] \triangleq \mathbb{E}_{(x,y) \sim \mathcal{D}}[\ell(x, y)] = \mathbb{E}_{\mathcal{D}}\|f(x) - y\|_2$ | population risk based on classifier $f$ |
| $\delta, \theta$ | additive input transformation on target data, parameterized by $\theta$ |
| $P(\cdot)$ | probability |

To bridge this gap, Yang et al. (2021b) proposed a novel approach, named *voice to series (V2S)*, for time series classification by reprogramming a pretrained acoustic model (AM), such as a spoken-terms recognition model. Unlike general time series tasks, modern AMs are trained on massive human voice datasets and are considered as a mature technology widely deployed in intelligent electronic devices. The rationale of V2S lies in the fact that voice data can be viewed as univariate temporal signals, and therefore a well-trained AM is likely to be reprogrammed as a powerful feature extractor for solving time series classification tasks. Fig. 18.1 shows a schematic illustration of the V2S framework, including (a) a trainable reprogram layer, (b) a pretrained AM, and (c) a specified label mapping function between source (human voice) and target (time series) labels.

*Trainable input transformation function.* Let $x_t \in \mathcal{X}_{\mathcal{T}} \subseteq \mathbb{R}^{d_{\mathcal{T}}}$ denote a univariate time series input from the target domain with $d_{\mathcal{T}}$ temporal features. V2S aims to find a trainable input transformation function $\mathcal{H}$ that is universal to all target data inputs, which serves the purpose of reprogramming $x_t$ into the source data space $\mathcal{X}_{\mathcal{S}} \subseteq \mathbb{R}^{d_{\mathcal{S}}}$, where $d_{\mathcal{T}} < d_{\mathcal{S}}$. Specifically, the

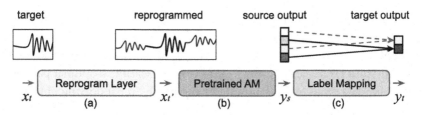

**Figure 18.1** Schematic illustration of the Voice2Series (V2S) framework (Yang et al., 2021b): (a) trainable reprogram layer; (b) pretrained acoustic model (AM); (c) source-target label mapping function.

reprogrammed sample $x_t'$ is formulated as

$$x_t' = \mathcal{H}(x_t; \theta) := \text{Pad}(x_t) + \underbrace{M \odot \theta}_{\triangleq \delta}, \qquad (18.1)$$

where $\text{Pad}(x_t)$ is a zero padding function that outputs a zero-padded time series of dimension $d_S$. The location of the segment $x_t$ to be placed in $x_t'$ is a design parameter as discussed by Yang et al. (2021b). The term $M \in \{0, 1\}^{d_S}$ is a binary mask that indicates the location of $x_t$ in its zero-padded input $\text{Pad}(x_t)$, where the $i$th entry of $M$ is 0 if $x_t$ is present (indicating that the entry is nonreprogrammable) and 1 otherwise (indicating that the entry is not occupied and thus reprogrammable). The operator $\odot$ denotes elementwise product. Finally, $\theta \in \mathbb{R}^{d_S}$ is a set of trainable parameters for aligning source and target domain data distributions. The term $\delta \triangleq M \odot \theta$ denotes the trainable additive input transformation for V2S reprogramming. For ease of representation, we will omit the padding notation and simply use $x_t + \delta$ to denote the reprogrammed target data by treating the operation "+" as a zero-padded broadcasting function.

*Pretrained model and output label mapping.* We select a pretrained deep acoustic classification model as the source model $f_S$ for model reprogramming. We assume that the source model has softmax as the final layer and outputs nonnegative confidence score (prediction probability) for each source label. With the transformed data inputs $\mathcal{H}(x_t; \theta)$ described in (18.1), we can obtain the class prediction of the source model $f_S$ on a reprogrammed target data sample $x_t$, denoted by

$$P(y_s | f_S(\mathcal{H}(x_t; \theta))) \text{ for } y_s \in \mathcal{Y}_S. \qquad (18.2)$$

Next, as illustrated in Fig. 18.1, we assign a (many-to-one) label mapping function $h$ to map source labels to target labels. For a target label

$y_t \in \mathcal{Y}_T$, its class prediction will be the averaged class prediction over the set of source labels assigned to it. We use the term $P(h(\mathcal{Y}_S)|f_S(\mathcal{H}(x_t; \theta)))$ to denote the prediction probability of the target task on the associated ground-truth target label $y_t = h(\mathcal{Y}_S)$. Finally, we learn the optimal parameters $\theta^*$ for data input reprogramming by optimizing the following objective:

$$\theta^* = \underset{\theta}{\operatorname{argmin}} \underbrace{- \log P(h(\mathcal{Y}_S)|f_S(\mathcal{H}(x_t; \theta)))}_{\text{V2S loss} \triangleq L}, \tag{18.3}$$

$$\text{where} \quad h(\mathcal{Y}_S) = y_t$$

The optimization will be implemented by minimizing the empirical loss (V2S loss $L$) evaluated on all target-domain training data pairs $\{x_t, y_t\}$ for solving $\theta^*$.

In practice, Yang et al. (2021b) found that a many-to-one label mapping can improve the reprogramming accuracy when compared to a one-to-one label mapping. Below we make a concrete example on how a many-to-one label mapping is used for V2S reprogramming. Consider the case of reprogramming spoken-term AM for ECG classification. We can choose to map multiple (but nonoverlapping) classes from the source task (e.g., "yes", "no", "up", "down" in AM classes) to every class from the target task (e.g., "Normal" or "Ischemia" in ECG classes), leading to a specified mapping function $h$. Let $\mathcal{B} \subset \mathcal{Y}_S$ denote the set of source labels mapping to the target label $y_t \in \mathcal{Y}_T$. Then the class prediction of $y_t$ based on V2S reprogramming is the aggregated prediction over the assigned source labels defined as

$$P(y_t|f_S(\mathcal{H}(x_t; \theta))) = \frac{1}{|\mathcal{B}|} \sum_{y_s \in \mathcal{B}} P(y_s|f_S(\mathcal{H}(x_t; \theta))), \tag{18.4}$$

where $|\mathcal{B}|$ denotes the number of labels in $\mathcal{B}$.

Algorithm 5 summarizes the training procedure of the V2S reprogramming.

*Experimental results.* Two pretrained voice models V2S$_a$ and V2S$_u$ are used as source models for reprogramming. Fig. 18.2 shows their end-to-end model architecture, and we refer for their details to (Yang et al., 2021b). Testing on a standard UCR time series classification benchmark (Dau et al., 2019), it is shown by Yang et al. (2021b) that V2S either outperforms or is tied with the best reported results on 19 out of 30 datasets, suggesting that V2S is a principled and effective approach for time series classification.

---

**Algorithm 5** Voice to Series (V2S) reprogramming.

---

1: **Inputs**: Pretrained acoustic model $f_S$, V2S loss $L$ in (18.3), target domain training data $\{x_t^{(i)}, y_t^{(i)}\}_{i=1}^n$, mask function $M$, multilabel mapping function $h(\cdot)$, maximum number of iterations $T$, initial learning rate $\alpha$

2: **Output**: Optimal reprogramming parameters $\theta^*$

3: Initialize $\theta$ randomly; set $t = 0$

4: **#Generate reprogrammed data input**

5: $\mathcal{H}(x_t^{(i)}; \theta) = \text{Pad}(x_t^{(i)}) + M \odot \theta \ \forall \ i = \{1, 2, \ldots, n\}$

6: **#Compute V2S loss $L$ from Eq. (18.3)**

7: $L(\theta) = -\frac{1}{n} \sum_{i=1}^n \log P(y_t^{(i)} | f_S(\mathcal{H}(x_t^{(i)}); \theta))$

8: **#Solve reprogramming parameters**

9: Use ADAM optimizer (Kingma and Ba, 2015) to solve for $\theta^*$ based on $L(\theta)$

---

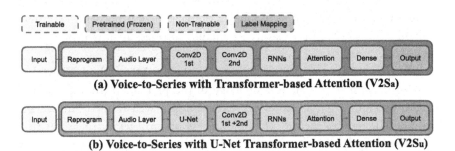

(a) Voice-to-Series with Transformer-based Attention (V2Sₐ)

(b) Voice-to-Series with U-Net Transformer-based Attention (V2Su)

**Figure 18.2** V2S model architectures: (a) V2S$_a$ (de Andrade et al., 2018) and (b) V2S$_u$ (Yang et al., 2021a).

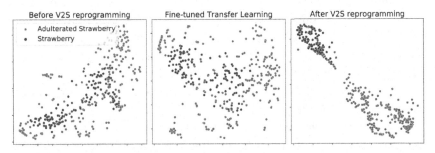

**Figure 18.3** tSNE plots of the logit representations using the Strawberry training set (Holland et al., 1998) and V2S$_a$ for the cases of before and after V2S reprogramming, and fine-tuned transfer learning (TF$_a$).

We use t-distributed stochastic neighbor embedding (tSNE) (Van der Maaten and Hinton, 2008) to visualize the logit representations of the

Strawberry training set (Holland et al., 1998) for the cases of before and after reprogramming, and the transfer learning baseline ($TF_a$). As shown in Fig. 18.3, after reprogramming, tSNE results show a clear separation between the embeddings from different target classes, suggesting that V2S indeed learns meaningful and discriminative data representations to reprogram the pretrained acoustic model for time series classification. On the other hand, the embedding visualization of transfer learning shows low classwise separability.

## 18.2 Reprogramming general image models for medical image classification

In this section, we introduce two capabilities of model reprogramming in terms of (i) the ability to reprogram a black-box model and (ii) the ability to reprogram general image models (e.g., deep neural network classifiers trained on ImageNet) for classifying medical images, as shown by Tsai et al. (2020).

*Black-box and resource-limited settings.* The vanilla AR method (Elsayed et al., 2019) assumes complete knowledge of the pretrained (source) model, which precludes the ability of reprogramming a well-trained but access-limited ML models such as prediction APIs or proprietary softwares that only reveal model outputs based on queried data inputs. Moreover, whereas data are crucial to most of ML tasks, in some scenarios such as medical applications, massive data collection can be expensive, if not impossible, especially when clinical trials, expert annotation, or privacy-sensitive data are involved. Consequently, without transfer learning, the practical limitation of data scarcity may hinder the strength of complex (large-scaled) ML models such as deep neural networks (DNNs). Finally, even with moderate amount of data, researchers may not have sufficient computation resources or budgets to train a DNN as large as a commercial ML model or perform transfer learning on a large pretrained ML model.

*Black-box reprogramming.* Fig. 18.4 provides an overview of the black-box adversarial reprogramming (BAR) method proposed by Tsai et al. (2020). To adapt to the black-box setting, zeroth-order optimization (Liu et al., 2020a) on iterative input–output model responses is used for optimizing the parameters associated with the input transformation functions, similarly to the methodology adopted for black-box evasion attacks in Chapter 3. Similarly to the end-to-end reprogramming framework in Section 18.1, we can use an input transformation function such as a universal trainable

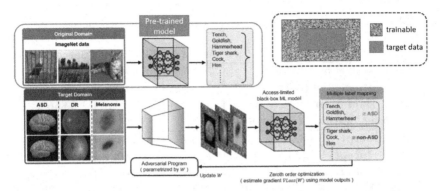

**Figure 18.4** Schematic overview of black-box adversarial reprogramming (BAR) proposed by Tsai et al. (2020).

additive input with a mask on the target data as the reprogrammed input, as well as a many-to-one label mapping function between the source and target domains, as demonstrated in Fig. 18.4.

*Experimental results.* Tsai et al. (2020) reprogram three pretrained ImageNet classifiers (1000-object recognition task), including ResNet 50, Inception V3, and DenseNet 121 models, for Autism Spectrum Disorder (ASD) classification (2-classes).[1] The dataset is split into 10 folds and contains 503 individuals suffering from ASD and 531 non-ASD samples. The data sample is a 200 × 200 brain-regional correlation graph of fMRI measurements, which is embedded in each color channel of ImageNet-sized inputs for reprogramming. The baselines comparisons include vanilla adversarial reprogramming (white-box AR), transfer learning via finetuning, training from scratch, and state-of-the-art (SOTA) results reported by the previous studies.

Table 18.2 reports the 10-fold cross validation test accuracy, where the averaged test data size is 104. The accuracy of BAR is comparable to white-box AR, and their accuracy outperforms the SOTA performance as reported in (Heinsfeld et al., 2018; Eslami et al., 2019). The performance of finetuning and training from scratch is merely close to random guessing due to limited data, and BAR's accuracy is 17%–18% better than that of transfer learning.

*Reprogramming real-life prediction APIs.* To demonstrate the practicality of BAR in reprogramming access-limited (black-box) ML models, Tsai et al. (2020) use two real-life online ML-as-a-Service (MLaaS) toolkits provided

[1] http://preprocessed-connectomes-project.org/abide.

**Table 18.2** Performance comparison (10-fold averaged test accuracy) on autism spectrum disorder classification task.

| Model | Accuracy | Sensitivity | Specificity |
|---|---|---|---|
| ResNet 50 (BAR) | **70.33%** | **69.94%** | **72.71%** |
| ResNet 50 (AR) | 72.99% | 73.03% | 72.13% |
| Train from scratch | 51.55% | 51.17% | 53.56% |
| Transfer Learning (finetuned) | 52.88% | 54.13% | 54.70% |
| Incept. V3 (BAR) | **70.10%** | **69.40%** | **70.00%** |
| Incept. V3 (AR) | 72.30% | 71.94% | 74.71% |
| Train from scratch | 50.20% | 51.43% | 52.67% |
| Transfer Learning (finetuned) | 52.10% | 52.65% | 54.42% |
| SOTA 1. Heinsfeld et al. (2018) | 65.40% | 69.30% | 61.10% |
| SOTA 2. Eslami et al. (2019) | 69.40% | 66.40% | 71.30% |

by Clarifai.com and Microsoft Custom Vision. For Clarifai.com, a regular user on an MLaaS platform can provide any data input (of the specified format) and observe a model prediction via Prediction API but has no information about the model and training data used. For Microsoft Custom Vision, it allows users to upload labeled datasets and trains an ML model for prediction, but the trained model is unknown to users. We aim to show how BAR can "unlock" the inference power of these unknown ML models and reprogram them for Autism spectrum disorder classification. Note that white-box AR and current transfer learning methods are inapplicable in this setting as acquiring input gradients or modifying the target model is inadmissible via prediction APIs.

Clarifai Moderation API can recognize whether images or videos have contents such as "gore", "drugs", "explicit nudity", or "suggestive nudity". It also has a class called "safe", meaning that it does not contain the aforementioned four moderation categories. Therefore, in total there are five output class labels for this API. Clarifai Not Safe For Work (NSFW) API can recognize images or videos with inappropriate contents (e.g., "porn", "sex", or "nudity"). It provides the prediction of two output labels "NSFW" and "SFW". Here we separate the ASD dataset into 930/104 samples for training and testing. The test accuracy, total number of queries, and expenses of reprogramming Clarifai.com are reported in Table 18.3. For instance, to achieve 67.32% accuracy for ASD task, BAR only costs $23.04 US dollars for reprogramming the Clarifai Moderation API. Setting a larger $q$ value (which uses $q$ random-vector querying in zeroth-order optimization as discussed in Chapter 3) for a more accurate gradient esti-

Table 18.3 Performance of BAR on Clarifai.com APIs.

| Orig. Task to New Task | q | # of query | Accuracy | Cost |
|---|---|---|---|---|
| NSFW to ASD | 15 | 12.8k | 64.04% | $14.24 |
| | 25 | 24k | **65.70%** | $23.2 |
| Moderation to ASD | 15 | 11.9k | 65.14% | $13.52 |
| | 25 | 23.8k | **67.32%** | $23.04 |

Table 18.4 Performance of BAR on Microsoft Custom Vision API.

| Orig. Task to New Task | q | # of query | Accuracy | Cost |
|---|---|---|---|---|
| Traffic sign classification to ASD | 1 | 1.86k | 48.15% | $3.72 |
| | 5 | 5.58k | 62.34% | $11.16 |
| | 10 | 10.23k | **67.80%** | $20.46 |

mation can indeed improve the accuracy but at the price of increased query and expense costs.

Microsoft Custom Vision API is used to obtain a black-box traffic sign image recognition model (with 43 classes) trained with GTSRB dataset (Stallkamp et al., 2012). BAR is then applied with different numbers of random vectors $q$ (1, 5, 10) and a fixed number of random label mapping ($m = 6$ labels) to reprogram it for ASD task. As shown in Table 18.4, the test accuracy achieves 69.15% when $q$ is set to 10 and the overall query cost is $20.46 US dollars.

## 18.3 Theoretical justification of model reprogramming

To provide theoretical justification on the effectiveness of model reprogramming, in what follows, we show a formal population risk analysis and prove that based on reprogramming, the population risk of the target task is upper bounded by the sum of the source population risk and the Wasserstein-1 distance between the logit representations of the source data and the reprogrammed target data. The analysis matches the intuition that a high-accuracy (low population risk) source model with a better source-target data alignment (small Wasserstein-1 distance) should exhibit better reprogramming performance.

Using the mathematical notation summarized in Table 18.1, the source model is a pretrained $K$-way neural network classifier $f_S(\cdot) = \eta(z_S(\cdot))$ with a softmax layer $\eta(\cdot)$ as the final model output. We omit the notation of the model parameters in our analysis because reprogramming does not change the pretrained model parameters. The notation $(x, y)$ is used to describe a data sample $x$ and its one-hot coded label $y$. We will use the subscript $s/t$ to denote source/target data when applicable. For the purpose of analysis, given a neural network classifier $f$, we consider the root mean squared error (RMSE) denoted by $\|f(x) - y\|_2$.

To put forth our analysis, we make the following assumptions based on the framework of reprogramming:

1. The source risk is $\epsilon_S$, that is, $\mathbb{E}_{\mathcal{D}_S}[\ell(x_s, y_s)] = \epsilon_S$.

2. The source-target label space has a specified surjective one-to-one label mapping function $h_t$ for every target label $t$, such that for all $y_t \in \mathcal{Y}_T$, $y_t = h_t(\mathcal{Y}_S) \triangleq y_s \in \mathcal{Y}_S$, and $h_t \neq h_{t'}$ if $t \neq t'$.

3. Based on reprogramming, the target loss function $\ell_T$ with an additive input transformation function $\delta$ can be represented as $\ell_T(x_t + \delta, y_t) \overset{(a)}{=} \ell_T(x_t + \delta, y_s) \overset{(b)}{=} \ell_S(x_t + \delta, y_s)$, where $(a)$ is induced by label mapping (Assumption 2), and $(b)$ is induced by reprogramming the source loss with target data.

4. The learned input transformation function for reprogramming is denoted by $\delta^* \triangleq \arg\min_\delta \mathbb{E}_{\mathcal{D}_T}[\ell_S(x_t + \delta, y_s)]$, which is the minimizer of the target population risk with the reprogramming loss objective.

5. Domain-independent drawing of source and target data: Let $\Phi_S(\cdot)$ and $\Phi_T(\cdot)$ denote the probability density functions of source and target data distributions over $\mathcal{X}_S$ and $\mathcal{X}_T$, respectively. The joint probability density function is the product of their marginals, i.e., $\Phi_{S,T}(x_s, x_t) = \Phi_S(x_s) \cdot \Phi_T(x_t)$.

For a given neural network classifier, the following lemma associates the expected RMSE of model predictions on two different domains with the Wasserstein-1 distance between their corresponding probability measures on the logit representations, which will play a key role in characterizing the population risk for reprogramming. The Wasserstein distance is a statistical distance between two probability measures $\mu$ and $\mu'$, widely used for studying optimal transport problems (Peyré and Cuturi, 2018). Specifically, for any $p \geq 1$, the Wasserstein-$p$ distance is defined as

$$\mathcal{W}_p(\mu, \mu') = \left( \inf_{\pi \in \Pi(\mu, \mu')} \int \|x - x'\|^p d\pi(x, x') \right)^{1/p},$$

where $\Pi(\mu, \mu')$ denotes all joint distributions $\pi$ that have marginals $\mu$ and $\mu'$.

**Lemma 6.** *Given a K-way neural network classifier $f(\cdot) = \eta(z(\cdot))$, let $\mu_z$ and $\mu'_z$ be the probability measures of the logit representations $\{z(x)\}$ and $\{z(x')\}$ from two data domains $\mathcal{D}$ and $\mathcal{D}'$, where $x \sim \mathcal{D}$ and $x' \sim \mathcal{D}'$. Assume independent draws for $x$ and $x'$, i.e., $\Phi_{\mathcal{D},\mathcal{D}'}(x, x') = \Phi_{\mathcal{D}}(x) \cdot \Phi_{\mathcal{D}'}(x')$. Then*

$$\mathbb{E}_{x \sim \mathcal{D}, \; x' \sim \mathcal{D}'} \|f(x) - f(x')\|_2 \le 2\sqrt{K} \cdot \mathcal{W}_1(\mu_z, \mu'_z),$$

*where $\mathcal{W}_1(\mu_z, \mu'_z)$ is the Wasserstein-1 distance between $\mu_z$ and $\mu'_z$.*

*Proof.* See Section 18.4. □

With Lemma 6, we now state the main theorem regarding an upper bound on population risk for reprogramming.

**Theorem 7.** *Let $\delta^*$ denote the learned additive input transformation for reprogramming (Assumption 4). The population risk for the target task via reprogramming a K-way source neural network classifier $f_S(\cdot) = \eta(z_S(\cdot))$, denoted by $\mathbb{E}_{\mathcal{D}_T}[\ell_T(x_t + \delta^*, y_t)]$, is upper bounded by*

$$\mathbb{E}_{\mathcal{D}_T}[\ell_T(x_t + \delta^*, y_t)] \le$$
$$\underbrace{\epsilon_S}_{\text{source risk}} + \underbrace{2\sqrt{K} \cdot \mathcal{W}_1(\mu(z_S(x_t + \delta^*)), \mu(z_S(x_s)))_{x_t \sim \mathcal{D}_T, \; x_s \sim \mathcal{D}_S}}_{\text{representation alignment loss via reprogramming}}.$$

*Proof.* See Section 18.4. □

Theorem 7 shows that the target population risk via reprogramming is upper bounded by the summation of two terms: (i) the source population risk $\epsilon_S$ and (ii) the representation alignment loss in the logit layer between the source data $z_S(x_s)$ and the reprogrammed target data $z_S(x_t + \delta^*)$ based on the same source neural network classifier $f_S(\cdot) = \eta(z_S(\cdot))$, measured by their Wasserstein-1 distance. The results suggest that reprogramming can attain better performance (lower risk) when the source model has a lower source loss and a smaller representation alignment loss.

In the extreme case, if the source and target representations can be fully aligned, then the Wasserstein-1 distance will become 0, and thus the target task via reprogramming can perform as well as the source task. On the other hand, if the representation alignment loss is large, then it may dominate the source risk and hinder the performance on the target task. We would also like to make a final remark that our risk analysis can be extended beyond the additive input transformation setting by considering a more complex function input transformation function $g(x_t)$ (e.g., an affine transformation).

*Numerical example.* As an illustration, we use the following experiments to empirically verify the representation alignment loss during V2S training and motivate its use for reprogramming performance assessment. Specifically, for computational efficiency, we use the sliced Wasserstein-2 distance (SWD) (Kolouri et al., 2018) to approximate the Wasserstein-1 distance in Theorem 7. SWD uses the one-dimensional (1D) random projection (we use 1,000 runs) to compute the sliced Wasserstein-2 distance by invoking 1D-optimal transport (OT), which possesses computational efficiency when compared to higher-dimensional OT problems (Peyré and Cuturi, 2018). Moreover, the Wasserstein-1 distance is upper bounded by the Wasserstein-2 distance (Peyré and Cuturi, 2018), and therefore the SWD will serve as a good approximation of the exact representation alignment loss.

*Sliced Wasserstein distance during training.* Using the DistalPhalanxTW dataset (Davis, 2013) and V2S$_a$ in Table 18.2, Fig. 18.5 shows the validation (test) accuracy, validation (test) loss, and SWD during V2S training. We can observe a similar trend between test loss and SWD, suggesting that V2S indeed learns to reprogram the target data representations by gradually making them closer to the source data distribution, as indicated by Theorem 7.

## 18.4 Proofs

*Proof of Lemma 6.* For brevity, we use $[K]$ to denote the integer set $\{1, 2, \ldots, K\}$. We have

$$\mathbb{E}_{x\sim\mathcal{D},\ x'\sim\mathcal{D}'}\|f(x) - f(x')\|_2$$

$$\overset{(a)}{=} \mathbb{E}_{x\sim\mathcal{D},\ x'\sim\mathcal{D}'}\|\eta(z(x)) - \eta(z(x'))\|_2 \tag{18.5}$$

$$\overset{(b)}{=} \int_{x\sim\mathcal{D},\ x'\sim\mathcal{D}'}\|\eta(z(x)) - \eta(z(x'))\|_2\Phi_{\mathcal{D},\mathcal{D}'}(x, x')dxdx' \tag{18.6}$$

$$\overset{(c)}{=} \int_{x\sim\mathcal{D},\ x'\sim\mathcal{D}'}\|\eta(z(x)) - \eta(z(x'))\|_2\Phi_{\mathcal{D}}(x)\cdot\Phi_{\mathcal{D}'}(x')dxdx' \tag{18.7}$$

$$\overset{(d)}{\leq} \sqrt{K}\cdot\int_{x\sim\mathcal{D},\ x'\sim\mathcal{D}'}\max_{k\in[K]}|[\eta(z(x))]_k - [\eta(z(x'))]_k|\Phi_{\mathcal{D}}(x)\cdot\Phi_{\mathcal{D}'}(x')dxdx'$$

$$\tag{18.8}$$

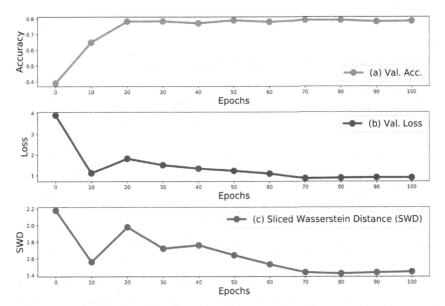

**Figure 18.5** Training-time reprogramming analysis using V2S$_a$ and DistalPhalanxTW dataset Davis (2013). All values are averaged over the test set. The rows are (a) validation (test) accuracy, (b) validation loss, and (c) sliced Wasserstein distance (SWD) (Kolouri et al., 2018).

$$\overset{(e)}{\leq} 2\sqrt{K} \cdot \sup_{g:\mathbb{R}^K \mapsto \mathbb{R}, \|g\|_{\mathrm{Lip}} \leq 1} \mathbb{E}_{x\sim\mathcal{D}}[g(z(x))] - \mathbb{E}_{x'\sim\mathcal{D}'}[g(z(x'))] \tag{18.9}$$

$$\overset{(f)}{=} 2\sqrt{K} \cdot \mathcal{W}_1(\mu_z, \mu'_z), \tag{18.10}$$

where (a) follows from the neural network model, (b) follows from the definition of expectation, (c) follows from the assumption of independent data drawing, (d) follows from $\|x\|_2 = \sqrt{\sum_i^d x_i^2} \leq \sqrt{d \cdot \max_i[x_i^2]} = \sqrt{d} \cdot \max_i |x_i|$, which yields $\|\eta - \eta'\|_2 \leq \sqrt{K} \cdot \max_k |[\eta - \eta']_k|$, and (e) holds by setting $k^+ = \arg\max_{k\in[K]}[\eta(z(x))]_k - [\eta(z(x'))]_k$ and $k^- = \arg\max_{k\in[K]}[\eta(z(x'))]_k - [\eta(z(x))]_k$. Then by definition $\max_{k\in[K]} |[\eta(z(x))]_k - [\eta(z(x'))]_k| \leq [\eta(z(x))]_{k^+} - [\eta(z(x'))]_{k^+} + [\eta(z(x'))]_{k^-} - [\eta(z(x))]_{k^-}$. We further make the following three notes: (i) $[\eta(z(x))]_{k^+} - [\eta(z(x'))]_{k^+} \geq 0$ and $[\eta(z(x))]_{k^-} - [\eta(z(x'))]_{k^-} \geq 0$; (ii) $|a| = \max\{a, -a\}$, and if $a, b \geq 0$, then $\max\{a, b\} \leq a + b$; (iii) There exists at least one $k$ such that $[\eta(x)]_k - [\eta(x)]_k \geq 0$. We can use a proof by contradiction to show that (iii) is true. If $[\eta(x)]_k - [\eta(x)]_k < 0$ for every $k$, then summing over $k$, we get a contradiction that $1 < 1$. Therefore

$$\int_{x\sim\mathcal{D},\ x'\sim\mathcal{D}'} \max_{k\in[K]} |[\eta(z(x))]_k - [\eta(z(x'))]_k| \Phi_{\mathcal{D}}(x) \cdot \Phi_{\mathcal{D}'}(x') dx dx' \qquad (18.11)$$

$$\leq \int_{x\sim\mathcal{D},\ x'\sim\mathcal{D}'} \left([\eta(z(x))]_{k^+} - [\eta(z(x))]_{k^-} + [\eta(z(x'))]_{k^-} - [\eta(z(x'))]_{k^+}\right)$$

$$\cdot \Phi_{\mathcal{D}}(x) \cdot \Phi_{\mathcal{D}'}(x') dx dx' \qquad (18.12)$$

$$= \mathbb{E}_{x\sim\mathcal{D}}[[\eta(z(x))]_{k^+} - [\eta(z(x))]_{k^-}] - \mathbb{E}_{x'\sim\mathcal{D}'}[[\eta(z(x'))]_{k^+} - [\eta(z(x'))]_{k^-}]$$

$$(18.13)$$

$$\leq 2 \cdot \sup_{g:\mathbb{R}^K\mapsto\mathbb{R},\ \|g\|_{\mathrm{Lip}}\leq 1} \mathbb{E}_{x\sim\mathcal{D}}[g(z(x))] - \mathbb{E}_{x'\sim\mathcal{D}'}[g(z(x'))], \qquad (18.14)$$

where $\|g\|_{\mathrm{Lip}}$ is defined as $\sup_{x,x'} |g(x) - g(x')|/\|x - x'\|_2$, and we use the fact that $[\eta(z)]_k$ is 1-Lipschitz for all $k \in [K]$ (Gao and Pavel, 2017) (so $[\eta]_{k^+} - [\eta]_{k^-}$ is 2-Lipschitz). Finally, (f) follows from the Kantorovich–Rubinstein theorem (Kantorovich and Rubinstein, 1958) of the dual representation of the Wasserstein-1 distance. $\qquad \square$

*Proof of Theorem 7.* First, we decompose the target risk function as

$$\ell_T(x_t + \delta^*, y_t) \overset{(a)}{=} \ell_S(x_t + \delta^*, y_s) \qquad (18.15)$$

$$\overset{(b)}{=} \|f_S(x_t + \delta^*) - y_s\|_2 \qquad (18.16)$$

$$\overset{(c)}{=} \|f_S(x_t + \delta^*) - f_S(x_s) + f_S(x_s) - y_s\|_2 \qquad (18.17)$$

$$\overset{(d)}{\leq} \underbrace{\|f_S(x_t + \delta^*) - f_S(x_s)\|_2}_{A} + \underbrace{\|f_S(x_s) - y_s\|_2}_{B}. \qquad (18.18)$$

(a) is based on Assumption 3, (b) is based on the definition of risk function, (c) is by subtracting and adding the same term $f_S(x_s)$, and (d) is based on the triangle inequality.

Note that by Assumption 1, $\mathbb{E}_{\mathcal{D}_S} B = \mathbb{E}_{\mathcal{D}_S}[\ell(x_s, y_s)] = \epsilon_S$. Next, we proceed to bound $\mathbb{E}_{\mathcal{D}_S,\mathcal{D}_T} A \triangleq \mathbb{E}_{x_s\sim\mathcal{D}_S, x_t\sim\mathcal{D}_T} A$. Using Lemma 6, we have

$$\mathbb{E}_{\mathcal{D}_S,\mathcal{D}_T} A \leq 2\sqrt{K} \cdot \mathcal{W}_1(\mu(z_S(x_t + \delta^*)), \mu(z_S(x_s)))_{x_t\sim\mathcal{D}_T,\ x_s\sim\mathcal{D}_S}. \qquad (18.19)$$

Finally, taking $\mathbb{E}_{\mathcal{D}_S,\mathcal{D}_T}$ on both sides of Eq. (18.18) completes the proof. $\qquad \square$

## 18.5  Extended reading

- A survey paper for model reprogramming: (Chen, 2022).
- Vinod et al. (2020) propose reprogramming language models for solving molecule learning tasks.
- Reprogramming in the natural language processing domains: (Neekhara et al., 2018; Hambardzumyan et al., 2021).
- Yen et al. (2021) use reprogramming for low-resource speech recognition.
- An active repository maintaining studies in model reprogramming: https://github.com/IBM/model-reprogramming.

# CHAPTER 19

# Contrastive explanations

Contrastive explanations aim to generate local explanations for neural networks of a given data input, in which, besides highlighting what is minimally sufficient (e.g., tall and long hair) in an input to justify its classification, we also want to identify contrastive characteristics or features that should be minimally and critically *absent* (e.g., glasses), so as to maintain the current classification and to distinguish it from another input that is "closest" to it but would be classified differently (e.g., Bob). We thus want to generate explanations of the form *An input x is classified in class y because features $f_i, \ldots, f_k$ are present and because features $f_m, \ldots, f_p$ are absent.*

There is a strong motivation to have such a form of explanations due to their presence in certain human-critical domains. In medicine and criminology, there is the notion of pertinent positives and pertinent negatives (Herman, 2016), which together constitute a complete explanation. *A pertinent positive (PP) is a factor whose presence is minimally sufficient in justifying the final classification. On the other hand, a pertinent negative (PN) is a factor whose absence is necessary in asserting the final classification.* For example, in medicine a patient showing symptoms of cough, cold and fever, but no sputum or chills, will most likely be diagnosed as having flu rather than having pneumonia. Cough, cold, and fever could imply both flu or pneumonia; however, the absence of sputum and chills leads to the diagnosis of flu. Thus sputum and chills are pertinent negatives, which along with the pertinent positives are critical and in some sense sufficient for an accurate diagnosis. The methods to identify such PPs and PNs can benefit from the study of generating and designing adversarial examples.

## 19.1 Contrastive explanations method

In this section, we detail the contrastive explanations method (CEM) proposed by Dhurandhar et al. (2018). Let $\mathcal{X}$ denote the feasible data space, and let $(x_0, t_0)$ denote an example $x_0 \in \mathcal{X}$ and its inferred class label $t_0$ obtained from a neural network model. The modified example $x \in \mathcal{X}$ based on $x_0$ is defined as $x = x_0 + \delta$, where $\delta$ is a perturbation applied to $x_0$. The method of finding pertinent positives/negatives is formulated as an optimization problem over the perturbation variable $\delta$ used to explain the model prediction results. We denote the prediction of the model on the example $x$ by $\mathrm{Pred}(x)$, where Pred is any function that outputs a vector of prediction scores for all classes, such as prediction probabilities and logits (unnormalized probabilities) widely used in neural networks, among others.

To ensure that the modified example $x$ is still close to the data manifold of natural examples, Dhurandhar et al. (2018) proposed to use an autoencoder to evaluate the closeness of $x$ to the data manifold. We denote by $\mathrm{AE}(x)$ the reconstructed example of $x$ using the autoencoder AE.

*Finding pertinent negatives (PNs).* For pertinent negative analysis, we are interested in what is missing in the model prediction. For any natural example $x_0$, we use the notation $\mathcal{X}/x_0$ to denote the space of missing parts with respect to $x_0$. We aim to find an interpretable perturbation $\delta \in \mathcal{X}/x_0$ to study the difference between the most probable class predictions in $\arg\max_i[\mathrm{Pred}(x_0)]_i$ and $\arg\max_i[\mathrm{Pred}(x_0 + \delta)]_i$. Given $(x_0, t_0)$, our method finds a pertinent negative by solving the following optimization problem:

$$\min_{\delta \in \mathcal{X}/x_0} c \cdot f_\kappa^{\mathrm{neg}}(x_0, \delta) + \beta \|\delta\|_1 + \|\delta\|_2^2 + \gamma \|x_0 + \delta - \mathrm{AE}(x_0 + \delta)\|_2^2. \quad (19.1)$$

We elaborate on the role of each term in the objective function (19.1) as follows. The first term $f_\kappa^{\mathrm{neg}}(x_0, \delta)$ is a designed loss function that encourages the modified example $x = x_0 + \delta$ to be predicted as a class different from $t_0 = \arg\max_i[\mathrm{Pred}(x_0)]_i$. The loss function is defined as

$$f_\kappa^{\mathrm{neg}}(x_0, \delta) = \max\{[\mathrm{Pred}(x_0 + \delta)]_{t_0} - \max_{i \neq t_0}[\mathrm{Pred}(x_0 + \delta)]_i, -\kappa\}, \quad (19.2)$$

where $[\mathrm{Pred}(x_0 + \delta)]_i$ is the $i$th class prediction score of $x_0 + \delta$. The hinge-like loss function favors the modified example $x$ to have a top-1 prediction class different from that of the original example $x_0$. The parameter $\kappa \geq 0$ is a confidence parameter that controls the separation between $[\mathrm{Pred}(x_0 + \delta)]_{t_0}$ and $\max_{i \neq t_0}[\mathrm{Pred}(x_0 + \delta)]_i$. The second and third terms $\beta \|\delta\|_1 + \|\delta\|_2^2$ in (19.1) are jointly called the elastic net regularizer, which is used for efficient feature selection in high-dimensional learning problems (Zou and Hastie, 2005). The last term $\|x_0 + \delta - \mathrm{AE}(x_0 + \delta)\|_2^2$ is an $L_2$ reconstruction error of $x$ evaluated by the autoencoder. This is relevant provided that a well-trained autoencoder for the domain is obtainable. The parameters $c, \beta, \gamma \geq 0$ are the associated regularization coefficients.

*Finding pertinent positives (PPs).* For pertinent positive analysis, we are interested in the critical features readily present in the input. Given a natural example $x_0$, we denote the space of its existing components by $\mathcal{X} \cap x_0$. Here

---

**Algorithm 6** Contrastive Explanations Method (CEM).

---

**Input:** example $(x_0, t_0)$, neural network model $\mathcal{N}$, and (optionally ($\gamma > 0$)) an autoencoder $AE$

1) Solve (19.1) and obtain

$\delta^{\text{neg}} \leftarrow \operatorname{argmin}_{\delta \in \mathcal{X}/x_0} c \cdot f_\kappa^{\text{neg}}(x_0, \delta) + \beta \|\delta\|_1 + \|\delta\|_2^2 + \gamma \|x_0 + \delta - AE(x_0 + \delta)\|_2^2$.

2) Solve (19.3) and obtain

$\delta^{\text{pos}} \leftarrow \operatorname{argmin}_{\delta \in \mathcal{X} \cap x_0} c \cdot f_\kappa^{\text{pos}}(x_0, \delta) + \beta \|\delta\|_1 + \|\delta\|_2^2 + \gamma \|\delta - AE(\delta)\|_2^2$.

**return** $\delta^{\text{pos}}$ and $\delta^{\text{neg}}$.

## Contrastive Explanation: Input $x_0$ is classified as class $t_0$ because features $\delta^{\text{pos}}$ are present and because features $\delta^{\text{neg}}$ are absent.

---

we aim at finding an interpretable perturbation $\delta \in \mathcal{X} \cap x_0$ such that after removing it from $x_0$, $\operatorname{argmax}_i[\text{Pred}(x_0)]_i = \operatorname{argmax}_i[\text{Pred}(\delta)]_i$; that is, $x_0$ and $\delta$ will have the same top-1 prediction class $t_0$, indicating that the removed perturbation $\delta$ is representative of the model prediction on $x_0$. Similarly to finding pertinent negatives, we formulate finding pertinent positives as the following optimization problem:

$$\min_{\delta \in \mathcal{X} \cap x_0} c \cdot f_\kappa^{\text{pos}}(x_0, \delta) + \beta \|\delta\|_1 + \|\delta\|_2^2 + \gamma \|\delta - AE(\delta)\|_2^2, \tag{19.3}$$

where the loss function $f_\kappa^{\text{pos}}(x_0, \delta)$ is defined as

$$f_\kappa^{\text{pos}}(x_0, \delta) = \max\{\max_{i \neq t_0}[\text{Pred}(\delta)]_i - [\text{Pred}(\delta)]_{t_0}, -\kappa\}. \tag{19.4}$$

In other words, for any given confidence $\kappa \geq 0$, the loss function $f_\kappa^{\text{pos}}$ is minimized when $[\text{Pred}(\delta)]_{t_0}$ is greater than $\max_{i \neq t_0}[\text{Pred}(\delta)]_i$ by at least $\kappa$.

*Algorithmic details.* A projected fast iterative shrinkage-thresholding algorithm (FISTA) (Beck and Teboulle, 2009) is applied to solve problems (19.1) and (19.3). FISTA is an efficient solver for optimization problems involving $\ell_1$ regularization. Take pertinent negative as an example, assume that $\mathcal{X} = [-1, 1]^p$ and $\mathcal{X}/x_0 = [0, 1]^p$, and let $g(\delta) = f_\kappa^{\text{neg}}(x_0, \delta) + \|\delta\|_2^2 + \gamma \|x_0 + \delta - AE(x_0 + \delta)\|_2^2$ denote the objective function of (19.1) without the $\ell_1$ regularization term. Given the initial iterate $\delta^{(0)} = 0$, projected FISTA iteratively updates the perturbation $I$ times by

$$\delta^{(k+1)} = \Pi_{[0,1]^p}\{S_\beta(y^{(k)} - \alpha_k \nabla g(y^{(k)}))\}, \tag{19.5}$$

$$y^{(k+1)} = \Pi_{[0,1]^p}\{\delta^{(k+1)} + \frac{k}{k+3}(\delta^{(k+1)} - \delta^{(k)})\}, \tag{19.6}$$

where $\Pi_{[0,1]^p}$ denotes the vector projection onto the set $\mathcal{X}/x_0 = [0,1]^p$, $\alpha_k$ is the step size, $y^{(k)}$ is a slack variable accounting for momentum acceleration with $y^{(0)} = \delta^{(0)}$, and $S_\beta : \mathbb{R}^p \mapsto \mathbb{R}^p$ is an elementwise shrinkage-thresholding function defined as

$$[S_\beta(z)]_i = \begin{cases} z_i - \beta & \text{if } z_i > \beta, \\ 0 & \text{if } |z_i| \le \beta, \\ z_i + \beta & \text{if } z_i < -\beta \end{cases} \qquad (19.7)$$

for $i \in \{1, \ldots, p\}$. The final perturbation $\delta^{(k^*)}$ for pertinent negative analysis is selected from the set $\{\delta^{(k)}\}_{k=1}^I$ such that $f_\kappa^{\text{neg}}(x_0, \delta^{(k^*)}) = 0$ and $k^* = \arg\min_{k \in \{1,\ldots,I\}} \beta \|\delta\|_1 + \|\delta\|_2^2$. A similar projected FISTA optimization approach is applied to pertinent positive analysis.

Eventually, as seen in Algorithm 6, both the pertinent negative $\delta^{\text{neg}}$ and the pertinent positive $\delta^{\text{pos}}$ obtained from the optimization methods are used to explain the model prediction. The last term in both (19.1) and (19.3) will be included only when an accurate autoencoder is available; otherwise, $\gamma$ is set to zero.

*Model-agnostic CEM.* It is worth noting that just like how white-box adversarial attacks can be extended to black-box adversarial attacks through the use of zeroth-order optimization techniques (Chen et al., 2017a; Liu et al., 2020a), contrastive explanations can be generated in a model-agnostic fashion by finding PPs/PNs through iterative queries with a black-box model, as proposed by Dhurandhar et al. (2019).

## 19.2 Contrastive explanations with monotonic attribute functions

Luss et al. (2021) address some limitations of the original CEM proposed by Dhurandhar et al. (2018). To identify PNs, addition is easy to define for grayscale images, where a pixel with zero value indicates no information, and so increasing its value toward 1 indicates addition. However, for color images with rich structure, it is not clear what is a "no-information" value for a pixel and consequently what does we mean by addition. By rich structure we mean that there exists an interpretable latent representation for the data; all faces have a particular shape, hair has a color, and even noses can be described by their shape (e.g., pointy or not). Defining addition in a naive way such as simply increasing the pixel or red-green-blue (RGB) channel intensities can lead to uninterpretable images as the relative structure may not be maintained with the added portion not necessarily being interpretable. Moreover, even for grayscaled images, just increasing values of pixels may not lead to humanly interpretable images, nor is there a guarantee that the added portion can be interpreted even if the overall image is realistic and lies on the data manifold.

To overcome these limitations, Luss et al. (2021) define "addition" in a novel way, which leads to realistic images with the additions also being interpretable and is called contrastive explanations method using monotonic attribute functions (CEM-MAF).

Given $k$ (available or learned) interpretable features (latent or otherwise), which represent meaningful concepts (viz. moustache, glasses, smile), let $g_i$, $i \in \{1, \ldots, k\}$, be the corresponding functions acting on these features with higher values indicating the presence of a certain visual concept, whereas lower values indicating its absence. For example, CelebA (Liu et al., 2015) has different high-level (interpretable) features for each image such as whether the person has black hair or high cheekbones. In this case, we can build binary classifiers for each of the features where 1 indicates the presence of black hair or high cheekbones, whereas 0 indicates its absence. These classifiers would be the functions $g_i$. On the other hand, for datasets with no high-level features, we can find latent features by learning disentangled representations and choose those latent features that are interpretable. Here the functions $g_i$ would be the identity (or negative identity) map depending on which direction adds a certain concept (viz. light to dark colored lesion).

Let $\mathcal{X}$ denote the feasible input space with $(x_0, t_0)$ being an example such that $x_0 \in \mathcal{X}$ and $t_0$ is the predicted label obtained from a classifier $f$, where $f$ is any function that outputs a vector of prediction scores for all classes. To make the final image realistic, CEM-MAF first learns a data manifold, denoted $\mathcal{D}$, using a generative adversarial network (GAN) or a variational autoencoder (VAE) on which we can perturb the image, so that the final image also lies on it after the necessary additions. Let $z$ denote the latent representation with $z_x$ denoting the latent representation corresponding to input $x$ such that $x = \mathcal{D}(z_x)$. This gives rise to the following optimization problem for finding PNs in CEM-MAF:

$$\min_{\delta \in \mathcal{X}} \gamma \sum_i \max\{g_i(x_0) - g_i(\mathcal{D}(z_\delta)), 0\} + \beta \|g(\mathcal{D}(z_\delta))\|_1$$

$$- c \cdot \min\{\max_{i \neq t_0}[f(\delta)]_i - [f(\delta)]_{t_0}, \kappa\} + \eta \|x_0 - \mathcal{D}(z_\delta)\|_2^2 + \nu \|z_{x_0} - z_\delta\|_2^2.$$

$$(19.8)$$

The first two terms in the objective function here are the novelty for PNs. The first term encourages the addition of attributes where we wants the $g_i$ for the final image to be no less than their original values. The second term encourages minimal addition of interpretable attributes. The third term is the PN loss from (Dhurandhar et al., 2018) and encourages the modified example $\delta$ to be predicted as a class different from $t_0 = \arg\max_i [f(x_0)]_i$, where $[f(\delta)]_i$ is the $i$th class prediction score of $\delta$. The hinge-like loss function pushes the modified example $\delta$ to lie in a class different from $x_0$. The parameter $\kappa \geq 0$ is a confidence parameter that controls the separation between $[f(\delta)]_{t_0}$ and $\max_{i \neq t_0}[f(\delta)]_i$. The fourth ($\eta > 0$) and fifth ($\nu > 0$) terms encourage the final image to be close to the original image in the input and latent spaces, respectively. In practice, we could have a threshold for each of the $g_i$, where only an increase in values beyond that threshold would imply a meaningful addition. The advantage of defining addition in this manner is that not only are the final images interpretable, but so are the additions, and we can clearly elucidate which (concepts) should be necessarily absent to maintain the original classification. Finally, we note that formulation (19.1) could be equivalently written as an optimization problem over the latent space since $\delta = \mathcal{D}(z_\delta)$.

To find PPs for CEM-MAF, we want to highlight a minimal set of important pixels or superpixels (from a segmentation of input $x_0$), which by themselves are sufficient for the classifier to output the same class as the original example. Let $\mathcal{M}$ denote a set of binary masks, which when applied to $x_0$ produce images $\mathcal{M}(x_0)$ by selecting the corresponding superpixels from the segmentation of $x_0$. Let $M_x$ denote the mask corresponding to the image $x = M_x(x_0)$ when applied on input $x_0$. The goal for example image $x_0$ is to find an image $\delta \in \mathcal{M}(x_0)$ such that $\arg\max_i[\text{Pred}(x_0)]_i = \arg\max_i[\text{Pred}(\delta)]_i$ (i.e., the same prediction) with $\delta$ containing as few superpixels and interpretable concepts from the original image as possible. This leads to the following optimization problem:

$$\min_{\delta \in \mathcal{M}(x_0)} \gamma \sum_i \max\{g_i(\delta) - g_i(x_0), 0\} + \beta \|M_\delta\|_1$$
$$- c \cdot \min\{[f(\delta)]_{t_0} - \max_{i \neq t_0}[f(\delta)]_i, \kappa\}. \tag{19.9}$$

The first term in the objective function here is the novelty for PPs and penalizes the addition of attributes since we seek a sparse explanation. The last term is the PP loss from (Dhurandhar et al., 2018) and is minimized when $[f(\delta)]_{t_0}$ is greater than $\max_{i \neq t_0}[f(\delta)]_i$ by at least $\kappa \geq 0$, which is a margin/confidence parameter. The parameters $\gamma, c, \beta \geq 0$ are the associated regularization coefficients. The optimization details for solving the PP and PN formulations (19.8) and (19.9) are discussed by Luss et al. (2021).

## 19.3 Empirical comparison

Dhurandhar et al. (2018) applied the CEM method to MNIST with a variety of examples illustrated in Fig. 19.1. The results using a convolutional autoencoder (CAE) to learn the pertinent positives and negatives are also displayed. Whereas results without CAE are quite convincing, CAE clearly improves the pertinent positives and negatives in many cases. Regarding pertinent positives, the cyan (light gray in print version) highlighted pixels in the column with CAE (CAE CEM PP) are a superset to the cyan-highlighted pixels in column without (CEM PP). Whereas these explanations are at the same level of confidence regarding the classifier, explanations using an AE are visually more interpretable. Take, for instance, the digit classified as a 2 in row 2. A small part of the tail of a 2 is used to explain the classifier without CAE, whereas the explanation using CAE has a much thicker tail and larger part of the vertical curve. In row 3, the explanation of the 3 is quite clear, but CAE highlights the same explanation but much thicker with more pixels. The same pattern holds for pertinent negatives. The horizontal line in row 4 that makes a 4 into a 9 is much more pronounced when using CAE. The change of a predicted 7 into a 9 in row 5 using the CAE is much more pronounced.

The two state-of-the-art methods used for explaining the classifier in Fig. 19.1 are LRP (Lapuschkin et al., 2016) and LIME (Ribeiro et al., 2016). LRP has a visually appealing explanation at the pixel level. Most pixels are deemed irrelevant (green (gray in print version)) to the classification (note the black background of LRP results was actually neutral). Positively relevant pixels (yellow (light gray in print version)/red (dark gray in print version)) are mostly consistent with our pertinent positives, though the pertinent positives do highlight more pixels for easier visualization. The most obvious such examples are row 3, where the yellow (light gray in print version) in LRP outlines a similar 3 to the pertinent positive, and row 6, where the yellow outlines most of what the pertinent positive provably deems necessary for the given prediction. There is little negative relevance in these examples, though we point out two interesting cases. In row 4, LRP shows that the little curve extending the upper left of the 4 slightly to the right has negative relevance (also shown by CEM as not being posi-

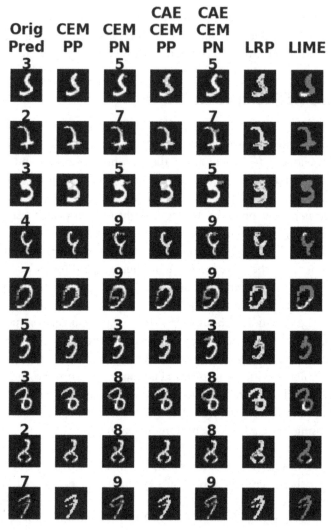

**Figure 19.1** CEM versus LRP and LIME on MNIST. PP/PN are highlighted in cyan (light gray in print version)/pink (mid gray in print version), respectively. For LRP, green (gray in print version) lightis neutral, red (dark gray in print version)/yellow (light gray in print version) is positive relevance, and blue (black in print version)is negative relevance. For LIME, red (dark gray in print version) is positive relevance, and white is neutral.

tively pertinent). Similarly, in row 3 the blue (black in print version) pixels in LRP are a part of the image that must obviously be deleted to see a clear 3. LIME is also visually appealing. However, the results are based on superpixels: the images were first segmented, and relevant segments were discovered. This explains why most of the pixels forming the digits are found relevant. Although both methods give important intuitions, neither illustrates what is necessary and sufficient about the classifier results as does our contrastive explanations method.

## 19.4  Extended reading

- Survey paper for explainability of machine learning models (Arya et al., 2019).

# CHAPTER 20

# Model watermarking and fingerprinting

Engineering a top-notch deep learning model is an expensive procedure, which involves collecting data, hiring human resources with expertise in machine learning, and providing high computational resources. For that reason, deep learning models are considered as valuable intellectual properties (IPs) of the model vendors. To ensure reliable commercialization of deep learning models, it is crucial to develop techniques to protect model vendors against IP infringements. One of such techniques, which recently has shown great promise, is *digital watermarking*.

Moreover, with the rapid development of machine learning and artificial intelligence, the efforts and resources spent in developing state-of-the-art machine learning models such as deep neural networks (DNNs) can be tremendous, and therefore it is of utmost importance to be able to claim the ownership of a well-trained model and its derived versions (e.g., pruned models). For instance, the cost of training current state-of-the-art transformer-based language model GPT-3 (Brown et al., 2020a) is estimated to be at least 4.6 million US dollars.[1] Imagine that an unethical model thief purposely pruned the pretrained GPT-3 model and attempted to claim the ownership of the resulting compressed model. The solution to the challenge of "how to protect IP for DNN models and reliably identify model ownership?" is literally worth million dollars. The methods for model watermarking and fingerprinting, as introduced in this chapter, are motivated from the study of adversarial robustness for DNNs.

## 20.1 Model watermarking

Aramoon et al. (2021) present GradSigns, a novel watermarking framework for deep neural networks (DNNs). GradSigns embeds the owner's signature into the gradient of the cross-entropy cost function with respect to inputs to the model. Their approach has a negligible impact on the performance of the protected model, and it allows model vendors to remotely verify the

---

[1] https://bdtechtalks.com/2020/08/17/openai-gpt-3-commercial-ai.

*Adversarial Robustness for Machine Learning*
https://doi.org/10.1016/B978-0-12-824020-5.00032-6

Copyright © 2023 Elsevier Inc.
All rights reserved.

227

watermark through prediction APIs. Table 20.1 lists the properties that an effective watermarking technique for deep learning models should have.

Table 20.1   Properties of an effective watermarking technique for deep learning models.

| Properties | Description |
| --- | --- |
| Loyalty | Watermark should have negligible overhead on the model's performance. |
| Robustness | Watermark must remain verifiable in the presence of antiwatermark attacks. |
| Reliability | Watermark verification should result in minimal false ownership claims. |
| Credibility | Finding or forging a fake (ghost) watermark should not be feasible. |
| Efficiency | Watermark extraction and verification should incur low costs. |
| Capacity | Watermarking technique should be able to embed large signatures. |

*Threat model.* The threat model includes two parties, *model vendor* and *adversary*. The model vendor owns model $M$, a DNN that they have engineered and trained for a certain task $T$ using the dataset $D$. The dataset $D$ is collected and owned by the model vendor. The second party, the adversary, is an entity that does not have the required resources for designing and training a top-notch model and wishes to make a profit out of model $M$ without paying any copyright fee to the model vendor. The adversary can be a company that has purchased the license of $M$ for one of their products and wants to deploy it on another one without paying additional copyright fees. They can also be any entity that has somehow got their hands on the model and wishes to sell it on the darknet. Model vendor's goal is to protect $M$ against IP infringements by means that enables the vendors to prove their ownership and possibly detect the source of theft. On the other hand, the adversary's ultimate goal is to continue profiting from $M$ without getting caught by law enforcement.

The threat model in (Aramoon et al., 2021) assumes the strongest adversary who has the expertise and the computation power required for training a model. However, the dataset that they have available for task $T$ is far smaller than dataset $D$ owned by the model vendor and therefore is not large enough for them to train a top-grade model from scratch. If the adversary had access to dataset $D$, then they would not need to hijack $M$ as they are capable of training the model themselves. Similarly to prior arts, it is assumed that the adversary is capable of trying any of the general antiwatermark attacks such as parameter pruning, model finetuning, and query invalidation and modification to remove the watermark or ob-

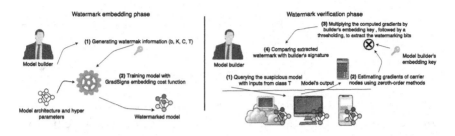

**Figure 20.1** Workflow of watermark embedding and verification using GradSigns proposed in (Aramoon et al., 2021).

struct verification. In addition, it is assumed that the adversary is aware of all existing watermarking techniques and is capable of designing adaptive antiwatermark schemes to target the deployed method. Due to such possible counter-watermark attempts, it is safe to assume that a hijacked model will go under modifications before being monetized by the adversary. The adversary accomplishes their goal if he can remove the vendor's signature or obstruct watermark verification without sacrificing too much on the performance of the model. Note that a counter-watermark attempt that drastically degrades the model's performance is not considered successful.

*Methodology of GradSigns.* Intuitively, GradSigns finds a solution, i.e., a set of model parameters, corresponding to a decision boundary that not only results in comparable performance on the original task but also fulfills an additional goal carrying the owner's watermark information. GradSigns works by embedding watermark information into the expected gradient of the cross-entropy cost function with respect to the model's input. For any input sample $x$, the gradient of the cost function with respect to the input is a vector tangent to the model's cost function surface and perpendicular to the decision boundary at point $x$. Therefore, by imposing a statistical bias on these gradients, GradSigns is essentially reshaping the decision boundary to incorporate the desired watermark information. For simplicity, we refer to the gradient of the cross-entropy cost function with respect to the input of the model as the *gradient of input* or *input gradient*. Fig. 20.1 illustrates the workflow of GradSigns.

*Watermark embedding.* Forcing a random statistical bias on the gradient of inputs to the model can drastically degrade its performance on the classification task. To ensure a successful marking without sacrificing the model's performance, the watermark needs to be embedded while optimizing the model for the original task. For that reason, Aramoon et al. (2021) embed the watermark into the host model by including a regularizer term in the model's training cost function. The final training cost function including the regularizer term is defined as

$$J(x|\theta, y) = J_{\text{cross-entropy}}(x|\theta, y) + \lambda J_{\text{embedding}}(x|\theta, y), \qquad (20.1)$$

where $\theta$ denotes the model's parameters, $x$ is an input sample, $y$ is the ground truth label for input sample $x$, $J_{\text{cross-entropy}}$ is the task-specific cost function, which is the cross-entropy function for classification problems, $\lambda$ is the trade-off hyperparameter, and $J_{\text{embedding}}$ is the watermark embedding regularizer term, which penalizes the distance between the expected value of input gradients and the desired watermark. Before defining the embedding regularizer term, we explain the steps that the model vendor needs to take prior to embedding the watermark. These steps are as follows:

*Step 1.* Generating an $N$-bit vector $b \in \{0, 1\}^N$ to be used as the watermark.

*Step 2.* Randomly selecting a set $C$ of input neurons to carry the watermark. We refer to set $C$ as the *watermark carrier set*, and to neurons in $C$ as *carrier nodes*. The gradient of inputs observed on neurons in the career set participates in embedding the watermark.

*Step 3.* Generating an *embedding key* $K^{N \times |C|} \in [-1, 1]^{N \times |C|}$. An embedding key is a transformation matrix that maps the expected gradient of carrier nodes to a binary vector of size $N$.

*Step 4.* Selecting a random target class $T$. Images from class $T$ are used to calculate the gradients of carrier nodes.

Note that generating the watermark $b$ and embedding key $K$ can either be done randomly by using a random number generator (RNG) or by hashing a message containing information that can be used to prove vendor's ownership. In GradSigns the watermark is successfully embedded if the following property holds:

$$\forall j \in \{0, 1, \ldots, N-1\}, \quad \chi_{[0,\infty)}\left(\sum_{i=0}^{|C|-1} K_{ji} G_i\right) = b_j, \qquad (20.2)$$

where $G \in \mathbb{R}^{|C|}$ is the expected gradient of cross-entropy function with respect to carrier nodes in $C$, measured over a sample of images from target class $T$, $K$ is the model vendor's embedding key, $b_j$ is $j$th watermark bit, and $\chi$ is a step function outputting one for values greater than zero.

For each watermark bit $j$, (20.2) denotes a linear inequality where the expected gradients of carrier nodes ($G$) are the variables, and the $j$th row of the embedding key $K$ is the coefficients, as shown in (20.3). This linear inequality is essentially denoting a half-space where acceptable values of expected gradients can reside for a successful embedding of watermark bit $j$:

$$(-1)^{b_j} \sum_{i=0}^{|C|-1} K_{ji} G_i < 0. \tag{20.3}$$

The task of embedding each watermark bit $j$ can also be viewed as a binary classification task with a single-layer perceptron (SLP), where the parameters of the perceptron layer are fixed to a constant value equal to the $j$th row of the embedding key $K$, and only the input of the SLP, i.e., the gradient of the carrier nodes, is being trained. To this end, we use a binary cross-entropy loss function in the embedding regularizer to embed each watermark bit:

$$J_{\text{embedding}}(\theta) = - \sum_{j=0}^{N-1} (b_j \log(y_j) + (1 - b_j) \log(1 - y_j)), \tag{20.4}$$

where $y_j = \sigma(\sum_i K_{ji} G_i)$ is the output of the SLP corresponding to the $j$th watermarking bit, and $\sigma$ is the sigmoid function.

*Watermark extraction.* To extract a watermark embedded by GradSigns, the first step that the model owner needs to take is computing the expected gradient of the carrier nodes. In the white-box setting, where the owner has access to the internal configurations of the suspicious model, the gradients can be calculated by backpropagation. However, in the black-box setting, computing gradients via backpropagation is not possible.

To enable watermark extraction in the black-box setting, the zeroth-order gradient estimation method (see Chapter 3) is used to calculate the expected gradients of the carrier nodes. Zeroth-order methods can estimate gradient with respect to any direction $v$ by evaluating the cost function value at two very close points located along this direction (Ghadimi and Lan, 2013; Liu et al., 2020a). The difference quotient is used to estimate the gradient of cost function with respect to carrier nodes as follows:

$$\widehat{G_c}(x) = \frac{\partial J(x)}{\partial x_c} \approx \frac{J(x + h e_c) - J(x)}{h}, \tag{20.5}$$

where $\widehat{G_c}(x)$ is the estimated gradient of carrier node $c$ at point $x$, $h$ is the estimation step length, $e_c$ is a standard basis vector with 1 at the component corresponding to career node $c$ and 0s elsewhere. Note that the value of cross-entropy function $J(x)$ can be computed in the black-box setting, given model's output and the ground truth label for input $x$.

In (20.5), for each input $x$, the gradient of a carrier node is calculated by evaluating the value of the cost function for two points whose coordinates are the same except for the one coordinate corresponding to the carrier node. The gradient estimation error of career nodes, not including the error introduced by limited numerical precision, is of order $O(|C|h^2)$ (Liu et al., 2018b). For any input $x$, we need to evaluate the cost function $|C| + 1$ times to estimate the gradients of all carrier nodes. Note that the watermark extraction naturally applies to more query-efficient gradient estimation methods such as (Liu et al., 2019c). After calculating the expected gradients for all carrier nodes, the model vendor can retrieve the embedded watermark by multiplying expected gradients with their embedding key. The model belongs to the vendor if the bit error rate (BER) of the extracted watermark is lower than a certain threshold.

We refer the readers to the detailed experiments and analysis in (Aramoon et al., 2021) for property evaluation of watermarking techniques with respect to Table 20.1 and for robustness assessment against counter-watermark attacks.

## 20.2 Model fingerprinting

Many existing DNN IP protection methods require intervention in training phase, which may cause performance degradation of the DNN (i.e., accuracy drop). Moreover, existing works may overlook the false positive problem of the DNN (i.e., mistakenly claiming the ownership of irrelevant models), which is of practical importance when designing fingerprints.

To address these limitations, Wang et al. (2021d) propose a novel approach to fingerprinting neural networks using *characteristic examples* (C-examples). Its advantages are as follows: (i) its generation process does not intervene with the training phase, and (ii) it does not require any realistic data from the training/testing set. By applying uniform random noise to the weights of the neural network with the combination of gradient mean descending technique, the proposed C-examples achieve high-robustness to the resulting models pruned from the base model where the fingerprints are extracted. When further equipped with a high-pass filter in the frequency domain of image data during the generation process, C-examples attain low-transferability to other models different from the base model. The C-examples are significantly different from widely known adversarial examples

(Szegedy et al., 2014; Goodfellow et al., 2015) causing model misprediction. Instead, C-examples are data-free and aim to achieve *high-robustness* for passing through pruned variants of the base model and *low-transferability* for screening out any other models different from the base model.

Wang et al. (2021d) consider three types of DNN models that are of interest in C-examples. ① *Base Model*: the pretrained model to fulfill some designated task, such as image classification. ② *Pruned Models*: the models pruned from the base model and implemented on the edge devices for inference execution. ③ *Other Models*: any other models that are neither ① nor ②. For example, if VGG16 is the base model, then VGG19, the ResNet family, etc. all belong to other models. The proposed DNN fingerprinting framework is as follows: The ① base model is used to generate C-examples with labels. Therefore C-examples have 100% accuracy on the base model. Then C-examples are used as fingerprints to test the models implemented on edge devices. A high accuracy is expected if the implemented model is ②, whereas a low accuracy is expected if the implemented model is ③. A systematic illustration of the C-example generation process is shown in Fig. 20.2.

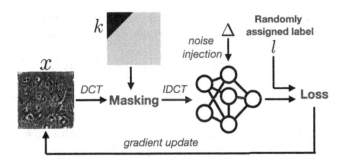

**Figure 20.2** A system diagram of generating LTRC-example proposed by Wang et al. (2021d).

*Vanilla C-examples.* Let $\mathbf{x} \in \mathbb{R}^{3 \times H \times W}$ denote a colored RGB image, where $H$ and $W$ are the image height and width, respectively. We scale pixel values of $\mathbf{x}$ to $[0, 1]$ for mathematical simplicity. $F_\theta$ denotes the base model, which outputs $\mathbf{y} = F_\theta(\mathbf{x})$ as a probability distribution for a total of $K$ classes. The element $y_i$ represents the probability that an input $\mathbf{x}$ belongs to the $i$th class. The base model $F_\theta$ parameterized with $\theta$ is pretrained. Then C-examples are generated from $F_\theta$. If we are given with a subset $\{l_1, l_2, \ldots, l_P\}$ of $P$ labels randomly chosen from the labels of training dataset, then a set of $\eta$-optimal C-examples $X^*$ can be characterized as

$$X^* = \left\{ (\mathbf{x}, l) \middle| \mathrm{Loss}_\theta(\mathbf{x}, l) < \eta, \mathbf{x} \in [0, 1]^n \right\}. \tag{20.6}$$

The term $\mathrm{Loss}_\theta$ denotes the loss function of $F_\theta$. A C-example $\mathbf{x}$ minimizing the loss for a specified label $l$ should satisfy the above constraint. To be independent of data when extracting the base model features, we simply use a random seed to generate a C-example, and therefore the generated C-examples are distinct from natural images for the human perception. A vanilla version C-example is shown in Fig. 20.3(a).

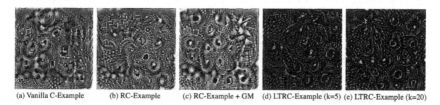

(a) Vanilla C-Example    (b) RC-Example    (c) RC-Example + GM    (d) LTRC-Example (k=5) (e) LTRC-Example (k=20)

**Figure 20.3** Characteristic examples visualized using different generation processes. The label assigned to all these image is "strawberry".

We can use the projected gradient descent (PGD) algorithm as introduced in Chapter 3 to find C-examples. The C-example generation problem (20.6) can be solved with the PGD algorithm as follows:

$$\mathbf{x}^{t+1} = \mathbf{Clip}\left(\mathbf{x}^t - \alpha \cdot \mathrm{sign}(\nabla_{\mathbf{x}}\mathrm{Loss}_\theta(\mathbf{x}^t, l))\right), \tag{20.7}$$

where $t$ is the iteration step index, $\mathbf{x}^0$ is the random starting point, $\alpha$ is the step size, sign returns the elementwise sign of a vector, $\nabla_{\mathbf{x}}$ calculates input gradients, and **Clip** denotes the clipping operation to satisfy the $\mathbf{x} \in [0, 1]^n$ constraint.

*Robust C-examples.* Wang et al. (2021d) further propose an enhancement named *Robust C-examples (RC-examples)* over the vanilla C-examples, by adding noise bounded by $\epsilon$ to the neural network parameters $\theta$ to mimic the model weight perturbation due to the model compression procedure. Here the loss is changed to $\mathrm{Loss}_{\theta+\Delta}$, where $\Delta$ presents the uniformly distributed weight perturbations within $[-\epsilon, \epsilon]$. Moreover, motivated by the expectation-over-transformation (EOT) method, (Athalye et al., 2018) toward stronger adversarial attacks (see Chapter 4 for details for EOT attack), the proposed RC-examples can be further enhanced by calculating the mean of the input gradients (the gradient mean (GM) method) in each iteration step over different random realizations of $\Delta$.

*LTRC-examples.* Finally, in addition to enhancing the robustness of C-examples on ② Pruned Models, it is desirable to exhibit low-transferability to ③ Other Models. Therefore the RC-examples are further improved by enforcing low transferability, named the *low-transferability RC-examples (LTRC-examples).* In this way, we can improve the capability of C-examples in detection for *false positive* cases, where positive means claiming the model ownership as ours in IP protection.

The frequency analysis (Guo et al., 2018; Sharma et al., 2019; Cheng et al., 2019b) suggests that low-frequency components can improve transferability of adversarial examples. Inspired by that, we propose to leverage high-frequency components to achieve C-examples with low transferability. Specifically, we can apply a frequency mask on the *discrete cosine transform* (DCT) (Rao and Yip, 2014) to implement a high-pass filter in the frequency domain of the C-example. As an important tool in signal processing, the DCT decomposes a given signal into cosine functions oscillating at different frequencies and amplitudes. For a 2D image, the DCT performed as $\omega = \text{DCT}(\mathbf{x})$ can transform the image $\mathbf{x}$ into the frequency domain, and $\omega_{(i,j)}$ is the magnitude of its corresponding cosine functions with the values of $i$ and $j$ representing frequencies, where smaller values mean lower frequencies. The DCT is invertible, and the inverse DCT (IDCT) is denoted as $\mathbf{x} = \text{IDCT}(\omega)$. Note that Wang et al. (2021d) apply DCT and IDCT for different color channels independently.

Inspired by the observation that the low frequencies play a more important role in machine classification and therefore are more transferable, Wang et al. (2021d) propose to filter out these components to effectively lower the fingerprint transferability. To demonstrate this, a high-pass frequency mask shown in Fig. 20.2 is imposed, where the high-frequency band size $k$ controls the range of the filtered low-frequency components. The frequency mask is designed to be a 2D matrix with elements being either 0 or 1, i.e., $\mathbf{m} \in \{0, 1\}^{H \times W}$, which performs elementwise product with the DCT of C-example. At each iteration step to generate the fingerprints, the high-pass mask sets the low-frequency components to 0, i.e., $\omega_{(i,j)} = 0$ if $1 \le i + j \le k$, while keeping the rest of the high-frequency components. By using the high-pass frequency mask the LTRC-example at the $(t+1)$th iteration step can be derived by

$$\mathbf{x}^{t+1} = \text{HighPass}\Big\{ \mathbf{Clip}\left(\mathbf{x}^t - \alpha \cdot \text{sign}(\nabla_{\mathbf{x}}\text{Loss}_{\theta+\Delta}(\mathbf{x}^t, 1))\right) \Big\}, \qquad (20.8)$$

where the HighPass filter is defined as

$$\text{HighPass}(\cdot) = \text{IDCT}(\text{FrequencyMask}(\text{DCT}(\cdot))). \qquad (20.9)$$

## 20.3 Empirical comparison

Here we compare different variants of the C-examples proposed by Wang et al. (2021d). Their visual comparisons are shown in Fig. 20.3.

In the experiment the accuracy of the C-examples on the pruned model is used to indicate its robustness and the accuracy on the variant model (with similar functionality to the base model, e.g., VGG-19 model to the base VGG-16 model) to indicate its transferability. Originally, the accuracy of all kinds of C-examples on the base model is 100% during generation. To effectively evaluate the trade-off between robustness of the pruned models and transferability to other variant models, we define the difference between the robustness and transferability as the *uniqueness score* (*uniqueness score* = *robustness* − *transferability*), where higher uniqueness score means that the C-examples are more robust to pruned models and less transferable to variant models. Intuitively, a better fingerprint method should achieve higher uniqueness score. The uniqueness score can also be used to indicate the false positive problem, i.e., if the uniqueness score is negative, then the corresponding fingerprint method is prone to make false model claims.

Table 20.2 demonstrates the effectiveness of C-examples, RC-examples, and LTRC-examples on different pruned models using the base VGG-16 model on ImageNet dataset with different pruning ratios for evaluating robustness. For testing transferability to other variant models (such as VGG-19, ResNet Family, DenseNet Family), as VGG-19 is the most similar architecture to VGG-16 and more transferable for fingerprints generated on VGG-16, we only report the transferability on VGG-19 and omit the transferability results on other models such as ResNet Family or DenseNet Family. Note that the transferability to other models should be lower than VGG-19, leading to better performance with higher uniqueness score.

As shown in Table 20.2, the uniqueness scores of RC-examples, RC-examples+GM, and LTRC-examples are higher than that of the baseline vanilla C-examples. We notice that C-examples suffer from negative uniqueness scores due to their high transferability to other models when the pruning ratios are 70% and 80%. We can observe that LTRC-examples with $\epsilon = 0.001$ achieve the best uniqueness scores with relatively large margins

**Table 20.2** Uniqueness Score of C-examples on implemented models by different weight pruning on the base VGG-16 model with ImageNet dataset: The base model has 70.85% top-1 accuracy and 90.10% top-5 accuracy. The base model is pruned by unstructured pruning (Han et al., 2015) with various pruning ratio, where it is pruned for 5 times at each pruning ratio with average accuracy degradation for pruning ratio 40%, 50%, 60%, 70%, and 80% are 0.26%, 0.45%, 0.38%, 0.61%, and 0.97%, respectively. The LTRC-examples are set with $k = 20$. The robustness at each pruning ratio can be obtained by the summation of *Uniqueness Score* and transferability. The experiment is evaluated on 100 C-examples generated from VGG-16.

| Method | $\epsilon$ | Base Model VGG-16 (%) | Transferability to VGG-19 (%) | Uniqueness Score (%) | | | | |
|---|---|---|---|---|---|---|---|---|
| | | | | 40% Pruned | 50% Pruned | 60% Pruned | 70% Pruned | 80% Pruned |
| Vanilla C-Example | 0 | 100 | 47 | +13 | +13 | +13 | −5 | −22 |
| RC-Example | 0.001 | 100 | 60 | +30 | +30 | +23 | +22 | +0 |
| | 0.003 | 100 | 88 | +6 | +11 | +5 | +2 | −3 |
| | 0.005 | 100 | 86 | +12 | +12 | +12 | +9 | +2 |
| | 0.007 | 100 | 95 | +4 | +4 | +3 | +2 | +3 |
| RC-Example+GM | 0.001 | 100 | 55 | +34 | +37 | +35 | +23 | −7 |
| | 0.003 | 100 | 67 | +30 | +38 | +38 | +21 | +19 |
| | 0.005 | 100 | 85 | +15 | +15 | +15 | +15 | +15 |
| | 0.007 | 100 | 100 | +0 | +0 | +0 | +0 | +0 |
| LTRC-Example | 0 | 100 | 16 | +53 | +51 | +50 | +23 | +13 |
| | 0.001 | 100 | 24 | **+65** | **+65** | **+65** | **+58** | **+32** |
| | 0.003 | 100 | 75 | +25 | +25 | +25 | +25 | +23 |
| | 0.005 | 100 | 96 | +4 | +4 | +4 | +4 | +3 |
| | 0.007 | 100 | 98 | +2 | +2 | +2 | +2 | +2 |

**Table 20.3**   False alarm analysis of C-examples using AUC and F1-score. $k = 20$ is used for LTRC-example.

| Method | $\epsilon$ | AUC | F1-score |
|---|---|---|---|
| Vanilla C-Example | 0 | 0.87 | 0.91 |
| RC-Example | 0.001 | 0.94 | 0.91 |
|  | 0.003 | 0.96 | 0.91 |
|  | 0.005 | 0.98 | 0.95 |
|  | 0.007 | 0.97 | 0.95 |
| RC-Example +GM | 0.001 | 0.97 | 0.95 |
|  | 0.003 | 0.99 | 0.95 |
|  | 0.005 | 0.99 | 0.95 |
|  | 0.007 | 0.86 | 0.95 |
| LTRC-Example | 0.001 | 1 | 1 |
|  | 0.003 | 1 | 1 |
|  | 0.005 | 1 | 1 |
|  | 0.007 | 1 | 1 |

(about 1.9×, 2.1×, and 5× that of the RC-examples+GM, RC-examples, and C-examples). In general, for a given method with fixed $\epsilon$, the uniqueness score decreases if the pruning ratio increases since larger pruning ratio degrades the test accuracy, leading to weaker model functionalities with less robustness after pruning. Meanwhile, we observe that with increasing $\epsilon$, there is more uncertainty in the model with larger random perturbations, leading to more general C-examples to incorporate larger uncertainty. Therefore they become more transferable to other variant models, resulting in increasing transferability and decreasing uniqueness score.

*False alarm and utility analysis.* Wang et al. (2021d) also evaluate the proposed C-examples under the false alarm scenario. Given a group of legally pruned models (test accuracy drop < 2%) and other widely used variant models on ImageNet dataset including VGG19, ResNet50, ResNet101, ResNet152, DenseNet121, DenseNet169, and DenseNet201, they evaluate the effectiveness of C-examples by calculating the receiver operating characteristic (ROC) curve of each method with different $\epsilon$ and report the area under the curve (AUC) and F1-score corresponding to each method, shown in Table 20.3. For the pruned models, five pruned models corresponding to pruning ratios of 40%, 50%, 60%, 70%, and 80% are used for testing. We can observe that with LTRC-examples, the AUC and F1-score both reached the ideal case of 1 with all $\epsilon$ values, meaning that with an appropriate threshold, LTRC-examples as fingerprints will not cause the false alarm problem (i.e., recognize other variant models as the base model). Meanwhile, we notice that incorporating enhanced robustness (RC-examples vs. C-examples), GM (RC-examples+GM vs. RC-examples) or low-transferability (LTRC-examples vs. RC-examples+GM) can help with false detection issues and improve the AUC and F1-score.

## 20.4 Extended reading

- Shao et al. (2021b) use adversarial examples to design robust text CAPTCHA (Completely Automated Public Truing test to tell Computers and Humans Apart), which is a widely used technology to distinguish real users and automated users such as bots.
- Shan et al. (2020) use data perturbations to improve the data privacy of facial recognition models.
- Sablayrolles et al. (2020) use data perturbations to detect whether a dataset is used for training or not.

# CHAPTER 21

# Data augmentation for unsupervised machine learning

In addition to studying the failure modes in machine learning models and systems, this chapter introduces how a type of adversarial examples can be used as an efficient data augmentation tool to improve the generalization and robustness for unsupervised machine learning tasks. When using these unsupervised adversarial examples as a simple plug-in data augmentation tool for model retraining, significant improvements are consistently observed across different unsupervised tasks and datasets, including data reconstruction, representation learning, and contrastive learning.

## 21.1 Adversarial examples for unsupervised machine learning models

Despite of a plethora of adversarial attacking algorithms, the design principle of existing methods is primarily for *supervised* learning models, requiring either the true label or a targeted objective (e.g., a specific class label or a reference sample). Some recent works have extended to the *semisupervised* setting by leveraging supervision from a classifier (trained on labeled data) and using the predicted labels on unlabeled data for generating (semisupervised) adversarial examples (Miyato et al., 2018; Zhang et al., 2019b; Stanforth et al., 2019; Carmon et al., 2019). On the other hand, recent advances in unsupervised and few-shot machine learning techniques show that task-invariant representations can be learned and contribute to downstream tasks with limited or even without supervision (Ranzato et al., 2007; Zhu and Goldberg, 2009; Zhai et al., 2019), which motivates the study by Hsu et al. (2022) regarding their robustness. The goal is to provide efficient robustness evaluation and data augmentation techniques for unsupervised (and self-supervised) machine learning models through *unsupervised* adversarial examples (UAEs). Table 21.1 summarizes the fundamental difference between conventional supervised adversarial examples and our UAEs. Notably, the UAE generation is supervision-free because it solely uses an information-theoretic similarity measure and the associated unsupervised learning objective function. It does not use any supervision such as label

*Adversarial Robustness for Machine Learning*
https://doi.org/10.1016/B978-0-12-824020-5.00033-8

information or prediction from other supervised models. The UAEs can be interpreted as "on-manifold" data samples having low training loss but are dissimilar to the training data, causing generalization errors. Therefore data augmentation and retraining with UAEs can improve model generalization (Stutz et al., 2019).

**Table 21.1** Illustration of adversarial examples for supervised/unsupervised machine learning tasks. Both settings use a native data sample $x$ as reference. For supervised setting, adversarial examples refer to *similar* samples of $x$ causing inconsistent predictions. For unsupervised setting, adversarial examples refer to *dissimilar* samples yielding smaller loss than $x$, relating to generalization errors on low-loss samples.

(I) *Mathematical notation*

$M^{\text{sup}}/M^{\text{unsup}}$: trained supervised/unsupervised machine learning models

$x/x_{\text{adv}}$: original/adversarial data sample

$\ell_x^{\text{sup}}/\ell_x^{\text{unsup}}$: supervised/unsupervised loss function in reference to $x$

| (II) *Supervised tasks* (e.g., classification) | (III) *Unsupervised tasks* (e.g., data reconstruction, contrastive learning) |
|---|---|
| $x_{\text{adv}}$ is **similar** to $x$, but $M^{\text{sup}}(x_{\text{adv}}) \neq M^{\text{sup}}(x)$ | $x_{\text{adv}}$ is **dissimilar** to $x$, but $\ell_x^{\text{unsup}}(x_{\text{adv}}\vert M^{\text{unsup}}) \leq \ell_x^{\text{unsup}}(x\vert M^{\text{unsup}})$ |

Hsu et al. (2022) propose a per-sample-based mutual information neural estimator (MINE) between a pair of original and modified data samples as an information-theoretic similarity measure and a supervision-free approach for generating UAE. Mutual information (MI) measures the mutual dependence between two random variables $X$ and $Z$, defined as $I(X, Z) = H(X) - H(X|Z)$, where $H(X)$ denotes the (Shannon) entropy of $X$, and $H(X|Z)$ denotes the conditional entropy of $X$ given $Z$. Computing MI can be difficult without knowing the marginal and joint probability distributions ($\mathbb{P}_X$, $\mathbb{P}_Z$, and $\mathbb{P}_{XZ}$). For efficient computation, the mutual information neural estimator (MINE) with consistency guarantees is proposed by Belghazi et al. (2018). Specifically, MINE aims to maximize the lower bound of the exact MI using a model parameterized by a neural network $\theta$ defined as $I_{\Theta}(X, Z) \leq I(X, Z)$, where $\Theta$ is the space of feasible parameters of a neural network, and $I_{\Theta}(X, Z)$ is the neural information quantity defined as $I_{\Theta}(X, Z) = \sup_{\theta \in \Theta} \mathbb{E}_{\mathbb{P}_{XZ}}[T_\theta] - \log(\mathbb{E}_{\mathbb{P}_X \otimes \mathbb{P}_Z}[e^{T_\theta}])$. The function $T_\theta$ is parameterized by a neural network $\theta$ based on the Donsker–Varadhan representation theorem (Donsker and Varadhan, 1983). MINE estimates the expectation of the quantities above by shuffling the samples from the joint distribution along the batch axis or using empirical samples $\{x_i, z_i\}_{i=1}^{n}$ from $\mathbb{P}_{XZ}$ and $\mathbb{P}_X \otimes \mathbb{P}_Z$ (the product of marginals). MINE has been successfully applied to improve representation learning (Hjelm et al., 2019; Zhu et al., 2020a) given a dataset. However, for generating an adversarial example for a given data sample, the vanilla MINE is not applicable because it only applies to a batch of data samples (so that empirical data distributions can be used for computing MI estimates) but not to single data sample.

*Per-sample MINE.* Given a data sample $x$ and its perturbed sample $x + \delta$, we can construct an auxiliary distribution using their random samples or convolution outputs to compute MI via MINE as a similarity measure, denoted as "per-sample MINE".

*Random sampling.* Using compressive sampling (Candès and Wakin, 2008), we perform independent Gaussian sampling of a given sample $x$ to obtain a batch of $K$ compressed samples $\{x_k, (x + \delta)_k\}_{k=1}^{K}$ for computing $I_\Theta(x, x + \delta)$ via MINE. We also note that random sampling is agnostic to the underlying machine learning model since it directly applies to the data sample.

*Convolution layer output.* When the underlying neural network model uses a convolution layer to process the input data (which is an almost granted setting for image data), we propose to use the output of the first convolution layer of a data input, denoted by *conv*, to obtain $K$ feature maps $\{conv(x)_k, conv(x + \delta)_k\}_{k=1}^{K}$ for computing $I_\Theta(x, x + \delta)$.

*Unified attack formulation.* We formalize the objectives for supervised and unsupervised adversarial examples using per-sample MINE. As summarized in Table 21.1, the supervised setting aims to find *most similar* examples causing prediction evasion, leading to an MINE *maximization* problem. The unsupervised setting aims to find *least similar* examples but having smaller training loss, leading to an MINE *minimization* problem. Both problems can be solved efficiently using a unified MinMax algorithm (Algorithm 7).

*Supervised adversarial example.* Let $(x, y)$ denote a pair of a data sample $x$ and its ground-truth label $y$. The objective of supervised adversarial example is to find a perturbation $\delta$ to $x$ such that the MI estimate $I_\Theta(x, x + \delta)$ is maximized while the prediction of $x + \delta$ is different from $y$ (or being a targeted class $y' \neq y$), which is formulated as

$$\underset{\delta}{\text{Maximize}} \quad I_\Theta(x, x + \delta)$$

$$\textit{such that } x + \delta \in [0, 1]^d, \ \delta \in [-\epsilon, \epsilon]^d \text{ and} f_x(x + \delta) \leq 0. \quad (21.1)$$

The constraint $x + \delta \in [0, 1]^d$ ensures that $x + \delta$ lies in the (normalized) data space of dimension $d$, and the constraint $\delta \in [-\epsilon, \epsilon]^d$ corresponds to the typical bounded $L_\infty$ perturbation norm. We include this bounded-norm constraint to make direct comparisons to other norm-bounded attacks. We can ignore this constraint by setting $\epsilon = 1$. Finally, the function $f_x^{sup}(x + \delta)$ is an attack success evaluation function, where $f_x^{sup}(x + \delta) \leq 0$ means that $x + \delta$ is a prediction-evasive adversarial example. For untargeted attack, we can use the attack function $f_x^{sup}$ designed by Carlini and Wagner (2017b), which is $f_x^{sup}(x') = \text{logit}(x')_y - \max_{j:j\neq y} \text{logit}(x')_j + \kappa$, where $\text{logit}(x')_j$ is the $j$th class output of the logit (pre-softmax) layer of a neural network, and $\kappa \geq 0$ is a tunable gap between the original prediction $\text{logit}(x')_y$ and the top prediction $\max_{j:j\neq y} \text{logit}(x')_j$ of all classes other than $y$. Similarly, the attack function for targeted attack with a class label $y' \neq y$ is $f_x^{sup}(x') = \max_{j:j\neq y'} \text{logit}(x')_j - \text{logit}(x')_{y'} + \kappa$.

*Unsupervised adversarial example.* Many machine learning tasks such as data reconstruction and unsupervised representation learning do not use data labels, which prevents the use of aforementioned supervised attack functions. Here we use an autoencoder $\Phi$ for data reconstruction to illustrate the unsupervised attack formulation. The design principle can naturally extend to other unsupervised tasks. The autoencoder $\Phi$ takes a data sample $x$ as an input and outputs a reconstructed data sample $\Phi(x)$. Different from the rationale of supervised attack, for unsupervised attack, we propose to use MINE to find the *least similar* perturbed data sample $x + \delta$ with respect to $x$ while ensuring that the reconstruction loss of $\Phi(x + \delta)$ is no greater than $\Phi(x)$ (i.e., the criterion of successful attack for data reconstruction). The unsupervised attack formulation is as follows:

$$\underset{\delta}{\text{Minimize}} \quad I_\Theta(x, x + \delta)$$

$$\textit{such that } x + \delta \in [0, 1]^d, \delta \in [-\epsilon, \epsilon]^d \text{ and } f_x(x + \delta) \leq 0. \quad (21.2)$$

The first two constraints regulate the feasible data space and the perturbation range. For the $L_2$-norm reconstruction loss, the unsupervised attack function is

$$f_x^{unsup}(x + \delta) = \|x - \Phi(x + \delta)\|_2 - \|x - \Phi(x)\|_2 + \kappa, \quad (21.3)$$

which means that the attack is successful (i.e., $f_x^{unsup}(x + \delta) \leq 0$) if the reconstruction loss of $x + \delta$ relative to the original sample $x$ is smaller than the native reconstruction loss minus a nonnegative margin $\kappa$, that is, $\|x - \Phi(x+\delta)\|_2 \leq \|x - \Phi(x)\|_2 - \kappa$. In other words, our unsupervised attack formulation aims to find that most dissimilar perturbed sample $x + \delta$ to $x$ measured by MINE while having smaller reconstruction loss (in reference to $x$) than $x$. Such UAEs thus relate to generalization errors on low-loss samples because the model is biased toward these unseen samples.

*MINE-based MinMax algorithm.* Here we introduce a unified MinMax algorithm for solving the aforementioned supervised and unsupervised attack formulations. Its algorithmic convergence proof is given in (Hsu et al., 2022). For simplicity, we will use $f_x$ to denote the attack criterion for $f_x^{sup}$ or $f_x^{unsup}$. Without loss of generality, we will analyze the supervised attack objective of maximizing $I_\Theta$ with constraints. The analysis also holds for the unsupervised case since minimizing $I_\Theta$ is equivalent to maximizing $I'_\Theta$, where $I'_\Theta = -I_\Theta$.

The attack generation via MINE can be reformulated as the following MinMax optimization problem with simple convex set constraints:

$$\min_{\delta: x+\delta \in [0,1]^d, \ \delta \in [-\epsilon,\epsilon]^d} \ \max_{c \geq 0} \ J(\delta, c) \triangleq c \cdot f_x^+(x+\delta) - I_\Theta(x, x+\delta). \quad (21.4)$$

The outer minimization problem finds the best perturbation $\delta$ with data and perturbation feasibility constraints $x + \delta \in [0, 1]^d$ and $\delta \in [-\epsilon, \epsilon]^d$, which are both convex sets with known analytical projection functions. The inner maximization associates a variable $c \geq 0$ with the original attack criterion $f_x(x + \delta) \leq 0$, where $c$ is multiplied by the ReLU activation function of $f_x$, denoted as $f_x^+(x + \delta) = \text{ReLU}(f_x(x + \delta)) = \max\{f_x(x + \delta), 0\}$. The use of $f_x^+$ means that when the attack criterion is not met (i.e., $f_x(x + \delta) > 0$), the loss term $c \cdot f_x(x + \delta)$ will appear in the objective function $F$. On the other hand, if the attack criterion is met (i.e., $f_x(x + \delta) \leq 0$), then $c \cdot f_x^+(x + \delta) = 0$, and the objective function $F$ only contains the similarity loss term $-I_\Theta(x, x + \delta)$. Therefore the design of $f_x^+$ balances the tradeoff between the two loss terms associated with attack success and MINE-based similarity. Hsu et al. (2022) propose to use alternative projected gradient descent between the inner and outer steps to solve the MinMax attack problem, which is summarized in Algorithm 7. The parameters $\alpha$ and $\beta$ denote the step sizes of the minimization and maximization steps, respectively. The gradient $\nabla f_x^+(x + \delta)$ with respect to $\delta$ is set to be 0 when $f_x(x + \delta) \leq 0$. The MinMax algorithm returns the successful adversarial example $x + \delta^*$ with the best MINE value $I_\Theta^*(x, x + \delta^*)$ over $T$ iterations.

## 21.2 Empirical comparison

With the MinMax attack algorithm and per-sample MINE for similarity evaluation, we can generate MINE-based unsupervised adversarial exam-

---

**Algorithm 7** MINE-based MinMax attack algorithm.

---

1: **Require:** data sample $x$, attack criterion $f_x$, step sizes $\alpha$ and $\beta$, perturbation bound $\epsilon$, # of iterations $T$

2: Initialize $\delta_0 = 0$, $c_0 = 0$, $\delta^* =$ null, $I_\Theta^* = -\infty$, $t = 1$

3: **for** $t$ in $T$ iterations **do**

4:      $\delta_{t+1} = \delta_t - \alpha \cdot (c \cdot \nabla f_x^+(x + \delta_t) - \nabla I_\Theta(x, x + \delta_t))$

5:      Project $\delta_{t+1}$ to $[-\epsilon, \epsilon]$ via clipping

6:      Project $x + \delta_{t+1}$ to $[0, 1]$ via clipping

7:      Compute $I_\Theta(x, x + \delta_{t+1})$

8:      Perform $c_{t+1} = (1 - \frac{\beta}{t/4}) \cdot c_t + \beta \cdot f_x^+(x + \delta_{t+1})$

9:      Project $c_{t+1}$ to $[0, \infty]$

10:      **if** $f_x(x + \delta_{t+1}) \leq 0$ and $I_\Theta(x, x + \delta_{t+1}) > I_\Theta^*$ **then**

11:          update $\delta^* = \delta_{t+1}$ and $I_\Theta^* = I_\Theta(x, x + \delta_{t+1})$

12:      **end if**

13: **end for**

14: **Return** $\delta^*$, $I_\Theta^*$

---

ples (MINE-UAEs). In what follows, we show novel applications of MINE-UAEs as a simple plug-in data augmentation tool to boost the model performance of several unsupervised machine learning tasks. We provide a brief summary of the datasets:

• *MNIST* consists of grayscale images of hand-written digits. The numbers of training/test samples are 60K/10K.

• *SVHN* is a color image dataset set of house numbers extracted from Google Street View images. The number of training/test samples are 73257/26302.

• *Fashion MNIST* contains grayscale images of 10 clothing items. The numbers of training/test samples are 60K/10K.

• *Isolet* consists of preprocessed speech data of people speaking the name of each letter of the English alphabet. The numbers of training/test samples are 6238/1559.

• *Coil-20* contains grayscale images of 20 multiviewed objects. The numbers of training/test samples are 1152/288.

• *Mice protein* consists of the expression levels (features) of 77 protein modifications in the nuclear fraction of cortex. The numbers of training/test samples are 864/216.

• *Human activity recognition* consists of sensor data collected from a smartphone for various human activities. The numbers of training/test samples are 4252/1492.

*Data reconstruction.* Data reconstruction using an autoencoder Φ that learns to encode and decode the raw data through latent representations is a standard unsupervised learning task. Here we use the default implementation of the following four autoencoders to generate UAEs based on the training data samples of MNIST and SVHN for data augmentation, retrain the model from scratch on the augmented dataset, and report the resulting reconstruction error on the original test set. All autoencoders use the $L_2$ reconstruction loss defined as $\|x - \Phi(x)\|_2$. The four autoencoders are summarized below.

• *Dense autoencoder (Cavallari et al., 2018).* The encoder and decoder have 1 dense layer separately, and the latent dimension is 128/256 for MNIST/SVHN.

• *Sparse autoencoder.* It has a sparsity enforcer ($L_1$ penalty on the training loss) that directs a network with a single hidden layer to learn the latent representations minimizing the error in reproducing the input while limiting the number of code words for reconstruction. We use the same architecture as Dense Autoencoder for MNIST and SVHN.

• *Convolutional autoencoder.*[1] The encoder uses convolution+relu+pooling layers. The decoder has reversed layer order with the pooling layer replaced by an upsampling layer.

• *Adversarial autoencoder (Makhzani et al., 2016).* It is composed of an encoder, a decoder, and a discriminator. The rationale is to force the distribution of the encoded values to be similar to the prior data distribution.

We also compare the performance of our proposed MINE-based UAE (MINE-UAE) with two baselines: (i) $L_2$-*UAE*, which replaces the objective of minimizing $I_\Theta(x, x + \delta)$ with maximizing the $L_2$ reconstruction loss $\|x - \Phi(x + \delta)\|_2$ in the MinMax attack algorithm while keeping the same attack success criterion; (ii) *Gaussian augmentation* (GA), which zero-mean Gaussian noise with a diagonal covariance matrix of the same constant $\sigma^2$ to the training data.

Table 21.2 shows the reconstruction loss and the ASR. The improvement of reconstruction error is measured with respect to the reconstruction loss of the original model (i.e., without data augmentation). We find that MINE-UAE can attain much higher ASR than $L_2$-UAE and GA in most

---

[1] https://github.com/shibuiwilliam/Keras_Autoencoder

cases. More importantly, data augmentation using MINE-UAE achieves consistent and significant reconstruction performance improvement across all models and datasets (up to 56.7% on MNIST and up to 73.5% on SVHN), validating the effectiveness of MINE-UAE for data augmentation. On the other hand, in several cases, $L_2$-UAE and GA lead to notable performance degradation. The results suggest that MINE-UAE can be an effective plug-in data augmentation tool for boosting the performance of unsupervised machine learning models.

Table 21.3 demonstrates that UAEs can further improve data reconstruction when the original model already involves conventional augmented training data such as flip, rotation, and Gaussian noise.

*Representation learning.* The concrete autoencoder (Balın et al., 2019) is an unsupervised feature selection method, which recognizes a subset of the most informative features through an additional *concrete select layer* with $M$ nodes in the encoder for data reconstruction. We apply MINE-UAE for data augmentation and use the same post-hoc classification evaluation procedure as in (Balın et al., 2019).

The six datasets and the resulting classification accuracy are reported in Table 21.4. We select $M = 50$ features for every dataset except for Mice Protein (we set $M = 10$) owing to its small data dimension. MINE-UAE can attain up to 11% improvement for data reconstruction and up to 1.39% increase in accuracy among five out of six datasets, corroborating the utility of MINE-UAE in representation learning and feature selection. The exception is Coil-20. A closer inspection shows that MINE-UAE has low ASR (<10%) for Coil-20 and the training loss after data augmentation is significantly higher than the original training loss. Therefore we conclude that the degraded performance in Coil-20 after data augmentation is likely due to the limitation of feature selection protocol and the model learning capacity.

*Contrastive learning.* The SimCLR algorithm (Chen et al., 2018e) is a popular contrastive learning framework for visual representations. It uses self-supervised data modifications to efficiently improve several downstream image classification tasks. We use the default implementation of SimCLR on CIFAR-10 and generate MINE-UAEs using the training data and the defined training loss for SimCLR. Table 21.5 shows the loss, ASR, and the resulting classification accuracy by training a linear head on the learned representations. We find that using MINE-UAE for additional data augmentation and model retraining can yield 7.8% improvement in contrastive loss and 1.58% increase in classification accuracy. Comparing to (Ho and

**Table 21.2** Comparison of data reconstruction by retraining the autoencoder on UAE-augmented data. The error is the average $L_2$ reconstruction loss of the test set. The improvement (in green (light gray in print version)/red (dark gray in print version)) is relative to the original model. The attack success rate (ASR) is the fraction of augmented training data having smaller reconstruction loss than the original loss (see Table 21.1 for definition).

| Autoencoder | Reconstruction Error (test set) | | | | | ASR (training set) | | | |
|---|---|---|---|---|---|---|---|---|---|
| | Original | MINE-UAE | $L_2$-UAE | GA ($\sigma = 0.01$) | GA ($\sigma = 10^{-3}$) | MINE-UAE | $L_2$-UAE | GA ($\sigma = 0.01$) | GA ($\sigma = 10^{-3}$) |
| **MNIST** | | | | | | | | | |
| Sparse | 0.00561 | 0.00243 (↑ 56.7%) | 0.00348 (↑ 38.0%) | 0.00280±2.60e-05 (↑ 50.1%) | 0.00280±3.71e-05 (↑ 50.1%) | 100% | 99.18% | 54.10% | 63.95% |
| Dense | 0.00258 | 0.00228 (↑ 11.6%) | 0.00286 (↑ 6.0%) | 0.00244±0.00014 (↑ 5.4%) | 0.00238±0.00012 (↑ 7.8%) | 92.99% | 99.94% | 48.53% | 58.47% |
| Convolutional | 0.00294 | 0.00256 (↑ 12.9%) | 0.00364 (↓ 23.8%) | 0.00301±0.00011 (↓ 2.4%) | 0.00304±0.00015 (↓ 3.4%) | 99.86% | 99.61% | 68.71% | 99.61% |
| Adversarial | 0.04785 | 0.04581 (↑ 4.3%) | 0.06098 (↓ 27.4%) | 0.05793±0.00501 (↓ 21%) | 0.05544±0.00567 (↓ 15.86%) | 98.46% | 43.54% | 99.79% | 99.83% |
| **SVHN** | | | | | | | | | |
| Sparse | 0.00887 | 0.00235 (↑ 73.5%) | 0.00315 (↑ 64.5%) | 0.00301±0.00137 (↑ 66.1%) | 0.00293±0.00078 (↑ 67.4%) | 100% | 72.16% | 72.42% | 79.92% |
| Dense | 0.00659 | 0.00421 (↑ 36.1%) | 0.00550 (↑ 16.5%) | 0.00858±0.00232 (↓ 30.2%) | 0.00860±0.00190 (↓ 30.5%) | 99.99% | 82.65% | 92.3% | 93.92% |
| Convolutional | 0.00128 | 0.00095 (↑ 25.8%) | 0.00121 (↑ 5.5%) | 0.00098 ± 3.77e-05 (↑ 25.4%) | 0.00104±7.41e-05 (↑ 18.8%) | 100% | 56% | 96.40% | 99.24% |
| Adversarial | 0.00173 | 0.00129 (↑ 25.4%) | 0.00181 (↓ 27.4%) | 0.00161±0.00061 (↑ 6.9%) | 0.00130±0.00037 (↑ 24.9%) | 94.82% | 58.98% | 97.31% | 99.85% |

**Table 21.3** Performance of data reconstruction when retraining with MINE-UAE and additional augmented training data.

### SVNH – Convolutional AE

| Augmentation | Aug. (test set) | Aug.+MINE-UAE (test set) |
|:---:|:---:|:---:|
| Flip + Rotation | 0.00285 | **0.00107** (↑ 62.46%) |
| Gaussian noise ($\sigma = 0.01$) | 0.00107 | **0.00095** (↑ 11.21%) |
| Flip + Rotation + Gaussian noise | 0.00307 | **0.00099** (↑ 67.75%) |

**Table 21.4** Performance of representation learning by the concrete autoencoder and the resulting classification accuracy.

| | Reconstruction Error (test set) | | Accuracy (test set) | | ASR |
|:---:|:---:|:---:|:---:|:---:|:---:|
| Dataset | Original | MINE-UAE | Original | MINE-UAE | MINE-UAE |
| MNIST | 0.01170 | **0.01142** (↑ 2.4%) | 94.97% | 95.41% | 99.98% |
| Fashion MMIST | 0.01307 | **0.01254** (↑ 4.1%) | 84.92% | 85.24% | 99.99% |
| Isolet | 0.01200 | **0.01159** (↑ 3.4%) | 81.98% | 82.93% | 100% |
| Coil-20 | **0.00693** | 0.01374 (↓ 98.3%) | 98.96% | 96.88% | 9.21% |
| Mice Protein | 0.00651 | **0.00611** (↑ 6.1%) | 89.81% | 91.2% | 40.24% |
| Activity | 0.00337 | **0.00300** (↑ 11.0%) | 83.38% | 84.45% | 96.52% |

**Table 21.5** Comparison of contrastive loss and the resulting accuracy on CIFAR-10 using Sim-CLR (Chen et al., 2018e) (ResNet-18 with batch size = 512). The attack success rate (ASR) is the fraction of augmented training data having smaller contrastive loss than original loss. For CLAE (Ho and Vasconcelos, 2020), we use the reported accuracy improvement (it shows negative gain in our implementation), though its base SimCLR model only has 83.27% test accuracy.

### CIFAR-10

| Model | Loss (test set) | Accuracy (test set) | ASR |
|:---:|:---:|:---:|:---:|
| Original | 0.29010 | 91.30% | – |
| MINE-UAE (Hsu et al., 2022) | **0.26755** (↑ 7.8%) | **+1.58%** | 100% |
| CLAE (Ho and Vasconcelos, 2020) | – | +0.05% | – |

Vasconcelos, 2020) using adversarial examples to improve SimCLR (named CLAE), the accuracy increase of MINE-UAE is 30 times higher. Moreover, MINE-UAE data augmentation also significantly improves adversarial robustness.

# References

Alzantot, Moustafa, Sharma, Yash, Elgohary, Ahmed, Ho, Bo-Jhang, Srivastava, Mani, Chang, Kai-Wei, 2018. Generating natural language adversarial examples. arXiv preprint. arXiv:1804.07998.

Alzantot, Moustafa, Sharma, Yash, Chakraborty, Supriyo, Zhang, Huan, Hsieh, Cho-Jui, Srivastava, Mani B., 2019. Genattack: practical black-box attacks with gradient-free optimization. In: Proceedings of the Genetic and Evolutionary Computation Conference, pp. 1111–1119.

Andriushchenko, Maksym, Hein, Matthias, 2019. Provably robust boosted decision stumps and trees against adversarial attacks. arXiv preprint. arXiv:1906.03526.

Aramoon, Omid, Chen, Pin-Yu, Qu, Gang, 2021. Don't forget to sign the gradients! Proceedings of Machine Learning and Systems 3.

Arya, Vijay, Bellamy, Rachel K.E., Chen, Pin-Yu, Dhurandhar, Amit, Hind, Michael, Hoffman, Samuel C., Houde, Stephanie, Liao, Q. Vera, Luss, Ronny, Mojsilović, Aleksandra, et al., 2019. One explanation does not fit all: a toolkit and taxonomy of AI explainability techniques. arXiv preprint. arXiv:1909.03012.

Athalye, Anish, Sutskever, Ilya, 2018. Synthesizing robust adversarial examples. In: International Conference on International Conference on Machine Learning.

Athalye, Anish, Carlini, Nicholas, Wagner, David, 2018. Obfuscated gradients give a false sense of security: circumventing defenses to adversarial examples. In: International Conference on International Conference on Machine Learning.

Aurenhammer, Franz, Klein, Rolf, 1999. Voronoi diagrams. Handbook of computational geometry 5 (10), 201–290.

Bagdasaryan, Eugene, Veit, Andreas, Hua, Yiqing, Estrin, Deborah, Shmatikov, Vitaly, 2018. How to backdoor federated learning. arXiv preprint. arXiv:1807.00459.

Balaji, Yogesh, Goldstein, Tom, Hoffman, Judy, 2019. Instance adaptive adversarial training: improved accuracy tradeoffs in neural nets. arXiv preprint. arXiv:1910.08051.

Balın, Muhammed Fatih, Abid, Abubakar, Zou, James, 2019. Concrete autoencoders: differentiable feature selection and reconstruction. In: International Conference on Machine Learning, pp. 444–453.

Beck, Amir, Teboulle, Marc, 2009. A fast iterative shrinkage-thresholding algorithm for linear inverse problems. SIAM Journal on Imaging Sciences 2 (1), 183–202.

Belghazi, Mohamed Ishmael, Baratin, Aristide, Rajeshwar, Sai, Ozair, Sherjil, Bengio, Yoshua, Courville, Aaron, Hjelm, Devon, 2018. Mutual information neural estimation. In: International Conference on Machine Learning, pp. 531–540.

Bhagoji, Arjun Nitin, Chakraborty, Supriyo, Mittal, Prateek, Calo, Seraphin, 2019. Analyzing federated learning through an adversarial lens. In: International Conference on Machine Learning, pp. 634–643.

Bhattad, Anand, Chong, Min Jin, Liang, Kaizhao, Li, Bo, Forsyth, David A., 2019. Big but imperceptible adversarial perturbations via semantic manipulation. arXiv preprint. arXiv:1904.06347.

Bishop, Christopher M., 2006. Pattern recognition and machine learning. Machine Learning 128 (9).

Blum, Avrim, Dick, Travis, Manoj, Naren, Zhang, Hongyang, 2020. Random smoothing might be unable to certify linf robustness for high-dimensional images. Journal of Machine Learning Research 21, 211–1.

Bogdan, Małgorzata, van den Berg, Ewout, Su, Weijie, Candès, Emmanuel Jean, 2013. Statistical Estimation and Testing via the Ordered $\ell_1$ Norm. Stanford University.

Boopathy, Akhilan, Weng, Tsui-Wei, Chen, Pin-Yu, Liu, Sijia, Daniel, Luca, 2019. CNN-cert: An efficient framework for certifying robustness of convolutional neural networks. In: Proceedings of the AAAI Conference on Artificial Intelligence, vol. 33, pp. 3240–3247.

Boopathy, Akhilan, Weng, Lily, Liu, Sijia, Chen, Pin-Yu, Zhang, Gaoyuan, Daniel, Luca, 2021. Fast training of provably robust neural networks by singleprop. In: Proceedings of the AAAI Conference on Artificial Intelligence, vol. 35, pp. 6803–6811.

Brendel, Wieland, Rauber, Jonas, Bethge, Matthias, 2018. Decision-based adversarial attacks: reliable attacks against black-box machine learning models. In: International Conference on Learning Representations.

Brown, Tom B., Mané, Dandelion, Roy, Aurko, Abadi, Martín, Gilmer, Justin, 2017. Adversarial patch. arXiv preprint. arXiv:1712.09665.

Brown, Tom B., Carlini, Nicholas, Zhang, Chiyuan, Olsson, Catherine, Christiano, Paul, Goodfellow, Ian, 2018. Unrestricted adversarial examples. arXiv preprint. arXiv:1809. 08352.

Brown, Tom B., et al., 2020a. Language models are few-shot learners. In: NeurIPS.

Brown, Tom B., Mann, Benjamin, Ryder, Nick, Subbiah, Melanie, Kaplan, Jared, Dhariwal, Prafulla, Neelakantan, Arvind, Pranav, Shyam, Sastry, Girish, Askell, Amanda, et al., 2020b. Language models are few-shot learners. arXiv preprint. arXiv:2005.14165.

Brunner, Thomas, Diehl, Frederik, Le Truong, Michael, Knoll, Alois, 2019. Guessing smart: biased sampling for efficient black-box adversarial attacks. In: Proceedings of the IEEE/CVF International Conference on Computer Vision, pp. 4958–4966.

Bunel, Rudy R., Turkaslan, Ilker, Torr, Philip, Kohli, Pushmeet, Mudigonda, Pawan K., 2018. A unified view of piecewise linear neural network verification. Advances in Neural Information Processing Systems 31.

Bunel, Rudy, De Palma, Alessandro, Desmaison, Alban, Dvijotham, Krishnamurthy, Kohli, Pushmeet, Torr, Philip, Kumar, M. Pawan, 2020a. Lagrangian decomposition for neural network verification. In: Conference on Uncertainty in Artificial Intelligence. PMLR, pp. 370–379.

Bunel, Rudy, Lu, Jingyue, Turkaslan, Ilker, Kohli, P., Torr, P., Mudigonda, P., 2020b. Branch and bound for piecewise linear neural network verification. Journal of Machine Learning Research 21 (2020).

Candès, Emmanuel J., Wakin, Michael B., 2008. An introduction to compressive sampling. IEEE Signal Processing Magazine 25 (2), 21–30.

Carion, Nicolas, Massa, Francisco, Synnaeve, Gabriel, Usunier, Nicolas, Kirillov, Alexander, Zagoruyko, Sergey, 2020. End-to-end object detection with transformers. In: European Conference on Computer Vision. Springer, pp. 213–229.

Carlini, Nicholas, Wagner, David, 2017a. Adversarial examples are not easily detected: bypassing ten detection methods. In: ACM Workshop on Artificial Intelligence and Security, pp. 3–14.

Carlini, Nicholas, Wagner, David, 2017b. Towards evaluating the robustness of neural networks. In: IEEE Symposium on Security and Privacy, pp. 39–57.

Carlini, Nicholas, Wagner, David, 2018. Audio adversarial examples: targeted attacks on speech-to-text. arXiv preprint. arXiv:1801.01944.

Carlini, Nicholas, Athalye, Anish, Papernot, Nicolas, Brendel, Wieland, Rauber, Jonas, Tsipras, Dimitris, Goodfellow, Ian, Madry, Aleksander, Kurakin, Alexey, 2019a. On evaluating adversarial robustness. arXiv preprint. arXiv:1902.06705.

Carlini, Nicholas, Liu, Chang, Erlingsson, Úlfar, Kos, Jernej, Song, Dawn, 2019b. The secret sharer: evaluating and testing unintended memorization in neural networks. In: 28th {USENIX} Security Symposium ({USENIX} Security 19), pp. 267–284.

Carlucci, Fabio M., D'Innocente, Antonio, Bucci, Silvia, Caputo, Barbara, Tommasi, Tatiana, 2019. Domain generalization by solving jigsaw puzzles. In: Proceedings of the IEEE Conference on Computer Vision and Pattern Recognition, pp. 2229–2238.

Carmon, Yair, Raghunathan, Aditi, Schmidt, Ludwig, Liang, Percy, Duchi, John C., 2019. Unlabeled data improves adversarial robustness. Neural Information Processing Systems.

Cavallari, Gabriel, Ribeiro, Leonardo, Ponti, Moacir, 2018. Unsupervised representation learning using convolutional and stacked auto-encoders: a domain and cross-domain feature space analysis. In: IEEE SIBGRAPI Conference on Graphics, Patterns and Images (SIBGRAPI), pp. 440–446.

Chen, Pin-Yu, 2022. Model reprogramming: resource-efficient cross-domain machine learning. arXiv preprint. arXiv:2202.10629.

Chen, Jinghui, Gu, Quanquan, 2020. Rays: A ray searching method for hard-label adversarial attack. In: Proceedings of the 26th ACM SIGKDD International Conference on Knowledge Discovery & Data Mining, pp. 1739–1747.

Chen, Xinlei, He, Kaiming, 2020. Exploring simple Siamese representation learning. arXiv preprint. arXiv:2011.10566.

Chen, Pin-Yu, Zhang, Huan, Sharma, Yash, Yi, Jinfeng, Hsieh, Cho-Jui, 2017a. Zoo: Zeroth order optimization based black-box attacks to deep neural networks without training substitute models. In: Proceedings of the 10th ACM Workshop on Artificial Intelligence and Security, pp. 15–26.

Chen, Xinyun, Liu, Chang, Li, Bo, Lu, Kimberly, Song, Dawn, 2017b. Targeted backdoor attacks on deep learning systems using data poisoning. arXiv preprint. arXiv:1712.05526.

Chen, Hongge, Zhang, Huan, Chen, Pin-Yu, Yi, Jinfeng, Hsieh, Cho-Jui, 2018a. Attacking visual language grounding with adversarial examples: a case study on neural image captioning. In: Proceedings of the 56th Annual Meeting of the Association for Computational Linguistics, vol. 1, pp. 2587–2597.

Chen, Pin-Yu, Sharma, Yash, Zhang, Huan, Yi, Jinfeng, Hsieh, Cho-Jui, 2018b. EAD: elastic-net attacks to deep neural networks via adversarial examples. In: Proceedings of the AAAI Conference on Artificial Intelligence.

Chen, Pin-Yu, Vinzamuri, Bhanukiran, Liu, Sijia, 2018c. Is ordered weighted $\ell_1$ regularized regression robust to adversarial perturbation? a case study on OSCAR. In: IEEE Global Conference on Signal and Information Processing (GlobalSIP), pp. 1174–1178.

Chen, Tian Qi, Rubanova, Yulia, Bettencourt, Jesse, Duvenaud, David K., 2018d. Neural ordinary differential equations. In: Advances in Neural Information Processing Systems, pp. 6572–6583.

Chen, Ting, Kornblith, Simon, Norouzi, Mohammad, Hinton, Geoffrey, 2018e. A simple framework for contrastive learning of visual representations. In: International Conference on Machine Learning.

Chen, Hongge, Zhang, Huan, Boning, Duane, Hsieh, Cho-Jui, 2019a. Robust decision trees against adversarial examples. In: International Conference on Machine Learning. PMLR, pp. 1122–1131.

Chen, Hongge, Zhang, Huan, Si, Si, Li, Yang, Boning, Duane, Hsieh, Cho-Jui, 2019b. Robustness verification of tree-based models. arXiv preprint. arXiv:1906.03849.

Chen, Jianbo, Jordan, Michael I., Wainwright, Martin J., 2020a. Hopskipjumpattack: a query-efficient decision-based attack. In: IEEE Symposium on Security and Privacy, pp. 1277–1294.

Chen, Mark, Radford, Alec, Child, Rewon, Wu, Jeffrey, Jun, Heewoo, Luan, David, Sutskever, Ilya, 2020b. Generative pretraining from pixels. In: International Conference on Machine Learning. PMLR, pp. 1691–1703.

Chen, Tianlong, Liu, Sijia, Chang, Shiyu, Cheng, Yu, Amini, Lisa, Wang, Zhangyang, 2020c. Adversarial robustness: from self-supervised pre-training to fine-tuning. In: Proceedings of the IEEE/CVF Conference on Computer Vision and Pattern Recognition, pp. 699–708.

Chen, Ting, Kornblith, Simon, Swersky, Kevin, Norouzi, Mohammad, Hinton, Geoffrey, 2020d. Big self-supervised models are strong semi-supervised learners. arXiv preprint. arXiv:2006.10029.

Chen, Xinlei, Fan, Haoqi, Girshick, Ross, He, Kaiming, 2020e. Improved baselines with momentum contrastive learning. arXiv preprint. arXiv:2003.04297.

Chen, Xiangning, Hsieh, Cho-Jui, Gong, Boqing, 2022. When vision transformers outperform ResNets without pre-training or strong data augmentations. In: International Conference on Learning Representations (ICLR).

Cheng, Chih-Hong, 2019. Towards robust direct perception networks for automated driving. arXiv preprint. arXiv:1909.13600.

Cheng, Minhao, Le, Thong, Chen, Pin-Yu, Yi, Jinfeng, Zhang, Huan, Hsieh, Cho-Jui, 2019a. Query-efficient hard-label black-box attack: an optimization-based approach. In: International Conference on Learning Representations.

Cheng, Shuyu, Dong, Yinpeng, Pang, Tianyu, et al., 2019b. Improving black-box adversarial attacks with a transfer-based prior. In: NeurIPS.

Cheng, Hao, Xu, Kaidi, Liu, Sijia, Chen, Pin-Yu, Zhao, Pu, Lin, Xue, 2020a. Defending against backdoor attack on deep neural networks. arXiv preprint. arXiv:2002.12162.

Cheng, Minhao, Lei, Qi, Chen, Pin-Yu, Dhillon, Inderjit, Hsie, Cho-Juih, 2020b. Cat: customized adversarial training for improved robustness. arXiv preprint. arXiv:2002.06789.

Cheng, Minhao, Singh, Simranjit, Chen, Patrick H., Chen, Pin-Yu, Liu, Sijia, Hsieh, Cho-Jui, 2020c. Sign-OPT: a query-efficient hard-label adversarial attack. In: International Conference on Learning Representations.

Cheng, Minhao, Yi, Jinfeng, Zhang, Huan, Chen, Pin-Yu, Hsieh, Cho-Jui, 2020d. Seq2sick: evaluating the robustness of sequence-to-sequence models with adversarial examples. In: Proceedings of the AAAI Conference on Artificial Intelligence.

Cheng, Minhao, Chen, Pin-Yu, Liu, Sijia, Chang, Shiyu, Hsieh, Cho-Jui, Das, Payel, 2021. Self-progressing robust training. In: Proceedings of the AAAI Conference on Artificial Intelligence.

Cohen, Jeremy M., Rosenfeld, Elan, Kolter, J. Zico, 2019. Certified adversarial robustness via randomized smoothing. In: International Conference on Machine Learning.

Croce, Francesco, Hein, Matthias, 2020. Reliable evaluation of adversarial robustness with an ensemble of diverse parameter-free attacks. In: International Conference on Machine Learning. PMLR, pp. 2206–2216.

Dai, Hanjun, Li, Hui, Tian, Tian, Huang, Xin, Wang, Lin, Zhu, Jun, Song, Le, 2018. Adversarial attack on graph structured data. In: International Conference on Machine Learning. PMLR, pp. 1115–1124.

Dau, Hoang Anh, Bagnall, Anthony, Kamgar, Kaveh, Yeh, Chin-Chia Michael, Zhu, Yan, Gharghabi, Shaghayegh, Ratanamahatana, Chotirat Ann, Keogh, Eamonn, 2019. The ucr time series archive. IEEE/CAA Journal of Automatica Sinica 6 (6), 1293–1305.

Davis, Luke M., 2013. Predictive modelling of bone ageing. PhD thesis. University of East Anglia.

Davis, Jason V., Kulis, Brian, Jain, Prateek, Sra, Suvrit, Dhillon, Inderjit S., 2007. Information-theoretic metric learning. In: International Conference on Machine Learning (ICML), pp. 209–216.

de Andrade, Douglas Coimbra, Leo, Sabato, Da Silva Viana, Martin Loesener, Bernkopf, Christoph, 2018. A neural attention model for speech command recognition. arXiv preprint. arXiv:1808.08929.

De Palma, Alessandro, Behl, Harkirat Singh, Bunel, Rudy, Torr, Philip H.S., Kumar, M. Pawan , 2021a. Scaling the convex barrier with active sets. In: International Conference on Learning Representations (ICLR).

De Palma, Alessandro, Bunel, Rudy, Desmaison, Alban, Dvijotham, Krishnamurthy, Kohli, Pushmeet, Philip Torr, H.S., Pawan Kumar, M., 2021b. Improved branch and bound for neural network verification via Lagrangian decomposition. arXiv preprint. arXiv: 2104.06718.

Deng, Jia, Dong, Wei, Socher, Richard, Li, Li-Jia, Li, Kai, Fei-Fei, Li, 2009. Imagenet: a large-scale hierarchical image database. In: 2009 IEEE Conference on Computer Vision and Pattern Recognition. IEEE, pp. 248–255.

Devlin, Jacob, Chang, Ming-Wei, Lee, Kenton, Toutanova, Kristina, 2018. Bert: pre-training of deep bidirectional transformers for language understanding. arXiv preprint. arXiv:1810.04805.

Dhillon, Guneet S., Azizzadenesheli, Kamyar, Lipton, Zachary C., Bernstein, Jeremy, Kossaifi, Jean, Khanna, Aran, Anandkumar, Anima, 2018. Stochastic activation pruning for robust adversarial defense. In: International Conference on Learning Representations.

Dhurandhar, Amit, Chen, Pin-Yu, Luss, Ronny, Tu, Chun-Chen, Ting, Paishun, Shanmugam, Karthikeyan, Das, Payel, 2018. Explanations based on the missing: towards contrastive explanations with pertinent negatives. Neural Information Processing Systems.

Dhurandhar, Amit, Pedapati, Tejaswini, Balakrishnan, Avinash, Chen, Pin-Yu, Shanmugam, Karthikeyan, Puri, Ruchir, 2019. Model agnostic contrastive explanations for structured data. arXiv preprint. arXiv:1906.00117.

Ding, Gavin Weiguang, Sharma, Yash, Chau Lui, Kry Yik, Huang, Ruitong, 2018. Mma training: direct input space margin maximization through adversarial training. arXiv preprint. arXiv:1812.02637.

Dong, Yinpeng, Liao, Fangzhou, Pang, Tianyu, Su, Hang, Zhu, Jun, Hu, Xiaolin, Li, Jianguo, 2018. Boosting adversarial attacks with momentum. In: Proceedings of the IEEE Conference on Computer Vision and Pattern Recognition, pp. 9185–9193.

Donsker, Monroe D., Varadhan, S.R. Srinivasa, 1983. Asymptotic evaluation of certain Markov process expectations for large time. iv. Communications on Pure and Applied Mathematics 36 (2), 183–212.

Dosovitskiy, Alexey, Beyer, Lucas, Kolesnikov, Alexander, Weissenborn, Dirk, Zhai, Xiaohua, Unterthiner, Thomas, Dehghani, Mostafa, Minderer, Matthias, Heigold, Georg, Gelly, Sylvain, et al., 2020. An image is worth 16x16 words: transformers for image recognition at scale. arXiv preprint. arXiv:2010.11929.

Dubey, Abhimanyu, van der Maaten, Laurens, Yalniz, Zeki, Li, Yixuan, Mahajan, Dhruv, 2019. Defense against adversarial images using web-scale nearest-neighbor search. In: Proceedings of the IEEE/CVF Conference on Computer Vision and Pattern Recognition, pp. 8767–8776.

Duchi, John, Hazan, Elad, Singer, Yoram, 2011. Adaptive subgradient methods for online learning and stochastic optimization. Journal of Machine Learning Research 12 (7).

Duchi, John C., Jordan, Michael I., Wainwright, Martin J., Wibisono, Andre, 2015. Optimal rates for zero-order convex optimization: the power of two function evaluations. IEEE Transactions on Information Theory 61 (5), 2788–2806.

Dvijotham, Krishnamurthy Dj, Hayes, Jamie, Balle, Borja, Kolter, Zico, Qin, Chongli, Gyorgy, Andras, Xiao, Kai, Gowal, Sven, Kohli, Pushmeet, 2020. A framework for robustness certification of smoothed classifiers using f-divergences.

Ehlers, Ruediger, 2017. Formal verification of piece-wise linear feed-forward neural networks. In: International Symposium on Automated Technology for Verification and Analysis. Springer, pp. 269–286.

Elsayed, Gamaleldin F., Goodfellow, Ian, Sohl-Dickstein, Jascha, 2019. Adversarial reprogramming of neural networks. In: International Conference on Learning Representations.

Engstrom, Logan, Tran, Brandon, Tsipras, Dimitris, Schmidt, Ludwig, Madry, Aleksander, 2017. A rotation and a translation suffice: fooling cnns with simple transformations. arXiv preprint. arXiv:1712.02779.

Engstrom, Logan, Ilyas, Andrew, Santurkar, Shibani, Tsipras, Dimitris, Tran, Brandon, Madry, Aleksander, 2019a. Learning perceptually-aligned representations via adversarial robustness. arXiv preprint. arXiv:1906.00945.

Engstrom, Logan, Tran, Brandon, Tsipras, Dimitris, Schmidt, Ludwig, Madry, Aleksander, 2019b. Exploring the landscape of spatial robustness. In: International Conference on Machine Learning, pp. 1802–1811.

Eslami, Taban, Mirjalili, Vahid, Fong, Alvis, Laird, Angela R., Saeed, Fahad, 2019. Asddiagnet: a hybrid learning approach for detection of autism spectrum disorder using fmri data. Frontiers in Neuroinformatics 13.

Evtimov, Ivan, Eykholt, Kevin, Fernandes, Earlence, Kohno, Tadayoshi, Li, Bo, Prakash, Atul, Rahmati, Amir, Song, Dawn, 2017. Robust physical-world attacks on machine learning models. arXiv preprint. arXiv:1707.08945.

Eykholt, Kevin, Evtimov, Ivan, Fernandes, Earlence, Li, Bo, Rahmati, Amir, Xiao, Chaowei, Prakash, Atul, Kohno, Tadayoshi, Song, Dawn, 2018. Robust physical-world attacks on deep learning visual classification. In: Proceedings of the IEEE Conference on Computer Vision and Pattern Recognition, pp. 1625–1634.

Fan, Lijie, Liu, Sijia, Chen, Pin-Yu, Zhang, Gaoyuan, Gan, Chuang, 2021. When does contrastive learning preserve adversarial robustness from pretraining to finetuning? Advances in Neural Information Processing Systems 34.

Fawzi, Alhussein, Frossard, Pascal, 2015. Manitest: Are classifiers really invariant? In: BMVC.

Feinman, Reuben, Curtin, Ryan R., Shintre, Saurabh, Gardner, Andrew B., 2017. Detecting adversarial samples from artifacts. In: International Conference on Machine Learning.

Finn, Chelsea, Abbeel, Pieter, Levine, Sergey, 2017. Model-agnostic meta-learning for fast adaptation of deep networks. arXiv preprint. arXiv:1703.03400.

Fong, Ruth, Patrick, Mandela, Vedaldi, Andrea, 2019. Understanding deep networks via extremal perturbations and smooth masks. In: Proceedings of the IEEE International Conference on Computer Vision, pp. 2950–2958.

Foret, Pierre, Kleiner, Ariel, Mobahi, Hossein, Neyshabur, Behnam, 2020. Sharpness-aware minimization for efficiently improving generalization. In: International Conference on Learning Representations (ICLR).

Freund, Yoav, Schapire, Robert E., 1997. A decision-theoretic generalization of on-line learning and an application to boosting. Journal of Computer and System Sciences 55 (1), 119–139.

Gan, Chuang, Gong, Boqing, Liu, Kun, Su, Hao, Guibas, Leonidas J., 2018. Geometry guided convolutional neural networks for self-supervised video representation learning. In: CVPR, pp. 5589–5597.

Gao, Bolin, Pavel, Lacra, 2017. On the properties of the softmax function with application in game theory and reinforcement learning. arXiv preprint. arXiv:1704.00805.

Gao, X., Jiang, B., Zhang, S., 2014. On the information-adaptive variants of the admm: an iteration complexity perspective. Optimization Online 12.

Garcia, Washington, Chen, Pin-Yu, Jha, Somesh, Clouse, Scott, Butler, Kevin R.B., 2021. Hard-label manifolds: unexpected advantages of query efficiency for finding on-manifold adversarial examples. arXiv preprint. arXiv:2103.03325.

Geiping, Jonas, Fowl, Liam, Huang, W. Ronny, Czaja, Wojciech, Taylor, Gavin, Moeller, Michael, Goldstein, Tom, 2021. Witches' brew: industrial scale data poisoning via gradient matching. In: International Conference on Learning Representations.

Ghadimi, Saeed, Lan, Guanghui, 2013. Stochastic first-and zeroth-order methods for nonconvex stochastic programming. SIAM Journal on Optimization 23 (4), 2341–2368.

Gidaris, Spyros, Singh, Praveer, Komodakis, Nikos, 2018. Unsupervised representation learning by predicting image rotations. arXiv preprint. arXiv:1803.07728.

Goldberger, Jacob, Hinton, Geoffrey E., Roweis, Sam T., Salakhutdinov, Ruslan R., 2004. Neighbourhood components analysis. In: Advances in Neural Information Processing Systems (NeurIPS), pp. 513–520.

Goldblum, Micah, Fowl, Liam, Goldstein, Tom, 2019. Adversarially robust few-shot learning: a meta-learning approach. ArXiv. ArXiv–1910.

Goldblum, Micah, Tsipras, Dimitris, Xie, Chulin, Chen, Xinyun, Schwarzschild, Avi, Song, Dawn, Madry, Aleksander, Li, Bo, Goldstein, Tom, 2022. Dataset security for machine learning: data poisoning, backdoor attacks, and defenses. IEEE Transactions on Pattern Analysis and Machine Intelligence.

Goodfellow, Ian, Pouget-Abadie, Jean, Mirza, Mehdi, Xu, Bing, Warde-Farley, David, Ozair, Sherjil, Courville, Aaron, Bengio, Yoshua, 2014. Generative adversarial nets. Advances in Neural Information Processing Systems 27.

Goodfellow, Ian J., Shlens, Jonathon, Szegedy, Christian, 2015. Explaining and harnessing adversarial examples. In: International Conference on Learning Representation.

Gowal, Sven, Dvijotham, Krishnamurthy, Stanforth, Robert, Bunel, Rudy, Qin, Chongli, Uesato, Jonathan, Mann, Timothy, Kohli, Pushmeet, 2018. On the effectiveness of interval bound propagation for training verifiably robust models. arXiv preprint. arXiv: 1810.12715.

Gowal, Sven, Huang, Po-Sen, van den Oord, Aaron, Mann, Timothy, Kohli, Pushmeet, 2021. Self-supervised adversarial robustness for the low-label, high-data regime. In: International Conference on Learning Representations. https://openreview.net/forum?id=bgQek2O63w.

Grill, Jean-Bastien, Strub, Florian, Altché, Florent, Tallec, Corentin, Richemond, Pierre H., Buchatskaya, Elena, Doersch, Carl, Avila, Bernardo Pires, Guo, Zhaohan Daniel, Azar, Mohammad Gheshlaghi, et al., 2020. Bootstrap your own latent: a new approach to self-supervised learning. arXiv preprint. arXiv:2006.07733.

Gu, Tianyu, Dolan-Gavitt, Brendan, Garg, Siddharth, 2017. Badnets: identifying vulnerabilities in the machine learning model supply chain. arXiv preprint. arXiv:1708.06733.

Gu, T., Liu, K., Dolan-Gavitt, B., Garg, S., 2019. BadNets: evaluating backdooring attacks on deep neural networks. IEEE Access 7, 47230–47244.

Guo, Chuan, Frank, Jared S., Kilian, Weinberger Q., 2018. Low frequency adversarial perturbation. arXiv preprint, arXiv:1809.08758.

Hambardzumyan, Karen, Khachatrian, Hrant, May, Jonathan, 2021. Warp: Word-level adversarial reprogramming. arXiv preprint. arXiv:2101.00121.

Han, Song, Pool, Jeff, Tran, John, Dally, William, 2015. Learning both weights and connections for efficient neural network. In: NeurIPS.

Hard, Andrew, Rao, Kanishka, Mathews, Rajiv, Beaufays, Françoise, Augenstein, Sean, Eichner, Hubert, Kiddon, Chloé, Ramage, Daniel, 2018. Federated learning for mobile keyboard prediction. arXiv preprint. arXiv:1811.03604.

He, Kaiming, Zhang, Xiangyu, Ren, Shaoqing, Sun, Jian, 2016. Deep residual learning for image recognition. In: Proceedings of the IEEE Conference on Computer Vision and Pattern Recognition, pp. 770–778.

He, Kaiming, Fan, Haoqi, Wu, Yuxin, Xie, Saining, Girshick, Ross, 2020. Momentum contrast for unsupervised visual representation learning. In: Proceedings of the IEEE/CVF Conference on Computer Vision and Pattern Recognition, pp. 9729–9738.

Heinsfeld, Anibal Sólon, Franco, Alexandre Rosa, Craddock, R. Cameron, Buchweitz, Augusto, Meneguzzi, Felipe, 2018. Identification of autism spectrum disorder using deep learning and the abide dataset. In: NeuroImage: Clinical.

Hendrycks, Dan, Zhao, Kevin, Basart, Steven, Steinhardt, Jacob, Song, Dawn, 2021. Natural adversarial examples. In: Proceedings of the IEEE/CVF Conference on Computer Vision and Pattern Recognition, pp. 15262–15271.

Herman, Amy, 2016. Are you visually intelligent? What you don't see is as important as what you do see. Medical Daily. http://www.medicaldaily.com/are-you-visually-intelligent-what-you-dont-see-important-what-you-do-see-397963.

Hjelm, R. Devon, Fedorov, Alex, Lavoie-Marchildon, Samuel, Grewal, Karan, Bachman, Phil, Trischler, Adam, Bengio, Yoshua, 2019. Learning deep representations by mutual information estimation and maximization. In: International Conference on Learning Representations.

Ho, Chih-Hui, Vasconcelos, Nuno, 2020. Contrastive learning with adversarial examples. In: Advances in Neural Information Processing Systems.

Holland, J.K., Kemsley, E.K., Wilson, R.H., 1998. Use of Fourier transform infrared spectroscopy and partial least squares regression for the detection of adulteration of strawberry purees. Journal of the Science of Food and Agriculture 76 (2), 263–269.

Hosseini, Hossein, Poovendran, Radha, 2018. Semantic adversarial examples. In: IEEE Conference on Computer Vision and Pattern Recognition Workshops, pp. 1614–1619.

Hsieh, Cheng-Yu, Yeh, Chih-Kuan, Liu, Xuanqing, Ravikumar, Pradeep, Kim, Seungyeon, Kumar, Sanjiv, Hsieh, Cho-Jui, 2020. Evaluations and methods for explanation through robustness analysis. arXiv preprint. arXiv:2006.00442.

Hsu, Chia-Yi, Chen, Pin-Yu, Lu, Songtao, Liu, Sijia, Yu, Chia-Mu, 2022. Adversarial examples can be effective data augmentation for unsupervised machine learning. In: AAAI.

Huang, Po-Sen, Wang, Chenglong, Singh, Rishabh, Yih, Wen-tau, He, Xiaodong, 2018. Natural language to structured query generation via meta-learning. arXiv preprint. arXiv:1803.02400.

Huang, Po-Sen, Stanforth, Robert, Welbl, Johannes, Dyer, Chris, Yogatama, Dani, Gowal, Sven, Dvijotham, Krishnamurthy, Kohli, Pushmeet, 2019. Achieving verified robustness to symbol substitutions via interval bound propagation. In: Proceedings of the 2019 Conference on Empirical Methods in Natural Language Processing and the 9th International Joint Conference on Natural Language Processing (EMNLP-IJCNLP), pp. 4074–4084.

Hubara, Itay, Courbariaux, Matthieu, Soudry, Daniel, El-Yaniv, Ran, Bengio, Yoshua, 2017. Quantized neural networks: training neural networks with low precision weights and activations. Journal of Machine Learning Research 18 (1), 6869–6898.

Ilyas, Andrew, Engstrom, Logan, Madry, Aleksander, 2019. Prior convictions: black-box adversarial attacks with bandits and priors. In: International Conference on Learning Representations.

Jagielski, Matthew, Oprea, Alina, Biggio, Battista, Liu, Chang, Nita-Rotaru, Cristina, Li, Bo, 2018. Manipulating machine learning: poisoning attacks and countermeasures for regression learning. In: IEEE Symposium on Security and Privacy, pp. 19–35.

Jia, Robin, Raghunathan, Aditi, Göksel, Kerem, Liang, Percy, 2019. Certified robustness to adversarial word substitutions. arXiv preprint. arXiv:1909.00986.

Jiang, Ziyu, Chen, Tianlong, Chen, Ting, Wang, Zhangyang, 2020. Robust pre-training by adversarial contrastive learning. arXiv preprint. arXiv:2010.13337.

Joshi, Ameya, Mukherjee, Amitangshu, Sarkar, Soumik, Hegde, Chinmay, 2019. Semantic adversarial attacks: parametric transformations that fool deep classifiers. arXiv preprint. arXiv:1904.08489.

Julian, Kyle D., Sharma, Shivam, Jeannin, Jean-Baptiste, Kochenderfer, Mykel J., 2019. Verifying aircraft collision avoidance neural networks through linear approximations of safe regions. arXiv preprint. arXiv:1903.00762.

Kantorovich, L.V., Rubinstein, G., 1958. On a space of completely additive functions. Vestnik Leningradskogo Universiteta 13 (7), 52–59.

Katz, Guy, Barrett, Clark, Dill, David L., Julian, Kyle, Kochenderfer, Mykel J., 2017. Reluplex: An efficient smt solver for verifying deep neural networks. In: International Conference on Computer Aided Verification. Springer, pp. 97–117.

Keskar, Nitish Shirish, Mudigere, Dheevatsa, Nocedal, Jorge, Smelyanskiy, Mikhail, Tang, Ping Tak Peter, 2017. On large-batch training for deep learning: generalization gap and sharp minima. In: International Conference on Learning Representations.

Khatri, Devvrit, Cheng, Minhao, Hsieh, Cho-Jui, Dhillon, Inderjit, et al., 2020. Voting based ensemble improves robustness of defensive models. arXiv preprint. arXiv:2011.14031.

Khosla, Prannay, Teterwak, Piotr, Wang, Chen, Sarna, Aaron, Tian, Yonglong, Isola, Phillip, Maschinot, Aaron, Liu, Ce, Krishnan, Dilip, 2020. Supervised contrastive learning. arXiv preprint. arXiv:2004.11362.

Kim, Minseon, Tack, Jihoon, Hwang, Sung Ju, 2020. Adversarial self-supervised contrastive learning. arXiv preprint. arXiv:2006.07589.

Kingma, Diederik, Ba, Jimmy, 2015. Adam: A method for stochastic optimization. In: International Conference on Learning Representations.

Kipf, T.N., Welling, M., 2016. Semi-supervised classification with graph convolutional networks. arXiv preprint. arXiv:1609.02907.

Ko, Ching-Yun, Lyu, Zhaoyang, Weng, Lily, Daniel, Luca, Wong, Ngai, Lin, Dahua, 2019. POPQORN: Quantifying robustness of recurrent neural networks. In: International Conference on Machine Learning (ICML).

Koch, Gregory, Zemel, Richard, Salakhutdinov, Ruslan, 2015. Siamese neural networks for one-shot image recognition. In: ICML Deep Learning Workshop. Lille, vol. 2.

Kolouri, Soheil, Rohde, Gustavo K., Hoffmann, Heiko, 2018. Sliced Wasserstein distance for learning Gaussian mixture models. In: Proceedings of the IEEE Conference on Computer Vision and Pattern Recognition, pp. 3427–3436.

Komkov, Stepan, Petiushko, Aleksandr, 2021. Advhat: Real-world adversarial attack on arcface face id system. In: 2020 25th International Conference on Pattern Recognition (ICPR). IEEE, pp. 819–826.

Kozlov, Mikhail K., Tarasov, Sergei P., Khachiyan, Leonid G., 1980. The polynomial solvability of convex quadratic programming. U.S.S.R. Computational Mathematics and Mathematical Physics 20 (5), 223–228.

Krizhevsky, Alex, Hinton, Geoffrey, et al., 2009. Learning multiple layers of features from tiny images. Technical report, Citeseer.

Krizhevsky, Alex, Sutskever, Ilya, Hinton, Geoffrey E., 2012. Imagenet classification with deep convolutional neural networks. In: Advances in Neural Information Processing Systems, pp. 1097–1105.

Kurakin, Alexey, Goodfellow, Ian, Bengio, Samy, 2016. Adversarial examples in the physical world. arXiv preprint. arXiv:1607.02533.

Kurakin, Alexey, Goodfellow, Ian, Bengio, Samy, 2017. Adversarial machine learning at scale. International Conference on Learning Representations.

Lapuschkin, Sebastian, Binder, Alexander, Montavon, Grégoire, Müller, Klaus-Robert, Samek, Wojciech, 2016. The lrp toolbox for artificial neural networks. Journal of Machine Learning Research 17 (114), 1–5. http://jmlr.org/papers/v17/15-618.html.

Lax, Peter D., Terrell, Maria Shea, 2014. Calculus with Applications. Springer.

LeCun, Yann, Bottou, Léon, Bengio, Yoshua, Haffner, Patrick, et al., 1998. Gradient-based learning applied to document recognition. Proceedings of the IEEE 86 (11), 2278–2324.

LeCun, Yann, Bengio, Yoshua, Hinton, Geoffrey, 2015. Deep learning. Nature 521 (7553), 436–444.

Lecuyer, Mathias, Atlidakis, Vaggelis, Geambasu, Roxana, Hsu, Daniel, Jana, Suman, 2019. Certified robustness to adversarial examples with differential privacy. In: 2019 IEEE Symposium on Security and Privacy (SP), pp. 656–672.

Lee, Kimin, Lee, Kibok, Lee, Honglak, Shin, Jinwoo, 2018. A simple unified framework for detecting out-of-distribution samples and adversarial attacks. Advances in Neural Information Processing Systems 31.

Lei, Qi, Wu, Lingfei, Chen, Pin-Yu, Dimakis, Alexandros G., Dhillon, Inderjit S., Witbrock, Michael, 2019. Discrete adversarial attacks and submodular optimization with applications to text classification. In: SysML.

Levenshtein, V.I., 1966. Binary codes capable of correcting deletions, insertions and reversals. Soviet Physics. Doklady 10 (1), 845–848.

Li, Jiwei, Monroe, Will, Jurafsky, Dan, 2016. Understanding neural networks through representation erasure. arXiv preprint. arXiv:1612.08220.

Li, Jinfeng, Ji, Shouling, Du, Tianyu, Li, Bo, Wang, Ting, 2018a. Textbugger: generating adversarial text against real-world applications. arXiv preprint. arXiv:1812.05271.

Li, Yao, Renqiang Min, Martin, Yu, Wenchao, Hsieh, Cho-Jui, Lee, Thomas C.M., Kruus, Erik, 2018b. Optimal transport classifier: defending against adversarial attacks by regularized deep embedding. arXiv preprint. arXiv:1811.07950.

Li, Bai, Chen, Changyou, Wang, Wenlin, Carin, Lawrence, 2019a. Certified adversarial robustness with additive noise. Neural Information Processing Systems.

Li, Juncheng, Schmidt, Frank, Kolter, Zico, 2019b. Adversarial camera stickers: a physical camera-based attack on deep learning systems. In: International Conference on Machine Learning. PMLR, pp. 3896–3904.

Li, Linyang, Ma, Ruotian, Guo, Qipeng, Xue, Xiangyang, Qiu, Xipeng, 2020a. Bert-attack: adversarial attack against bert using bert. arXiv preprint. arXiv:2004.09984.

Li, Qizhang, Guo, Yiwen, Chen, Hao, 2020b. Practical no-box adversarial attacks against dnns. In: Advances in Neural Information Processing Systems.

Lin, Chang-Sheng, Hsu, Chia-Yi, Chen, Pin-Yu, Yu, Chia-Mu, 2021. Real-world adversarial examples involving makeup application. arXiv preprint. arXiv:2109.03329.

Liu, Ziwei, Luo, Ping, Wang, Xiaogang, Tang, Xiaoou, 2015. Deep learning face attributes in the wild. In: ICCV 2015.

Liu, Yannan, Wei, Lingxiao, Luo, Bo, Xu, Qiang, 2017a. Fault injection attack on deep neural network. In: IEEE/ACM International Conference on Computer-Aided Design (ICCAD), pp. 131–138.

Liu, Yanpei, Chen, Xinyun, Liu, Chang, Song, Dawn, 2017b. Delving into transferable adversarial examples and black-box attacks. In: International Conference on Learning Representations.

Liu, Sijia, Chen, Jie, Chen, Pin-Yu, Hero, Alfred O., 2018a. Zeroth-order online alternating direction method of multipliers: Convergence analysis and applications. AISTATS.

Liu, Sijia, Kailkhura, Bhavya, Chen, Pin-Yu, Ting, Paishun, Chang, Shiyu, Amini, Lisa, 2018b. Zeroth-order stochastic variance reduction for nonconvex optimization. In: Advances in Neural Information Processing Systems, pp. 3727–3737.

Liu, Xuanqing, Cheng, Minhao, Zhang, Huan, Hsieh, Cho-Jui, 2018c. Towards robust neural networks via random self-ensemble. In: Proceedings of the European Conference on Computer Vision (ECCV), pp. 369–385.

Liu, Changliu, Arnon, Tomer, Lazarus, Christopher, Strong, Christopher, Barrett, Clark, Kochenderfer, Mykel J., 2019a. Algorithms for verifying deep neural networks. arXiv preprint. arXiv:1903.06758.

Liu, Hsueh-Ti Derek, Tao, Michael, Li, Chun-Liang, Nowrouzezahrai, Derek, Jacobson, Alec, 2019b. Beyond pixel norm-balls: parametric adversaries using an analytically differentiable renderer. In: International Conference on Learning Representations.

Liu, Sijia, Chen, Pin-Yu, Chen, Xiangyi, Hong, Mingyi, 2019c. Signsgd via zeroth-order oracle. In: International Conference on Learning Representations.

Liu, Xuanqing, Li, Yao, Wu, Chongruo, Hsieh, Cho-Jui, 2019d. Adv-BNN: improved adversarial defense through robust Bayesian neural network. In: International Conference on Learning Representations.

Liu, Yinhan, Ott, Myle, Goyal, Naman, Du, Jingfei, Joshi, Mandar, Chen, Danqi, Levy, Omer, Lewis, Mike, Zettlemoyer, Luke, Stoyanov, Veselin, 2019e. Roberta: a robustly optimized bert pretraining approach. arXiv preprint. arXiv:1907.11692.

Liu, Sijia, Chen, Pin-Yu, Kailkhura, Bhavya, Zhang, Gaoyuan, Hero, Alfred, Varshney, Pramod K., 2020a. A primer on zeroth-order optimization in signal processing and machine learning. IEEE Signal Processing Magazine.

Liu, Sijia, Lu, Songtao, Chen, Xiangyi, Feng, Yao, Xu, Kaidi, Al-Dujaili, Abdullah, Hong, Mingyi, O'Reilly, Una-May, 2020b. Min-max optimization without gradients: convergence and applications to black-box evasion and poisoning attacks. In: International Conference on Machine Learning, pp. 6282–6293.

Liu, Xuanqing, Si, Si, Cao, Qin, Kumar, Sanjiv, Hsieh, Cho-Jui, 2020c. How does noise help robustness? Explanation and exploration under the neural sde framework. In: Proceedings of the IEEE/CVF Conference on Computer Vision and Pattern Recognition, pp. 282–290.

Liu, Yong, Siqi, Mai, Chen, Xiangning, Hsieh, Cho-Jui, You, Yang, 2022. Towards efficient and scalable sharpness-aware minimization. In: IEEE Conference on Computer Vision and Pattern Recognition, 2022. CVPR 2022.

Lu, Jingyue, Kumar, M. Pawan, 2020. Neural network branching for neural network verification. In: International Conference on Learning Representation (ICLR).

Luss, Ronny, Chen, Pin-Yu, Dhurandhar, Amit, Sattigeri, Prasanna, Zhang, Yunfeng, Shanmugam, Karthikeyan, Tu, Chun-Chen, 2021. Leveraging latent features for local explanations. In: Proceedings of the 27th ACM SIGKDD Conference on Knowledge Discovery & Data Mining, pp. 1139–1149.

Ma, Xingjun, Li, Bo, Wang, Yisen, Erfani, Sarah M., Wijewickrema, Sudanthi, Schoenebeck, Grant, Song, Dawn, Houle, Michael E., Bailey, James, 2018. Characterizing adversarial subspaces using local intrinsic dimensionality. In: International Conference on Learning Representations.

Madry, Aleksander, Makelov, Aleksandar, Schmidt, Ludwig, Tsipras, Dimitris, Vladu, Adrian, 2017. Towards deep learning models resistant to adversarial attacks. arXiv preprint. arXiv:1706.06083.

Madry, Aleksander, Makelov, Aleksandar, Schmidt, Ludwig, Tsipras, Dimitris, Vladu, Adrian, 2018. Towards deep learning models resistant to adversarial attacks. In: International Conference on Learning Representations.

Maicas, Gabriel, Bradley, Andrew P., Nascimento, Jacinto C., Reid, Ian, Carneiro, Gustavo, 2018. Training medical image analysis systems like radiologists. In: International Conference on Medical Image Computing and Computer-Assisted Intervention. Springer, pp. 546–554.

Makhzani, Alireza, Shlens, Jonathon, Jaitly, Navdeep, Goodfellow, Ian, Frey, Brendan, 2016. Adversarial autoencoders. In: ICLR Workshop.

McMahan, Brendan, Moore, Eider, Ramage, Daniel, Hampson, Seth, Aguera y Arcas, Blaise, 2017. Communication-efficient learning of deep networks from decentralized data. In: Proceedings of the 20th International Conference on Artificial Intelligence and Statistics. In: Proceedings of Machine Learning Research, vol. 54. PMLR, pp. 1273–1282.

Mehra, Akshay, Kailkhura, Bhavya, Chen, Pin-Yu, Hamm, Jihun, 2021a. How robust are randomized smoothing based defenses to data poisoning? In: Proceedings of the IEEE/CVF Conference on Computer Vision and Pattern Recognition, pp. 13244–13253.

Mehra, Akshay, Kailkhura, Bhavya, Chen, Pin-Yu, Hamm, Jihun, 2021b. Understanding the limits of unsupervised domain adaptation via data poisoning. In: Thirty-Fifth Conference on Neural Information Processing Systems.

Meng, Dongyu, Chen, Hao, 2017. Magnet: a two-pronged defense against adversarial examples. In: ACM SIGSAC Conference on Computer and Communications Security, pp. 135–147.

Mikolov, Tomas, Sutskever, Ilya, Chen, Kai, Corrado, Greg S., Dean, Jeff, 2013. Distributed representations of words and phrases and their compositionality. Advances in Neural Information Processing Systems 26.

Miyato, Takeru, Maeda, Shin-ichi, Koyama, Masanori, Ishii, Shin, 2018. Virtual adversarial training: a regularization method for supervised and semi-supervised learning. IEEE Transactions on Pattern Analysis and Machine Intelligence 41 (8), 1979–1993.

Mohapatra, Jeet, Weng, Tsui-Wei, Chen, Pin-Yu, Liu, Sijia, Daniel, Luca, 2020. Towards verifying robustness of neural networks against a family of semantic perturbations. In:

Proceedings of the IEEE/CVF Conference on Computer Vision and Pattern Recognition, pp. 244–252.

Moosavi-Dezfooli, Seyed-Mohsen, Fawzi, Alhussein, Fawzi, Omar, Frossard, Pascal, 2017. Universal adversarial perturbations. In: Proceedings of the IEEE Conference on Computer Vision and Pattern Recognition, pp. 1765–1773.

Munkhdalai, Tsendsuren, Yu, Hong, 2017. Meta networks. Proceedings of Machine Learning Research 70, 2554.

Neekhara, Paarth, Hussain, Shehzeen, Dubnov, Shlomo, Koushanfar, Farinaz, 2018. Adversarial reprogramming of text classification neural networks. arXiv preprint. arXiv: 1809.01829.

Nesterov, Yurii, Spokoiny, Vladimir, 2017. Random gradient-free minimization of convex functions. Foundations of Computational Mathematics 17 (2), 527–566.

Neyshabur, Behnam, Bhojanapalli, Srinadh, McAllester, David, Srebro, Nati, 2017. Exploring generalization in deep learning. In: Advances in Neural Information Processing Systems, pp. 5947–5956.

Nguyen, Anh, Tran, Anh, 2020. Input-aware dynamic backdoor attack. In: Neural Information Processing Systems.

Nichol, Alex, Achiam, Joshua, Schulman, John, 2018. On first-order meta-learning algorithms. arXiv preprint. arXiv:1803.02999.

Noroozi, Mehdi, Favaro, Paolo, 2016. Unsupervised learning of visual representations by solving jigsaw puzzles. In: European Conference on Computer Vision. Springer, pp. 69–84.

Novak, Joseph D., Gowin, D. Bob, 1984. Learning How to Learn. Cambridge University Press.

Papernot, Nicolas, McDaniel, Patrick, 2018. Deep k-nearest neighbors: towards confident, interpretable and robust deep learning. arXiv preprint. arXiv:1803.04765.

Papernot, Nicolas, McDaniel, Patrick, Goodfellow, Ian, 2016. Transferability in machine learning: from phenomena to black-box attacks using adversarial samples. arXiv preprint. arXiv:1605.07277.

Papernot, Nicolas, McDaniel, Patrick, Goodfellow, Ian, Jha, Somesh, Celik, Z. Berkay, Swami, Ananthram, 2017. Practical black-box attacks against machine learning. In: ACM Asia Conference on Computer and Communications Security, pp. 506–519.

Paul, Sayak, Chen, Pin-Yu, 2022. Vision transformers are robust learners. In: Proceedings of the AAAI Conference on Artificial Intelligence.

Pennington, Jeffrey, Socher, Richard, Manning, Christopher D., 2014. Glove: global vectors for word representation. In: Proceedings of the 2014 Conference on Empirical Methods in Natural Language Processing (EMNLP), pp. 1532–1543.

Peyré, G., Cuturi, M., 2018. Computational optimal transport. arXiv preprint. arXiv:1803. 00567.

Purushwalkam, Senthil, Gupta, Abhinav, 2020. Demystifying contrastive self-supervised learning: invariances, augmentations and dataset biases. arXiv preprint. arXiv:2007. 13916.

Qin, Yao, Carlini, Nicholas, Cottrell, Garrison, Goodfellow, Ian, Raffel, Colin, 2019. Imperceptible, robust, and targeted adversarial examples for automatic speech recognition. In: International Conference on Machine Learning. PMLR, pp. 5231–5240.

Qin, Yunxiao, Xiong, Yuanhao, Yi, Jinfeng, Hsieh, Cho-Jui, 2021. Training meta-surrogate model for transferable adversarial attack. arXiv preprint. arXiv:2109.01983.

Raghu, Aniruddh, Raghu, Maithra, Bengio, Samy, Vinyals, Oriol, 2019. Rapid learning or feature reuse? Towards understanding the effectiveness of maml. arXiv preprint. arXiv: 1909.09157.

Raghunathan, Aditi, Steinhardt, Jacob, Liang, Percy S., 2018. Semidefinite relaxations for certifying robustness to adversarial examples. In: Advances in Neural Information Processing Systems, pp. 10877–10887.

Raghuram, Jayaram, Chandrasekaran, Varun, Jha, Somesh, Banerjee, Suman, 2020. Detecting anomalous inputs to DNN classifiers by joint statistical testing at the layers. arXiv preprint. arXiv:2007.15147.

Ranzato, Marc'Aurelio, Huang, Fu Jie, Boureau, Y-Lan, LeCun, Yann, 2007. Unsupervised learning of invariant feature hierarchies with applications to object recognition. In: IEEE Conference on Computer Vision and Pattern Recognition, pp. 1–8.

Rao, K. Ramamohan, Yip, Ping, 2014. Discrete Cosine Transform: Algorithms, Advantages, Applications. Academic Press.

Ravi, Sachin, Larochelle, Hugo, 2016. Optimization as a model for few-shot learning.

Ribeiro, Marco, Singh, Sameer, Guestrin, Carlos, 2016. "why should I trust you?" explaining the predictions of any classifier. In: ACM SIGKDD Intl. Conference on Knowledge Discovery and Data Mining.

Russakovsky, Olga, Deng, Jia, Su, Hao, Krause, Jonathan, Satheesh, Sanjeev, Ma, Sean, Huang, Zhiheng, Karpathy, Andrej, Khosla, Aditya, Bernstein, Michael, et al., 2015. Imagenet large scale visual recognition challenge. International Journal of Computer Vision 115 (3), 211–252.

Sablayrolles, Alexandre, Douze, Matthijs, Schmid, Cordelia, Jégou, Hervé, 2020. Radioactive data: tracing through training. In: International Conference on Machine Learning. PMLR, pp. 8326–8335.

Salman, Hadi, Yang, Greg, Li, Jerry, Zhang, Pengchuan, Zhang, Huan, Razenshteyn, Ilya, Bubeck, Sebastien, 2019a. Provably robust deep learning via adversarially trained smoothed classifiers. arXiv preprint. arXiv:1906.04584.

Salman, Hadi, Yang, Greg, Zhang, Huan, Hsieh, Cho-Jui, Zhang, Pengchuan, 2019b. A convex relaxation barrier to tight robustness verification of neural networks. Advances in Neural Information Processing Systems 32.

Salman, Hadi, Ilyas, Andrew, Engstrom, Logan, Vemprala, Sai, Madry, Aleksander, Kapoor, Ashish, 2020a. Unadversarial examples: designing objects for robust vision. arXiv preprint. arXiv:2012.12235.

Salman, Hadi, Sun, Mingjie, Yang, Greg, Kapoor, Ashish, Kolter, J. Zico, 2020b. Denoised smoothing: provable defense for pretrained classifiers. Advances in Neural Information Processing Systems 33, 21945–21957.

Samangouei, Pouya, Kabkab, Maya, Chellappa, Rama, 2018. Defense-gan: protecting classifiers against adversarial attacks using generative models. arXiv preprint. arXiv:1805.06605.

Santoro, Adam, Bartunov, Sergey, Botvinick, Matthew, Wierstra, Daan, Lillicrap, Timothy, 2016. Meta-learning with memory-augmented neural networks. In: International Conference on Machine Learning, pp. 1842–1850.

Shafahi, Ali, Huang, W. Ronny, Najibi, Mahyar, Suciu, Octavian, Studer, Christoph, Dumitras, Tudor, Goldstein, Tom, 2018. Poison frogs! Targeted clean-label poisoning attacks on neural networks. In: Advances in Neural Information Processing Systems, pp. 6103–6113.

Shafahi, Ali, Najibi, Mahyar, Ghiasi, Amin, Xu, Zheng, Dickerson, John, Studer, Christoph, Davis, Larry S., Taylor, Gavin, Goldstein, Tom, 2019. Adversarial training for free!. arXiv preprint. arXiv:1904.12843.

Shan, Shawn, Wenger, Emily, Zhang, Jiayun, Li, Huiying, Zheng, Haitao, Zhao, Ben Y., 2020. Fawkes: protecting privacy against unauthorized deep learning models. In: 29th {USENIX} Security Symposium ({USENIX} Security 20), pp. 1589–1604.

Shao, Rulin, Shi, Zhouxing, Yi, Jinfeng, Chen, Pin-Yu, Hsieh, Cho-Jui, 2021a. On the adversarial robustness of vision transformers. arXiv preprint. arXiv:2103.15670.

Shao, Rulin, Shi, Zhouxing, Yi, Jinfeng, Chen, Pin-Yu, Hsieh, Cho-Jui, 2021b. Robust text captchas using adversarial examples. arXiv preprint. arXiv:2101.02483.

Sharif, Mahmood, Bhagavatula, Sruti, Bauer, Lujo, Reiter, Michael K., 2016. Accessorize to a crime: real and stealthy attacks on state-of-the-art face recognition. In: Proceedings of the 2016 Acm Sigsac Conference on Computer and Communications Security, pp. 1528–1540.

Sharma, Yash, Ding, Gavin Weiguang, Brubaker, Marcus A., 2019. On the effectiveness of low frequency perturbations. In: AAAI.

Shi, Zhouxing, Zhang, Huan, Chang, Kai-Wei, Huang, Minlie, Hsieh, Cho-Jui, 2020. Robustness verification for transformers. In: International Conference on Learning Representations (ICLR).

Shi, Zhouxing, Wang, Yihan, Zhang, Huan, Yi, Jinfeng, Hsieh, Cho-Jui, 2021. Fast certified robust training via better initialization and shorter warmup. In: NeurIPS.

Simonyan, Karen, Zisserman, Andrew, 2014. Very deep convolutional networks for large-scale image recognition. arXiv preprint. arXiv:1409.1556.

Singh, Gagandeep, Gehr, Timon, Mirman, Matthew, Püschel, Markus, Vechev, Martin, 2018a. Fast and effective robustness certification. In: Advances in Neural Information Processing Systems, pp. 10802–10813.

Singh, Gagandeep, Gehr, Timon, Püschel, Markus, Vechev, Martin, 2018b. Boosting robustness certification of neural networks. In: International Conference on Learning Representations.

Singh, Gagandeep, Ganvir, Rupanshu, Püschel, Markus, Vechev, Martin, 2019a. Beyond the single neuron convex barrier for neural network certification. In: Advances in Neural Information Processing Systems (NeurIPS).

Singh, Gagandeep, Gehr, Timon, Püschel, Markus, Vechev, Martin, 2019b. An abstract domain for certifying neural networks. Proceedings of the ACM on Programming Languages 3 (POPL), 41.

Sitawarin, Chawin, Wagner, David, 2019. Defending against adversarial examples with k-nearest neighbor. arXiv preprint. arXiv:1906.09525.

Smith, Virginia, Chiang, Chao-Kai, Sanjabi, Maziar, Talwalkar, Ameet S., 2017. Federated multi-task learning. In: Advances in Neural Information Processing Systems, pp. 4424–4434.

Snell, Jake, Swersky, Kevin, Zemel, Richard, 2017. Prototypical networks for few-shot learning. In: Advances in Neural Information Processing Systems, pp. 4077–4087.

Stallkamp, Johannes, Schlipsing, Marc, Salmen, Jan, Igel, Christian, 2012. Man vs. computer: benchmarking machine learning algorithms for traffic sign recognition. Neural Networks 32, 323–332.

Stanforth, Robert, Fawzi, Alhussein, Kohli, Pushmeet, et al., 2019. Are labels required for improving adversarial robustness? Neural Information Processing Systems.

Stutz, David, Hein, Matthias, Schiele, Bernt, 2019. Disentangling adversarial robustness and generalization. In: Proceedings of the IEEE Conference on Computer Vision and Pattern Recognition, pp. 6976–6987.

Stutz, David, Chandramoorthy, Nandhini, Hein, Matthias, Schiele, Bernt, 2020. Bit error robustness for energy-efficient dnn accelerators. arXiv preprint. arXiv:2006.13977.

Su, Dong, Zhang, Huan, Chen, Hongge, Yi, Jinfeng, Chen, Pin-Yu, Gao, Yupeng, 2018. Is robustness the cost of accuracy?—a comprehensive study on the robustness of 18 deep image classification models. In: Proceedings of the European Conference on Computer Vision (ECCV), pp. 631–648.

Su, Jiawei, Vargas, Danilo Vasconcellos, Sakurai, Kouichi, 2019. One pixel attack for fooling deep neural networks. IEEE Transactions on Evolutionary Computation 23 (5), 828–841.

Sugiyama, Masashi, 2007. Dimensionality reduction of multimodal labeled data by local Fisher discriminant analysis. Journal of Machine Learning Research 8, 1027–1061.

Sun, Lichao, Dou, Yingtong, Yang, Carl, Wang, Ji, Yu, Philip S., He, Lifang, Li, Bo, 2018. Adversarial attack and defense on graph data: a survey. arXiv preprint. arXiv:1812.10528.

Sun, Xiaowu, Khedr, Haitham, Shoukry, Yasser, 2019a. Formal verification of neural network controlled autonomous systems. In: Proceedings of the 22nd ACM International Conference on Hybrid Systems: Computation and Control, pp. 147–156.

Sun, Yu, Wang, Shuohuan, Li, Yukun, Feng, Shikun, Chen, Xuyi, Zhang, Han, Tian, Xin, Zhu, Danxiang, Tian, Hao, Wu, Hua, 2019b. Ernie: Enhanced representation through knowledge integration. arXiv preprint. arXiv:1904.09223.

Sutskever, Ilya, Vinyals, Oriol, Le, Quoc V., 2014. Sequence to sequence learning with neural networks. In: Advances in Neural Information Processing Systems, pp. 3104–3112.

Szegedy, Christian, Zaremba, Wojciech, Sutskever, Ilya, Bruna, Joan, Erhan, Dumitru, Goodfellow, Ian, Fergus, Rob, 2014. Intriguing properties of neural networks. In: International Conference on Learning Representations.

Szegedy, Christian, Vanhoucke, Vincent, Ioffe, Sergey, Shlens, Jon, Wojna, Zbigniew, 2016. Rethinking the inception architecture for computer vision. In: IEEE Conference on Computer Vision and Pattern Recognition (CVPR), pp. 2818–2826.

Thrun, Sebastian, Pratt, Lorien, 2012. Learning to Learn. Springer Science & Business Media.

Thys, Simen, Van Ranst, Wiebe, Goedemé, Toon, 2019. Fooling automated surveillance cameras: adversarial patches to attack person detection. In: Proceedings of the IEEE/CVF Conference on Computer Vision and Pattern Recognition Workshops.

Tian, Yonglong, Sun, Chen, Poole, Ben, Krishnan, Dilip, Schmid, Cordelia, Isola, Phillip, 2020. What makes for good views for contrastive learning. arXiv preprint. arXiv:2005.10243.

Tibshirani, Robert, 1996. Regression shrinkage and selection via the lasso. Journal of the Royal Statistical Society, Series B, Methodological, 267–288.

Tjandraatmadja, Christian, Anderson, Ross, Huchette, Joey, Ma, Will, Patel, Krunal Kishor, Vielma, Juan Pablo, 2020. The convex relaxation barrier, revisited: tightened single-neuron relaxations for neural network verification. Advances in Neural Information Processing Systems 33, 21675–21686.

Tramer, Florian, Boneh, Dan, 2019. Adversarial training and robustness for multiple perturbations. In: Advances in Neural Information Processing Systems.

Tramer, Florian, Carlini, Nicholas, Brendel, Wieland, Madry, Aleksander, 2020. On adaptive attacks to adversarial example defenses. arXiv preprint. arXiv:2002.08347.

Trinh, Trieu H., Luong, Minh-Thang, Le, Quoc V., 2019. Selfie: self-supervised pretraining for image embedding. arXiv preprint. arXiv:1906.02940.

Tsai, Yun-Yun, Chen, Pin-Yu, Ho, Tsung-Yi, 2020. Transfer learning without knowing: reprogramming black-box machine learning models with scarce data and limited resources. In: International Conference on Machine Learning, pp. 9614–9624.

Tsai, Yu-Lin, Hsu, Chia-Yi, Yu, Chia-Mu, Chen, Pin-Yu, 2021a. Formalizing generalization and adversarial robustness of neural networks to weight perturbations. Advances in Neural Information Processing Systems 34.

Tsai, Yu-Lin, Hsu, Chia-Yi, Yu, Chia-Mu, Chen, Pin-Yu, 2021b. Non-singular adversarial robustness of neural networks. In: ICASSP 2021-2021 IEEE International Conference on Acoustics, Speech and Signal Processing (ICASSP). IEEE, pp. 3840–3844.

Tsai, Yun-Yun, Hsiung, Lei, Chen, Pin-Yu, Ho, Tsung-Yi, 2022. Towards compositional adversarial robustness: generalizing adversarial training to composite semantic perturbations. arXiv preprint. arXiv:2202.04235.

Tu, Chun-Chen, Ting, Paishun, Chen, Pin-Yu, Liu, Sijia, Zhang, Huan, Yi, Jinfeng, Hsieh, Cho-Jui, Cheng, Shin-Ming, 2019. Autozoom: Autoencoder-based zeroth order optimization method for attacking black-box neural networks. In: Proceedings of the AAAI Conference on Artificial Intelligence, vol. 33, pp. 742–749.

van den Oord, Aaron, Li, Yazhe, Vinyals, Oriol, 2018. Representation learning with contrastive predictive coding. arXiv preprint. arXiv:1807.03748.

Van der Maaten, Laurens, Hinton, Geoffrey, 2008. Visualizing data using t-sne. Journal of Machine Learning Research 9 (11).

Vaswani, Ashish, Shazeer, Noam, Parmar, Niki, Uszkoreit, Jakob, Jones, Llion, Gomez, Aidan N., Kaiser, Lukasz, Polosukhin, Illia, 2017. Attention is all you need. arXiv preprint. arXiv:1706.03762.

Vinod, Ria, Chen, Pin-Yu, Das, Payel, 2020. Reprogramming language models for molecular representation learning. arXiv preprint. arXiv:2012.03460.

Vinyals, Oriol, Toshev, Alexander, Bengio, Samy, Erhan, Dumitru, 2015. Show and tell: a neural image caption generator. In: Proceedings of the IEEE Conference on Computer Vision and Pattern Recognition, pp. 3156–3164.

Wang, Tongzhou, Isola, Phillip, 2020. Understanding contrastive representation learning through alignment and uniformity on the hypersphere. arXiv preprint. arXiv: 2005.10242.

Wang, Shiqi, Pei, Kexin, Whitehouse, Justin, Yang, Junfeng, Jana, Suman, 2018a. Efficient formal safety analysis of neural networks. In: Advances in Neural Information Processing Systems, pp. 6367–6377.

Wang, Yining, Du, Simon, Balakrishnan, Sivaraman, Singh, Aarti, 2018b. Stochastic zeroth-order optimization in high dimensions. In: AISTATS.

Wang, Bao, Shi, Zuoqiang, Osher, Stanley, 2019a. Resnets ensemble via the Feynman-Kac formalism to improve natural and robust accuracies. Advances in Neural Information Processing Systems 32.

Wang, Bolun, Yao, Yuanshun, Shan, Shawn, Li, Huiying, Viswanath, Bimal, Zheng, Haitao, Ben Zhao, Y., 2019b. Neural cleanse. Identifying and Mitigating Backdoor Attacks in Neural Networks.

Wang, Lu, Liu, Xuanqing, Yi, Jinfeng, Zhou, Zhi-Hua, Hsieh, Cho-Jui, 2019c. Evaluating the robustness of nearest neighbor classifiers: a primal-dual perspective. arXiv preprint. arXiv:1906.03972.

Wang, Yisen, Ma, Xingjun, Bailey, James, Yi, Jinfeng, Zhou, Bowen, Gu, Quanquan, 2019d. On the convergence and robustness of adversarial training. In: Proceedings of the 36th International Conference on Machine Learning. In: Proceedings of Machine Learning Research, vol. 97. PMLR, pp. 6586–6595.

Wang, Xiao, Wang, Siyue, Chen, Pin-Yu, Wang, Yanzhi, Kulis, Brian, Lin, Xue, Chin, Sang, 2019e. Protecting neural networks with hierarchical random switching: towards better robustness-accuracy trade-off for stochastic defenses. In: Proceedings of the Twenty-Eighth International Joint Conference on Artificial Intelligence (IJCAI), pp. 6013–6019.

Wang, Guangting, Luo, Chong, Sun, Xiaoyan, Xiong, Zhiwei, Zeng, Wenjun, 2020a. Tracking by instance detection: a meta-learning approach. In: Proceedings of the IEEE/CVF Conference on Computer Vision and Pattern Recognition, pp. 6288–6297.

Wang, Haohan, Wu, Xindi, Huang, Zeyi, Xing, Eric P., 2020b. High-frequency component helps explain the generalization of convolutional neural networks. In: Proceedings of the IEEE/CVF Conference on Computer Vision and Pattern Recognition, pp. 8684–8694.

Wang, Lu, Liu, Xuanqing, Yi, Jinfeng, Jiang, Yuan, Hsieh, Cho-Jui, 2020c. Provably robust metric learning. arXiv preprint. arXiv:2006.07024.

Wang, Ren, Zhang, Gaoyuan, Liu, Sijia, Chen, Pin-Yu, Xiong, Jinjun, Wang, Meng, 2020d. Practical detection of trojan neural networks: data-limited and data-free cases. In: European Conference on Computer Vision, pp. 222–238.

Wang, Yihan, Zhang, Huan, Chen, Hongge, Boning, Duane, Hsieh, Cho-Jui, 2020e. On lp-norm robustness of ensemble decision stumps and trees. In: International Conference on Machine Learning. PMLR, pp. 10104–10114.

Wang, Zifan, Yang, Yilin, Shrivastava, Ankit, Rawal, Varun, Ding, Zihao, 2020f. Towards frequency-based explanation for robust cnn. arXiv preprint. arXiv:2005.03141.

Wang, Jingkang, Zhang, Tianyun, Liu, Sijia, Chen, Pin-Yu, Xu, Jiacen, Fardad, Makan, Li, Bo, 2021a. Adversarial attack generation empowered by min-max optimization. Advances in Neural Information Processing Systems 34.

Wang, Ren, Xu, Kaidi, Liu, Sijia, Chen, Pin-Yu, Weng, Tsui-Wei, Gan, Chuang, Wang, Meng, 2021b. On fast adversarial robustness adaptation in model-agnostic meta-learning. In: International Conference on Learning Representations.

Wang, Shiqi, Zhang, Huan, Xu, Kaidi, Lin, Xue, Jana, Suman, Hsieh, Cho-Jui, Kolter, J. Zico, 2021c. Beta-crown: Efficient bound propagation with per-neuron split constraints for complete and incomplete neural network verification. arXiv preprint. arXiv:2103.06624.

Wang, Siyue, Wang, Xiao, Chen, Pin-Yu, Zhao, Pu, Lin, Xue, 2021d. Characteristic examples: high-robustness, low-transferability fingerprinting of neural networks. In: Proceedings of the Thirtieth International Joint Conference on Artificial Intelligence, IJCAI, pp. 575–582.

Weinberger, Kilian Q., Saul, Lawrence K., 2009. Distance metric learning for large margin nearest neighbor classification. Journal of Machine Learning Research 10, 207–244.

Weng, Tsui-Wei, Zhang, Huan, Chen, Hongge, Song, Zhao, Hsieh, Cho-Jui, Boning, Duane, Dhillon, Inderjit S., Daniel, Luca, 2018a. Towards fast computation of certified robustness for relu networks. In: International Conference on International Conference on Machine Learning.

Weng, Tsui-Wei, Zhang, Huan, Chen, Pin-Yu, Yi, Jinfeng, Su, Dong, Gao, Yupeng, Hsieh, Cho-Jui, Daniel, Luca, 2018b. Evaluating the robustness of neural networks: an extreme value theory approach. In: International Conference on Learning Representations.

Weng, Lily, Chen, Pin-Yu, Nguyen, Lam, Squillante, Mark, Boopathy, Akhilan, Oseledets, Ivan, Daniel, Luca, 2019. PROVEN: Verifying robustness of neural networks with a probabilistic approach. In: International Conference on Machine Learning, PMLR, pp. 6727–6736.

Weng, Tsui-Wei, Zhao, Pu, Liu, Sijia, Chen, Pin-Yu, Lin, Xue, Daniel, Luca, 2020. Towards certificated model robustness against weight perturbations. In: Proceedings of the AAAI Conference on Artificial Intelligence, pp. 6356–6363.

Wong, Eric, Kolter, J. Zico, 2017. Provable defenses against adversarial examples via the convex outer adversarial polytope. arXiv preprint. arXiv:1711.00851.

Wong, Eric, Kolter, Zico, 2018. Provable defenses against adversarial examples via the convex outer adversarial polytope. In: International Conference on Machine Learning, pp. 5286–5295.

Wong, Eric, Rice, Leslie, Kolter, J. Zico, 2020a. Fast is better than free: revisiting adversarial training. arXiv preprint. arXiv:2001.03994.

Wong, Eric, Schneider, Tim, Schmitt, Joerg, Schmidt, Frank R., Kolter, J. Zico, 2020b. Neural network virtual sensors for fuel injection quantities with provable performance specifications. arXiv preprint. arXiv:2007.00147.

Wu, Dongxian, Wang, Yisen, Xia, Shu-Tao, Bailey, James, Ma, Xingjun, 2020a. Skip connections matter: on the transferability of adversarial examples generated with resnets. In: International Conference on Learning Representations.

Wu, Dongxian, Xia, Shu-tao, Wang, Yisen, 2020b. Adversarial weight perturbation helps robust generalization. In: NeurIPS.

Xiao, Chaowei, Zhu, Jun-Yan, Li, Bo, He, Warren, Liu, Mingyan, Song, Dawn, 2018. Spatially transformed adversarial examples. In: International Conference on Learning Representations.

Xiao, Chang, Zhong, Peilin, Zheng, Changxi, 2019a. Enhancing adversarial defense by k-winners-take-all. arXiv preprint. arXiv:1905.10510.

Xiao, Kai Y., Tjeng, Vincent, Shafiullah, Nur Muhammad, Madry, Aleksander, 2019b. Training for faster adversarial robustness verification via inducing relu stability. In: ICLR.

Xie, Cihang, Wang, Jianyu, Zhang, Zhishuai, Ren, Zhou, Yuille, Alan, 2017. Mitigating adversarial effects through randomization. arXiv preprint. arXiv:1711.01991.

Xie, Cihang, Zhang, Zhishuai, Zhou, Yuyin, Bai, Song, Wang, Jianyu, Ren, Zhou, Yuille, Alan L., 2019. Improving transferability of adversarial examples with input diversity. In: Proceedings of the IEEE/CVF Conference on Computer Vision and Pattern Recognition, pp. 2730–2739.

Xie, Chulin, Huang, Keli, Chen, Pin-Yu, Li, Bo, 2020. DBA: Distributed backdoor attacks against federated learning. In: International Conference on Learning Representations.

Xu, Kaidi, Chen, Hongge, Liu, Sijia, Chen, Pin-Yu, Weng, Tsui-Wei, Hong, Mingyi, Lin, Xue, 2019a. Topology attack and defense for graph neural networks: an optimization perspective. In: IJCAI.

Xu, Kaidi, Liu, Sijia, Zhao, Pu, Chen, Pin-Yu, Zhang, Huan, Fan, Quanfu, Erdogmus, Deniz, Wang, Yanzhi, Lin, Xue, 2019b. Structured adversarial attack: towards general implementation and better interpretability. In: International Conference on Learning Representations.

Xu, Kaidi, Liu, Sijia, Chen, Pin-Yu, Sun, Mengshu, Ding, Caiwen, Kailkhura, Bhavya, Lin, Xue, 2020a. Towards an efficient and general framework of robust training for graph neural networks. In: ICASSP.

Xu, Kaidi, Shi, Zhouxing, Zhang, Huan, Wang, Yihan, Chang, Kai-Wei, Huang, Minlie, Kailkhura, Bhavya, Lin, Xue, Hsieh, Cho-Jui, 2020b. Automatic perturbation analysis for scalable certified robustness and beyond. Advances in Neural Information Processing Systems (NeurIPS).

Xu, Kaidi, Zhang, Gaoyuan, Liu, Sijia, Fan, Quanfu, Sun, Mengshu, Chen, Hongge, Chen, Pin-Yu, Wang, Yanzhi, Lin, Xue, 2020c. Adversarial t-shirt! Evading person detectors in a physical world. In: European Conference on Computer Vision, pp. 665–681.

Xu, Kaidi, Zhang, Huan, Wang, Shiqi, Wang, Yihan, Jana, Suman, Lin, Xue, Hsieh, Cho-Jui, 2021. Fast and complete: enabling complete neural network verification with rapid and massively parallel incomplete verifiers. In: International Conference on Learning Representations (ICLR).

Yan, Xueting, Misra, Ishan, Gupta, Abhinav, Ghadiyaram, Deepti, Mahajan, Dhruv, 2020. Clusterfit: improving generalization of visual representations. In: Proceedings of the IEEE/CVF Conference on Computer Vision and Pattern Recognition, pp. 6509–6518.

Yang, Timothy, Andrew, Galen, Eichner, Hubert, Sun, Haicheng, Li, Wei, Kong, Nicholas, Ramage, Daniel, Beaufays, Françoise, 2018. Applied federated learning: improving Google keyboard query suggestions. arXiv preprint. arXiv:1812.02903.

Yang, Qiang, Liu, Yang, Chen, Tianjian, Tong, Yongxin, 2019a. Federated machine learning: concept and applications. ACM Transactions on Intelligent Systems and Technology (TIST) 10 (2), 12.

Yang, Zhilin, Dai, Zihang, Yang, Yiming, Carbonell, Jaime, Salakhutdinov, Ruslan, Le, Quoc V., 2019b. Xlnet: Generalized autoregressive pretraining for language understanding. arXiv preprint. arXiv:1906.08237.

Yang, Zhuolin, Li, Bo, Chen, Pin-Yu, Song, Dawn, 2019c. Characterizing audio adversarial examples using temporal dependency. In: International Conference on Learning Representations.

Yang, Chao-Han, Qi, Jun, Chen, Pin-Yu, Ma, Xiaoli, Lee, Chin-Hui, 2020a. Characterizing speech adversarial examples using self-attention u-net enhancement. In: ICASSP 2020-2020 IEEE International Conference on Acoustics, Speech and Signal Processing (ICASSP). IEEE, pp. 3107–3111.

Yang, Chao-Han Huck, Qi, Jun, Chen, Pin-Yu, Ouyang, Yi, Hung, I., Danny, Te, Lee, Chin-Hui, Ma, Xiaoli, 2020b. Enhanced adversarial strategically-timed attacks against deep reinforcement learning. In: ICASSP.

Yang, Greg, Duan, Tony, Hu, J. Edward, Salman, Hadi, Razenshteyn, Ilya, Li, Jerry, 2020c. Randomized smoothing of all shapes and sizes. In: International Conference on Machine Learning. PMLR, pp. 10693–10705.

Yang, Puyudi, Chen, Jianbo, Hsieh, Cho-Jui, Wang, Jane-Ling, Jordan, Michael, 2020d. Ml-loo: Detecting adversarial examples with feature attribution. In: Proceedings of the AAAI Conference on Artificial Intelligence, vol. 34, pp. 6639–6647.

Yang, Puyudi, Chen, Jianbo, Hsieh, Cho-Jui, Wang, Jane-Ling, Jordan, Michael I., 2020e. Greedy attack and Gumbel attack: generating adversarial examples for discrete data. Journal of Machine Learning Research 21 (43), 1–36.

Yang, Yao-Yuan, Rashtchian, Cyrus, Wang, Yizhen, Chaudhuri, Kamalika, 2020f. Robustness for non-parametric classification: a generic attack and defense. In: International Conference on Artificial Intelligence and Statistics. PMLR, pp. 941–951.

Yang, Chao-Han Huck, Qi, Jun, Chen, Samuel Yen-Chi, Chen, Pin-Yu, Marco Siniscalchi, Sabato, Ma, Xiaoli, Lee, Chin-Hui, 2021a. Decentralizing feature extraction with quantum convolutional neural network for automatic speech recognition. In: ICASSP 2021-2021 IEEE International Conference on Acoustics, Speech and Signal Processing (ICASSP). IEEE, pp. 6523–6527.

Yang, Chao-Han Huck, Tsai, Yun-Yun, Chen, Pin-Yu, 2021b. Voice2series: reprogramming acoustic models for time series classification. In: International Conference on Machine Learning.

Yang, Chao-Han Huck, Hung, I., Danny, Te, Ouyang, Yi, Chen, Pin-Yu, 2022. Training a resilient Q-network against observational interference. In: Proceedings of the AAAI Conference on Artificial Intelligence.

Yao, Yuanshun, Li, Huiying, Zheng, Haitao, Ben Zhao, Y., 2019. Latent backdoor attacks on deep neural networks. In: Proceedings of the 2019 ACM SIGSAC Conference on Computer and Communications Security, pp. 2041–2055.

Yen, Hao, Ku, Pin-Jui, Huck Yang, Chao-Han, Hu, Hu, Marco Siniscalchi, Sabato, Chen, Pin-Yu, Tsao, Yu, 2021. A study of low-resource speech commands recognition based on adversarial reprogramming. arXiv preprint. arXiv:2110.03894.

Yin, Chengxiang, Tang, Jian, Xu, Zhiyuan, Wang, Yanzhi, 2018. Adversarial meta-learning.

Yuan, Xuejing, Chen, Yuxuan, Zhao, Yue, Long, Yunhui, Liu, Xiaokang, Chen, Kai, Zhang, Shengzhi, Huang, Heqing, Wang, Xiaofeng, Gunter, Carl A., 2018. Commandersong: A systematic approach for practical adversarial voice recognition. arXiv preprint. arXiv:1801.08535.

Zantedeschi, Valentina, Nicolae, Maria-Irina, Rawat, Ambrish, 2017. Efficient defenses against adversarial attacks. In: Proceedings of the 10th ACM Workshop on Artificial Intelligence and Security, pp. 39–49.

Zawad, Syed, Ali, Ahsan, Chen, Pin-Yu, Anwar, Ali, Zhou, Yi, Baracaldo, Nathalie, Tian, Yuan, Yan, Feng, 2021. Curse or redemption? How data heterogeneity affects the robustness of federated learning. In: Proceedings of the AAAI Conference on Artificial Intelligence.

Zeiler, M.D., Fergus, R., 2014. Visualizing and understanding convolutional networks. In: ECCV. Springer, pp. 818–833.

Zeng, Xiangrong, Figueiredo, Mário AT, 2014a. Decreasing weighted sorted $\ell_1$ regularization. IEEE Signal Processing Letters 21 (10), 1240–1244.

Zeng, Xiangrong, Figueiredo, Mario AT, 2014b. Solving oscar regularization problems by fast approximate proximal splitting algorithms. Digital Signal Processing 31, 124–135.

Zhai, Xiaohua, Oliver, Avital, Kolesnikov, Alexander, Beyer, Lucas, 2019. S4l: self-supervised semi-supervised learning. In: Proceedings of the IEEE International Conference on Computer Vision, pp. 1476–1485.

Zhang, Chiyuan, Bengio, Samy, Hardt, Moritz, Recht, Benjamin, Vinyals, Oriol, 2017. Understanding deep learning requires rethinking generalization. In: International Conference on Learning Representations.

Zhang, Huan, Weng, Tsui-Wei, Chen, Pin-Yu, Hsieh, Cho-Jui, Daniel, Luca, 2018. Efficient neural network robustness certification with general activation functions. In: Advances in Neural Information Processing Systems, pp. 4944–4953.

Zhang, Dinghuai, Zhang, Tianyuan, Lu, Yiping, Zhu, Zhanxing, Dong, Bin, 2019a. You only propagate once: accelerating adversarial training via maximal principle. arXiv preprint. arXiv:1905.00877.

Zhang, Hongyang, Yu, Yaodong, Jiao, Jiantao, Xing, Eric, El Ghaoui, Laurent, Jordan, Michael, 2019b. Theoretically principled trade-off between robustness and accuracy. In: International Conference on Machine Learning. PMLR, pp. 7472–7482.

Zhang, Huan, Chen, Hongge, Xiao, Chaowei, Li, Bo, Boning, Duane, Hsieh, Cho-Jui, 2020a. Towards stable and efficient training of verifiably robust neural networks. In: International Conference on Learning Representations (ICLR).

Zhang, Wei Emma, Sheng, Quan Z., Alhazmi, Ahoud, Li, Chenliang, 2020b. Adversarial attacks on deep-learning models in natural language processing: a survey. ACM Transactions on Intelligent Systems and Technology (TIST) 11 (3), 1–41.

Zhang, Gaoyuan, Lu, Songtao, Zhang, Yihua, Chen, Xiangyi, Chen, Pin-Yu, Fan, Quanfu, Martie, Lee, Horesh, Lior, Hong, Mingyi, Liu, Sijia, 2022. Distributed adversarial training to robustify deep neural networks at scale. In: The Conference on Uncertainty in Artificial Intelligence.

Zhao, Yue, Li, Meng, Lai, Liangzhen, Suda, Naveen, Civin, Damon, Chandra, Vikas, 2018. Federated learning with non-iid data. arXiv preprint. arXiv:1806.00582.

Zhao, Pu, Liu, Sijia, Chen, Pin-Yu, Hoang, Nghia, Xu, Kaidi, Kailkhura, Bhavya, Lin, Xue, 2019a. On the design of black-box adversarial examples by leveraging gradient-free optimization and operator splitting method. In: IEEE International Conference on Computer Vision, pp. 121–130.

Zhao, Pu, Wang, Siyue, Gongye, Cheng, Wang, Yanzhi, Fei, Yunsi, Lin, Xue, 2019b. Fault sneaking attack: a stealthy framework for misleading deep neural networks. In: ACM/IEEE Design Automation Conference (DAC), pp. 1–6.

Zhao, Pu, Chen, Pin-Yu, Das, Payel, Ramamurthy, Karthikeyan Natesan, Lin, Xue, 2020a. Bridging mode connectivity in loss landscapes and adversarial robustness. In: International Conference on Learning Representations.

Zhao, Pu, Chen, Pin-Yu, Wang, Siyue, Lin, Xue, 2020b. Towards query-efficient black-box adversary with zeroth-order natural gradient descent. In: Proceedings of the AAAI Conference on Artificial Intelligence.

Zhu, Xiaojin, Goldberg, Andrew B., 2009. Introduction to semi-supervised learning. Synthesis Lectures on Artificial Intelligence and Machine Learning 3 (1), 1–130.

Zhu, Chen, Huang, W. Ronny, Li, Hengduo, Taylor, Gavin, Studer, Christoph, Goldstein, Tom, 2019a. Transferable clean-label poisoning attacks on deep neural nets. In: Proceedings of the 36th International Conference on Machine Learning, pp. 7614–7623.

Zhu, Chen, Huang, W. Ronny, Li, Hengduo, Taylor, Gavin, Studer, Christoph, Goldstein, Tom, 2019b. Transferable clean-label poisoning attacks on deep neural nets. In: International Conference on Machine Learning. PMLR, pp. 7614–7623.

Zhu, Sicheng, Zhang, Xiao, Evans, David, 2020a. Learning adversarially robust representations via worst-case mutual information maximization. In: International Conference on Machine Learning.

Zhu, Xizhou, Su, Weijie, Lu, Lewei, Li, Bin, Wang, Xiaogang, Dai, Jifeng, 2020b. Deformable detr: deformable transformers for end-to-end object detection. arXiv preprint. arXiv:2010.04159.

Zhuang, Juntang, Gong, Boqing, Yuan, Liangzhe, Cui, Yin, Adam, Hartwig, Dvornek, Nicha, Tatikonda, Sekhar, Duncan, James, Liu, Ting, 2022. Surrogate gap minimization improves sharpness-aware training. In: International Conference on Learning Representations (ICLR).

Zou, Hui, Hastie, Trevor, 2005. Regularization and variable selection via the elastic net. Journal of the Royal Statistical Society, Series B, Statistical Methodology 67 (2), 301–320.

Zügner, Daniel, Günnemann, Stephan, 2019. Adversarial attacks on graph neural networks via meta learning. In: International Conference on Learning Representations.

Zügner, Daniel, Akbarnejad, Amir, Günnemann, Stephan, 2018. Adversarial attacks on neural networks for graph data. In: Proceedings of the 24th ACM SIGKDD International Conference on Knowledge Discovery & Data Mining, pp. 2847–2856.

# Index

## A

Accuracy
  certified robust, 114
  classification, 10, 195, 248
  clean, 114, 155
  drop, 232
  increase, 250
  prediction, 7, 8, 128
  reprogramming, 204
  standard, 8, 187, 189, 195
Acoustic model (AM), 202–204, 206
Adaptive
  antiwatermark schemes, 229
  attacks, 24, 146
Advanced
  attacks, 146
  finetuning techniques, 189
AdvCL, 189, 191, 194, 197, 198
AdvCL framework, 191
Adversarial
  agent models, 66
  attack, 15–18, 29, 48, 59, 62, 64, 73, 95, 138, 143, 146, 148, 185, 234
  attack formulation, 47
  attacking algorithms, 241
  audio, 148
    attacks, 149
    examples, 155
    inputs, 146
  autoencoder, 247
  characteristics, 148
  context, 189, 193
  contrastive
    pretraining framework, 189
    training, 195
  detection, 143, 144, 146
  example, 8, 15–20, 30, 31, 35, 38–40, 47, 48, 60, 62–64, 73, 74, 113–117, 119, 120, 127, 143–145, 159, 186, 188, 191, 232, 241, 243
    detection, 143

for unsupervised machine learning, 241
from natural examples, 144
transferability, 38, 235
inputs, 147
instances, 148
loss, 180
network, 97
perturbation, 15, 22, 23, 41, 43, 66, 73, 74, 116, 127, 147, 153, 158, 160, 162, 164, 193, 194
purposes, 201
robustness, 7–10, 12, 24, 59, 68, 73, 76, 113, 115, 130, 132, 170, 183, 184, 186, 188, 189, 250
  for machine learning, 7
  in machine learning algorithms, 3
  in MAML, 183, 184
targets, 148
threats, 3
timing attacks, 66
unsupervised example, 244
view, 193
Adversarial full finetuning (AFF), 189–191, 195, 197
Adversarial linear finetuning (ALF), 189, 191, 198
Adversarial machine learning (AdvML), 3, 201
Adversarial reprogramming (AR), 201, 206
Adversarial training (AT), 10, 114, 115, 117, 119, 121, 122, 128, 131, 180, 185, 189–191
  algorithm, 20
  fast, 121
  method, 107, 129
  process, 120
Adversarially robust metric learning (ARML), 168, 170
  algorithm, 170
  certified robustness, 170
Adversary, 228, 229
Aggregated prediction, 204

Printed in the United States
by Baker & Taylor Publisher Services